EVERYMAN, I will go with thee,

and be thy guide,

In thy most need to go by thy side

RICHARD FORD

Born in 1796. Educated at Winchester and
Trinity College, Oxford. Spent three years,
1830–3, travelling in Spain. On his return
settled at Heavitree, near Exeter. Contributed
to the *Quarterly* and other reviews from 1837
onwards. Published *Handbook for Spain*, 1845,
Gatherings from Spain, 1846. Formed a collection of Spanish pictures, Italian bronzes and
maiolica. As the result of his writings such
artists as Velasquez and Murillo became better
known in Britain. Died in 1858.

RICHARD FORD

Gatherings from Spain

INTRODUCTION BY
BRINSLEY FORD

DENT: LONDON
EVERYMAN'S LIBRARY
DUTTON: NEW YORK

INTRODUCTION

It has long been my hope that Richard Ford's writings on Spain would be reprinted as the difficulty of obtaining copies of his books must have prevented a great many people from reading them. His great work, the *Handbook for Travellers in Spain*, was published in two volumes in 1845. An abridged edition, reduced to one volume, was issued two years later. A third edition, partly rewritten and incorporating new material, appeared in two volumes in 1855. This was the last edition to be brought out in Ford's lifetime. None of the later editions is worth reading since the excisions and additions have mutilated his masterpiece. Quoting one of Ford's own phrases, Mr Ian Robertson has described the changes made by various editors as 'like Niagara passed through a jelly-bag'.

Unfortunately the first edition of the *Handbook* had become so scarce that it could only be bought by rich bibliophiles who were prepared to pay a rarity value for it. Now, however, thanks to the courage of the Centaur Press, the first edition has once again become available. It was reissued in its entirety in three volumes in 1966. Besides a foreword written by Sir John Balfour, who was British ambassador to Spain from 1951 until 1954, it contains an extremely valuable introduction by Mr Robertson, who also undertook the laborious and exacting task of checking that the text of 1,500 pages was identical with that of the original version. The *Gatherings from Spain* has been out of print for over twenty years, and it is very welcome news that the publishers have decided to reissue their Everyman edition, first published in 1906 with an introduction by Thomas Okey.

Richard Ford was born in Sloane Street on 21st April 1796. He was the eldest son of Sir Richard Ford (1758–1806) who, after representing East Grinstead and Appleby in the House of Commons, became Chief Police Magistrate at Bow Street. If Sir Richard has any claim to fame, it is as the creator of the mounted police force of London. Sir Richard married Marianne, the daughter of Benjamin Booth, who had formed an important collection of paintings by Richard Wilson, and it was from her that their son inherited his love of the fine arts as well as his gifts as an amateur draughtsman.

Richard Ford was educated at Winchester and Trinity College, Oxford; he was called to the Bar at Lincoln's Inn in 1822, but never practised. As a young man of independent means he was free to follow his own inclinations. These led him to travel on the Continent, which had for so long been closed to Englishmen by the Napoleonic wars. His passports show that he made four tours abroad between 1815 and 1819, in the course of which he visited France, the Netherlands, Germany, Switzerland and Italy. Ford has left no account of those travels, but they had a great influence in forming his tastes. Ford's first publication, a paper written on his return from Italy in 1819 when he was only twenty-two, was a privately printed description of a picture which he had bought at Naples in the previous year. In this paper he set out to prove that the picture he had acquired was Corregio's original *modello* for the frescoed cupola in the cathedral at Parma. Although his evidence for this attribution sounds authentic, it must have been fabricated by the Neapolitan dealer, as one of the greatest authorities on Corregio has convinced me that the picture is a seventeenth-century copy. But, if Ford's connoisseurship was at fault, this picture does at least establish the early age at which he became a collector and a writer. It was not long before he was to try his hand at drawing. On his visits to the Continent, and in London, he had formed a collection of etchings and engravings by and after Parmigianino and Andrea Meldolla. In 1822 he published a book containing twelve plates which he had etched from the originals in his collection. These etchings, which he described as 'the first attempts of an amateur', were accompanied by the entries he had written about the plates. Fifteen years were to elapse before he next appeared in print.

In 1824 Richard Ford married as his first wife Harriet, a natural daughter of George, 5th Earl of Essex, the patron of Girtin and Turner. Her portrait by Hayter, painted before marriage, shows that she was an enchantingly pretty young woman. She was an accomplished musician and had learnt to draw very skilfully. Little is known about the first six years of their married life as no letters dating from this period have been preserved.

In 1830 Ford decided that it was necessary for the sake of his wife's health to spend a winter or two in a warm climate, and they chose the south of Spain. With his wife and their three small children, and with three female retainers, Ford sailed from Plymouth on 9th October 1830 and reached Gibraltar on the 29th. From Gibraltar they went by sea to Cadiz and thence by steamer to Seville, where they established themselves for the winter. They spent three winters at Seville and two summers at Granada. The rest of the time Ford spent travelling about Spain. He made one or two expeditions with his wife, but most of his tours were made alone on horseback accompanied by an attendant.

Ford rode over two thousand miles in Spain on Jaca Cordovese, his favourite horse, which, like its master, was drawn by John Frederick Lewis. It is possible to trace all his tours over the peninsula by examining his passports, which contain over one hundred and fifty entries. Ford says that the system of passports and police surveillance was introduced by the French, and retained as a substitute for the inquisition by Ferdinand VII. He advises travellers to submit to this annoyance with a good grace and to consider it as one of the penalties of foreign travel. Ford was provided with a passport by the 'redoubtable' Conde de España, and he describes in the *Gatherings* (page 297) the advantages of being armed with such a recommendation. If his passports had not been preserved, his tours could still be traced from the dated drawings that he made of the places he visited. While making these sketches Ford ran the risk of arousing the suspicions of the local authorities. In the *Gatherings* (page 295) he points out that the foreigner who made

drawings in the untrodden parts of Spain was always in
danger of being arrested as a spy, and he mentions an
occasion when he was marched off to a guard-house for
sketching a Roman ruin.

Ford made over five hundred drawings during the three
years he spent in Spain. They are contained in two large
albums in my possession. As none of the Spanish artists
made drawings of the cities they lived in, Ford's accurate
drawings constitute an invaluable record of Spain in the
1830s, and they provide a visual complement to the *Handbook*. Their importance has now been recognized by the
Spaniards. Ford spent more of his time in Seville and
Granada than anywhere else, and it follows that by far
the largest number of his drawings were done in these two
cities. His drawings of Granada were published, with an
introduction by the late Don Alfonso Gámir, by the
Patronato of the Alhambra in 1955. This volume is largely
devoted to Ford's drawings of the Alhambra in which he
lived. The Alhambra has changed a great deal less than
Seville in the last hundred and forty years. The drawings
of Seville provide a precious record of the city when many
of the Moorish walls were still standing. They also record
many monuments that have since disappeared, including
some beautiful gateways which, ironically, have been
pulled down to allow for the greater influx of tourist
traffic! On the initiative of Professor Angulo, the present
Director of the Prado, these drawings were published by
the Instituto Diego Velazquez in 1963. Professor Angulo
also wrote the learned notes on the illustrations. My
introduction, which describes Ford's life in Seville, was
translated into Spanish by my friend, Professor de Salas,
the Deputy Director of the Prado.

Ford had no sooner arrived in Seville than he threw himself with whole-hearted zest into the enjoyment of the
colourful spectacle of Spanish life. It was at this period
that he began a lifelong correspondence with his friend
Henry Unwin Addington, who was then Envoy Extraordinary and Plenipotentiary at Madrid. I possess some
four hundred and fifty letters from Ford to Addington,

Introduction

which are preserved in three volumes splendidly bound in
Spanish leather. A selection from these letters was published
by John Murray in 1905. They were edited by Rowland E.
Prothero, whose text, interspersed with the letters, is the
best biography of Ford that has yet been written, and it can
be warmly recommended to those who are curious to know
more about his life.

Ford has dealt with many different aspect of Spanish
life in the *Gatherings*. Few men can have explored a foreign
country so thoroughly in so short a time, or have acquired
such insight into the characteristics of the people and their
customs. In Chapter IX he discusses the advantages of
adopting the dress worn by the natives. Amongst the
portraits of him in my possession are three water-colours
by J. Becquer, which were painted in Seville in 1832. In
one of them Ford is represented wearing the black sheepskin jacket which he wore on all his riding tours. Thus
attired he was able to mix freely with the inhabitants. His
account in Chapter XV of a night spent in a *venta* shows
how well he got to know the lower classes of Spaniards,
whose courtesy he greatly admired. He was prepared to
share their hardships, and was rewarded by the scenes he
witnessed, which reminded him of antiquity.

None of Ford's admirers will deny that his opinions are
often biased by his Protestant and patriotic convictions.
But, if his book is to be enjoyed, his prejudices must be
swallowed like some of the less agreeable ingredients in the
Spanish national dish, the *olla*, which the French have
described as consisting of two cigars boiled in three gallons
of water. But just as the true *olla*, which is concocted of
countless excellent ingredients and highly flavoured, can
only be made by a cook who has thrown 'his whole soul
into the pan', so Ford has poured into the *Gatherings* the
wealth of all his accumulated Spanish experiences. 'In this
volume,' wrote Thomas Okey, the author 'gave free rein to
his genius, and drew lavishly on his wide and curious
reading, on his rich memories and warm imagination.' Ford
was gifted with powers of description which enabled him
to bring to life any scene, however varied, that had

excited his interest. To appreciate this gift, it is only necessary to compare his joyous evocation of the *Majo* and *Maja* dancing the bolero with his macabre account of the execution of El Veneno (pages 349 and 224). But what makes the *Gatherings* so readable is not only the wide range of subjects discussed with so much wit, humour and learning, but also the racy style in which it is written, a style spiced with happy phrases and unexpected metaphors.

The story of how the *Handbook* and the *Gatherings* came to be written has been fully told by Prothero, and it can only be recounted here in the barest outline. On his return to England in 1833, Ford settled at Exeter, where in the summer of the following year he bought Heavitree House, which he gradually hispaniolized. As early as 1834 he had planned to write a book about Spain, but it came to nothing. Instead he amused himself with his Spanish books, and spent much of his time in laying out the gardens in the Spanish style, planting the terraces 'with pines and cypresses from historical groves by the Xenil and Guadal-quivir', and building in the grounds a Moorish tower, all of which have been demolished since the last war to make room for bungalows. From 1837 onwards he became a regular contributor to the *Quarterly Review*, in which he wrote chiefly on Spanish subjects. It was on the strength of these articles that John Murray asked him to recommend someone to write a Spanish guide-book. Ford replied, almost in jest, that he would do it himself and thought no more of the matter until he received a formal offer. He started work on the *Handbook* in 1840. Instead of the six months he had estimated to write the book, it took him nearly five years.

Sir William Stirling of Keir, who was one of the friends admitted to the 'den' at Heavitree, the garden-house where the work was accomplished, later recalled the 'long deal shelves laden with parchment-clad folios and quartos, the inky deal table, the crammed pigeon-holes, and the piles of manuscript which encumbered the chairs and the floor, and the kindly, lively author, in his black jacket of Spanish sheepskin, doing the honours of his book-rarities, pouring

Introduction

forth his humorous complaints of the slavery to which he had unwittingly condemned himself—complaints diversified with Spanish proverb and English jest'.

When, in 1845, the *Handbook* eventually appeared, it was an immediate success. In a review, written for the *Quarterly* but never published, Borrow declared that the *Handbook* was one of the best books ever written about Spain. He praised the iron application that had been required for the task, the years of enormous labour which must have been spent in carrying it into effect even after the necessary materials had been collected. 'But here is the book before us;' he wrote, 'the splendid result of the toil, travel, genius, and learning of one man and that man an Englishman.' He feared that with so unpretentious a title the *Handbook* might never be appreciated at its proper value. 'What a pity that his delightful book does not bear a more romantic sounding title—"Wanderings in Spain", for example; or yet better, "The Wonders of the Peninsula".'

Ford was aware that, in spite of its success, the *Handbook* was printed in a form 'which rendered its perusal irksome' to ladies. It was for their distraction, as he explains in his preface, that he produced the *Gatherings from Spain*, in which 'to lighten the narrative, the Author has removed much lumber of learning, and has not scrupled occasionally to throw Strabo, and even Saint Isidore himself, overboard'. He composed the *Gatherings*, partly by selecting extracts from the introductory essays in the *Handbook*, and partly by adding new material. He informed Addington that he had 'almost written a new book as to half of it'. The *Gatherings* was published towards the end of 1846. On 10th January 1847 Ford wrote to Addington: 'The *Gatherings* have taken wonderfully. All the critics praise without exception: so I have sacked £210 for two months work, and not damaged my literary reputation.' When he wrote this letter, Ford had probably just received one, dated 5th January, from J. G. Lockhart, the editor of the *Quarterly*. 'You may,' Lockhart wrote, 'live fifty years without turning out any more delightful thing than the *Gatherings*. Tho' I had read the *Handbook* pretty well, I found the full zest of novelty in these Essays, and such, I think, is the nearly universal feeling. Fergusson was at Lord Clarendon's in Herts at Christmas. Lord Clarendon said that he had had a Spanish party a few days before—all highly pleased. One said it would take, to get together the knowledge of this book, four of the most accomplished of Spaniards. "Ah!" said another, "but where could you get *one* that could put it all together in a form so readable?" I forget their names; but they were men of mark.'

Since 1846 there have been four English and two American editions of the *Gatherings*. Under the title *Cosas de España*, it was translated by Enrique de Mesa, and published in two volumes in Madrid in 1923. This edition has long been exhausted. The only other Spanish edition that has yet appeared was produced for the Banco Ibérico in 1968. This edition, which is richly illustrated with Ford's drawings, was destined for the friends of the bank and was limited to three hundred copies. The publishers who were responsible for this sumptuous volume have informed me that they intend to bring out a cheap edition of the *Cosas de España*.

Richard Ford's first wife died in 1837. She was the mother of my grandfather, Sir Clare Ford, who was ambassador at Madrid from 1885 until 1892. In 1838 Ford married Eliza, the sister of the tenth Lord Cranstoun. After her death he married, in 1851, Mary, the sister of the radical politician, Sir William Molesworth, from whom she inherited Pencarrow in Cornwall in 1855. She survived Richard Ford, who died in 1858, by half a century, during which she continued to reside at his house in Park Street, where she entertained the statesmen and men of letters of her day. Born in 1816, she lived on until 1910, when as a small child I was allowed the privilege of gazing up at this living monument of the past.

BRINSLEY FORD.

London, 1970.

BIBLIOGRAPHY

WORKS. *An account of the original Design by Correggio for his painting in fresco in the Cathedral at Parma*, privately printed, 1819. *An Historical Enquiry into the unchangeable Character of a War in Spain*, 1837. *The Hand-Book for Travellers in Spain, and Readers at Home . . .* , suppressed edition printed in 1844 (only twenty to twenty-five copies are said to survive, the remainder having been destroyed by Ford); first edition, 2 vols., 1845 (Centaur Press edition, 3 vols., 1966); second edition, 1 vol., 1847; third edition, 2 vols., 1855. *Gatherings from Spain*, 1846; new edition, 1861; Everyman's Library edition, 1906, with introduction by Thomas Okey, reprinted 1913, 1927. The first American edition, entitled *The Spaniards and their Country*, was published in 1847; another American edition, 1848. A Spanish edition, *Cosas de España*, translated by Enrique de Mesa, was published in 2 vols., 1923; another Spanish edition (300 copies), illustrated with Ford's drawings, was produced for the Banco Ibérico in 1968. *The Life of Diego Rodriguez de Silva y Velasquez*, limited edition of twenty-five copies, 1851 (originally published in the Penny Cyclopaedia, 1843). *A Guide to the Diorama of the Campaigns of the Duke of Wellington*, 1852. *Tauromachia, or The Bull Fights of Spain*, 1852. *Apsley House and Walmer Castle*, 1853.

CONTRIBUTIONS TO JOURNALS. Between 1837 and 1857 Ford contributed more than fifty articles to the *Quarterly Review*, the *Edinburgh Review*, the *Foreign Quarterly*, the *Athenaeum*, *The Times*, the *Westminster Review*, etc. See Brinsley Ford, 'Richard Ford's Articles and Reviews', in *Book Handbook*, 1948, No. 7.

DRAWINGS. Ford's drawings of Granada were published by the Patronato of the Alhambra in 1955; those of Seville by the Instituto Diego Velasquez in 1963. The first of these volumes has an introduction by Alfonso Gámir; the second an introduction by Brinsley Ford and notes by Professor Angulo.

LETTERS. *The Letters of Richard Ford*, edited by Rowland E. Prothero (later Lord Ernle), London and New York, 1905.

CONTENTS

Contents

Contents

CHAPTER XV

CHAPTER XVI

CHAPTER XVII

CHAPTER XVIII

CHAPTER XIX

CHAPTER XX

Contents

GATHERINGS FROM SPAIN

PREFACE

MANY ladies, some of whom even contemplate a visit to Spain, having condescended to signify to the publisher their regrets, that the Handbook was printed in a form, which rendered its perusal irksome, and also to express a wish that the type had been larger, the Author, to whom this distinguished compliment was communicated, has hastened to submit to their indulgence a few extracts and selections, which may throw some light on the character of a country and people, always of the highest interest, and particularly so at this moment, when their independence is once more threatened by a crafty and aggressive neighbour.

In preparing these compilations for the press much new matter has been added, to supply the place of portions omitted ; for, in order to lighten the narrative, the Author has removed much lumber of learning, and has not scrupled occasionally to throw Strabo, and even Saint Isidore himself, overboard. Progress is the order of the day in Spain, and its advance is the more rapid, as she was so much in arrear of other nations. Transition is the present condition of the country, where yesterday is effaced by to-morrow. There the relentless march of European intellect is crushing many a native wild flower, which, having no value save colour and sweetness, must be rooted up before cotton-mills are constructed and breadstuffs substituted ; many a trait of nationality in manners and costume is already effaced ; monks are gone, and mantillas are going, alas ! going.

In the changes that have recently taken place, many descriptions of ways and things now presented to the public will soon become almost matters of history and antiquarian interest. The passages here reprinted will be omitted in the forthcoming new edition of the Handbook, to which these pages may form a companion; but their chief object has been to offer a few hours' amusement, and may be of instruction, to those who remain at home; and should the humble attempt meet with the approbation of fair readers, the author will bear, with more than Spanish resignation, whatever animadversions bearded critics may be pleased to inflict on this or on the other side of the water.

CHAPTER I

THE kingdom of Spain, which looks so compact on the map, is composed of many distinct provinces, each of which in earlier times formed a separate and independent kingdom; and although all are now united under one crown by marriage, inheritance, conquest, and other circumstances, the original distinctions, geographical as well as social, remain almost unaltered. The language, costume, habits, and local character of the natives, vary no less than the climate and productions of the soil. The chains of mountains which intersect the whole peninsula, and the deep rivers which separate portions of it, have, for many years, operated as so many walls and moats, by cutting off intercommunication, and by fostering that tendency to isolation which must exist in all hilly countries, where good roads and bridges do not abound. As similar circumstances led the people of ancient Greece to split into small principalities, tribes and clans, so in Spain, man, following the example of the nature by which he is surrounded, has little in common with the inhabitant of the adjoining district; and these differences are increased and perpetuated by the ancient jealousies and inveterate dislikes, which petty and contiguous states keep up with such tenacious memory. The general comprehensive term "Spain," which is convenient for geographers and politicians, is calculated to mislead the traveller, for it would be far from easy to predicate any single thing of Spain or Spaniards which will be equally applicable to all its heterogeneous component parts. The north-western provinces are more rainy than Devonshire, while the centre plains are more calcined than those of the deserts of Arabia, and the

littoral south or eastern coasts altogether Algerian.
The rude agricultural Gallician, the industrious manu-
facturing artisan of Barcelona, the gay and voluptuous
Andalucian, the sly vindictive Valencian, are as essentially different from each other as so many distinct
characters at the same masquerade.   It will therefore
be more convenient to the traveller to take each province by itself and treat it in detail, keeping on the
look-out for those peculiarities, those social and
natural characteristics or idiosyncrasies which particularly belong to each division, and distinguish it from its
neighbours.   The Spaniards who have written on their
own geography and statistics, and who ought to be
supposed to understand their own country and institutions the best, have found it advisable to adopt this
arrangement from feeling the utter impossibility of
treating Spain (where union is not unity) as a whole.
There is no king of *Spain:* among the infinity of kingdoms, the list of which swells out the royal style, that
of " Spain " is not found; he is King of the Spains,
Rex Hispaniarum, *Rey de las Españas,* not " *Rey de
España.*"   Philip II., called by his countrymen *el pru-
dente,* the prudent, wishing to fuse down his hetero-
geneous subjects, was desirous after his conquest of
Portugal, which consolidated his dominion, to call himself King of Spain, which he then really was; but this
alteration of title was beyond the power of even his
despotism; such was the opposition of the kingdoms
of Arragon and Navarre, which never gave up the
hopes of shaking off the yoke of Castile, and recover-
ing their former independence, while the empire provinces of New and Old Castile refused in anywise to
compromise their claims of pre-eminence.   They from
early times, as now, took the lead in national nomenclature; hence " *Castellano,*" Castilian, is synonymous
with Spaniard, and particularly with the proud genuine
older stock.   " *Castellano á las derechas,*" means a
Spaniard to the backbone; " *Hablar Castellano,*" to
speak Castilian, is the correct expression for speaking
the Spanish language.   Spain again was long without the advantage of a fixed metropolis, like Rome,

Paris, or London, which have been capitals from their foundation, and recognised and submitted to as such; here, the cities of Leon, Burgos, Toledo, Seville, Valladolid, and others, have each in their turns been the capitals of the kingdom. This constant change and short-lived pre-eminence has weakened any prescriptive superiority of one city over another, and has been a cause of national weakness by raising up rivalries and disputes about precedence, which is one of the most fertile sources of dissension among a punctilious people. In fact the king was the state, and wherever he fixed his head-quarters was the court, *La Corte*, a word still synonymous with Madrid, which now claims to be the only residence of the Sovereign—the residenz, as Germans would say; otherwise, when compared with the cities above mentioned, it is a modern place; from not having a bishop or cathedral, of which latter some older cities possess two, it has not even the rank of a *ciudad*, or city, but is merely denominated *villa*, or town. In moments of national danger it exercises little influence over the Peninsula: at the same time, from being the seat of the court and government, and therefore the centre of patronage and fashion, it attracts from all parts those who wish to make their fortune; yet the capital has a hold on the ambition rather than on the affections of the nation at large. The inhabitants of the different provinces think, indeed, that Madrid is the greatest and richest court in the world, but their hearts are in their native localities. " *Mi paisano,*" my fellow-countryman, or rather my fellow-countyman, fellow-parishioner, does not mean Spaniard, but Andalucian, Catalonian, as the case may be. When a Spaniard is asked, Where do you come from? the reply is, " *Soy hijo de Murcia—hijo de Granada,*" " I am a son of Murcia—a son of Granada," etc. This is strictly analogous to the " Children of Israel," the " Beni " of the Spanish Moors, and to this day the Arabs of Cairo call themselves *children* of that town, " *Ibn el Musr,*" etc. ; and just as the Milesian Irishman is " a *boy* from Tipperary," etc., and ready to fight with any one who is so also, against all who

are not of that ilk; similar too is the clanship of the
Highlander; indeed, everywhere, not perhaps to the
same extent as in Spain, the being of the same province or town creates a powerful freemasonry; the
parties cling together like old school-fellows. It is a
home and really binding feeling. To the spot of their
birth all their recollections, comparisons, and eulogies
are turned; nothing to them comes up to their particular province, that is, their real country. " *La Patria*,"
meaning Spain at large, is a subject of declamation,
fine words, *palabras*—palaver, in which all, like
Orientals, delight to indulge, and to which their
grandiloquent idiom lends itself readily; but their
patriotism is parochial, and self is the centre of Spanish
gravity. Like the German, they may sing and spout
about *Fatherland*: in both cases the theory is splendid,
but in practice each Spaniard thinks his own province
or town the best in the Peninsula, and himself the
finest fellow in it. From the earliest period down to
the present all observers have been struck with this
localism as a salient feature in the character of the
Iberians, who never would amalgamate, never would,
as Strabo said, put their shields together—never would
sacrifice their own local private interest for the general
good; on the contrary, in the hour of need they had,
as at present, a constant tendency to separate into
distinct *juntas*, " *collective* " assemblies, each of which
only thought of its own views, utterly indifferent to
the injury thereby occasioned to what ought to have
been the common cause of all. Common danger and
interest scarcely can keep them together, the tendency
of each being rather to repel than to attract the other:
the common enemy once removed, they instantly fall
to loggerheads among each other, especially if there
be any spoil to be divided: scarcely ever, as in the East,
can the energy of one individual bind the loose staves
by the iron power of a master mind; remove the band,
and the centrifugal members instantaneously disunite.
Thus the virility and vitality of the noble people have
been neutralised: they have, indeed, strong limbs and
honest hearts; but, as in the Oriental parable, " a

head " is wanting to direct and govern : hence Spain
is to-day, as it always has been, a bundle of small
bodies tied together by a rope of sand, and, being without union, is also without strength, and has been beaten
in detail. The much-used phrase *Españolismo* expresses rather a " dislike of foreign dictation," and the
" self-estimation " of Spaniards, *Españoles sobre
todos*, than any real patriotic love of country, however
highly they rate its excellences and superiority to every
other one under heaven : this opinion is condensed in one
of those pithy proverbs which, nowhere more than in
Spain, are the exponents of popular sentiment : it runs
thus,—" *Quien dice España, dice todo*," which means,
" Whoever says Spain, says everything." A foreigner
may perhaps think this a trifle too comprehensive and
exclusive ; but he will do well to express no doubts on
the subject, since he will only be set down by every
native as either jealous, envious, or ignorant, and
probably all three.

To boast of Spain's strength, said the Duke of Wellington, is the national weakness. Every infinitesimal
particle which constitutes *nosotros*, or ourselves, as
Spaniards term themselves, will talk of his country as
if the armies were still led to victory by the mighty
Charles V., or the councils managed by Philip II.
instead of Louis-Philippe. Fortunate, indeed, was it,
according to a Castilian preacher, that the Pyrenees
concealed Spain when the Wicked One tempted the
Son of Man by an offer of all the kingdoms of the
world, and the glory of them. This, indeed, was predicated in the mediæval or dark ages, but few peninsular congregations, even in these enlightened times,
would dispute the inference. It was but the other day
that a foreigner was relating in a *tertulia*, or conver-
sazione of Madrid, the well-known anecdote of Adam's
revisit to the earth. The narrator explained how our
first father on lighting in Italy was perplexed and taken
aback ; how, on crossing the Alps into Germany, he
found nothing that he could understand—how matters
got darker and stranger at Paris, until on his reaching England he was altogether lost, confounded, and

abroad, being unable to make out any thing. Spain was his next point, where, to his infinite satisfaction, he found himself quite at home, so little had things changed since his absence, or indeed since the sun at its creation first shone over Toledo. The story concluded, a distinguished Spaniard, who was present, hurt perhaps at the somewhat protestant-dissenting tone of the speaker, gravely remarked, the rest of the party coinciding,—*Si Señor, y tenia razon; la España es Paradiso*—"Adam, Sir, was right, for Spain is paradise;" and in many respects this worthy, zealous gentleman was not wrong, although it is affirmed by some of his countrymen that some portions of it are inhabited by persons not totally exempt from original sin; thus the Valencians will say of their ravishing *huerta*, or garden, *Es un paradiso habitado por demonios*,—"It is an Eden peopled by subjects of his Satanic Majesty." Again, according to the natives, Murcia, a land overflowing with milk and honey, where Flora and Pomona dispute the prize with Ceres and Bacchus, possesses a *cielo y suelo bueno, el entresuelo malo*, has "a sky and soil that are good, while all between is indifferent;" which the *entresol* occupant must settle to his liking.

Another little anecdote, like a straw thrown up in the air, will point out the direction in which the wind blows. Monsieur Thiers, the great historical romance writer, in his recent hand-gallop tour through the Peninsula, passed a few days only at Madrid; his mind being, as logicians would say, of a *subjective* rather than an *objective* turn, that is, disposed rather to the consideration of the *ego*, and to things relating to self, than to those that do not, he scarcely looked more at any thing there, than he did during his similar run through London : "Behold," said the Spaniards, "that little *gabacho;* he dares not remain, nor raise his eyes from the ground in this land, whose vast superiority wounds his personal and national vanity." There is nothing new in this. The old Castilian has an older saying :—*Si Dios no fuese Dios, seria rey de las Españas, y el de Francia su cocinero*—"If God were not

God, he would make himself king of the Spains, with him of France for his cook." Lope de Vega, without derogating one jot from these paradisiacal pretensions, used him of England better. His sonnet on the romantic trip to Madrid ran thus :—

> " Carlos Stuardo soy,
>   Que siendo amor mi guia,
>   Al *cielo de España* voy,
>   Por ver mi estrella Maria."

" I am Charles Stuart, who, with love for my guide, hasten to the heaven Spain to see my star Mary." The Virgin, it must be remembered, after whom this infanta was named, is held by every Spaniard to be the brightest luminary, and the sole empress of heaven.

CHAPTER II

FROM Spain being the most southern country in Europe, it is very natural that those who have never been there, and who in England criticise those who have, should imagine the climate to be even more delicious than that of Italy or Greece. This is far from being the fact; some, indeed, of the sea coasts and sheltered plains in the S. and E. provinces are warm in winter, and exposed to an almost African sun in summer, but the N. and W. districts are damp and rainy for the greater part of the year, while the interior is either cold and cheerless, or sunburnt and wind-blown : winters have occurred at Madrid of such severity that sentinels have been frozen to death; and frequently all communication is suspended by the depth of the snow in the elevated roads over the mountain passes of the Castiles. All, therefore, who are about to travel through the Peninsula, are particularly cautioned to consider well their line of route beforehand,

and to select certain portions to be visited at certain seasons, and thus avoid every local disadvantage.

One glance at a map of Europe will convey a clearer notion of the relative position of Spain in regard to other countries than pages of letter-press: this is an advantage which every school-boy possesses over the Plinys and Strabos of antiquity; the ancients were content to compare the shape of the Peninsula to that of a bull's hide, nor was the comparison ill chosen in some respects. We will not weary readers with details of latitude and longitude, but just mention that the whole superficies of the Peninsula, including Portugal, contains upwards of 19,000 square leagues, of which somewhat more than 15,500 belong to Spain; it is thus almost twice as large as the British Islands, and only one-tenth smaller than France; the circumference or coast-line is estimated at 750 leagues. This compact and isolated territory, inhabited by a fine, hardy, warlike population, ought, therefore, to have rivalled France in military power, while its position between those two great seas which command the commerce of the old and new world, its indented line of coast, abounding in bays and harbours, offered every advantage of vying with England in maritime enterprise.

Nature has provided commensurate outlets for the infinite productions of a country which is rich alike in everything that is to be found either on the face or in the bowels of the earth; for the mines and quarries abound with precious metals and marbles, from gold to iron, from the agate to coal, while a fertile soil and every possible variety of climate admit of unlimited cultivation of the natural productions of the temperate or tropical zones: thus in the province of Granada the sugar-cane and cotton-tree luxuriate at the base of ranges which are covered with eternal snow: a wide range is thus afforded to the botanist, who may ascend by zones, through every variety of vegetable strata, from the hothouse plant growing wild, to the hardiest lichen. It has, indeed, required the utmost ingenuity and bad government of man to neutralise the prodigality of advantages which Providence has lavished on this highly favoured land, and which, while under the dominion of the Romans and Moors, resembled an Eden, a garden of plenty and delight, when in the words of an old author, there was nothing idle, nothing barren in Spain—"nihil otiosum, nihil sterile in Hispaniâ." A sad change has come over this fair vision, and now the bulk of the Peninsula offers a picture of neglect and desolation, moral and physical, which it is painful to contemplate: the face of nature and the mind of man have too often been dwarfed and curtailed of their fair proportions; they have either been neglected and their inherent fertility allowed to run into vice and luxuriant weeds, which it will show against any country in the world, or their energies have been misdirected, and a capability of all good converted into an element equally powerful for evil; but pride and laziness are here as everywhere the keys to poverty, *altivez y pereza, llaves de pobreza.*

The geological construction of Spain is very peculiar, and unlike that of most other countries; it is almost one mountain or agglomeration of mountains, as those of our countrymen who are speculating in Spanish railroads are just beginning to discover. The interior rises on every side from the sea, and the central portions are higher than any other table-lands in Europe, ranging on an average from two to three thousand feet above the level of the sea, while from this elevated plain chains of mountains rise again to a still greater height. Madrid, which stands on this central plateau, is situated about 2000 feet above the level of Naples, which lies in the same latitude; the mean temperature of Madrid is 59°, while that of Naples is 63° 30'; it is to this difference of elevation that the extraordinary difference of climate and vegetable productions between the two capitals is to be ascribed. Fruits which flourish on the coasts of Provence and Genoa, which lie four degrees more to the north than any portion of Spain, are rarely to be met with in the elevated interior of the Peninsula: on the other hand, the low and sunny maritime belts abound with productions of a tropical vegetation. The mountainous

character and general aspect of the coast are nearly
analogous throughout the circuit which extends from
the Basque Provinces to Cape Finisterre; and offer a
remarkable contrast to those sunny alluvial plains which
extend, more or less, from Cadiz to Barcelona, and
which closely resemble each other in vegetable productions, such as the fig, orange, pomegranate, aloe, and
carob tree, which grow everywhere in profusion, except
in those parts where the mountains come down abruptly
into the sea itself. Again, the central districts, composed of vast plains and steppes, *Parameras, Tierras de
campo, y Secanos*, closely resemble each other in their
monotonous denuded aspect, in their scarcity of fruit
and timber, and their abundance of cereal productions.

Spanish geographers have divided the Peninsula into
seven distinct chains of mountains. These commence
with the Pyrenees and end with the Bœtican or Andalucian ranges: these *cordilleras*, or lines of lofty ridges,
arise on each side of intervening plains, which once
formed the basins of internal lakes, until the accumulated waters, by bursting through the obstructions by
which they were dammed up, found a passage to the
ocean: the dip or inclination of the country lies from
the east towards the west, and, accordingly, the chief
rivers which form the drains and principal water-sheds
of the greater parts of the surface, flow into the
Atlantic: their courses, like the basins through which
they pass, lie in a transversal and almost a parallel
direction; thus the Duero, the Tagus, the Guadiana,
and the Guadalquivir, all flow into their recipient between their distinct chains of mountains. The sources
of the supply to these leading arteries arise in the lon-
gitudinal range of elevations which descends all through
the Peninsula, approaching rather to the eastern than
to the western coast, whereby a considerably greater
length is obtained by each of these four rivers, when
compared to the Ebro, which disembogues in the
Mediterranean.

The Moorish geographer Alrasi was the first to take
difference of climate as the rule of dividing the Peninsula into distinct portions; and modern authorities,

carrying out this idea, have drawn an imaginary line, which runs north-east to south-west, thus separating the Peninsula into the northern, or the boreal and temperate, and the southern or the torrid, and sub-dividing these two into four zones : nor is this division altogether fanciful, for there is no caprice or mistake in tests derived from the vegetable world; manners may make man, but the sun alone modifies the plant: man may be fused down by social appliances into one uniform mass, but the rude elements are not to be civilised, nor can nature be made cosmopolitan, which heaven forfend.

The first or northern zone is the *Cantabrian*, the European; this portion skirts the base of the Pyrenees, and includes portions of Catalonia, Arragon, and Navarre, the Basque provinces, the Asturias, and Gallicia. This is the region of humidity, and as the winters are long, and the springs and autumns rainy, it should only be visited in the summer. It is a country of hill and dale, is intersected by numerous streams which abound in fish, and which irrigate rich meadows for pastures. The valleys form the now improving dairy country of Spain, while the mountains furnish the most valuable and available timber of the Peninsula. In some parts corn will scarcely ripen, while in others, in addition to the cerealia, cider and an ordinary wine are produced. It is inhabited by a hardy, independent, and rarely subdued population, since the mountainous country offers natural means of defence to brave high-landers. It is useless to attempt the conquest with a small army, while a large one would find no means of support in the hungry localities.

The second zone is the Iberian or eastern, which, in its maritime portions, is more Asiatic than European, and where the lower classes partake of the Greek and Carthaginian character, being false, cruel, and trea-cherous, yet lively, ingenious, and fond of pleasure: this portion commences at Burgos, and includes the southern portion of Catalonia and Arragon, with parts of Castile, Valencia, and Murcia. The sea-coasts should be visited in the spring and autumn, when they are delicious; but they are intensely hot in the summer, and infested with myriads of moskitoes. The districts about Burgos are among the coldest in Spain, and the thermometer sinks very much below the ordinary average of our more temperate climate; and as they have little at any time to attract the traveller, he will do well to avoid them except during the summer months. The population is grave, sober, and Castilian. The elevation is very considerable; thus the upper valley of the Miño and some of the north-western portions of Old Castile and Leon are placed more than 6000 feet above the level of the sea, and the frosts often last for three months at a time.

The third zone is the Lusitanian, or western, which is by far the largest, and includes the central parts of Spain and all Portugal. The interior of this portion, and especially the provinces of the two Castiles and La Mancha, both in the physical condition of the soil and the moral qualities of the inhabitants, presents a very unfavourable view of the Peninsula, as these inland steppes are burnt up by summer suns, and are tempest and wind-rent during winter. The general absence of trees, hedges, and enclosures exposes these wide unprotected plains to the rage and violence of the elements : poverty-stricken mud houses, scattered here and there in the desolate extent, afford a wretched home to a poor, proud, and ignorant population; but these localities, which offer in themselves neither pleasure nor profit to the stranger, contain many sites and cities of the highest interest, which none who wish to understand Spain can possibly pass by unnoticed. The best periods for visiting this portion of Spain are May and June, or September and October.

The more western districts of this Lusitanian zone are not so disagreeable. There in the uplands the ilex and chestnut abound, while the rich plains produce vast harvests of corn, and the vineyards powerful red wines. The central table-land, which closely resembles the plateau of Mexico, forms nearly one-half of the entire area of the Peninsula. The peculiarity of the climate is its dryness; it is not, however, unhealthy,

being free from the agues and fevers which are prevalent in the lower plains, river-swamps, and rice-grounds
of parts of Valencia and Andalucia. Rain, indeed, is
so comparatively scarce on this table-land, that the
annual quantity on an average does not amount to more
than ten inches. The least quantity falls in the mountain regions near Guadalupe, and on the high plains
of Cuenca and Murcia, where sometimes eight or nine
months pass without a drop falling. The occasional
thunder-storms do but just lay the dust, since here
moisture dries up quicker even than woman's tears.
The face of the earth is tanned, tawny, and baked into
a veritable terra cotta : everything seems dead and
burnt on a funeral pile. It is all but a miracle how
the principle of life in the green herb is preserved,
since the very grass appears scorched and dead ; yet
when once the rains set in, vegetation springs up,
phœnix-like, from the ashes, and bursts forth in an
inconceivable luxuriance and life. The ripe seeds which
have fallen on the soil are called into existence, carpet-
ing the desert with verdure, gladdening the eye with
flowers, and intoxicating the senses with perfume. The
thirsty chinky dry earth drinks in these genial showers,
and then rising like a giant refreshed with wine, puts
forth all its strength ; and what vegetation is, where
moisture is combined with great heat, cannot even be
guessed at in lands of stinted suns. The periods of
rains are the winter and spring, and when these are
plentiful, all kinds of grain, and in many places wines,
are produced in abundance. The olive, however, is
only to be met with in a few favoured localities.

The fourth zone is the Bœtican, which is the most
southern and African ; it coasts the Mediterranean,
basking at the foot of the mountains which rise behind
and form the mass of the Peninsula : this mural barrier
offers a sure protection against the cold winds which
sweep across the central region. Nothing can be more
striking than the descent from the table elevations into
these maritime strips ; in a few hours the face of nature
is completely changed, and the traveller passes from
the climate and vegetation of Europe into that of

Africa. This region is characterised by a dry burning atmosphere during a large part of the year. The
winters are short and temperate, and consist rather in
rain than in cold, for in the sunny valleys ice is scarcely
known except for eating; the springs and autumns
delightful beyond all conception. Much of the cultivation depends on artificial irrigation, which was carried by the Moors to the highest perfection: indeed
water, under this forcing, vivifying sun, is the blood of
the earth, and synonymous with fertility: the productions are tropical; sugar, cotton, rice, the orange,
lemon, and date. The *algarrobo*, the carob tree, and
the *adelfa*, the oleander, may be considered as forming
boundary marks between this the *tierra caliente*, or
torrid district, and the colder regions by which it is
encompassed.

Such are the geographical divisions of nature with
which the vegetable and animal productions are closely
connected; and we shall presently enter somewhat more
fully into the *climate* of Spain, of which the natives are
as proud as if they had made it themselves. This
Bœtican zone, Andalucia, which contains in itself many
of the most interesting cities, sites, and natural beauties
of the Peninsula, will always take precedence in any
plan of the traveller, and each of these points has its
own peculiar attractions. These embrace a wide range
of varied scenery and objects; and Andalucia, easy of
access, may be gone over almost at every portion of
the year. The winters may be spent at Cadiz, Seville,
or Malaga; the summers in the cool mountains of
Ronda, Aracena, or Granada. April, May, and June,
or September, October, and November, are, however,
the most preferable. Those who go in the spring
should reserve June for the mountains; those who go
in the autumn should reverse the plan, and commence
with Ronda and Granada, ending with Seville and
Cadiz.

Spain, it has thus been shown, is one mountain, or
rather a jumble of mountains,—for the principal and
secondary ranges are all more or less connected with
each other, and descend in a serpentising direction

throughout the Peninsula, with a general inclination to the west. Nature, by thus dislocating the country, seems to have suggested, nay, almost to have forced, localism and isolation to the inhabitants, who each in their valleys and districts are shut off from their neighbours, whom to love, they are enjoined in vain.

The internal communication of the Peninsula, which is thus divided by the mountain-walls, is effected by some good roads, few and far between, and which are carried over the most convenient points, where the natural dips are the lowest, and the ascents and descents the most practicable. These passes are called *Puertos—portæ*, or gates. There are, indeed, mule-tracks and goat-paths over other and intermediate portions of the chain, but they are difficult and dangerous, and being seldom provided with ventas or villages, are fitter for smugglers and bandits than honest men : the farthest and fairest way about will always be found the best and shortest road.

The Spanish mountains in general have a dreary and harsh character, yet not without a certain desolate sublimity : the highest are frequently capped with snow, which glistens in the clear sky. They are rarely clad with forest trees ; the scarped and denuded ridges cut with a serrated outline the clean clear blue sky. The granitic masses soar above the green valley or yellow corn-plains in solitary state, like the castles of a feudal baron, that lord it over all below, with which they are too proud to have aught in common. These mountains are seen to greatest advantage at the rise and setting of the sun, for during the day the vertical rays destroy all form by removing shadows.

These geographical peculiarities of Spain, and particularly the existence of the great central elevation, when once attained are apt to be forgotten. The country rises from the coast, directly in the north-western provinces, and in some of the southern and eastern, with an intervening alluvial strip and swell : but when once the ascent is accomplished, no *real* descent ever takes place—we are then on the summit of a vast elevated mass. The roads indeed *apparently*

ascend and descend, but the mean height is seldom
diminished : the interior hills or plains are undulations
of one mountain. The traveller is often deceived at
the apparent low level of snow-clad ranges, such as the
Guadarrama; this will be accounted for by adding the
great elevation of their bases above the level of the
sea. The palace of the Escorial, which is placed at
the foot of the Guadarrama, and at the head of a seem-
ing plain, stands in reality at 2725 feet above Valencia,
while the summer residence of the king at *La Granja*,
in the same chain, is thirty feet higher than the summit of Vesuvius. This, indeed, is a castle in the air—
a château en Espagne, and worthy of the most German
potentate to whom that element belongs, as the sea
does to Britannia. The mean temperature on the
plateau of Spain is as 15° Réaumur, while that of the
coast is as 18° and 19°, in addition to the protection
from cutting winds which their mountainous back-
grounds afford; nor is the traveller less deceived as
regards the heights of the interior mountains than he
is with the champaigns, or table-land plains. The eye
wanders over a vast level extent bounded only by the
horizon, or a faint blue line of other distant sierras;
this space, which appears one townless level, is intersected with deep ravines, *barrancos*, in which villages
lie concealed, and streams, *arroyos*, flow unperceived.
Another important effect of this central elevation is
the searching dryness and rarefication of the air. It
is often highly prejudicial to strangers; the least exposure, which is very tempting under a burning sun, will
often bring on ophthalmia, irritable colics, and inflammatory diseases of the lungs and vital organs. Such
are the causes of the *pulmonia*, which carries off the
invalid in a few days, and is the disease of Madrid.
The frozen blasts descending from the snow-clad
Guadarrama catch the incautious passenger at the
turning of streets which are roasting under a fierce
sun. Is it to be wondered at, that this capital should
be so very insalubrious? in winter you are frozen alive,
in summer baked. A man taking a walk for the benefit
of his health, crosses with his pores open from an oven

to an ice-house; catch-cold introduces the Spanish doctor, who soon in his turn presents the undertaker.

As the Pyrenees possess an European interest at this moment when the Napoleon of Peace proposes to annihilate their existence, which defied Louis XIV. and Buonaparte, some details may be not unacceptable. This gigantic barrier, which divides Spain and France, is connected with the dorsal chain which comes down from Tartary and Asia. It stretches far beyond the transversal spine, for the mountains of the Basque Provinces, Asturias, and Gallicia, are its continuation. The Pyrenees, properly speaking, extend E. to W., in length about 270 miles, being both broadest and highest in the central portions, where the width is about 60 miles, and the elevations exceed 11,000 feet. The spurs and offsets of this great transversal spine penetrate on both sides into the lateral valleys like ribs from a backbone. The central nucleus slopes gradually E. to the gentle Mediterranean, and W. to the fierce Atlantic, in a long uneven swell.

This range of mountains was called by the Romans *Montes* and *Saltus Pyrenei*, and by the Greeks Πυρηνη, probably from a local Iberian word, but which they, as usual, catching at sound, not sense, connected with their Πυρ, and then bolstered up their erroneous derivation by a legend framed to fit the name, asserting that it either alluded to *a fire* through which certain precious metals were discovered, or because the lofty summits were often struck with lightning, and dislocated by the volcanos. According to the Iberians, Hercules, when on his way to " lift " Geryon's cattle, was hospitably received by Bebryx, a petty ruler in these mountains; whereupon the demigod got drunk, and ravished his host's daughter *Pyrene*, who died of grief, when Hercules, sad and sober, made the whole range re-echo with her name; a legend which, like some others in Spain, requires confirmation, for the Phœnicians called these ranges *Purani*, from the forests, *Pura* meaning wood in Hebrew. The Basques have, of course, their etymology, some saying that the real root *is Biri*, an elevation, while others prefer *Bierri enac*, the " two countries," which, separated by the range, were ruled by Tubal; but when Spaniards once begin with Tubal, the best plan is to shut the book.

The *Maledêta* is the loftiest peak, although the *Pico del Mediodia* and the *Canigú*, because rising at once out of plains and therefore having the greatest apparent altitudes, were long considered to be the highest; but now these French usurpers are dethroned. Seen from a distance, the range appears to be one mountain-ridge, with broken pinnacles, but, in fact, it consists of two distinct lines, which are parallel, but not continuous. The one which commences at the ocean is the most forward, being at least 30 miles more in advance towards the south than the corresponding line, which commences from the Mediterranean. The centre is the point of dislocation, and here the ramifications and reticulations are the most intricate, as it is the key-stone of the system, which is buttressed up by *Las Tres Sorellas*, the three sisters *Monte Perdido*, *Cylindro, and Marboré*. Here is the source of the Garonne, *La Garona;* here the scenery is the grandest, and the lateral valleys the longest and widest. The smaller spurs enclose valleys, down each of which pours a stream : thus the Ebro, Garona, and Bidasoa are fed from the mountain source. These tributaries are generally called in France *Gaves*,[1] and in some parts on the

---

[1] The word *Gabacho*, which is the most offensive vituperative of the Spaniard against the Frenchman, and has by some been thought to mean " those who dwell on Gaves," is the Arabic *Cabach*, detestable, filthy, or " qui prava indole est, moribusque." In fact the real meaning cannot be further alluded to beyond referring to the clever tale of *El Frances y Español*, by Quevedo. The antipathy to the Gaul is natural and national, and dates far beyond history. This nickname was first given in the eighth century, when Charlemagne, the Buonaparte of his day, invaded Spain, on the abdication and cession of the crown by the chaste Alonso, the prototype of the wittol Charles IV. ; then the Spanish Moors and Christians, foes and friends, forgot their hatreds of creeds in the greater loathing for the abhorred intruder, whose " peerage fell " in the memorable passes of Roncesvalles. The true derivation of the word *Gabacho*, which now resounds from these Pyrenees to the Straits, is blinked in the royal academical dictionary, such was the servile adulation of the members to

Spanish side *Gabas;* but *Gav* signifies a " river," and
may be traced in our *Avon;* and Humboldt derives it
from the Basque *Gav,* a " hollow or ravine;" cavus.
The parting of these waters, or their flowing down
either N. or S., should naturally mark the line of division between France and Spain : such, however, is not
the case, as part of *Cerdaña* belongs to France, while
Aran belongs to Spain; thus each country possesses a
key in its neighbour's territory. It is singular that this
obvious inconvenience should not have been remedied
by some exchange when the long-disputed boundary-
question was settled between Charles IV. and the
French republic.

Most of the passes over this Alpine barrier are impracticable for carriages, and remain much in the same
state as in the time of the Moors, who from them called
the Pyrenean range *Albort,* from the Roman *Portæ,* the
ridge of " gates." Many of the wild passes are only
known to the natives and smugglers, and are often impracticable from the snow; while even in summer they
are dangerous, being exposed to mists and the hurricanes
of mighty rushing winds. The two best carriageable
lines of intercommunication are placed at each extremity : that to the west passes through Irun; that to the
east through Figueras.

The Spanish Pyrenees offer few attractions to the
lovers of the fleshly comforts of cities; but the scenery,
sporting, geology, and botany are truly Alpine, and will
well repay those who can " rough it " considerably. The
contrast which the unfrequented Spanish side offers to
the crowded opposite one is great. In Spain the mountains themselves are less abrupt, less covered with
snow, while the numerous and much frequented baths
in the French Pyrenees have created roads, diligences,

---

their French patron Philip V. *Mueran los Gabachos,* " Death to
the miscreants," was the rally cry of Spain after the inhuman
butcheries of the terrorist Murat; nor have the echoes died
away; a spark may kindle the prepared mine : of what an
unspeakable value is a national war-cry which at once gives to
a whole people a shibboleth, a rallying watch-word to a
common cause ! *Vox populi vox Dei.*

hotels, tables-d'hôte, cooks, Ciceronis, donkeys, and so
forth; for the Badauds de Paris who babble about green
fields and *des belles horreurs*, but who seldom go beyond
the immediate vicinity and hackneyed " lions." A want
of good taste and real perception of the sublime and
beautiful is nowhere more striking, says Mr. Erskine
Murray, than on the French side, where mankind remains profoundly ignorant of the real beauties of the
Pyrenees, which have been chiefly explored by the English, who love nature with all their heart and soul, who
worship her alike in her shyest retreats and in her
wildest forms. Nevertheless, on the north side many
comforts and appliances for the tourist are to be had;
nay, invalids and ladies in search of the picturesque can
ascend to the *Brèche de Roland*. Once, however, cross
the frontier, and a sudden change comes over all facilities of locomotion. Stern is the first welcome of the
" hard land of Iberia," scarce is the food for body or
mind, and deficient the accommodation for man or beast,
and simply because there is small demand for either.
No Spaniard ever comes here for pleasure; hence the
localities are given up to the smuggler and izard.

The Oriental inæsthetic incuriousness for *things*, old
stones, wild scenery, etc., is increased by political
reasons and fears. The neighbour, from the time of the
Celt down to to-day, has ever been the coveter, ravager,
and terror of Spain: her " knavish tricks," fire and
rapine are too numerous to be blinked or written away,
too atrocious to be forgiven: to revenge becomes a
sacred duty. However governments may change, the
policy of France is immutable. Perfidy, backed by
violence, " ruse doublée de force," is the state maxim
from Louis XIV. and Buonaparte down to Louis-
Philippe: the principle is the same, whether the instrument employed be the sword or wedding ring. The
weaker Spain is thus linked in the embrace of her
stronger neighbour, and has been made alternately her
dupe and victim, and degraded into becoming a mere
satellite, to be dragged along by fiery Mars. France
has forced her to share all her bad fortune, but never
has permitted her to participate in her success. Spain

has been tied to the car of her defeats, but never has
been allowed to mount it in the day of triumph. Her
friendship has always tended to denationalise Spain,
and by entailing the forced enmity of England, has
caused to her the loss of her navies and colonies in the
new world.

" The Pyrenean boundary," says the Duke of Wellington, "is the most vulnerable frontier of France,
probably the only vulnerable one;" accordingly she has
always endeavoured to dismantle the Spanish defences
and to foster insurrections and *pronunciamientos* in
Catalonia, for Spain's infirmity is her opportunity, and
therefore the " sound policy " of the rest of Europe is
to see Spain strong, independent, and able to hold her
own Pyrenean key.

While France therefore has improved her means of
approach and invasion, Spain, to whom the past is pro-
phetic of the future, has raised obstacles, and has left
her protecting barrier as broken and hungry as when
planned by her tutelar divinity. Nor are her highlanders
more practicable than their granite fastnesses. Here
dwell the smuggler, the rifle sportsman, and all who
defy the law : here is bred the hardy peasant, who, accustomed to scale mountains and fight wolves, becomes a
ready raw materials for the *guerrilleros*, and none were
ever more formidable to Rome or France than those
marshalled in these glens by Sertorius and Mina. When
the tocsin bell rings out, a hornet swarm of armed men,
the weed of the hills, starts up from every rock and
brake. The hatred of the Frenchman, which the Duke
said formed "part of a Spaniard's nature," seems to
increase in intensity in proportion to vicinity, for as they
touch, so they fret and rub each other : here it is the
antipathy of an antithesis; the incompatibility of the
saturnine and slow, with the mercurial and rapid; of the
proud, enduring, and ascetic, against the vain, the fickle,
and sensual; of the enemy of innovation and change, to
the lover of variety and novelty; and however tyrants
and tricksters may assert in the gilded galleries of Ver-
sailles that *Il n'y a plus de Pyrénées*, this party-wall of
Alps, this barrier of snow and hurricane, does and will

exist for ever : placed there by Providence, as was said
by the Gothic prelate Saint Isidore, they ever have forbidden and ever will forbid the banns of an unnatural
alliance, as in the days of Silius Italicus :

> " Pyrene celsâ nimbosi verticis arce
> Divisos Celtis laté prospectat Hiberos
> Atque æterna tenet magnis *divortia* terris."

If the eagle of Buonaparte could never build in the Arragonese Sierra, the lily of the Bourbon assuredly will not
take root in the Castilian plain ; so sings Ariosto :

> ———— " Che non lice
> Che 'l giglio in quel terreno habbia radice !"

This inveterate condition either of pronounced hostility, or at best of armed neutrality, has long rendered
these localities disagreeable to the man of the note-book.
The rugged mountain frontiers consist of a series of
secluded districts, which constitute the entire world to
the natives, who seldom go beyond the natural walls by
which they are bounded, except to smuggle. This voca-
tion is the curse of the country ; it fosters a wild reliance
on self-defence, a habit of border foray and insurrection,
which seems as necessary to them as a moral excitement
and combustible element, as carbon and hydrogen are in
their physical bodies. Their habitual suspicion against
prying foreigners, which is an Oriental and Iberian instinct, converts a curious traveller into a spy or partisan.
Spanish authorities, who seldom do these things except
on compulsion, cannot understand the gratuitous braving
of hardship and danger for its own sake—the botanizing
and geologising, etc., of the nature and adventure-loving
English. The *impertinente curioso* may possibly escape
observation in a Spanish city and crowd, but in these
lonely hills it is out of the question : he is the observed
of all observers; and they, from long smuggling and
sporting habits, are always on the look-out, and are
keen-sighted as hawks, gipseys, and beasts of prey.
Latterly some who, by being placed immediately under
the French boundary, have seen the glitter of our

tourists' coin, have become more humanised, and
anxious to obtain a share in the profits of the season.

The geology and botany have yet to be properly in-
vestigated. In the metal-pregnant Pyrenees rude forges
of iron abound, but everything is conducted on a small,
unscientific scale, and probably after the unchanged
primitive Iberian system. Fuel is scarce, and transport
of ores on muleback expensive. The iron is at once
inferior to the English and much dearer : the tools and
implements used on both sides of the Pyrenees are at
least a century behind ours; while absurd tariffs, which
prevent the importation of a cheaper and better article,
retard improvements in agriculture and manufactures,
and perpetuate poverty and ignorance among backward,
half-civilised populations. The timber, moreover, has
suffered much from the usual neglect, waste, and improvidence of the natives, who destroy more than they
consume, and never replant. The sporting in these lonely
wild districts is excellent, for where man seldom penetrates the feræ naturæ multiply : the bear is, however,
getting scarce, as a premium is placed on every head destroyed. The grand object is the *Cabra Montanez*, or
Rupicapra, German Steinbock, the Bouquetin of the
French, the Izard (*Ibex*, becco, bouc, bock, buck). The
fascination of this pursuit, like that of the Chamois in
Switzerland, leads to constant and even fatal accidents,
as this shy animal lurks in almost inaccessible localities,
and must be stalked with the nicest skill. The sporting
on the north side is far inferior, as the cooks of the table-
d'hôtes have waged a *guerra al cuchillo*, a war to the
knife, and fork too, against even *les petits oiseaux;* but
your French *artiste* persecutes even minnows, as all
sport and fair play is scouted, and everything gives way
for the pot. The Spaniards, less mechanical and gastronomic, leave the feathered and finny tribes in comparative peace. Accordingly the streams abound with trout,
and those which flow into the Atlantic with salmon. The
lofty Pyrenees are not only alembics of cool crystal
streams, but contain, like the heart of Sappho, sources
of warm springs under a bosom of snow. The most
celebrated issue on the north side, or at least those which

are the most known and frequented, for the Spaniard is a small bather, and no great drinker of medicinal waters. Accommodations at the baths on his side scarcely exist, while even those in France are paltry when compared to the spas of Germany, and dirty and indecent when contrasted with those of England. The scenery is alpine, a jumble of mountain, precipice, glacier, and forest, enlivened by the cataract or hurricane. The natives, when not smugglers or *guerrilleros*, are rude, simple, and pastoral they are poor and picturesque, as people are who dwell in mountains. *Plains* which produce " bread stuffs " may be richer, but what can a traveller or painter do with their monotonous commonplace?

In these wild tracts the highlanders in summer lead their flocks up to mountain huts and dwell with their cattle, struggling against poverty and wild beasts, and endeavouring really to keep the wolf from the door : their watch-dogs are magnificent; the sheep are under admirable control—being, as it were, in the presence of the enemy, they know the voice of their shepherds, or rather the peculiar whistle and cry : their wool is largely smuggled into France, and when manufactured in the shape of coarse cloth is then re-smuggled back again.

CHAPTER III

THERE are six great rivers in Spain,—the arteries which run between the seven mountain chains, the vertebræ of the geological skeleton. These water-sheds are each intersected in their extent by others on a minor scale, by valleys and indentations, in each of which runs its own stream. Thus the rains and melted snows are all collected in an infinity of ramifications, and are carried by these tributary conduits into one of the main trunks, which all, with the exception of the Ebro, empty themselves into the Atlantic. The Duero and Tagus, unfortunately for Spain, disembogue in Portugal, and thus become a portion of a foreign dominion exactly where their commercial importance is the greatest. Philip II. saw the true value of the possession of an angle which rounded Spain, and insured to her the possession of these valuable outlets of internal produce, and inlets for external commerce. Portugal annexed to Spain gave more real power to his throne than the dominion of entire continents across the Atlantic, and is the secret object of every Spanish government's ambition. The *Miño*, which is the shortest of these rivers, runs through a bosom of fertility. The *Tajo*, Tagus, which the fancy of poets has sanded with gold and embanked with roses, tracks much of its dreary way through rocks and comparative barrenness. The *Guadiana* creeps through lonely Estremadura, infecting the low plains with miasma. The *Guadalquivir* eats out its deep banks amid the sunny olive-clad regions of Andalucia, as the Ebro divides the levels of Arragon. Spain abounds with brackish streams, *Salados*, and with salt-mines, or saline deposits after the evaporation of the sea-waters; indeed, the soil of the central portions is so strongly impregnated with " villainous saltpetre," that the small province of La Mancha alone could furnish materials to blow up the world; the surface of these regions, always arid, is every day becoming more so, from the singular antipathy which the inhabitants of the interior have against trees. There is nothing to check the power of rapid evaporation, no shelter to protect or preserve moisture. The soil becomes more and more parched and dried up, insomuch that in some parts it has almost ceased to be available for cultivation : another serious evil, which arises from want of plantations, is, that the slopes of hills are everywhere liable to constant denudation of soil after heavy rain. There is nothing to break the descent of the water; hence the naked, barren stone summits of many of the sierras, which have been pared and peeled of every particle capable of nourishing vegetation : they are skeletons where life is extinct; not only is the soil thus lost, but the detritus washed down either forms bars at the mouths of rivers, or chokes up and raises their beds; they are thus rendered liable to overflow their banks, and convert the adjoining plains into pestilential swamps. The supply of water, which is afforded by periodical rains, and which ought to support the reservoirs of rivers, is carried off at once in violent floods, rather than in a gentle gradual disembocation. From its mountainous character Spain has very few lakes, as the fall is too considerable to allow water to accumulate; the exceptions which do exist might with greater propriety be termed lochs—not that they are to be compared in size or beauty to some of those in Scotland. The volume in the principal rivers of Spain has diminished, and is diminishing; thus some which once were navigable, are so no longer, while the artificial canals which were to have been substituted remain unfinished : the progress of deterioration advances, while little is done to counteract or amend what every year must render more difficult and expensive, while the means of repair and correction will diminish in equal proportion, from the poverty occasioned by the evil, and by the fearful extent which it will be allowed to attain. However, several grand water-companies have been lately formed, who are to dig Artesian wells, finish canals, navigate rivers with steamers, and *issue shares at a premium*, which will be effected if nothing else is.

The rivers which are really adapted to navigation are, however, only those which are perpetually fed by those tributary streams that flow down from mountains which are covered with snow all the year, and these are not many. The majority of Spanish rivers are very scanty of water during the summer time, and very rapid in their flow when filled by rains or melting snow : during these periods they are impracticable for boats. They are, moreover, much exhausted by being drained off, *sangrado*—that is, bled, for the purpose of artificial irrigation; thus, at Madrid and Valencia, the wide beds of the Manzanares and the Turia are frequently dry as the sands of the seashore when the tide is out. They seem only to be entitled to be called rivers by courtesy, because they have so many and such splendid bridges; as numerous are the jokes cut by the newly-arrived stranger, who advises the townsfolk to sell one of them to purchase water, or compares their thirsting arches to the rich man in torments, who prays for one drop; but a heavy rain in the mountains soon shows the necessity for their strength and length, for their wide and lofty arches, their buttress-like piers, which before had appeared to be rather the freaks of architectural magnificence than the works of public utility. Those who live in a comparatively level country can scarcely form an idea of the rapidity and fearful destruction of the river inundations in this land of mountains. The deluge rolls forth in an avalanche, the rising water coming down tier above tier like a flight of steps let loose. These tides carry everything before them—scarring and gullying up the earth, tearing down rocks, trees, and houses, and strewing far and wide the relics of ruin; but the fierce fury is short-lived, and is spent in its own violence; thus the traveller at Madrid, if he wishes to see its Thames, should run down or take the 'bus as he can, when it rains, or the river will be gone before he gets there. When the Spaniards, under those blockheads Blake and Cuesta, lost the battle of *Rio Seco*, which gave Madrid to Buonaparte, the French soldiers, in crossing the *dry river* bed in pursuit of the fugitives, exclaimed,—" Why, Spanish rivers run away too!"

Many of these beds serve in remote districts, where highways and bridges are thought to be superfluous luxuries, for the double purposes of a river when there is water in them, and as a road when there is not. Again, in this land of anomalies, some streams have no bridges, while other bridges have no streams; the most remarkable of these *pontes asinorum* is at Coria, where the Alagon is crossed at an inconvenient, and often dangerous ferry, while a noble bridge of five arches stands high and dry in the meadows close by. This has arisen from the river having quitted its old channel in some inundation; or, as Spaniards say, *salido de su madre*, gone out from its mother, who does not seem to know that it is out, or certainly does not care, since no steps have ever been taken by the Corians to coax it back again under its old arches; they call on Hercules to turn this Alpheus, and rely in the meantime on their proverb, that all fickle, unfaithful rivers repent and return to their legitimate beds after a thousand years, for nothing is hurried in Spain, *Despues de anos mil, vuelve el rio a su cubil*. On the fishing in these wandering streams we shall presently say something.

The navigation of Spanish rivers is Oriental, classical, and imperfect; the boats, barges, and bargemen carry one back beyond the mediæval ages, and are better calculated for artistical than commercial purposes. The "great river," the Guadalquivir, which was navigable in the time of the Romans as far as Cordova, is now scarcely practicable for sailing-vessels of a moderate size even up to Seville. Passengers, however, have facilities afforded them by the steamers which run backwards and forwards between this capital and Cadiz; these conveniences, it need not be said, were introduced from England, although the first steamer that ever paddled in waters was of Spanish invention, and was launched at Barcelona in 1543; but the Spanish Chancellor of the Exchequer of the time was a poor red tapist, and opposed the whole thing, which, as usual, fell to the ground. The steamers on the Guadalquivir are safe; indeed, in our times, the advertisements always stated that a mass was said before starting in the heretical contrivance, just as to this day Birmingham locomotives, when a railway is first opened in France, are sprinkled with holy water, and blessed by a bishop, which may be a new "wrinkle" to Mr. Hudson and the primate of York.

There is considerable talk in Arragon about rendering the Ebro navigable, and it has been surveyed this year by two engineers—English of course. The local newspapers compared the astonishment of the herns and peasantry, created on the banks by this arrival, as second only to that occasioned when Don Quixote and Sancho ventured near the same spot into the enchanted bark.

There has been still older and greater talk about establishing a water communication between Lisbon and Toledo, by means of the Tagus. This mighty river, which is in everybody's mouth, because the capital of the kingdom of Port wine is placed at its embouchure, is in fact almost as little known in Spain and out of it, as the Niger. It has been our fate to behold it in many places and various phases of its most poetical and picturesque course—first green and arrowy amid the yellow corn fields of New Castile; then freshening the sweet Tempe of Aranjuez, clothing the gardens with verdure, and filling the nightingale-tenanted glens with groves; then boiling and rushing around the granite ravines of rock-built Toledo, hurrying to escape from the cold shadows of its deep prison, and dashing joyously into light and liberty, to wander far away into silent plains, and on to Talavera, where its waters were dyed with brave blood, and gladly reflected the flash of the victorious bayonets of England,—triumphantly it rolls thence, under the shattered arches of Almaraz, down to desolate Estremadura, in a stream as tranquil as the azure sky by which it is curtained, yet powerful enough to force the mountains at Alcantra. There the bridge of Trajan is worth going a hundred miles to see; it stems the now fierce condensed stream, and ties the rocky gorges together; grand, simple, and solid, tinted by the tender colours of seventeen centuries, it looms like the grey skeleton of Roman power, with all the sentiment of loneliness, magnitude, and the interest of the past and present. Such are the glorious scenes we have beheld and sketched; such are the sweet waters in which we have refreshed our dusty and weary limbs.

How stern, solemn, and striking is this Tagus of Spain! No commerce has ever made it its highway—no English steamer has ever civilised its waters like those of France and Germany. Its rocks have witnessed battles, not peace; have reflected castles and dungeons, not quays or warehouses: few cities have risen on its banks, as on those of the Thames and Rhine; it is truly a river of Spain—that isolated and solitary land. Its waters are without boats, its banks without life; man has never laid his hand upon its billows, nor enslaved their free and independent gambols.

It is impossible to read Tom Campbell's admirable description of the Danube before its poetry was discharged by the smoke of our ubiquitous countrymen's Dampf Schiff, without applying his lines to this uncivilised Tagus :—

" Yet have I loved thy wild abode,
    Unknown, unploughed, untrodden shore,
Where scarce the woodman finds a road,
    And scarce the fisher plies an oar ;
For man's neglect I love thee more,
    That art nor avarice intrude
To tame thy torrent's thunder shock,
Or prune the vintage of thy rock,
    Magnificently rude !"

As rivers in a state of nature are somewhat scarce in
Great Britain, one more extract may be perhaps pardoned, and the more as it tends to illustrate Spanish
character, and explain *las cosas de España,* or the things
of Spain, which it is the object of these humble pages to
accomplish.

The Tagus rises in that extraordinary jumble of mountains, full of fossil bones, botany, and trout, that rise
between Cuenca and Teruel, and which being all but unknown, clamour loudly for the disciples of Isaac Walton
and Dr. Buckland. It disembogues into the sea at Lisbon, having flowed 375 miles in Spain, of which nature
destined it to be the aorta. The Toledan chroniclers
derive the name from Tagus, fifth king of Iberia, but
Bochart traces it to *Dag,* Dagon, a fish, as besides being
considered auriferous, the ancients pronounced it to be
piscatory. Not that the present Spaniards trouble their
head more about the fishes here than if they were croco-
diles. Grains of gold are indeed found, but barely
enough to support a poet, by amphibious paupers, called
artesilleros from their baskets, in which they collect the
sand, which is passed through a sieve.

The Tagus might easily be made navigable to the sea,
and then with the Xarama connect Madrid and Lisbon,
and facilitate importation of colonial produce, and exportation of wine and grain. Such an act would confer
more benefits upon Spain than ten thousand *charters* or
paper constitutions, guaranteed by the sword of Narvaez,
or the word and honour of Louis-Philippe. The performance has been contemplated by many *foreigners,* the
Toledans looking lazily on; thus in 1581, Antonelli, a
Neapolitan, and Juanelo Turriano, a Milanese, suggested
the scheme to Philip II., then master of Portugal; but

money was wanting—the old story—for his revenues
were wasted in relic-removing and in building the useless
Escorial, and nothing was made except water parties,
and odes to the " wise and great king " who *was* to
perform the deed, to the tune of Macbeth's witches, " *I'll
do, I'll do, I'll do*," for here the future is preferred to the
present tense. The project dozed until 1641, when two
other *foreigners*, Julio Martelli and Luigi Carduchi, in
vain roused Philip IV. from his siesta, who soon after
losing Portugal itself, forthwith forgot the Tagus.
Another century glided away, when in 1755 Richard
Wall, an Irishman, took the thing up; but Charles III.,
busy in waging French wars against England, wanted
cash. The Tagus has ever since, as it roared over its
rocky bed, like an unbroken barb, laughed at the Toledan
who dreamily angles for impossibilities on the bank, in-
voking Brunel, Hercules, and Rothschild, instead of putting his own shoulder to the water-wheel. In 1808 the
scheme was revived : Fro. Xavier de Cabanas, who had
studied in England our system of canals, published a
survey of the whole river; this folio ' *Memoria sobre la
Navigacion del Tajo*,' or, ' Memoir on the Navigation
of the Tagus,' Madrid, 1829, reads like the blue book of
one discovering the source of the Nile, so desert-like are
the unpeopled, uncultivated districts between Toledo and
Abrantes. Ferd. VII. thereupon issued an approving
paper decree, and so there the thing ended, although
Cabanas had engaged with Messrs. Wallis and Mason
for the machinery, etc. Recently the project has been
renewed by Señor Bermudez de Castro, an intelligent
gentleman, who, from long residence in England, has
imbibed the schemes and energy of the foreigner. *Veré-
mos !* " we shall see ;" for hope is a good breakfast but a
bad supper, says Bacon ; and in Spain things are begun
late in the day, and never finished ; so at least says the
proverb :—*En España se empieza tarde, y se acaba
nunca.*

CHAPTER IV

IN the divisions of the Peninsula which are effected by mountains, rivers, and climate, a leading principle is to be traced throughout, for it is laid down by the unerring hand of nature. The artificial, political, and conventional arrangement into kingdoms and provinces is entirely the work of accident and absence of design.

These provincial divisions were formed by the gradual union of many smaller and previously independent portions, which have been taken into Spain as a whole, just as our inconvenient counties constitute the kingdom of England; for the inconveniences of these results of the ebb and flow of the different tides in the affairs of man's dominion—these boundaries not fixed by the lines and rules of theodolite-armed land surveyors, use had provided remedies, and long habit had reconciled the inhabitants to divisions which suited them better than any new arrangement, however scientifically calculated, according to statistical and geographical principles.

The French, during their intrusive rule, were horrified at this " chaos administratif," this apparent irregularity, and introduced their own system of *départements*, by which districts were neatly squared out and people rearranged, as if Spain were a chess-board and Spaniards mere pawns—*peones*, or footmen, which this people, calling itself one of *caballeros*, that is, riders on horses *par excellence*, assuredly is not : nor, indeed, in this paradise of the church militant, can the moves of any Spanish bishop or knight be calculated on with mathematical certainty, since they seldom will take the steps to-morrow which they did yesterday.

Accordingly, however specious the theory, it was found to be no easy matter to carry departementalization out in practice : individuality laughs at the solemn nonsense of in-door pedants, who would class men like ferns or shells. The failure in this attempt to remodel ancient demarcations and recombine antipathetic populations was utter and complete. No sooner, therefore, had the Duke cleared the Peninsula of *doctrinaires* and invaders than

the Lion of Castile shook off their papers from his mane,
and reverted like the Italian, on whom the same experiment was tried, to his own pre-existing divisions, which,
however defective in theory, and unsightly and inconvenient on the map, had from long habit been found
practically to suit better. Recently, in spite of this experience among other newfangled transpyrenean reforms, innovations, and botherations, the Peninsula has again
been parcelled out into forty-nine provinces, instead of
the former national divisions of thirteen kingdoms, principalities, and lordships; but long will it be before these
deeply impressed divisions, which have grown with the
growth of the monarchy, and are engraved in the re-
tentive memories of the people, can be effaced.

Those who are curious in statistical details are referred
to the works of Paez, Antillon, and others, who are considered by Spaniards to be authorities on vast subjects,
which are fitter for a gazetteer or a handbook than for
volumes destined like these for lighter reading; and assuredly the pages of the respectable Spaniards just named
are duller than the high-roads of Castile, which no tiny
rivulet the cheerful companion of the dusty road ever
freshens, no stray flower adorns, no song of birds gladdens—"dry as the remainder of the biscuit after the
voyage."

The thirteen divisions have grand and historical
names : they belong to an old and monarchical country,
not to a spick and span vulgar democracy, without title-
deeds. They fill the mouth when named, and conjure up
a thousand recollections of the better and more glorious
times of Spain's palmy power, when there were giants in
the land, not pigmies in Parisian *paletots*, whose only
ambition is to ape the foreigner, and disgrace and denationalise themselves.

First and foremost *Andalucia* presents herself, crowned
with a quadruple, not a triple tiara, for the name *los
cuatro reinos*, "the four kingdoms," is her synonym.
They consist of those of Seville, Cordova, Jaen, and
Granada. There is magic and birdlime in the very
letters. Secondly advances the kingdom of *Murcia*, with
its silver-mines, barilla, and palms. Then the gentle

kingdom of *Valencia* appears, all smiles, with fruits and silk. The principality of grim and truculent *Catalonia* scowls next on its fair neighbour. Here rises the smoky factory chimney; here cotton is spun, vice and discontent bred, and revolutions concocted. The proud and stiff-necked kingdom of *Arragon* marches to the west with this Lancashire of Spain, and to the east with the king-dom of Navarre, which crouches with its green valleys under the Pyrenees. The three *Basque Provinces* which abut thereto, are only called *El Senorio*, " The Lord-ship," for the king of all the Spains is but simple lord of this free highland home of the unconquered descend-ants of the aboriginal man of the Peninsula. Here there is much talk of bullocks and *fueros*, or " privileges;" for when not digging and delving, these gentlemen by the mere fact of being born here, are fighting and uphold-ing their good rights by the sword. The empire province of the *Castiles* furnishes two coronets to the royal brow; to wit, that of the older portion, where the young monarchy was nursed, and that of the newer portion, which was wrested afterwards from the infidel Moor. The ninth division is desolate *Estremadura*, which has no higher title than a province, and is peopled by locusts, wandering sheep, pigs, and here and there by human bipeds. *Leon*, a most time-honoured kingdom, stretches higher up, with its corn-plains and venerable cities, now silent as tombs, but in auld lang syne the scenes of mediæval chivalry and romance. The kingdom of *Gal-licia* and the principality of the *Asturias* form the sea-board to the west, and constitute Spain's breakwater against the Atlantic.

It is not very easy to ascertain the exact population of any country, much less that of one which does not yet possess the advantages of public registrars; the people at large, for whom, strange to say, the pleasant studies of statistics and political economy have small charms, consider any attempt to number them as boding no good; they have a well-grounded apprehension of ulterior objects. To " number the people " was a crime in the East, and many moral and practical difficulties exist in arriving at a true census of Spain. Thus, while some writers on statistics hope to flatter the powers that be, by a glowing exaggeration of national strength, "to boast of which," says the Duke, "is the national weakness," the suspicious *many*, on the other hand, are disposed to conceal and diminish the truth. We should be always on our guard when we hear accounts of the past or present population, commerce, or revenue of Spain. The better classes will magnify them both, for the credit of their country; the poorer, on the other hand, will appeal *ad misericordiam*, by representing matters as even worse than they really are. They never afford any opening, however indirect, to information which may lead to poll-taxes and conscriptions..

The population and the revenue have generally been exaggerated, and all statements may be much discounted; the present population, at an approximate calculation, may be taken at about eleven or twelve millions, with a slow tendency to increase. This is a low figure for so large a country, and for one which, under the Romans, is said to have swarmed with inhabitants as busy and industrious as ants; indeed, the longest period of rest and settled government which this ill-fated land has ever enjoyed was during the three centuries that the Roman power was undisputed. The Peninsula is then seldom mentioned by authors; and how much happiness is inferred by that silence, when the blood-spattered page of history was chiefly employed to register great calamities, plagues, pestilences, wars, battles, or the freaks of men, at which angels weep! Certainly one of the causes which have changed this happy state of things, has been the numerous and fierce invasions to which Spain has been exposed; fatal to her has been her gift of beauty and wealth, which has ever attracted the foreign ravisher and spoiler. The Goths, to whom a worse name has been given than they deserved in Spain, were ousted by the Moors, the real and wholesale destroyers; bringing to the darkling West the luxuries, arts and sciences of the bright East, they had nothing to learn from the conquered; to them the Goth was no instructor, as the Roman had been to him; they despised both of their predecessors, with whose wants and works they had no sympathy, while they abhorred their creed as idolatrous

and polytheistic—down went altar and image. There
was no fair town which they did not destroy; they exterminated, say their annals, the fowls of the air.

The Gotho-Spaniard in process of time retaliated, and
combated the invader with his own weapons, bettering
indeed the destructive lesson which was taught. The
effects of these wars, carried on without treaty, without
quarter, and waged for country and creed, are evident in
those parts of Spain which were their theatre. Thus,
vast portions of Estremadura, the south of Toledo and
Andalucia, by nature some of the richest and most fertile
in the world, are now *dehesas y desploblados*, depopulated wastes, abandoned to the wild bee for his heritage;
the country remains as it was left after the discomfiture
of the Moor. The early chronicles of both Spaniard and
Moslem teem with accounts of the annual forays inflicted on each other, and to which a frontier-district was
always exposed. The object of these border *guerrilla*-
warfares was extinction, *talar, quemar y robar*, to desolate, burn, and rob, to cut down fruit-trees, to " harry,"
to " razzia." [1] The internecine struggle was that of
rival nations and creeds. It was truly Oriental, and such
as Ezekiel, who well knew the Phœnicians, has described : " Go ye after him through the city and smite;
let not your eye have pity, neither have ye pity; slay
utterly old and young, both maids and little children and
women." The religious duty of smiting the infidel pre-
cluded mercy on both sides alike, for the Christian foray
and crusade was the exact counterpart of the Moslem
algara and *algihad;* while, from military reasons, everything was turned into a desert, in order to create a
frontier Edom of starvation, a defensive glacis, through
which no invading army could pass and live; the " beasts
of the field alone increased." Nature, thus abandoned,
resumed her rights, and has cast off every trace of former cultivation; and districts the granaries of the Roman
and the Moor, now offer the saddest contrasts to that
former prosperity and industry.

[1] *Razzia* is derived from the Arabic *Al ghazia*, a word which
expresses these raids of a ferocious, barbarous age. It has been
introduced to European dictionaries by the Pelissiers, who thus
civilise Algeria. They make a solitude, and call it peace.

To these horrors succeeded the thinning occasioned by causes of a bigoted and political nature : the expulsion of the Jews deprived poor Spain of her bankers, while the final banishment of the Moriscoes, the remnant of the Moors, robbed the soil of its best and most industrious agriculturists.

Again, in our time, have the fatal scenes of contending Christian and Moor been renewed in the struggle for national independence, waged by Spaniards against the Buonapartist invaders, by whom neither age nor sex was spared—neither things sacred nor profane; the land is everywhere scarred with ruins; a few hours' Vandalism sufficed to undo the works of ages of piety, wealth, learning and good taste. The French retreat was worse than their advance : then, infuriated by disgrace and disaster, the Soults and Massénas vented their spite on the unarmed villagers and their cottages. But let General Foy describe their progress—" Ainsi que la neige précipitée des sommets des Alpes dans les vallons, nos armées innombrables détruisaient en quelques heures, par leur seul passage, les ressources de toute une contrée ; elles bivouaquaient habituellement, et à chaque gîte nos soldats démolissaient les maisons bâties depuis un demi-siècle, pour construire avec les décombres ces longs villages alignés qui souvent ne devaient durer qu'un jour : au défaut du bois des forêts les arbres fruitiers, les végétaux précieux, comme le mûrier, l'olivier, l'oranger, servaient à les réchauffer ; les conscrits irrités à la fois par le besoin et par le danger contractaient *une ivresse morale* dont nous ne cherchions pas à les guérir."

" So France gets drunk with blood to vomit crime,
And fatal ever have her saturnalia been."

Who can fail to compare this habitual practice of Buonaparte's legions with the terrible description in Hosea of the " great people and strong " who execute the dread judgments of heaven?—" A fire devoureth before them, and behind them a flame burneth ; the land is the garden of Eden before them, and behind them a desolate wilderness, yea, and nothing shall escape them."

No sooner were they beaten out by the Duke, than population began to spring up again, as the bruised flowerets do when the iron heel of marching hordes has passed on. Then ensued the civil fratricide wars, drain-ing the land of its males, from which bleeding Spain has not yet recovered. Insecurity of property and person will ever prove bars to marriage and increased population.

Again, a deeper and more permanent curse has steadily operated for the last two centuries, at which Spanish authors long have not dared to hint. They have ascribed the depopulation of Estremadura to the swarm of colonist adventurers and emigrants who departed from this province of Cortes and Pizarro to seek for fortune in the new world of gold and silver; and have attributed the similar want of inhabitants in Andalucia to the similar outpouring from Cadiz, which, with Seville, engrossed the traffic of the Americas. But colonisation never thins a vigorous, well-conditioned mother state—witness the rapid and daily increase of population in our own island, which, like Tyre of old, is ever sending forth her outpouring myriads, and wafts to the uttermost parts of the sea, on the white wings of her merchant fleets, the blessings of peace, religion, liberty, order, and civilisation, to disseminate which is the mission of Great Britain.

The real permanent and standing cause of Spain's thinly peopled state, want of cultivation, and abomina-tion of desolation, is BAD GOVERNMENT, civil and re-ligious; this all who run may read in her lonely land and silent towns. But Spain, if the anecdote which her children love to tell be true, will never be able to remove the incubus of this fertile origin of every evil. When Ferdinand III. captured Seville and died, being a saint he escaped purgatory, and Santiago presented him to the Virgin, who forthwith desired him to ask any favours for beloved Spain. The monarch petitioned for oil, wine, and corn—conceded; for sunny skies, brave men, and pretty women—allowed; for cigars, relics, garlic, and bulls—by all means; for a *good government*—" Nay, nay," said the Virgin, " that never can be granted; for

were it bestowed, not an angel would remain a day
longer in heaven."

The present revenue may be taken at about 12,000,000*l.*
or 13,000,000*l.* sterling; but money is compared by
Spaniards to oil; a little will stick to the fingers of those
who measure it out; and such is the robbing and jobbing,
the official mystification and peculation, that it is difficult
to get at *facts* whenever cash is in question. The
revenue, moreover, is badly collected, and at a ruinous
per centage, and at no time during this last century has
been sufficient for the national expenses. Recourse has
been had to the desperate experiments of usurious loans
and wholesale confiscations. At one time church pillage
and appropriation was almost the only item in the
governmental budget. The recipients were ready to
" prove from Vatel exceedingly well " that the first duty
of a rich clergy was to relieve the necessitous, and the
more when the State was a pauper: croziers are no
match for bayonets. This system necessarily cannot
last. Since the reign of Philip II. every act of dishonesty
has been perpetrated. Public securities have been " repudiated," interest unpaid, and principal spunged out.
No country in the Old World, or even New drab-coated
World, stands lower in financial discredit. Let all be
aware how they embark in Spanish speculations : however promising in the prospectus, they will, sooner or
later, turn out to be deceptions; and whether they
assume the form of loans, lands, or rails, none are *real*
securities : they are mere castles in the air, *châteaux en
Espagne:* " The earth has bubbles as the water has,
and these are of them."

For the benefit and information of those who have
purchased Iberian stock, it may be stated that an Exchange, or *Bolsa de Comercio,* was established at Madrid
in 1831. It may be called the *coldest* spot in the hot
capital, and the *idlest,* since the usual " city article " is
short and sweet, " *sin operaciones,*" or nothing has
been bought or sold. It might be likened to a tomb,
with " Here *lies* Spanish credit " for its epitaph. If
there be a thing which " *La perfide Albion,*" " a nation
of shopkeepers," dislikes, worse even than a French

assignat, it is a bankrupt.   One circumstance is clear,
that Castilian *pundonor*, or point of honour, will rather
settle its debts with cold iron and warm abuse than with
gold and thanks.

The Exchange at Madrid was first held at *St. Martin's*,
a saint who divided his cloak with a supplicant.   As
comparisons are odious, and bad examples catching, it
has been recently removed to the *Calle del Desengaño*,
the street of " finding out fallacious hopes," a locality
which the bitten will not deem ill-chosen.

As all men in power use their official knowledge in
taking advantage of the turn of the market, the *Bolsa*
divides with the court and army the moving influence of
every *situacion* or crisis of the moment : clever as are
the ministers of Paris, they are mere tyros when compared to their colleagues of Madrid in the arts of working
the telegraph, gazette, etc., and thereby feathering their
own nests.

The Stock Exchange is open from ten to three o'clock,
where those who like Spanish funds may buy them as
cheap as stinking mackerel; for when the 3 per cents.
of perfidious Albion are at 98, surely Spanish fives at
22 are a tempting investment. The stocks are numerous,
and suited to all tastes and pockets, whether those
funded by Aguado, Ardouin, Toreno, Mendizabal, or
Mon, " all honourable men," and whose punctuality is
un-remitting, for in some the principal is consolidated,
in others the interest is deferred; the grand financial
object in all having been to receive as much as possible,
and pay back in an inverse ratio—their leading principle
being to bag both principal and interest.   As we have
just said, in measuring out money and oil a little will
stick to the cleanest fingers—the Madrid ministers and
contractors made fortunes, and actually " did " the
Hebrews of London, as their forefathers spoiled the
Egyptians.   But from Philip II. downwards, theologians
have never been wanting in Spain to prove the religious,
however painful, duty of bankruptcy, and particularly
in contracts with usurious heretics.   The stranger, when
shown over the Madrid bank, had better evince no im-
pertinent curiosity to see the " Dividend *pay* office," as

it might give offence. Whatever be our dear reader's pursuit in the Peninsula, let him—

> "Neither a borrower nor lender be,
> For loan oft loseth both itself and friend."

Beware of Spanish stock, for in spite of official reports, *documentos*, and arithmetical mazes, which, intricate as an arabesque pattern, look well on paper without being intelligible; in spite of ingenious conversions, fundings of interest, coupons—some active, some passive, and other repudiatory terms and tenses, the present excepted —the thimblerig is always the same; and this is the question, since national credit depends on national good faith and surplus income, how can a country pay interest on debts, whose revenues have long been, and now are, miserably insufficient for the ordinary expenses of government? You cannot get blood from a stone; *ex nihilo nihil fit.*

Mr. Macgregor's report on Spain, a truthful exposition of commercial ignorance, habitual disregard of treaties and violation of contracts, describes her public *securities*, past and present. Certainly they had very imposing names and titles—*Juros Bonos, Vales reales, Titulos*, etc.,—much more royal, grand, and poetical than our prosaic *Consols;* but no oaths can attach real value to dishonoured and good-for-nothing paper. According to some financiers, the public debts of Spain, previously to 1808, amounted to 83,763,966*l.*, which have since been increased to 279,083,089*l.*, farthings omitted, for we like to be accurate. This possibly may be exaggerated, for the government will give no information as to its own peculation and mismanagement: according to Mr. Henderson, 78,649,675*l.* of this debt is due to English creditors alone, and we wish they may get it, when he gets to Madrid. In the time of James I., Mr. Howell was sent there on much such an errand; and when he left it, his "pile of unredressed claims was higher than himself." At all events, Spain is over head and ears in debt, and irremediably insolvent. And yet few countries, if we regard the fertility of her soil, her golden possessions at home and abroad, her frugal temperate population, ought to have been less embarrassed;

but Heaven has granted her every blessing, except a
good and honest government. It is either a bully or a
craven : satisfaction in twenty-four hours *à la Bresson*,
or a line-of-battle ship off Malaga—Cromwell's receipt—
is the only argument which these semi-Moors understand : conciliatory language is held to be weakness :
you may obtain at once from their fears what never will
be granted by their sense of justice.

CHAPTER V

OF the many misrepresentations regarding Spain, few
are more inveterate than those which refer to the dangers
and difficulties that are there supposed to beset the
traveller. This, the most romantic, racy, and peculiar
country of Europe, may in reality be visited by sea and
land, and throughout its length and breadth, with ease
and safety, as all who have ever been there well know,
the nonsense with which Cockney critics who never have
been there scare delicate writers in albums and lady-bird
tourists, to the contrary notwithstanding : the steamers
are regular, the mails and diligences excellent, the roads
decent, and the mules sure-footed; nay, latterly, the
posadas, or inns, have been so increased, and the robbers
so decreased, that some ingenuity must be evinced in
getting either starved or robbed. Those, however, who
are dying for new excitements, or who wish to make a
picture or chapter, in short, to get up an adventure for
the home-market, may manage by a great exhibition of
imprudence, chattering, and a holding out luring baits,
to gratify their hankering, although it would save some
time, trouble, and expense to try the experiment much
nearer home.

As our readers live in an island, we will commence
with the sea and steamers.

The Peninsular and Oriental Navigation Company depart regularly three times a month from Southampton
for Gibraltar. They often arrive at Corunna in seventy

hours, from whence a mail starts directly to Madrid, which it reaches in three days and a half. The vessels are excellent sea-boats, are manned by English sailors, and propelled by English machinery. The passage to Vigo has been made in less than three days, and the voyage to Cadiz—touching at Lisbon included—seldom exceeds six. The change of climate, scenery, men, and manners effected by this week's trip, is indeed remarkable. Quitting the British Channel we soon enter the "sleepless Bay of Biscay," where the stormy petrel is at home, and where the gigantic swell of the Atlantic is first checked by Spain's iron-bound coast, the mountain break-water of Europe. Here *The Ocean* will be seen in all its vast majesty and solitude : grand in the tempest-lashed storm, grand in the calm, when spread out as a mirror; and never more impressive than at night, when the stars of heaven, free from earth-born mists, sparkle like diamonds over those "who go down to the sea in ships, and behold the works of the Lord, and his wonders in the deep." The land has disappeared, and man feels alike his weakness and his strength; a thin plank separates him from another world; yet he has laid his hand upon the billow, and mastered the ocean; he has made it the highway of commerce, and the binding link of nations.

The steamers which navigate the Eastern coast from Marseilles to Cadiz and back again, are cheaper indeed in their fares, but by no means such good sea-boats; nor do they keep their time—the essence of business—with English regularity. They are foreign built, and worked by Spaniards and Frenchmen. They generally stop a day at Barcelona, Valencia, and other large towns, which gives them an opportunity to replenish coal, and to smuggle. A rapid traveller is also thus enabled to pay a flying visit to the cities on the seaboard; and thus those lively authors who comprehend foreign nations with an intuitive eagle-eyed glance, obtain materials for sundry octavos on the history, arts, sciences, literature, and genius of Spaniards. But as Mons. Feval remarks of some of his gifted countrymen, they have merely to scratch their head, according to the Horatian expression, and out come a number of volumes, ready bound in calf, as Minerva issued forth armed from the temple of Jupiter.

The Mediterranean is a dangerous, deceitful sea, fair and false as Italia; the squalls are sudden and terrific; then the crews either curse the sacred name of God, or invoke St. Telmo, according as their notion may be. We have often been so caught when sailing on these perfidious waters in these foreign craft, and think, with the Spaniards, that escape is a miracle. The hilarity excited by witnessing the jabber, confusion, and lubber proceedings, went far to dispel all present apprehension, and future also. Some of our poor blue-jackets in case of a war may possibly escape the fate with which they are threatened in this French lake. But no wise man will ever go by sea when he can travel by land, nor is viewing Spain's coasts with a telescope from the deck, and passing a few hours in a sea-port, a very satisfactory mode of becoming acquainted with the country.

The roads of Spain, a matter of much importance to a judicious traveller, are somewhat a modern luxury, having been only regularly introduced by the Bourbons. The Moors and Spaniards, who rode on horses and not in carriages, suffered those magnificent lines with which the Romans had covered the Peninsula to go to decay; of these there were no less than twenty-nine of the first order, which were absolutely necessary to a nation of conquerors and colonists to keep up their military and commercial communications. The grandest of all, which like the Appian might be termed the Queen of Roads, ran from Merida, the capital of Lusitania, to Salamanca. It was laid down like a Cyclopean wall, and much of it remains to this day, with the grey granite line stretching across the aromatic wastes, like the vertebræ of an extinct mammoth. We have followed for miles its course, which is indicated by the still standing miliary columns that rise above the cistus underwood; here and there tall forest trees grow out of the stone pavement, and show how long it has been abandoned by man to Nature ever young and gay, who thus by uprooting and displacing the huge blocks slowly recovers her rights.

She festoons the ruins with necklaces of flowers and
creepers, and hides the rents and wrinkles of odious, all-
dilapidating Time, or man's worse neglect, as a pretty
maid decorates a shrivelled dowager's with diamonds.
The Spanish muleteer creeps along by its side in a track
which he has made through the sand or pebbles; he
seems ashamed to trample on this lordly way, for which,
in his petty wants, he has no occasion. Most of the
similar roads have been taken up by monks to raise
convents, by burgesses to build houses, by military men
to construct fortifications—thus even their ruins have
perished.

The mediæval Spanish roads were the works of the
clergy; and the long-bearded monks, here as elsewhere,
were the pioneers of civilisation; they made straight,
wide, and easy the way which led to their convent, their
high place, their miracle shrine, or to whatever point of
pilgrimage that was held out to the devout; traffic was
soon combined with devotion, and the service of mam-
mon with that of God. This imitation of the Oriental
practice which obtained at Mecca, is evidenced by language in which the Spanish term *Feria* signifies at once
a religious function, a holiday, and a fair. Even saints
condescended to become waywardens, and to take title
from the highway. Thus *Santo Domingo de la Calzada*,
" St. Domenick of the *Paved Road*," was so called from
his having been the first to make one through a part of
Old Castile for the benefit of pilgrims on their way to
Compostella, and this town yet bears the honoured
appellation.

This feat and his legend have furnished Southey with
a subject of a droll ballad. The saint having finished
his road, next set up an inn or *Venta*, the Maritornes of
which fell in love with a handsome pilgrim, who resisted;
whereupon she hid some spoons in this Joseph's saddle-
bags, who was taken up by the Alcalde, and forthwith
hanged. But his parents some time afterwards passed
under the body, which told them that he was innocent,
alive, and well, and all by the intercession of the sainted
road-maker; thereupon they proceeded forthwith to the
truculent Alcalde, who was going to dine off two roasted

fowls, and, on hearing their report, remarked, You
might as well tell me that this cock (pointing to his rôti)
would crow; whereupon it did crow, and was taken with
its hen to the cathedral, and two chicks have ever since
been regularly hatched every year from these respectable
parents, of which a travelling ornithologist should secure
one for the Zoological Garden. The cock and hen were
duly kept near the high altar, and their white feathers
were worn by pilgrims in their caps. Prudent bagsmen
will, however, put a couple of ordinary roast fowls into
their "provend," for hungry is this said road to
Logroño.

In this land of miracles, anomalies, and contradictions,
the roads to and from this very *Compostella* are now
detestable. In other provinces of Spain, the star-paved
milky way in heaven is called *El Camino de Santiago,*
the road of St. James; but the Gallicians, who know
what their roads really are, namely, the worst on earth,
call the milky way *El Camino de Jerusalem,* "the road
to Jerusalem," which it assuredly is not. The ancients
poetically attributed this phenomenon to some spilt milk
of Juno.

Meanwhile the roads in Gallicia, although under the
patronage of Santiago, who has replaced the Roman
Hermes, are, like his milky-way in heaven, but little
indebted to mortal repairs. The Dean of Santiago is
waywarden by virtue of his office or dignity, and especially "protector." The chapter, however, now chiefly
profess to make smooth the road to a better world. They
have altogether degenerated from their forefathers,
whose grand object was to construct roads for the
pilgrim; but since the cessation of offering-making
Hadjis, little or nothing has been done in the turnpike-
trust line.

Some of the finest roads in Spain lead either to the
sitios or royal pleasure-seats of the king, or wind gently
up some elevated and monastery-crowned mountain like
Monserrat. The ease of the despot was consulted, while
that of his subjects was neglected; and the Sultan was
the State, Spain was his property, and Spaniards his
serfs, and willing ones, for as in the East, their perfect

equality amongst each other was one result of the im-
measurable superiority of the master of all. Thus, while
he rolled over a road hard and level as a bowling-green,
and rapidly as a galloping team could proceed, to a mere
summer residence, the communication between Madrid
and Toledo, that city on which the sun shone on the day
light was made, has remained a mere track ankle-deep
in mud during winter and dust-clouded during summer,
and changing its direction with the caprice of wandering sheep and muleteers; but Bourbon Royalty never
visited this widowed capital of the Goths. The road
therefore was left as it existed if not before the time of
Adam, at least before Mac Adam. There is some talk
just now of beginning a regular road; when it will be
finished is another affair.

The church, which shared with the state in dominion,
followed the royal example in consulting its own comforts as to roads. Nor could it be expected in a torrid
land, that holy men, whose abdomens occasionally were
prominent and pendulous, should lard the stony or sandy
earth like goats, or ascend heaven-kissing hills so expe-
ditiously as their prayers. In Spain the primary consideration has ever been the souls, not the bodies, of
men, or legs of beasts. It would seem, indeed, from the
indifference shown to the sufferings of these quadrupedal
blood-engines, *Maquinas de sangre*, as they are called,
and still more from the reckless waste of biped life, that
a man was of no value until he was dead; then what
admirable contrivances for the rapid travelling of his
winged spirit, first to purgatory, next out again, and
thence from stage to stage to his journey's end and
blessed rest! More money has been thus expended in
masses than would have covered Spain with railroads,
even on a British scale of magnificence and extravagance.

To descend to the roads of the peninsular earth, the
principal lines are nobly planned. These geographical
arteries, which form the circulation of the country,
branch in every direction from Madrid, which is the
centre of the system. The road-making spirit of Louis
XIV. passed into his Spanish descendants, and during
the reigns of Charles III. and Charles IV. communica-

tions were completed between the capital and the principal cities of the provinces. These causeways, " *Arre-
cifes* "—these royal roads, " *Caminos reales* "—were
planned on an almost unnecessary scale of grandeur,
in regard both to width, parapets, and general execution.
The high road to La Coruña, especially after entering
Leon, will stand comparison with any in Europe; but
when Spaniards finish anything it is done in a grand
style, and in this instance the expense was so enormous
that the king inquired if it was paved with silver, alluding
to the common Spanish corruption of the old Roman via
lata into " camino de *plata*," of plate. This and many
of the others were constructed from fifty to seventy years
ago, and very much on the M'Adam system, which,
having been since introduced into England, has rendered
our roads so very different from what they were not very
long since. The war in the Peninsula tended to deteriorate the Spanish roads—when bridges and other conveniences were frequently destroyed for military reasons,
and the exhausted state of the finances of Spain, and
troubled times, have delayed many of the more costly
reparations; yet those of the first class were so admirably constructed at the beginning, that, in spite of the
injuries of war, ruts, and neglect, they may, as a whole,
be pronounced equal to many of the Continent, and are
infinitely more pleasant to the traveller from the absence
of pavement. The roads in England have, indeed, latterly been rendered so excellent, and we are so apt to
compare those of other nations with them, that we forget
that fifty years ago Spain was in advance in that and
many other respects. Spain remains very much what
other countries were : she has stood on her old ways,
moored to the anchor of prejudice, while we have progressed, and consequently now appears behindhand in
many things in which she set the fashion to England.

The grand royal roads start from Madrid, and run to
the principal frontier and sea-port towns. Thus the
capital may be compared to a spider, as it is the centre
of the Peninsula web. These diverging fan-like lines are
sufficiently convenient to all who are about to journey
to any single terminus, but inter-communications are

almost entirely wanting between any one terminus with another. This scanty condition of the Peninsular roads accounts for the very limited portions of the country which are usually visited by foreigners, who—the French especially—keep to one beaten track, the high road, and follow each other like wild geese; a visit to Burgos, Madrid, and Seville, and then a steam trip from Cadiz to Valencia and Barcelona, is considered to be making the grand tour of Spain; thus the world is favoured with volumes that reflect and repeat each other, which tell us what we know already, while the rich and rare, the untrodden, unchanged, and truly Moro-Hispanic portions are altogether neglected, except by the exceptional few, who venture forth like Don Quixote on their horses, in search of adventures and the picturesque.

The other roads of Spain are bad, but not much more so than in other parts of the Continent, and serve tolerably well in dry weather. They are divided into those which are practicable for wheel-carriages, and those which are only bridle-roads, or as they call them, " of horseshoe," on which all thought of going with a carriage is out of the question; when these horse or mule tracks are very bad, especially among the mountains, they compare them to roads for partridges. The cross roads are seldom tolerable; it is safest to keep the high-road—or, as we have it in English, the furthest way round is the nearest way home—for there is no short cut without hard work, says the Spanish proverb, " ho hay atajo, sin trabajo."

All this sounds very unpromising, but those who adopt the customs of the country will never find much practical difficulty in getting to their journey's end; slowly, it is true, for where leagues and hours are convertible terms —the Spanish *hora* being the heavy German *stunde*— the distance is regulated by the day-light. Bridle-roads and travelling on horseback, the former systems of Europe, are very Spanish and Oriental; and where people journey on horse and mule back, the road is of minor importance. In the remoter provinces of Spain the population is agricultural and poverty-stricken, unvisiting and unvisited, not going much beyond their

chimney's smoke.   Each family provides for its simple
habits and few wants; having but little money to buy
foreign commodities, they are clad and fed, like the
Bedouins, with the productions of their own fields and
flocks. There is little circulation of persons; a neighbouring fair is the mart where they obtain the annual supply
of whatever luxury they can indulge in, or it is brought to
their cottages by wandering muleteers, or by the smuggler, who is the type and channel of the really active
principle of trade in three-fourths of the Peninsula.   It
is wonderful how soon a well-mounted traveller becomes
attached to travelling on horseback, and how quickly he
becomes reconciled to a state of roads which, startling
at first to those accustomed to carriage highways, are
found to answer perfectly for all the purposes of the
place and people where they are found.

Let us say a few things on Spanish railroads, for the
mania of England has surmounted the Pyrenees,
although confined rather more to words than deeds; in
fact, it has been said that no rail exists, in any country
of either the new world or the old one, in which the
Spanish language is spoken, probably from other objections than those merely philological.   Again, in other
countries roads, canals, and traffic usher in the rail,
which in Spain is to precede and introduce them.   Thus,
by the prudent delays of national caution and procrastination, much of the trouble and expense of these intermediate stages will be economised, and Spain will jump
at once from a mediæval condition into the comforts and
glories of Great Britain, the land of restless travellers.
Be that as it may, just now there is much talk of *railroads*, and splendid official and other *documentos* are
issued, by which the " whole country is to be intersected
(on paper) with a net-work of rapid and bowling-green
communications," which are to create a " perfect homo-
geneity among Spaniards;" for great as have been the
labours of Herculean steam, this amalgamation of the
Iberian rope of sand has properly been reserved for the
crowning performance.

It would occupy too much space to specify the infinite
lines which are in contemplation, which may be described

when completed. Suffice it to say, that they almost all are to be effected by the iron and gold of England. However this *estrangerismo*, this influence of the foreigner, may offend the sensitive pride, the *Españolismo* of Spain, the power of resistance offered by the national indolence and dislike to change, must be propelled by British steam, with a dash of French revolution. Yet our speculators might, perhaps, reflect that Spain is a land which never yet has been able to construct or support even a sufficient number of common roads or canals for her poor and passive commerce and circulation. The distances are far too great, and the traffic far too small, to call yet for the rail; while the geological formation of the country offers difficulties which, if met with even in England, would baffle the colossal science and extravagance of our first-rate engineers. Spain is a land of mountains, which rise everywhere in Alpine barriers, walling off province from province, and district from district. These mighty cloud-capped *sierras* are solid masses of hard stone, and any tunnels which ever perforate their ranges will reduce that at Box to the delving of the poor mole. You might as well cover Switzerland and the Tyrol with a net-work of *level* lines, as those caught in the aforesaid net will soon discover to their cost. The outlay of this up-hill work may be in an inverse ratio to the remuneration, for the one will be enormous, and the other paltry. The parturient mountains may produce a most musipular interest, and even that may be " deferred."

Spain, again, is a land of *dehesas y despoblados :* in these wild unpeopled wastes, next to travellers, commerce and cash are what is scarce, while even Madrid, the capital, is without industry or resources, and poorer than many of our provincial cities. The Spaniard, a creature of routine and foe to innovations, is not a moveable or locomotive ; local, and a parochial fixture by nature, he hates moving like a Turk, and has a particular horror of being hurried ; long, therefore, here has an ambling mule answered all the purposes of transporting man and his goods. Who again is to do the work even if Engand will pay the wages? The native, next

to disliking regular sustained labour himself, abhors
seeing the foreigner toiling even in his service, and wast-
ing his gold and sinews in the thankless task. The villagers, as they always have done, will rise against the
stranger and heretic who comes to " suck the wealth of
Spain." Supposing, however, by the aid of Santiago and
Brunel, that the work were possible and were completed,
how is it to be secured against the fierce action of the
sun, and the fiercer violence of popular ignorance? The
first cholera that visits Spain will be set down as a passenger per rail by the dispossessed muleteer, who now
performs the functions of steam and rail. He constitutes
one of the most numerous and finest classes in Spain,
and is the legitimate channel of the semi-Oriental caravan system. He will never permit the bread to be taken
out of his mouth by this Lutheran locomotive : deprived
of means of earning his livelihood, he, like the smuggler,
will take to the road in another line, and both will become either robbers or patriots. Many, long, and lonely
are the leagues which separate town from town in the
wide deserts of thinly-peopled Spain, nor will any preventive service be sufficient to guard the rail against
the *guerrilla* warfare that may then be waged. A handful
of opponents in any cistus-overgrown waste, may at any
time, in five minutes, break up the road, stop the train,
stick the stoker, and burn the engines in their own fire,
particularly smashing the luggage-train. What, again,
has ever been the recompense which the foreigner has
met with from Spain but breach of promise and ingrati-
tude? He will be used, as in the East, until the native
thinks that he has mastered his arts, and then he will
be abused, cast out, and trodden under foot ; and who
then will keep up and repair the costly artificial undertaking?—certainly not the Spaniard, on whose pericra-
nium the bumps of operative skill and mechanical
construction have yet to be developed.

The lines which are the least sure of failure will be
those which are the shortest, and pass through a level
country of some natural productions, such as oil, wine,
and coal. Certainly, if the rail can be laid down in
Spain by the gold and science of England, the gift,

like that of steam, will be worthy of the Ocean's Queen,
and of the world's real leader of civilisation; and what
a change will then come over the spirit of the Peninsula! how the siestas of torpid man-vegetation, will be
disturbed by the shrill whistle and panting snort of the
monster engine! how the seals of this long hermet-
ically shut-up land will be broken! how the cloistered
obscure, and dreams of treasures in heaven, will be
enlightened by the flashing fire-demon of the wide-
awake money-worshipper! what owls will be vexed,
what bats dispossessed, what drones, mules, and asses
will be scared, run over, and annihilated! Those who
love Spain, and pray, like the author, daily for her
prosperity, must indeed hope to see this "net-work of
rails" concluded, but will take especial care at the
same time not to invest one farthing in the imposing
speculation.

Recent results have fully justified during this year
what was prophesied last year in the Handbook: our
English agents and engineers were received with
almost divine honours by the Spaniards, so incensed
were they with flattery and cigars. Their shares were
instantaneously subscribed for, and directors nominated, with names and titles longer even than the lines,
and the smallest contributions in cash were thankfully
accepted:—

"L'argent dans une bourse entre agréablement;
Mais le terme venu, quand il faut le rendre,
C'est alors que les douleurs commencent à nous prendre."

When the period for booking up, for making the first
instalments, arrived, the Spanish shareholders were
found somewhat wanting: they repudiated; for in the
Peninsula it has long been easier to promise than to
pay. Again, on the only line which seems likely to be
carried out at present, that of Madrid to Aranjuez, the
first step taken by them was to dismiss all English
engineers and *navvies*, on the plea of encouraging
native talent and industry rather than the foreigner.
Many of the English home proceedings would border
on the ridiculous, were not the laugh of some speculators rather on the wrong side. The City capitalists

certainly have our pity, and if their plethora of wealth
required the relief of bleeding, it could not be better performed than by a Spanish *Sangrado*. How different some
of the windings-up, the final reports, to the magnificent
beginnings and grandiloquent prospectuses put forth as
baits for John Bull, who hoped to be tossed at once, or
elevated, from haberdashery to a throne, by being
offered a "potentiality of getting rich beyond the
dreams of avarice!" Thus, to clench assertion by
example, the London directors of the Royal Valencia
Company made known by an advertisement only last
July, that they merely required 240,000,000 reals to
connect the seaport of Valencia—where there is none
—to the capital Madrid, with 800,000 inhabitants,—
there not being 200,000. One brief passage alone
seemed ominous in the lucid array of prospective profit
—"The line has not yet been minutely surveyed;" this
might have suggested to the noble Marquis whose attractive name heads the provisional committee list, the
difficulty of Sterne's traveller, of whom, when observing how much better things were managed on the Continent than in England, the question was asked, "Have
you, sir, ever been there?"

A still wilder scheme was broached, to connect Aviles
on the Atlantic with Madrid, the Asturian Alps and
the Guadarrama mountains to the contrary notwithstanding. The originator of this ingenious idea was
to receive 40,000*l.* for the cession of his plan to the
company, and actually did receive 25,000*l.*, which, considering the difficulties, natural and otherwise, must
be considered an inadequate remuneration. Although
the original and captivating prospectus stated "*that
the line had been surveyed, and presented no engineer-
ing difficulties,*" it was subsequently thought prudent
to obtain some notion of the actual localities, and Sir
Joshua Walmsley was sent forth with competent assistance to spy out the land, which the Jewish practice
of old was rather to do before than after serious undertakings. A sad change soon came over the spirit of
the London dream by the discovery that a country
which looked level as Arrowsmith's map in the pro-

spectus, presented such trifling obstacles to the rail
as sundry leagues of mountain ridges, which range
from 6000 to 9000 feet high, and are covered with snow
for many months of the year. This was a damper.
The report of the special meeting (see 'Morning
Chronicle,' Dec. 18, 1845) should be printed in letters
of gold, from the quantity of that article which it will
preserve to our credulous countrymen. Then and there
the chairman observed, with equal *naïveté* and pathos,
"that had he known as much before as he did now,
he would have been the last man to carry out a railway in Spain." This experience cost him, he observed, 5000*l.*, which is paying dear for a Spanish rail
whistle. He might for five pounds have bought the
works of Townshend and Captain Cook : our modesty
prevents the naming another red book, in which these
precise localities, these mighty Alps, are described by
persons who had ridden, or rather soared, over them.
At another meeting of another Spanish rail company,
held at the London Tavern, October 20, 1846, another
chairman announced "a fact of which he was not before aware, that it was impossible to surmount the
Pyrenees." Meanwhile, the Madrid government had
secured 30,000*l.* from them by way of *caution* money ;
but caution disappears from our capitalists, whenever
excess of cash mounts from their pockets into their
heads ; loss of common sense and dollars is the natural
result. But it is the fate of Spain and her things, to
be judged of by those who have never been there, and
who feel no shame at the indecency of the nakedness
of their geographical ignorance. When the blind lead
the blind, beware of hillocks and ditches.

CHAPTER VI

A SYSTEM of post, both for the despatch of letters
and the conveyance of couriers, was introduced into
Spain under Philip and Juana, that is, towards the end

of the reign of our Henry VII. ; whereas it was scarcely organised in England before the government of Cromwell. Spain, which in these matters, as well as in many others, was once so much in advance, is now compelled to borrow her improvements from those nations of which she formerly was the instructress : among these may be reckoned all travelling in carriages, whether public or private.

The post-office for letters is arranged on the plan common to most countries on the Continent : the delivery is pretty regular, but seldom daily—twice or three times a-week. Small scruple is made by the authorities in opening private letters, whenever they suspect the character of the correspondence. It is as well, therefore, for the traveller to avoid expressing the whole of his opinions of the powers that be. The minds of men have been long troubled in Spain ; civil war has rendered them very distrustful and guarded in their *written* correspondence—" *carta canta*," " a letter speaks."

There is the usual continental bother in obtaining post-horses, which results from there being a monopoly of government. There must be a passport, an official order, notice of departure, etc. ; next ensue vexatious regulations in regard to the number of passengers, horses, luggage, style of carriage, and so forth. These, and other spokes put into the wheel, appear to have been invented by clerks who sit at home devising how to impede rather than facilitate posting at all.

Post-horses and mules are paid at the rate of seven reals each for each post. The Spanish postillions generally, and especially if well paid, drive at a tremendous pace, often amounting to a gallop ; nor are they easily stopped, even if the traveller desires it—they seem only to be intent on arriving at their stages' end, in order to indulge in the great national joy of then doing nothing : to get there, they heed neither ruts nor ravines ; and when once their cattle are started the inside passenger feels like a kettle tied to the tail of a mad dog, or a comet ; the wild beasts think no more of him than if he were Mazeppa : thus money makes the mare and its driver to go, as surely in Spain as in all other countries.

Another mode of travelling is by riding post, accompanied by a mounted postillion, who is changed with the cattle at each relay. It is an expeditious but fatiguing plan; yet one which, like the Tartar courier of the East, has long prevailed in Spain. Thus our Charles 1. rode to Madrid under the name of John Smith, by which he was not likely to be identified. The delight of Philip II., who boasted that he governed the world from the Escorial, was to receive frequent and early intelligence; and this desire to hear something new is still characteristic of the Spanish government. The cabinet-couriers have the preference of horses at every relay. The particular distances they have to perform are all timed, and so many leagues are required to be done in a fixed time; and, in order to encourage despatch, for every hour gained on the allowed time, an additional sum was paid to them: hence the common expression " *ganando horas*," gaining hours —equivalent to our old " post haste—haste for your life."

The usual mode of travelling for the affluent is in the public conveyances, which are the fashion from being novelties and only introduced under Ferdinand VII.; previously to their being allowed at all, serious objections were started, similar to those raised by his late Holiness to the introduction of railways into the papal states; it was said that these tramontane facilities would bring in foreigners, and with them philosophy, heresy, and innovations, by which the wisdom of Spain's ancestors might be upset. These scruples were ingeniously got over by bribing the monarch with a large share of the profits. Now that the royal monopoly is broken down, many new and competing companies have sprung up; this mode of travelling is the cheapest and safest, nor is it thought at all beneath the dignity of " the best set," nay royalty itself goes by the coach. Thus the Infante Don Francisco de Paula constantly hires the whole of the diligence to convey himself and his family from Madrid to the sea-coast; and one reason gravely given for Don Enrique's not coming to marry the Queen, was that his Royal Highness could not get a place, as the dilly was booked full. The public carriages of Spain are quite as good as those of France, and the company who travel in them generally more respectable and better bred. This is partly accounted for by the expense : the fares are not very high, yet still form a serious item to the bulk of Spaniards; consequently those who travel in the public carriages in Spain are the class who would in other countries travel per post. It must, however, be admitted that all travelling in the public conveyances of the Continent necessarily implies great discomfort to those accustomed to their own carriages; and with every possible precaution the long journeys in Spain, of three to five hundred miles at a stretch, are such as few English ladies can undergo, and are, even with men, undertakings rather of necessity than of pleasure. The mail is organised on the plan of the French malle-poste, and offers, to those who can stand the bumping, shaking, and churning of continued and rapid travelling without halting, a means of locomotion which leaves nothing to be desired. The diligences also are imitations of the lumbering French model. It will be in vain to expect in them the neatness, the well-appointed turn-out, the quiet, time-keeping, and infinite facilities of the English original. These matters when passed across the water are modified to the heroic Continental contempt for doing things in style; cheapness, which is their great principle, prefers rope-traces to those of leather, and a carter to a regular coachman; the usual foreign drags also exist, which render their slow coaches and bureaucratic absurdities so hateful to free Britons; but when one is once booked and handed over to the conductor, you arrive in due time at the journey's end. The "guards" are realities; they consist of stout, armed, most picturesque, robber-like men and no mistake, since many, before they were pardoned and pensioned, have frequently taken a purse on the Queen's highway; for the foreground of your first sketch, they are splendid fellows, and worth a score of marshals. They are provided with a complete arsenal of swords and blunderbusses, so that the cumbrous machine rolling over the sea of plains looks like a man-of-war, and has been compared to a marching citadel. Again in suspicious localities a mounted escort of equally suspicious look gallops alongside, nor is the primitive practice of black mail altogether neglected : the consequence of these admirable precautions is, that the diligences are seldom or never robbed ; the thing, however, is possible.

The whole of this garrisoned Noah's ark is placed under the command of the *Mayoral* or conductor, who like all Spanish men in authority is a despot, and yet, like them, is open to the conciliatory influences of a bribe. He regulates the hours of toil and sleep, which latter—blessings, says Sancho, on the man who invented it !—is uncertain, and depends on the early or late arrival of the diligence and the state of the roads, for all that is lost of the fixed time on the road is made up for by curtailing the time allowed for repose. One of the many good effects of setting up diligences is the bettering the inns on the road ; and it is a safe and general rule to travellers in Spain, whatever be their vehicle, always to inquire in every town which is the *posada* that the diligence stops at. Persons were dispatched from Madrid to the different stations on the great lines, to fit up houses, bed-rooms, and kitchens, and provide everything for table service; cooks were sent round to teach the innkeepers to set out and prepare a proper dinner and supper. Thus, in villages in which a few years before the use of a fork was scarcely known, a table was laid out, clean, well served, and abundant. The example set by the diligence inns has produced a beneficial effect, since they offer a model, create competition, and suggest the existence of many comforts, which were hitherto unknown among Spaniards, whose abnegation of material enjoyments at home, and praiseworthy endurance of privations of all kinds on journeys, are quite Oriental.

In some of the new companies every expense is calculated in the fare, to wit, journey, postillions, inns, etc., which is very convenient to the stranger, and pre-

vents the loss of much money and temper. A chapter
on the dilly is as much a standing dish in every Peninsular tour as a bullfight or a bandit adventure, for which
there is a continual demand in the home-market; and
no doubt in the long distances of Spain, where men and
women are boxed up for three or four mortal days together (the nights not being omitted), the plot thickens,
and opportunity is afforded to appreciate costume and
character; the farce or tragedy may be spun out into
as many acts as the journey takes days. In general the
order of the course is as follows: the breakfast consists
at early dawn of a cup of good stiff chocolate, which
being the favourite drink of the church and allowable
even on fast days, is as nutritious as delicious. It is
accompanied by a bit of roasted or fried bread, and is
followed by a glass of cold water, to drink which is an
axiom with all wise men who respect the efficient condition of their livers. After rumbling on, over a given
number of leagues, when the passengers get well shaken
together and hungry, a regular knife and fork breakfast is provided that closely resembles the dinner or
supper which is served up later in the evening; the table
is plentiful, and the cookery to those who like oil and
garlic excellent. Those who do not, can always fall
back on the bread and eggs, which are capital; the wine
is occasionally like purple blacking, and sometimes
serves also as vinegar for the salad, as the oil is said to
be used indifferently for lamps or stews; a bad dinner,
especially if the bill be long, and the wine sour, does
not sweeten the passengers' tempers; they become
quarrelsome, and if they have the good luck, a little
robber skirmish gives vent to ill-humour.

At nightfall after supper, a few hours are allowed on
your part to steal whatever rest the *mayoral* and certain *voltigeurs*, creeping and winged, will permit; the
beds are plain and clean; sometimes the mattresses may
be compared to sacks of walnuts, but there is no pillow
so soft as fatigue; the beds are generally arranged in
twos, threes, and fours, according to the size of the
room. The traveller should immediately on arriving
secure his, and see that it is comfortable, for those who

neglect to get a good one must sleep in a bad. Generally speaking, by a little management, he may get a room to himself, or at least select his companions. There is, moreover, a real civility and politeness shown by all classes of Spaniards, on all occasions, towards strangers and ladies; and that even failing, a small tip, "*una gratificacioncita*," given beforehand to the maid, or the waiter, seldom fails to smooth all difficulties. On these, as on all occasions in Spain, most things may be obtained by good humour, a smile, a joke, a proverb, a cigar, or a bribe, which, though last, is by no means the least resource, since it will be found to mollify the hardest heart and smooth the greatest difficulties, after civil speeches had been tried in vain, for *Dadivas quebrantan peñas, y entra sin barrenas*, gifts break rocks, and penetrate without gimlets; again, *Mas ablanda dinero que palabras de Caballero*, cash softens more than a gentleman's palaver. The mode of driving in Spain, which is so unlike our way of handling the ribbons, will be described presently.

Means of conveyance for those who cannot afford the diligence are provided by vehicles of more genuine Spanish nature and discomfort; they may be compared to the neat accommodation for man and beast which is doled out to third-class passengers by our monopolist railway kings, who have usurped her Majesty's highway, and fleece her lieges by virtue of act of Parliament.

First and foremost comes the *galera,* which fully justifies its name; and even those who have no value for their time or bones will, after a short trial of the rack and dislocation, exclaim,—" *que diable allais-je faire dans cette galère?*" These machines travel periodically from town to town, and form the chief public and carrier communication between most provincial cities; they are not much changed from that classical cart, the *rheda,* into which, as we read in Juvenal, the whole family of Fabricius was conveyed. In Spain these primitive locomotives have stood still in the general advance of this age of progress, and carry us back to our James I., and Fynes Moryson's accounts of

" carryers who have long covered waggons, in which
they carry passengers from city to city; but this kind
of journeying is so tedious, by reason they must take
waggons very early and come very late to their innes,
none but women and people of inferior condition used
to travel in this sort." So it is now in Spain.

This *galera* is a long cart without springs; the sides
are lined with matting, while beneath hangs a loose
open net, as under the calesinas of Naples, in which lies
and barks a horrid dog, who keeps a Cerberus watch
over iron pots and sieves, and suchlike gipsey utensils,
and who is never to be conciliated. These *galeras* are
of all sizes; but if a *galera* should be a larger sort of
vehicle than is wanted, then a "*tartana*," a sort of
covered tilted cart, which is very common in Valencia,
and which is so called from a small Mediterranean craft
of the same name, will be found convenient.

The packing and departure of the *galera*, when hired
by a family who remove their goods, is a thing of Spain;
the heavy luggage is stowed in first, and beds and mattresses spread on the top, on which the family repose
in admired disorder. The *galera* is much used by the
" poor students " of Spain, a class unique of its kind,
and full of rags and impudence; their adventures have
the credit of being rich and picturesque, and recall some
of the accounts of " waggon incidents " in ' Roderick
Random,' and Smollett's novels.

Civilisation, as connected with the wheel, is still at
a low ebb in Spain, notwithstanding the numerous
political revolutions. Except in a few great towns, the
quiz vehicles remind us of those caricatures at which one
laughed so heartily in Paris in 1814; and in Madrid,
even down to Ferdinand VII.'s decease, the *Prado*—
its rotton row—was filled with antediluvian carriages—
grotesque coachmen and footmen to match, which with
us would be put into the British Museum; they are
now, alas for painters and authors ! worn out, and replaced by poor French imitations of good English
originals.

As the genuine older Spanish ones were built in
remote ages, and before the invention of folding steps,

the ascent and descent were facilitated by a three-legged
footstool, which dangled, strapped up near the door, as
appears in the hieroglyphics of Egypt 4000 years ago;
a pair of long-eared fat mules, with hides and tails fan-
tastically cut, were driven by a superannuated postillion
in formidable jackboots, and not less formidable cocked
hat of oilcloth. In these, how often have we seen
Spanish grandees with pedigrees as old-fashioned,
gravely taking the air and dust! These slow coaches
of old Spain have been rapidly sketched by the clever
young American; such are the ups and downs of
nations and vehicles. Spain for having discovered
America has in return become her butt; she cannot go
a-head; so the great dust of Alexander may stop a
bung-hole, and we too join in the laugh and forget that
our ancestors—see Beaumont and Fletcher's ' Maid of
the Inn '—talked of " *hurrying* on featherbeds that
move upon four-wheel Spanish *caroches*."

While on these wheel subjects it may be observed that
the carts and other machines of Spanish rural locomotion and husbandry have not escaped better; when not
Oriental they are Roman; rude in form and material,
they are always odd, picturesque, and inconvenient.
The peasant, for the most part, scratches the earth with
a plough modelled after that invented by Triptolemus,
beats out his corn as described by Homer, and carries
his harvest home in strict obedience to the rules in the
Georgics. The iron work is iniquitous, but both sides
of the Pyrenees are centuries behind England; there,
absurd tariffs prohibit the importation of our cheap and
good work in order to encourage their own bad and
dear wares—thus poverty and ignorance are perpetuated.

The carts in the north-west provinces are the unchanged *plaustra*, with solid wheels, the Roman *tym-
pana* which consist of mere circles of wood, without
spokes or axles, much like mill-stones or Parmesan
cheeses, and precisely such as the old Egyptians used,
as is seen in hieroglyphics, and no doubt much resem-
bling those sent by Joseph for his father, which are still
used by the Affghans and other unadvanced coach-

makers. The whole wheel turns round together with a piteous creaking; the drivers, whose leathern ears are as blunt as their edgeless teeth, delight in this excruciating *Chirrio*, Arabicè *charrar*, to make a *noise*, which they call music, and delight in, because it is cheap and plays to them of itself; they, moreover, think it frightens wolves, bears, and the devil himself, as Don Quixote says, which it well may, for the wheel of Ixion, although damned in hell, never whined more piteously. The doleful sounds, however, serve like our waggoners' lively bells, as warnings to other drivers, who, in narrow paths and gorges of rocks, where two carriages cannot pass, have this notice given them, and draw aside until the coast is clear.

We have reserved some details and the mode of driving for the *coche de colleras*, the *caroche* of horse-collars, which is the real coach of Spain, and in which we have made many a pleasant trip; it too is doomed to be scheduled away, for Spaniards are descending from these coaches and six to a chariot and pair, and by degrees beautifully less, to a fly.

Mails and diligences, we have said, are only established on the principal high roads connected with Madrid : there are but few local coaches which run from one provincial town to another, where the necessity of frequent and certain intercommunication is little called for. In the other provinces, where these modern conveniences have not been introduced, the earlier mode of travelling is the only resource left to families of children, women, and invalids, who are unable to perform the journey on horseback. This is the *festina lentè*, or voiturier system; and from its long continuance in Italy and Spain, in spite of all the improvements adopted in other countries, it would appear to have something congenial and peculiarly fitted to the habits and wants of those cognate nations of the south, who have a Gotho-Oriental dislike to be hurried—*no corre priesa*, there is plenty of time. *Sie haben zeit genug*.

The Spanish vetturino, or " *Calesero*," is to be found, as in Italy, standing for hire in particular and well-known places in every principal town. There is not much necessity for hunting for *him*; he has the Italian instinctive perception of a stranger and traveller, and the same importunity in volunteering himself, his cattle, and carriage, for any part of Spain. The man, however, and his equipage are peculiarly Spanish; his carriage and his team have undergone little change during the last two centuries, and are the representatives of the former ones of Europe; they resemble those vehicles once used in England, which may still be seen in the old prints of country-houses by Kip; or, as regards France, in the pictures of Louis XIV.'s journeys and campaigns by Vandermeulen. They are the remnant of the once universal " coach and six," in which according to Pope, who was not infallible, British fair were to delight for ever. The " *coche de colleras* " is a huge cumbrous machine, built after the fashion of a reduced lord mayor's coach, or some of the equipages of the old cardinals at Rome. It is ornamented with rude sculpture, gilding, and painting of glaring colour, but the modern pea-jacket and round hat spoil the picture which requires passengers dressed in brocade and full-bottomed wigs; the forewheels are very low, the hind ones very high, and both remarkably narrow in the tire; remember when they stick in the mud, and the drivers call upon Santiago, to push the vehicle out *backwards*, as the more you draw it forwards the deeper you get into the mire. The pole sticks out like the bowsprit of a ship, and contains as much wood and iron work as would go to a small waggon. The interior is lined with gay silk and gaudy plush, adorned with lace and embroidery, with doors that open indifferently and windows that do not shut well; latterly the general poverty and *prose* of transpyrenean civilisation has effaced much of these ornate nationalities, both in coach and drivers; better roads and lighter vehicles require fewer horses, which were absolutely necessary formerly to drag the heavy concern through heavier ways.

The luggage is piled up behind, or stowed away in a front boot. The management of driving this vehicle is conducted by two persons. The master is called the "*mayoral;*" his helper or cad the "*mozo*," or, more properly, "*el zagal*," from the Arabic, "a strong active youth." The costume is peculiar, and is based on that of Andalucia, which sets the fashion all over the Peninsula, in all matters regarding bull-fighting, horse-dealing, robbing, smuggling, and so forth. He wears on his head a gay-coloured silk handkerchief, tied in such a manner that the tails hang down behind; over this remnant of the Moorish turban he places a high-peaked sugarloaf-shaped hat with broad brims; his jaunty jacket is made either of black sheepskin, studded with silver tags and filigree buttons, or of brown cloth, with the back, arms, and particularly the elbows, welted and tricked out with flowers and vases, cut in patches of different-coloured cloth and much embroidered. When the jacket is not worn, it is usually hung over the left shoulder, after the hussar fashion. The waistcoat is made of rich fancy silk; the breeches of blue or green velvet plush, ornamented with stripes and filigree buttons, and tied at the knee with silken cords and tassels; the neck is left open, and the shirt collar turned down, and a gaudy neck-handkerchief is worn, oftener passed through a ring than tied in a knot; his waist is girt with a red sash, or with one of a bright yellow. This "*faja*," [1] a *sine quâ non*, is the old Roman zona; it serves also for a purse, "girds the loins," and keeps up a warmth over the abdomen, which is highly beneficial in hot climates, and wards off any tendency to irritable colic; in the sash is stuck the "*navaja*," the knife, which is part and parcel of a Spaniard, and behind the "*zagal*" usually places his stick. The richly embroidered gaiters are left open at the outside to show a handsome stocking; the shoes are yellow, like those of our cricketers, and are generally made of untanned calfskin, which being the colour of dust require no

[1] Faja; the Hhezum of Cairo. Atrides tightens his sash when preparing for action—Iliad xi. 15. The Roman soldiers kept their money in it. Ibit qui *zonam* perdidit.—Hor. ii. Ep. 2. 40. The Jews used it for the same purpose—Matthew x. 9; Mark vi. 8. It is loosened at night. "None shall slumber or sleep, neither shall the girdle of their loins be loosed."—Isaiah v. 27.

cleaning. The *caleseros* on the eastern coast wear the Valencian stocking, which has no feet to it—being open at bottom, it is likened by wags to a Spaniard's purse; instead of top boots they wear the ancient Roman sandals, made of the *esparto* rush, with hempen soles, which are called " *alpargatas*," Arabicè *Alpalgah*. The " *zagal* " follows the fashion in dress of the " *mayoral*," as nearly as his means will permit him. He is the servant of all-work, and must be ready on every occasion; nor can any one who has ever seen the hard and incessant toil which these men undergo, justly accuse them of being indolent—a reproach which has been cast somewhat indiscriminately on all the lower classes of Spain; he runs by the side of the carriage, picks up stones to pelt the mules, ties and unties knots, and pours forth a volley of blows and oaths from the moment of starting to that of arrival. He sometimes is indulged with a ride by the side of the mayoral on the box, when he always uses the tail of the hind mule to pull himself up into his seat. The harnessing the six animals is a difficult operation; first the tackle of ropes is laid out on the ground, then each beast is brought into his portion of the rigging. The start is always an important ceremony, and, as our royal mail used to do in the country, brings out all the idlers in the vicinity. When the team is harnessed, the mayoral gets all his skeins of ropes into his hand, the " *zagal* " his sash full of stones, the helpers at the venta their sticks; at a given signal all fire a volley of oaths and blows at the team, which, once in motion, away it goes, pitching over ruts deep as routine prejudices, with its pole dipping and rising like a ship in a rolling sea, and continues at a brisk pace, performing from twenty-five to thirty miles a-day. The hours of starting are early, in order to avoid the mid-day heat; in these matters the Spanish customs are pretty much the same with the Italian; the *calesero* is always the best judge of the hours of departure and these minor details, which vary according to circumstances.

Whenever a particularly bad bit of road occurs, notice is given to the team by calling over their names, and

by crying out " *arré, arré*," gee-up, which is varied with
" *firmé, firmé*," steady, boy, steady ! The names of the
animals are always fine-sounding and polysyllabic; the
accent is laid on the last syllable, which is always dwelt
on and lengthened out with a particular emphasis—
Căpĭtănā-ā—Băndŏlĕrā-ā—Gĕnĕrălā-ā—Vălĕrŏsā-ā. All
this vocal driving is performed at the top of the voice,
and, indeed, next to scaring away crows in a field,
must be considered the best possible practice for the
lungs. The team often exceeds six in number, and
never is less ; the proportion of females predominates :
there is generally one male mule making the seventh,
who is called " *el macho*," the male par excellence, like
the Grand Turk, or a substantive in a speech in Cortes,
which seldom has less than half a dozen epithets ; he
invariably comes in for the largest share of abuse and
ill usage, which, indeed, he deserves the most, as the
male mule is infinitely more stubborn and viciously inclined than the female. Sometimes there is a horse of
the Rosinante breed ; he is called " *el cavallo*," or
rather, as it is pronounced, " *el căvăl yō-ō.*" The horse
is always the best used of the team ; to be a rider,
" *caballero*," is the Spaniard's synonym for gentleman ;
and it is their correct mode of addressing each other,
and is banded gravely among the lower orders, who
never have crossed any quadruped save a mule or a
jackass.

The driving a *coche de colleras* is quite a science of
itself, and is observed in conducting *diligences ;* it
amuses the Spanish " *majo* " or fancy-man as much as
coach-driving does the fancy-man of England ; the great
art lies not in handling the ribbons, but in the proper
modulation of the voice, since the cattle are always
addressed individually by their names ; the first syllables
are pronounced very rapidly ; the " *macho*," the male
mule, who is the most abused, is the only one who is
not addressed by any names beyond that of his sex :
the word is repeated with a voluble iteration ; in order
to make the two syllables longer, they are strung together thus, *măchŏ—măchŏ—măchŏ—māchŏ-ō :* they
begin in semiquavers, flowing on crescendo to a semi-

breve or breve, so the four words are compounded into one polysyllable. The horse, *caballo*, is simply called so; he has no particular name of his own, which the female mules are never without, and which they perfectly know—indeed, the owners will say that they understand them, and all bad language, as well as Christian women, "*como Cristianas;*" and, to do the beasts justice, they seem more shocked and discomfited thereby than the bipeds who profess the same creed. If the animal called to does not answer by pricking up her ears, or by quickening her pace, the threat of "*lǎ vǎrā,*" the stick, is added—the last argument of Spanish drivers, men in office, and schoolmasters, with whom there is no sort of reason equal to that of the bastinado, "*no hay tal razon, como la del baston.*" It operates on the timorous more than "unadorned eloquence." The Moors thought so highly of the bastinado, that they held the stick to be a special gift from Allah to the faithful. It holds good, *à priori* and *à posteriori*, to mule and boy, "*al hijo y mulo, para el culo;*" and if the "*macho*" be in fault, and he is generally punished to encourage the others, some abuse is added to blows, such as "*que pĕrrō-ō,*" "what a dog!" or some unhandsome allusion to his mother, which is followed by throwing a stone at the leaders, for no whip could reach them from the coach-box. When any particular mule's name is called, if her companion be the next one to be abused, she is seldom addressed by her name, but is spoken to as "*a la ŏtrā-ā,*" "*aquella ŏtrā-ā,*" "Now for that other one," which from long association is expected and acknowledged. The team obeys the voice and is in admirable command. Few things are more entertaining than driving them, especially over bad roads; but it requires much practice in Spanish speaking and swearing.

Among the many commandments that are always broken in Spain, that of "swear not at all" is not the least. "Our army swore lustily in Flanders," said Uncle Toby. But few nations can surpass the Spaniards in the language of vituperation: it is limited only by the extent of their anatomical, geographical, astronomi-

cal, and religious knowledge; it is so plentifully bestowed on their animals—" un muletier à ce jeu vaut
trois rois "—that oaths and imprecations seem to be
considered as the only language the mute creation can
comprehend; and as actions are generally suited to
the words, the combination is remarkably effective. As
much of the traveller's time on the road must be passed
among beasts and muleteers, who are not unlike them,
some knowledge of their sayings and doings is of great
use : to be able to talk to them in their own lingo, to
take an interest in them and in their animals, never
fails to please; " *Por vida del demonio, mas sabe Usia
que nosotros;*" " by the life of the devil, your honour
knows more than we," is a common form of compliment. When once equality is established, the master
mind soon becomes the real master of the rest. The
great oath of Spain, which ought never to be written
or pronounced, practically forms the foundation of the
language of the lower orders; it is a most ancient
remnant of the phallic abjuration of the evil eye, the
dreaded fascination which still perplexes the minds of
Orientals, and is not banished from Spanish and Neapolitan superstitions.[1] The word terminates in *ajo,* on
which great stress is laid : the *j* is pronounced with a
most Arabic, guttural aspiration. The word *ajo* means
also garlic, which is quite as often in Spanish mouths,

[1] The dread of the fascination of the evil eye, from which
Solomon was not exempt (Proverbs xxiii. 6), prevails all over the
East ; it has not been extirpated from Spain or from Naples,
which so long belonged to Spain. The lower classes in the
Peninsula hang round the necks of their children and cattle a
horn tipped with silver ; this is sold as an amulet in the silver-
smith's shops ; the cord by which it is attached *ought* to be
braided from a black mare's tail. The Spanish gipsies, of whom
Borrow has given us so complete an account, thrive by disarming
the *mal de ojo,* " *querelar nasula,*" as they term it. The dread
of the " *Ain ara* " exists among all classes of the Moors. The
better classes of Spaniards make a joke of it ; and often, when
you remark that a person has put on or wears something strange
about him, the answer is, " *Es para que no me hagan mal de
ojo.*" Naples is the head-quarters for charms and coral
amulets : all the learning has been collected by the Canon Jorio
and the Marques Arditi.

and is exactly what Hotspur liked, a "mouth-filling oath," energetic and Michael Angelesque. The pun has been extended to onions : thus, "*ajos y cebollas*" means oaths and imprecations. The sting of the oath is in the "*ajo;*" all women and quiet men, who do not wish to be particularly objurgatory, but merely to enforce and give a little additional vigour, un soupçon d'ail, or a shotting to their discourse, drop the offensive "*ajo*," and say "*car*," "*carai*," "*caramba*." The Spanish oath is used as a verb, as a substantive, as an adjective, just as it suits the grammar or the wrath of the utterer. It is equivalent also to a certain place and the person who lives there. "*Vaya Usted al C—ajo*" is the worst form of the angry "*Vaya Usted al demonio*," or "*á los infiernos*," and is a whimsical mixture of courtesy and transportation. "Your Grace may go to the devil, or to the infernal regions !"

Thus these imprecatory vegetables retain in Spain their old Egyptian flavour and mystical charm; as on the Nile, according to Pliny, onions and garlic were worshipped as adjuratory divinities. The Spaniards have also added most of the gloomy northern Gothic oaths, which are imprecatory, to the Oriental, which are grossly sensual. Enough of this. The traveller who has much to do with Spanish mules and asses, biped or quadruped, will need no hand-book to teach him the sixty-five or more "*serments espaignols*" on which Mons. de Brantome wrote a treatise. More becoming will it be to the English gentleman to swear not at all; a reasonable indulgence in *Caramba* is all that can be permitted; the custom is more honoured in the breach than in the observance, and bad luck seldom deserts the house of the imprecator. "*En la casa del que jura, no falta desaventura.*"

Previously to hiring one of these "coaches of collars," which is rather an expensive amusement, every possible precaution should be taken in clearly and minutely specifying everything to be done, and the price; the Spanish "*caleseros*" rival their Italian colleagues in that untruth, roguery, and dishonesty, which seem everywhere to combine readily with jockeyship, and distinguishes those who handle the whip, "do job-bings," and conduct mortals by horses; the fee to be given to the drivers should never be included in the bargain, as the keeping this important item open and dependent on the good behaviour of the future recipients offers a sure check over master and man, and other road-classes. In justice, however, to this class of Spaniards, it may be said that on the whole they are civil, good-humoured, and hard-working, and, from not having been accustomed to either the screw bargaining or alternative extravagance of the English travellers in Italy, are as tolerably fair in their transactions as can be expected from human nature brought in constant contact with four-legged and four-wheeled temptations. They offer to the artist an endless subject of the picturesque; everything connected with them is full of form, colour, and originality. They can do nothing, whether sitting, driving, sleeping, or eating, that does not make a picture; the same may be said of their animals and their habits and harness; those who draw will never find the midday halt long enough for the infinite variety of subject and scenery to which their travelling equipage and attend-ants form the most peculiar and appropriate fore-ground: while our modern poetasters will consider them quite as worthy of being sung in immortal verse as the Cambridge carrier Hobson, who was Milton's choice.

CHAPTER VII

WE now proceed to Spanish quadrupeds, having placed the wheel-carriages before the horses. That of Andalucia takes precedence of all; he fetches the highest price, and the Spaniards in general value no other breed; they consider his configuration and qualities as perfect, and in some respects they are right, for no horse is more elegant or more easy in his motions, none are more gentle or docile, none are more quick in ac-quiring showy accomplishments, or in performing feats

of Astleyan agility; he has very little in common with
the English blood-horse; his mane is soft and silky, and
is frequently plaited with gay ribbons; his tail is of
great length, and left in all the proportions of nature,
not cropped and docked, by which Voltaire was so much
offended :—

> " Fiers et bizarres Anglais, qui des mêmes ciseaux
>   Coupez la tête aux rois, et la queue aux chevaux."

It often trails to the very ground, while the animal has
perfect command over it, lashing it on every side as a
gentleman switches his cane; therefore, when on a
journey, it is usual to double and tie it up, after the
fashion of the ancient pig-tails of our sailors. The
Andalucian horse is round in his quarters, though inclined to be small in the barrel; he is broad-chested, and
always carries his head high, especially when going a
good pace; his length of leg adds to his height, which
sometimes reaches to sixteen hands; he never, however,
stretches out with the long graceful sweep of the English thorough-bred; his action is apt to be loose and
shambling, and he is given to *dishing* with the feet.
The pace is, notwithstanding, perfectly delightful.
From being very long in the pastern, the motion is
broken as it were by the springs of a carriage; their
pace is the peculiar "*paso Castellano*," which is something more than a walk, and less than a trot, and it is
truly sedate and sedan-chair-like, and suits a grave Don,
who is given, like a Turk, to tobacco and contemplation.
Those Andalucian horses which fall when young into
the hands of the officers at Gibraltar acquire a very
different action, and lay themselves better down to their
work, and gain much more in speed from the English
system of training than they would have done had they
been managed by Spaniards. Taught or untaught, this
pace is most gentlemanlike, and well did Beaumont and
Fletcher

> " Think it noble, as Spaniards do in riding,
>   In managing a great horse, which is princely;"

and as has been said, is the only attitude in which the

kings of the Spains, true φιλιπποι, ought ever to be painted, witching the world with noble horsemanship.

Many other provinces possess breeds which are more useful, though far less showy, than the Andalucian. The horse of Castile is a strong, hardy animal, and the best which Spain produces for mounting heavy cavalry. The ponies of Gallicia, although ugly and uncouth, are admirably suited to the wild hilly country and laborious population; they require very little care or grooming, and are satisfied with coarse food and Indian corn. The horses of Navarre, once so celebrated, are still esteemed for their hardy strength; they have, from neglect, degenerated into ponies, which, however, are beautiful in form, hardy, docile, sure-footed, and excellent trotters. In most of the large towns of Spain there is a sort of market, where horses are publicly sold; but Ronda fair, in May, is the great Howden and Horncastle of the four provinces of Seville, Cordova, Jaen, and Granada, and the resort of all the picturesque-looking rogues of the south. The reader of Don Quixote need not be told that the race of Gines Passamonte is not extinct; the Spanish *Chalanes,* or horse-dealers, have considerable talents; but the cleverest is but a mere child when compared to the perfection of rascality to which a real English professor has attained in the mysteries of lying, chaunting, and making up a horse.

The breeding of horses was carefully attended to by the Spanish government previously to the invasion of the French, by whom the entire horses and brood-mares were either killed or stolen, and the buildings and stables burnt.

The saddles used commonly in Spain are Moorish; they are made with high peak and croup behind; the stirrup-irons are large triangularly-shaped boxes. The food is equally Oriental, and consists of " barley and straw," as mentioned in the Bible. We well remember the horror of our Andalucian groom, on our first reaching Gallicia, when he rushed in, exclaiming that the beasts would perish, as nothing was to be had there but oats and hay. After some difficulty he was persuaded to see if they would eat it, which to his surprise they actually did; such, however, is habit, that they soon fell out of condition, and did not recover until the damp mountains were quitted for the arid plains of Castile.

Spaniards in general prefer mules and asses to the horse, which is more delicate, requires greater attention, and is less sure-footed over broken and precipitous ground. The mule performs in Spain the functions of the camel in the East, and has something in his morale (besides his physical suitableness to the country) which is congenial to the character of his masters; he has the same self-willed obstinacy, the same resignation under burdens, the same singular capability of endurance of labour, fatigue, and privation. The mule has always been much used in Spain, and the demand for them very great; yet, from some mistaken crotchet of Spanish political economy (which is very Spanish), the breeding of the mule has long been attempted to be prevented, in order to encourage that of the horse. One of the reasons alleged was, that the mule was a non-reproductive animal; an argument which might or ought to apply equally to the monk; a breed for which Spain could have shown for the first prize, both as to number and size, against any other country in all Christendom. This attempt to force the production of an animal far less suited to the wants and habits of the people has failed, as might be expected. The difficulties thrown in the way have only tended to raise the prices of mules, which are, and always were, very dear; a good mule will fetch from 25*l.* to 50*l.,* while a horse of relative goodness may be purchased for from 20*l.* to 40*l.* Mules were always very dear; thus Martial, like a true Andalucian Spaniard, *talks* of one which cost more than a house. The most esteemed are those bred from the mare and the ass, or " *garañon,*" [1] some of which are of extraordinary size; and one which Don Carlos had in his stud-house at Aranjuez in 1832 ex-

---

[1] The *garañon* is also called " *burro padre,*" ass father, not " *padre burro.*" " *Padre,*" the prefix of paternity, is the common title given in Spain to the clergy and the monks. " Father jackass " might in many instances, when applied to the latter, be too morally and physically appropriate, to be consistent with the respect due to the celibate cowl and cassock.

ceeded fifteen hands in height.   This colossal ass and
a Spanish infante were worthy of each other.

The mules in Spain, as in the East, have their coats
closely shorn or clipped; part of the hair is usually left
on in stripes like the zebra, or cut into fanciful patterns,
like the tattooings of a New Zealand chief.   This process of shearing is found to keep the beast cooler and
freer from cutaneous disorders.   The operation is performed in the southern provinces by gipsies, who are
the same tinkers, horse-dealers, and vagrants in Spain
as elsewhere.   Their clipping recalls the " mulo curto,"
on which Horace could amble even to Brundusium.
The operators rival in talent those worthy Frenchmen
who cut the hair of poodles on the Pont Neuf, in the
heart and brain of European civilisation.   Their Spanish
colleagues may be known by the shears, formidable and
classical-shaped as those of Lachesis and her sisters,
which they carry in their sashes.   They are very particular in clipping the heels and pasterns, which they say
ought to be as free from superfluous hair as the palm
of a lady's hand.

Spanish asses have been immortalised by Cervantes;
they are endeared to us by Sancho's love and talent of
imitation; he brayed so well, be it remembered, that
all the long-eared chorus joined a performer who, in
his own modest phrase, only wanted a tail to be a perfect donkey.   Spanish mayors, according to Don
Quixote, have a natural talent for this braying; but,
save and except in the west of England, their right
worshipfuls may be matched elsewhere.

The humble ass, " burro," " borrico," is the rule,
the as in præsenti, and part and parcel of every Spanish
scene: he forms the appropriate foreground in streets
or roads.   Wherever two or three Spaniards are collected together in the market, junta, or " congregation," there is quite sure to be an ass among them; he
is the hardworked companion of the lower orders, to
whom to work is the greatest misfortune; sufferance
is indeed the common virtue of both tribes.   They may,
perhaps, both wince a little when a new burden or a
new tax is laid on them by Señor Mon, but they soon,

when they see that there is no remedy, bear on and
endure : from this fellow-feeling, master and animal
cherish each other at heart, though from the blows and
imprecations bestowed openly, the former may be
thought by hasty observers to be ashamed of confess-
ing these predilections in public. Some under-current,
no doubt, remains of the ancient prejudices of chivalry ;
but Cervantes, who thoroughly understood human
nature in general, and Spanish nature in particular,
has most justly dwelt on the dear love which Sancho
Panza felt for his " *Rucio*," and marked the reciprocity of the brute, affectionate as intelligent. In fact,
in the *Sagra* district, near Toledo, he is called *El vecino*,
one of the householders ; and none can look a Spanish
ass in the face without remarking a peculiar expression, which indicates that the hairy fool considers himself, like the pig in a cabin of the " first gem of the
sea," to be one of the family, *de la familia*, or *de nosotros*. La Mancha is the paradise of mules and asses ;
many a Sancho at this moment is there fondling and
embracing his ass, his " *chato chatito*," " *romo*," or
other complimentary variations of *Snub*, with which,
when not abusing him, he delights to nickname his
helpmate. In Spain, as Sappho says, Love is γλυκυ-
πικρον, an alternation of the agro-dolce ; nor is there
any Prevention of Cruelty Society towards animals ;
every Spaniard has the same right in law and equity
to kick and beat his own ass to his own liking, as a
philanthropical Yankee has to wallop his own nigger ;
no one ever thinks of interposing on these occasions,
any more than they would in a quarrel between a man
and his wife. The *words* are, at all events, on one
side. It is, however, recorded *in piam memoriam*, of
certain Roman Catholic asses of Spain, that they tried
to throw off one Tomas Trebiño and some other heretics, when on the way to be burnt, being horror-struck
at bearing such monsters. Every Spanish peasant is
heart-broken when injury is done to his ass, as well he
may be, for it is the means by which he lives ; nor has
he much chance, if he loses him, of finding a crown
when hunting for him, as was once done, or even a

government like Sancho. Sterne would have done better to have laid the venue of his sentimentalities over a dead ass in Spain, rather than in France, where the quadruped species is much rarer. In Spain, where small carts and wheel-barrows are almost unknown, and the drawing them is considered as beneath the dignity of the Spanish man, the substitute, an ass, is in constant employ; sometimes it is laden with sacks of corn, with wine-skins, with water-jars, with dung, or with dead robbers, slung like sacks over the back, their arms and legs tied under the animal's belly. Asses' milk, "*leche de burra*," is in much request during the spring season. The brown sex drink it in order to fine their complexions and cool their blood, "*refrescar la sangre;*" the clergy and men in office, "*los empleados*," to whom it is mother's milk, swallow it in order that it may give tone to their gastric juices. Riding on assback was accounted a disgrace and a degradation to the Gothic hidalgo, and the Spaniards, in the sixteenth century, mounted unrepining cuckolds, "*los cornudos pacientes*," on asses. Now-a-days, in spite of all these unpleasant associations, the grandees and their wives, and even grave ambassadors from foreign parts, during the royal residence at Aranjuez, much delight in elevating themselves on this beast of ill omen, and "*borricadas*" or donkey parties are all the fashion.

The muleteer of Spain is justly renowned; his generic term is *arriero*, a gee-uper, for his *arre arre* is pure Arabic, as indeed are almost all the terms connected with his craft, as the Moriscoes were long the great carriers of Spain. To travel with the muleteer, when the party is small or a person is alone, is both cheap and safe; indeed, many of the most picturesque portions of Spain, Ronda and Granada for instance, can scarcely be reached except by walking or riding. These men, who are constantly on the road, and going backwards and forwards, are the best persons to consult for details; their animals are generally to be hired, but a muleteer's stud is not pleasant to ride, since their beasts always travel in single files. The leading animal is furnished with a copper bell with a wooden clapper, to give notice of their march, which is shaped like an ice-mould, sometimes two feet long, and hangs from the neck, being contrived, as it were, on purpose to knock the animal's knees as much as possible, and to emit the greatest quantity of the most melancholy sounds, which, according to the pious origin of all bells, were meant to scare away the Evil One. The bearer of all this tintinnabular clatter is chosen from its superior docility and knack in picking out a way. The others follow their leader, and the noise he makes when they cannot see him. They are heavily but scientifically laden. The cargo of each is divided into three portions; one is tied on each side, and the other placed between. If the cargo be not nicely balanced, the muleteer either unloads or adds a few stones to the lighter portion—the additional weight being compensated by the greater comfort with which a well-poised burden is carried. These "sumpter" mules are gaily decorated with trappings full of colour and tags. The head-gear is composed of different coloured worsteds, to which a multitude of small bells are affixed; hence the saying, "*muger de mucha campanilla*," a woman of many bells, of much show, much noise, or pretension. The muleteer either walks by the side of his animal or sits aloft on the cargo, with his feet dangling on the neck, a seat which is by no means so uncomfortable as it would appear. A rude gun, "but 'twill serve," and is loaded with slugs, hangs always in readiness by his side, and often with it a guitar; these emblems of life and death paint the unchanged reckless condition of Iberia, where extremes have ever met, where a man still goes out of the world like a swan, with a song. Thus accoutred, as Byron says, with "all that gave, promise of pleasure or a grave," the approach of the caravan is announced from afar by his cracked or guttural voice : " How carols now the lusty muleteer!" For when not engaged in swearing or smoking, the livelong day is passed in one monotonous high-pitched song, the tune of which is little in harmony with the import of the words, or his cheerful humour, being most unmusical and melancholy; but

such is the true type of Oriental *melody*, as it is called.
The same absence of thought which is shown in England by whistling is displayed in Spain by singing.
" *Quien canta sus males espanta:*" he who sings frightens away ills, a philosophic consolation in travel as old and as classical as Virgil :—" Cantantes licet usque, minus via tædet, eamus,'' which may be thus translated for the benefit of country gentlemen :—

> If we join in doleful chorus,
> The dull highway will much less bore us.

The Spanish muleteer is a fine fellow; he is intelligent, active, and enduring; he braves hunger and thirst, heat and cold, mud and dust; he works as hard as his cattle, never robs or is robbed; and while his betters in this land put off everything till to-morrow except bankruptcy, he is punctual and honest, his frame is wiry and sinewy, his costume peculiar; many are the leagues and long, which we have ridden in his caravan, and longer his robber yarns, to which we paid no attention; and it must be admitted that these cavalcades are truly national and picturesque. Mingled with droves of mules and mounted horsemen, the zig-zag lines come threading down the mountain defiles, now tracking through the aromatic brushwood, now concealed amid rocks and olive-trees, now emerging bright and glittering into the sunshine, giving life and movement to the lonely nature, and breaking the usual stillness by the tinkle of the bell and the sad ditty of the muleteer—sounds which, though unmusical in themselves, are in keeping with the scene, and associated with wild Spanish rambles, just as the harsh whetting of the scythe is mixed up with the sweet spring and newly-mown hay-meadow.

There is one class of muleteers which are but little known to European travellers—the *Maragatos*, whose head-quarters are at *San Roman*, near *Astorga;* they, like the Jew and gipsy, live exclusively among their own people, preserving their primeval costume and customs, and never marrying out of their own tribe. They are as perfectly nomad and wandering as the Bedouins,

the mule only being substituted for the camel; their
honesty and industry are proverbial.   They are a
sedate, grave, dry, matter-of-fact, business-like people.
Their charges are high, but the security counterbalances, as they may be trusted with untold gold.
They are the channels of all traffic between Gallicia and
the Castiles, being seldom seen in the south or east
provinces.   They are dressed in leathern jerkins, which
fit tightly like a cuirass, leaving the arms free.   Their
linen is coarse but white, especially the shirt collar; a
broad leather belt, in which there is a purse, is fastened
round the waist.   Their breeches, like those of the
Valencians, are called *Zaraguelles*, a pure Arabic word
for kilts or wide drawers, and no burgomaster of
Rembrandt is more broad-bottomed.   Their legs are
encased in long brown cloth gaiters, with red garters;
their hair is generally cut close—sometimes, however,
strange tufts are left. A huge, slouching, flapping hat
completes the most inconvenient of travelling dresses,
and it is too Dutch to be even picturesque; but these
fashions are as unchangeable as the laws of the Medes
and Persians were; nor will any Maragato dream of
altering his costume until those dressed models of
painted wood do which strike the hours of the clock on
the square of *Astorga: Pedro Mato*, also, another
figure *costumée*, who holds a weathercock at the cathedral, is the observed of all observers; and, in truth, this
particular costume is, as that of Quakers used to be,
a guarantee of their tribe and respectability; thus even
Cordero, the rich Maragato deputy, appeared in Cortes
in this local costume.

The dress of the Maragata is equally peculiar: she
wears, if married, a sort of head-gear, *El Caramiello*,
in the shape of a crescent, the round part coming over
the forehead, which is very Moorish, and resembles
those of the females in the basso-rilievos at Granada.
Their hair flows loosely on their shoulders, while their
apron or petticoat hangs down open before and behind, and is curiously tied at the back with a sash, and
their bodice is cut square over the bosom.   At their
festivals they are covered with ornaments of long chains

of coral and metal, with crosses, relics, and medals in silver. Their earrings are very heavy, and supported by silken threads, as among the Jewesses in Barbary. A marriage is the grand feast; then large parties assemble, and a president is chosen, who puts into a waiter whatever sum of money he likes, and all invited must then give as much. The bride is enveloped in a mantle, which she wears the whole day, and never again except on that of her husband's death. She does not dance at the wedding-ball. Early next morning two roast chickens are brought to the bed-side of the happy pair. The next evening ball is opened by the bride and her husband, to the tune of the *gaita*, or Moorish bagpipe. Their dances are grave and serious; such indeed is their whole character. The *Maragatos*, with their honest, weather-beaten countenances, are seen with files of mules all along the high road to La Coruña. They generally walk, and, like other Spanish *arrieros*, although they sing and curse rather less, are employed in one ceaseless shower of stones and blows at their mules.

The whole tribe assembles twice a year at Astorga, at the feasts of Corpus and the Ascension, when they dance *El Canizo*, beginning at two o'clock in the afternoon, and ending precisely at three. If any one not a *Maragato* joins, they all leave off immediately. The women never wander from their homes, which their undomestic husbands always do. They lead the hard-worked life of the Iberian females of old, and now, as then, are to be seen everywhere in these west provinces toiling in the fields, early before the sun has risen, and late after it has set; and it is most painful to behold them drudging at these unfeminine vocations.

The origin of the *Maragatos* has never been ascertained. Some consider them to be a remnant of the Celtiberian, others of the Visigoths; most, however, prefer a Bedouin, or caravan descent. It is in vain to question these ignorant carriers as to their history or origin; for like the gipsies, they have no traditions, and know nothing. *Arrieros*, at all events, they are; and that word, in common with so many others relating to the barb and carrier-caravan craft, is Arabic, and proves whence the system and science were derived by Spaniards.

The *Maragatos* are celebrated for their fine beasts of burden; indeed, the mules of Leon are renowned, and the asses splendid and numerous, especially the nearer one approaches to the learned university of Salamanca. The *Maragatos* take precedence on the road; they are the lords of the highway, being *the* channels of commerce in a land where mules and asses represent luggage rail trains. They know and feel their importance, and that they are the rule, and the traveller for mere pleasure is the exception. Few Spanish muleteers are much more polished than their beasts, and however picturesque the scene, it is no joke meeting a string of laden beasts in a narrow road, especially with a precipice on one side, *cosa de España*. The *Maragatos* seldom give way, and their mules keep doggedly on; as the baggage projects on each side, like the paddles of a steamer, they sweep the whole path. But all wayfaring details in the genuine Spanish interior are calculated for the *pack*, as in England a century back; and there is no thought bestowed on the foreigner, who is not wanted, nay is disliked. The inns, roads, and right sides, suit the natives and their brutes; nor will either put themselves out of their way to please the fancies of a stranger. The racy Peninsula is too little travelled over for its natives to adopt the mercenary conveniences of the Swiss, that nation of innkeepers and coach-jobbers.

CHAPTER VIII

A MAN in a public carriage ceases to be a private individual: he is merged into the fare, and becomes a number according to his place; he is booked like a parcel, and is delivered by the guard. How free, how lord and master of himself, does the same dependent gentleman mount his eager barb, who by his neighing and pawing exhibits his joyful impatience to be off too! How fresh and sweet the free breath of heaven, after the frousty atmosphere of a full inside of foreigners, who, from the narcotic effects of tobacco, forget the existence of soap, water, and clean linen! Travelling on horseback, so unusual a gratification to Englishmen, is the ancient, primitive, and once universal mode of travelling in Europe, as it still is in the East; mankind, however, soon gets accustomed to a changed state of locomotion, and forgets how recent is its introduction. Fynes Moryson gave much the same advice two centuries ago to travellers in England, as must be now suggested to those who in Spain desert the coach-beaten highways for the delightful bye-ways, and thus explore the rarely visited, but not the least interesting portions of the Peninsula. It has been our good fortune to perform many of these expeditions on horseback, both alone and in company; and on one occasion to have made the pilgrimage from Seville to Santiago, through Estremadura and Gallicia, returning by the Asturias, Biscay, Leon, and the Castiles; thus riding nearly two thousand miles on the same horse, and only accompanied by one Andalucian servant, who had never before gone out of his native province. The same tour was afterwards performed by two friends with two servants; nor did they or ourselves ever meet with any real impediments or difficulties, scarcely indeed sufficient of either to give the flavour of adventure, or the dignity of danger, to the undertaking. It has also been our lot to make an extended tour of many months, accompanied by an English lady, through Granada, Murcia, Valencia, Catalonia, and Arragon, to say nothing of repeated excursions through every nook and corner of Andalucia. The result of all this experience, combined with that of many friends, who have *ridden over* the Peninsula, enables us to recommend this method to the young, healthy, and adventurous, as by far the most agreeable plan of proceeding; and, indeed, as we have said, as regards two-thirds of the Peninsula, the only practicable course.

The leading royal roads which connect the capital

with the principal seaports are, indeed, excellent; but they are generally drawn in a straight line, whereby many of the most ancient cities are thus left out, and these, together with sites of battles and historical incident, ruins and remains of antiquity, and scenes of the greatest natural beauty, are accessible with difficulty, and in many cases only on horseback. Spain abounds with wide tracts which are perfectly unknown to the Geographical Society. Here, indeed, is fresh ground open to all who aspire in these threadbare days to book something new; here is scenery enough to fill a dozen portfolios, and subject enough for a score of quartos. How many flowers pine unbotanised, how many rocks harden ungeologised; what views are dying to be sketched; what bears and deer to be stalked; what trout to be caught and eaten; what valleys expand their bosoms, longing to embrace their visitor; what virgin beauties hitherto unseen await the happy member of the Travellers' Club, who in ten days can exchange the bore of eternal Pall Mall for these untrodden sites; and then what an accession of dignity in thus discovering a terra incognita, and rivalling Mr. Mungo Park! Nor is a guide wanting, since our good friend John Murray, the grand monarque of Handbooks, has proclaimed from Albemarle Street, *Il n'y a plus de Pyrénées.*

As the wide extent of country which intervenes between the radii of the great roads is most indifferently provided with public means of inter-communication; as there is little traffic, and no demand for modern conveyances—even mules and horses are not always to be procured, and we have always found it best to set out on these distant excursions with our own beasts: the comfort and certainty of this precaution have been corroborated beyond any doubt by frequent comparisons with the discomforts undergone by other persons, who trusted to chance accommodations and means of locomotion in ill-provided districts and out-of-the-way excursions: indeed, as a general rule, the traveller will do well to carry with him everything with which from habit he feels that he cannot dispense. The chief object will be to combine in as small a space as possible the greatest quantity of portable comfort, taking care to select the really essential; for there is no worse mistake than lumbering oneself with things that are never wanted. This mode of travelling has not been much detailed by the generality of authors, who have rarely gone much out of the beaten track, or undertaken a long-continued riding tour, and they have been rather inclined to overstate the dangers and difficulties of a plan which they have never tried. At the same time this plan is not to be recommended to fine ladies nor to delicate gentlemen, nor to those who have had a touch of rheumatism, or who tremble at the shadows which coming gout casts before it.

Those who have endurance and curiosity enough to face a tour in Sicily, may readily set out for Spain; rails and post-horses certainly get quicker over the country; but the pleasure of the remembrance and the benefits derived by travel are commonly in an inverse ratio to the ease and rapidity with which the journey is performed. In addition to the accurate knowledge which is thus acquired of the country (for there is no map like this mode of surveying), and an acquaintance with a considerable, and by no means the worst portion of its population, a riding expedition to a civilian is almost equivalent to serving a campaign. It imparts a new life, which is adopted on the spot, and which soon appears quite natural, from being in perfect harmony and fitness with everything around, however strange to all previous habits and notions; it takes the conceit out of a man for the rest of his life—it makes him bear and forbear. It is a capital practical school of moral discipline, just as the hardiest mariners are nurtured in the roughest seas. Then and there will be learnt golden rules of patience, perseverance, good temper, and good fellowship: the individual man must come out, for better or worse. On these occasions, where wealth and rank are stripped of the aids and appurtenances of conventional superiority, a man will draw more on his own resources, moral and physical, than on any letter of credit; his wit will be sharpened by invention-suggesting necessity.

Then and there, when up, about, and abroad, will be shaken off dull sloth; action—Demosthenic action—will be the watchword. The traveller will blot out from his dictionary the fatal Spanish phrase of procrastination *by and by*, a street which leads to the house of *never*, for " *por la calle de despues, se va a la casa de nunca.* " Reduced to shift for himself, he will see the evil of waste —the folly of improvidence and want of order. He will whistle to the winds the paltry excuse of idleness, the Spanish " *no se puede,* " " *it is impossible.* " He will soon learn, by grappling with difficulties, how surely they are overcome,—how soft as silk becomes the nettle when it is sternly grasped, which would sting the tender-handed touch,—how powerful a principle of realising the object proposed, is the moral conviction that we can and will accomplish it. He will never be scared by shadows thin as air, for when one door shuts another opens, and he who pushes on arrives. And after all, a dash of hardship may be endured by those accustomed to loll in easy britzskas, if only for the sake of novelty; what a new relish is given to the palled appetite by a little unknown privation!—hunger being, as Cervantes says, the best of sauces, which, as it never is wanting to the poor, is the reason why eating is their huge delight.

Again, these sorts of independent expeditions are equally conducive to health of body: after the first few days of the new fatigue are got over, the frame becomes of iron, " *hecho de bronze,* " and the rider, a centaur not fabulous. The living in the pure air, the sustaining excitement of novelty, exercise, and constant occupation, are all sweetened by the willing heart, which renders even labour itself a pleasure; a new and vigorous life is infused into every bone and muscle: early to bed and early to rise, if it does not make all brains wise, at least invigorates the gastric juices, makes a man forget that he has a liver, that storehouse of mortal misery— bile, blue pill, and blue devils. This health is one of the secrets of the amazing charm which seems inherent to this mode of travelling, in spite of all the apparent hardships with which it is surrounded in the abstract. Oh!

the delight of this gipsy, Bedouin, nomade life, seasoned with unfettered liberty! We pitch our tent wherever we please, and there we make our home—far from letters "requiring an immediate answer," and distant dining-outs, visits, ladies' maids, band-boxes, butlers, bores, and button-holders.

Escaping from the meshes of the west end of London, we are transported into a new world; every day the out-of-door panorama is varied; now the heart is cheered and the countenance made glad by gazing on plains overflowing with milk and honey, or laughing with oil and wine, where the orange and citron bask in the glorious sunbeams, the palm without the desert, the sugar-cane without the slave. Anon we are lost amid the silence of cloud-capped glaciers, where rock and granite are tost about like the fragments of a broken world, by the wild magnificence of Nature, who, careless of mortal admiration, lavishes with proud indifference her fairest charms where most unseen, her grandest forms where most inaccessible. Every day and everywhere we are unconsciously funding a stock of treasures and pleasures of memory, to be hived in our bosoms like the honey of the bee, to cheer and sweeten our after-life, when we settle down like wine-dregs in our cask, which, delightful even as in the reality, wax stronger as we grow in years, and feel that these feats of our youth, like sweet youth itself, can never be our portion again. Of one thing the reader may be assured,—that dear will be to him, as is now to us, the remembrance of those wild and weary rides through tawny Spain, where hardship was forgotten ere undergone: those sweet-aired hills—those rocky crags and torrents—those fresh valleys which communicated their own freshness to the heart—that keen relish for hard fare, gained and seasoned by hunger sauce, which Ude did not invent—those sound slumbers on harder couch, earned by fatigue, the downiest of pillows—the braced nerves—the spirits light, elastic, and joyous—that freedom from care—that health of body and soul which ever rewards a closer communion with Nature—and the shuffling off of the frets and factitious wants of the thick-pent artificial city.

Whatever be the number of the party, and however they travel, whether on wheels or horseback, admitting even that a pleasant friend pro vehiculo est, that is, is better than a postchaise, yet no one should ever dream of making a pedestrian tour in Spain. It seldom answers anywhere, as the walker arrives at the object of his promenade tired and hungry, just at the moment when he ought to be the freshest and most up to intellectual pleasures. The deipnosophist Athenæus long ago discovered that there was no love for the sublime and beautiful in an empty stomach, æsthetics yield then to gastronomics, and there is no prospect in the world so fine as that of a dinner and a nap, or *siesta* afterwards. The pedestrian in Spain, where fleshly comforts are rare, will soon understand why, in the real journals of our Peninsular soldiers, so little attention is paid to those objects which most attract the well-provided traveller. In cases of bodily hardship, the employment of the mental faculties is narrowed into the care of supplying mere physical wants, rather than expanded into searching for those of a contemplative or intellectual gratification; the footsore and way-worn require, according to

> " The unexempt condition
> By which all mortal frailty must subsist,
> Refreshment after toil, ease after pain."

Walking is the manner by which beasts travel, who have therefore four legs; those bipeds who follow the example of the brute animals will soon find that they will be reduced to their level in more particulars than they imagined or bargained for. Again, as no Spaniard ever walks for pleasure, and none ever perform a journey on foot except trampers and beggars, it is never supposed possible that any one else should do so except from compulsion. Pedestrians therefore are either ill-received, or become objects of universal suspicion; for a Spanish authority, judging of others by himself, always takes the worst view of the stranger, whom he considers as guilty until he proves himself innocent.

Before the pleasures of a riding tour through Spain are mentioned, a few observations on the choice of companions may be made.

Those who travel in public conveyances or with muleteers are seldom likely to be left alone.   It is the
horseman who strikes into out-of-the way, unfrequented
districts, who will feel the want of that important item
—a travelling companion, on which, as in choosing a
wife, it is easy enough to give advice.   The patient must,
however, administer to himself, and the selection will
depend, of course, much on the taste and idiosyncrasy
of each individual; those unfortunate persons who are
accustomed to have everything their own way, or those,
happy ones, who are never less alone than when alone,
and who possess the alchymy of finding resources and
amusements in themselves, may perhaps find that plan
to be the best; at all events, no company is better than
bad company : " *mas vale ir solo, que mal acompañado.*"
A solitary wanderer is certainly the most unfettered as
regards his notions and motions, " *no tengo padre ni
madre, ni perro que me ladre.*"   He who has " neither
father, mother, nor dog to bark at him," can read the
book of Spain, as it were, in his own room, dwelling on
what he likes, and skipping what he does not, as with a
red Murray.

Every coin has, however, its reverse, and every rose
its thorn.   Notwithstanding these and other obvious advantages, and the tendency that occupation and even
hardships have to drive away imaginary evils, this freedom will be purchased by occasional moments of depres-
sion; a dreary, forsaken feeling will steal over the most
cheerful mind.   It is not good for man to be alone; and
this social necessity never comes home stronger to the
warm heart than during a long-continued solitary ride
through the rarely visited districts of the Peninsula.
The sentiment is in perfect harmony with the abstract
feeling which is inspired by the present condition of unhappy Spain, fallen from her high estate, and blotted
almost from the map of Europe.   Silent, sad, and lonely
is her face, on which the stranger will too often gaze;
her hedgeless, treeless tracts of corn-field, bounded only
by the low horizon; her uninhabited, uncultivated
plains, abandoned to the wild flower and the bee, and
which are rendered still more melancholy by ruined

castle, or village, which stand out bleaching skeletons
of a former vitality. The dreariness of this abomination
of desolation is increased by the singular absence of
singing birds, and the presence of the vulture, the eagle,
and lonely birds of prey. The wanderer, far from home
and friends, feels doubly a stranger in this strange land,
where no smile greets his coming, no tear is shed at his
going,—where his memory passes away, like that of a
guest who tarrieth but a day,—where nothing of human
life is seen, where its existence only is inferred by the
rude wooden cross or stone-piled cairn, which marks
the unconsecrated grave of some traveller who has been
waylaid there alone, murdered, and sent to his account
with all his imperfections on his head.

However confidently we have relied on past experience
that such would not be our fate, yet these sorts of
Spanish milestones marked with memento mori, are
awkward evidences that the thing is not altogether impossible. It makes a single gentleman, whose life is
not insured, not only trust to Santiago, but keep his
powder dry, and look every now and then if his percus-
sion cap fits. On these occasions the falling in with
any of the nomade half-Bedouin natives is a sort of godsend; their society is quite different from that of a
regular companion, for better or worse until death us
do part, as it is casual, and may be taken up or dropped
at convenience. The habits of all Spaniards when on
the road are remarkably gregarious; a common fear acts
as a cement, while the more they are in number the
merrier. It is hail! well met, fellow-traveller! and the
being glad to see each other is an excellent introduction.
The sight of passengers bound our way is like speaking
a strange sail on the Atlantic, *Hola Camara!* ship a-hoy.
This predisposition tends to make all travellers write
so much and so handsomely of the lower classes of
Spaniards, not indeed more than they deserve, for they
are a fine, noble race. Something of this arises, because
on such occasions all parties meet on an equality; and
this levelling effect, perhaps unperceived, induces many
a foreigner, however proud and reserved at home, to
unbend, and that unaffectedly. He treats these acci-

dental acquaintances quite differently from the manner
in which he would venture to treat the lower orders of
his own country, who, probably, if conciliated by the
same condescension of manner, would appear in a more
amiable light, although they are inferior to the Spaniard
in his Oriental goodness of manner, his perfect tact, his
putting himself and others into their proper place, without either self-degradation or vulgar assumption of
social equality or superior physical powers.

A long solitary ride is hardly to be recommended; it
is not fair to friends who have been left anxious behind,
nor is it prudent to expose oneself, without help, to the
common accidents to which a horse and his rider are
always liable. Those who have a friend with whom they
feel they can venture to go in double harness, had better
do so. It is a severe test, and the trial becomes greater
in proportion as hardships abound and accommodations
are scanty—causes which sour the milk of human kindness, and prove indifferent restorers of stomach or temper. It is on these occasions, on a large journey and in
a small *venta*, that a man finds out what his friend really
is made of. While in the more serious necessities of
danger, sickness, and need—a friend is one indeed, and
the one thing wanting, with whom we share our last
morsel and cup gladly. The salt of good fellowship, if
it cannot work miracles as to quantity, converts the
small loaf into a respectable abstract feed, by the zest
and satisfaction with which it flavours it.

Nothing, moreover, cements friendships for the future
like having made one of these conjoint rambles, provided
it did not end in a quarrel. The mere fact of having
travelled *at all* in Spain has a peculiarity which is denied
to the more hackneyed countries of Europe. When we
are introduced to a person who has visited these spell-
casting sites, we feel as if we knew him already. There
is a sort of freemasonry in having done something in
common, which is not in common with the world at
large. Those who are about to qualify themselves for
this exclusive quality will do well not to let the party
exceed five in number, three masters and two servants;
two masters with two servants are perhaps more likely

to be better accommodated; a third person, however, is often of use in trying journeys, as an arbiter elegantiarum et rixarum, a referee and arbitrator; for in the best regulated teams it must happen that some one will occasionally start, gib, or bolt, when the majority being against him brings the offender to his proper senses. Four eyes, again, see better than two, " *mas ven cuatro ojos que dos.*"

By attending to a few simple rules, a tour of some months' duration, and over thousands of miles, may be performed on one and the same horse, who with his rider will at the end of the journey be neither sick nor sorry, but in such capital condition as to be ready to start again. We presume that the time will be chosen when the days are long and Nature has thrown aside her wintry garb. Fine weather is the joy of the wayfarer's soul, and nothing can be more different than the aspect of Spanish villages in good or in bad weather; as in the East, during wintry rains they are the acmes of mud and misery, but let the sun shine out, and all is gilded. It is the smile which lights up the habitually sad expression of a Spanish woman's face. The blessed beam cheers poverty itself, and by its stimulating, exhilarating action on the system of man, enables him to buffet against the moral evils to which countries the most favoured by climate seem, as if it were from compensation, to be more exposed than those where the skies are dull, and the winds bleak and cold.

As in our cavalry regiments, where real service is required, a perfect animal is preferred, a rider should choose a mare rather than a gelding; the use of entire horses is, however, so general in Spain, that one of such had better be selected than a mare. The day's journey will vary according to circumstances from twenty-five to forty miles. The start should be made before daybreak, and the horse well fed at least an hour before the journey is commenced, during which Spaniards, if they can, go to church, for they say that no time is ever lost on a journey by feeding horses and men and hearing masses, *misa y cebada no estorban jornada.*

The hours of starting, of course, depend on the distance

and the district. The sooner the better, as all who wish to cheat the devil must get up very early. " *Quien al demonio quiere engañar, muy temprano levantarse ha.*" It is a great thing for the traveller to reach his night quarters as soon as he can, for the first comers are the best served : borrow therefore an hour of the morning rather than from the night; and that hour, if you lose it at starting, you will never overtake in the day. Again, in the summer it is both agreeable and profitable to be under way and off at least an hour or two before sunrise, as the heat soon gets insupportable, and the stranger is exposed to the *tabardillo*, the coup de soleil, which, even in a smaller degree, occasions more ill health in Spain than is generally imagined, and especially by the English, who brave it either from ignorance or foolhardiness. The head should be well protected with a silk handkerchief, tied after a turban fashion, which all the natives do; in addition to which we always lined the inside of our hats with thickly doubled brown paper. In Andalucia, during summer, the muleteers travel by night, and rest during the day-heat, which, however, is not a satisfactory method, except for those who wish to see nothing. We have never adopted it. The early mornings and cool afternoons and evenings are infinitely preferable; while to the artist the glorious sunrises and sunsets, and the marking of mountains, and definition of forms from the long shadows, are magnificent beyond all conception. In these almost tropical countries, when the sun is high, the effect of shadow is lost, and everything looks flat and unpicturesque.

The journey should be divided into two portions, and the longest should be accomplished the first : the pace should average about five miles an hour, it being an object not to keep the animal unnecessarily on his legs : he may be trotted gently, and even up easy hills, but should always be walked down them; nay, if led, so much the better, which benefits both horse and rider. It is surprising how a steady, continued slow pace gets over the ground : *Chi va piano, va sano, é lontano*, says the Italian; *paso a paso va lejos*, step by step goes far, responds the Castilian. The end of the journey each day is settled before starting, and there the traveller is sure to arrive with the evening. Spaniards never fidget themselves to get quickly to places where nobody is expecting them : nor is there any good to be got in trying to hurry man or beast in Spain; you might as well think of hurrying the Court of Chancery. The animals should be rested, if possible, every fourth day, and not used during halts in towns, unless they exceed three days' sojourn.

On arriving at every halting-place, look first at the feet, and pick out any pebbles or dirt, and examine the nails and shoes carefully, to see that nothing is loose; let this inspection become a habit; do not wash the feet too soon, as the sudden chill sometimes produces fever in them : when they are cool, clean them and grease the hoof well; after that you may wash as much as you please. The best thing, however, is to feed your horse at once, before thinking of his toilet; the march will have given an appetite, while the fatigue requires immediate restoration. If a horse is to be worried with cleaning, etc., he often loses heart and gets off his feed : he may be rubbed down when he has done eating, and his bed should be made up as for night, the stable darkened, and the animal left quite quiet, and the longer the better : feed him well again an hour before starting for the afternoon stage, and treat him on coming in exactly as you did in the morning. The food must be regulated by the work : when that is severe, give corn with both hands, and stint the hay and other lumber : what you want is to concentrate support by quality, not quantity. The Spaniards will tell you that one mouthful of beef is worth ten of potatoes. If your horse is an English one, it must be remembered that eight pounds' weight of barley is equal to ten of oats, as containing less husk and more mucilage or starch, which our horse-dealers know when they want to *make up* a horse; overfeeding a horse in the hot climate of Spain, like overfeeding his rider, renders both liable to fevers and sudden inflammatory attacks, which are much more prevalent in Gibraltar than elsewhere in Spain, because our countrymen will go on exactly as if they were at home.

At all events, feed your horse well with *something or other*, or your Spanish squire will rain proverbs on you, like Sancho Panza; the belly must be filled with hay or straw, for it in reality carries the feet, *O paja o heno el vientre lleno—tripas llevan á pies*, and so forth. The Spaniards when on a journey allow their horses to drink copiously at every stream, saying that there is no juice like that of flints; and indeed they set the example, for they are all down on their bellies at every brook, swilling water, according to the proverb, like an ox, and wine when they can get it, like a king. If therefore you are riding a Spanish horse which has been accustomed to this continual tippling, let him drink, otherwise he will be fevered. If the horse has been treated in the English fashion, give him his water only after his meals, otherwise he will break out into weakening sweats. Should the animal ever arrive distressed, a tepid gruel, made with oatmeal or even flour, will comfort him much. At nightfall stop the feet with wet tow, or with horse dung, for that of cows will seldom be to be had in Spain, where goats furnish milk, and Dutchmen butter.

Let the feet be constantly attended to; the horse having twice as many as his rider, requires double attention, and of what use to a traveller is a quadruped that has not a leg to go upon? This is well known to those commercial gentlemen, who are the only persons now-a-days in England who make riding journeys. It is the shoe that makes or mars the horse, and no wise man, in Spain or out, who has got a four-footed hobby, or three half-crowns, should delay sending to Longman's for that admirable "Miles on the Horse's Foot." "Every knight errant," says Don Quixote, "ought to be able to shoe his own *Rosinante* himself." *Rosin* is pure Arabic for a hackney—at least he should know how this calceolation ought to be done. As a general rule, always take your quadruped to the forge, where the shoes can be fitted to his feet, not the feet to ready-made shoes; and if you value the comfort, the extension of life and service of your steed—*fasten the fore shoes with five nails at most in the outside, and with two only in the inside, and those near the toe;* do not in mercy fix by nails all round an unyielding rim of dead iron, to an expanding living hoof; remember also always to take with you a spare set of shoes, with nails and a hammer— for the want of a nail the shoe was lost; for the want of a shoe the rider was tost. In many parts of Spain, where there are no fine modern roads, you might almost do without any shoes at all, as the ancients did, and is done in parts of Mexico; but no unprotected hoof can stand the constant wear and tear, the filing of a mac- adamised highway.

The horse will probably be soon in such condition as to want no more physic than his rider; a lump, how- ever, of rock-salt, and a bit of chalk put at night into his manger, answers the same purposes as Epsoms and soda do to the master. You should wash out the long tail and mane, which is the glory of a Spanish horse, as fine hair is to a woman, with soda and water; the alkali combining with the animal grease forms a most search- ing detergent. A grand remedy for most of the acci- dents to which horses are liable on a journey, such as kicks, cuts, strains, etc., is a constant fomentation with hot water, which should be done under the immediate superintendence of the master, or it will be either done insufficiently, or not done at all; hot water, according to the groom genus, having been created principally as a recipient of something stronger. A crupper and breast- plate are almost indispensable, from the steep ascents and descents in the mountains. The *mosquero*, the fly- flapper, is a great comfort to the horse, as, being in perpetual motion, and hanging between his eyes, it keeps off the flies; the head-stall, or night halter, never should be removed from the bridle, but be rolled up during the day, and fastened along the side of the cheek. The long tail is also rolled up when the ways are miry, just as those of our blue jackets and horse-guards used to be.

CHAPTER IX

THE rider's costume and accoutrements require consideration; his great object should be to pass in a crowd, either unnoticed, or be taken for " one of us," *Uno de Nosotros*, and a member of the Iberian family—*de la Familia*: this is best effected by adopting the dress, that is usually worn by the natives when they travel on horseback, or journey by any of their national conveyances, among which Anglo-Franco mails and diligences are not yet to be reckoned; all classes of Spaniards, on getting outside the town-gate, assume country habits, and eschew the long-tailed coats and civilisation of the city; they drop pea-jackets and foreign fashions, which would only attract attention, and expose the wearers to the ridicule, or coarser marks of consideration from the peasantry, muleteers, and other gentry, who rule on the road, hate novelties, and hold fast to the ways and jackets of their forefathers; the best hat, therefore, is the common *sombrero calanes*, which resemble those worn at Astley's by banditti, being of a conical shape, is edged with black velvet, ornamented with silken tufts, and looks equally well on a cockney from London, or on a squire from Devonshire. The jacket should be the universal fur *Zamarra*, which is made of black sheepskin, in its ordinary form, and of lambskin for those who can pay; a sash round the waist should never be forgotten, being most useful both in reality and metaphor : it sustains the loins, and keeps off the dangerous colics of Spain, by maintaining an equable heat over the abdomen; hence, to be Homerically well girt is half the battle for the Peninsular traveller.

The *capa* the cloak, or the *manta* a striped plaid, and saddle-bags, the *Alforjas*, are absolute essentials, and should be strapped on the pommel of the saddle, as being there less heating to the horse than when placed on his flanks, and being in front, they are more handy for sudden use, since in the mountains and valleys, the rider is

constantly exposed to sudden variations of wind and
weather; when Æolus and Sol contend for his cloak, as
in Æsop's Fables, and the buckets of heaven are emptied
on him as soon as the god of fire thinks him sufficiently
baked.

These saddle-bags are most classical, Oriental, and
convenient; they indeed constitute the genus *bagsman*,
and have given their name to our riding travellers; they
are the *Sarcinæ* of Cato the Censor, the *Bulgæ* of Luci-
lius, who made an epigram thereon :—

> " Cum *bulgâ* cœnat, dormit, lavat, omnis in unâ.
>   Spes hominis *bulga* hâc devincta est cætera vita :"

which, as these indispensables are quite as necessary to
the modern Spaniard, may be thus translated :—

> " A good roomy bag delighteth a Roman,
>   He is never without this appendage a minute;
> In bed, at the bath, at his meals,—in short no man
>   Should fail to stow life, hope, and self away in it."

The countrymen of Sancho Panza, when on the road,
make the same use of their wallets as the Romans did;
they still (the washing excepted) live and die with these
bags, in which their hearts are deposited with their
bread and cheese.

These Spanish *alforjas*, in name and appearance, are
the Moorish *al horeh*. (The F and H, like the B and V,
X and J, are almost equivalent, and are used indiscriminately in Spanish cacography.) They are generally composed of cotton and worsted, and are embroidered in
gaudy colours and patterns; the *correct* thing is to have
the owner's name worked in on the edge, which ought to
be done by the delicate hand of his beloved mistress.
Those made at Granada are very excellent; the Moorish,
especially those from Morocco, are ornamented with an
infinity of small tassels. Peasants, when dismounted,
mendicant monks, when foraging for their convents,
sling their *alforjas* over their shoulders when they come
into villages.

Among the contents which most people will find it
convenient to carry in the *right-hand bag*, as the easiest
to be got at, a pair of blue gauze wire spectacles or

goggles will be found useful, as ophthalmia is very common in Spain, and particularly in the calcined central plains. The constant glare is unrelieved by any verdure, the air is dry, and the clouds of dust highly irritating from being impregnated with nitre. The best remedy is to bathe the eyes frequently with hot water, and *never to rub them when inflamed*, except with the elbows, *los ojos con los codos*. Spaniards never jest with their eyes or faith; of the two perhaps they are seriously fondest of the former, not merely when sparkling beneath the arched eyebrow of the dark sex, but when set in their own heads. "I love thee like my eyes," is quite a hackneyed form of affection; nor, however wrathful and imprecatory, do they under any circumstances express the slightest uncharitable wishes in regard to the visual organs of their bitterest foe.

The whole art of the *alforjas* is the putting into them what you want the most often, and in the most handy and accessible place. Keep here, therefore, a supply of small money for the halt and the blind, for the piteous cases of human suffering and poverty by which the traveller's eye will be pained in a land where soup-dispensing monks are done away with, and assistant new poor law commissioners not yet appointed; such charity from God's purse, *bolsa de Dios*, never impoverishes that of man, and a cheerful giver, however opposed to modern political economists, is commended in that old-fashioned book called the Bible. The left half of the *alforjas* may be apportioned to the writing and dressing cases, and the smaller each are the better.

Food for the mind must not be neglected. The travelling library, like companions, should be select and good; *libros y amigos pocos y buenos*. The duodecimo editions are the best, as a large heavy book kills horse, rider, and reader. Books are a matter of taste; some men like Bacon, others prefer Pickwick; stow away at all events a pocket edition of the Bible, Shakespeare, and Don Quixote: and if the advice of dear Dr. Johnson be worth following, one of those books that can be taken in *the hand*, and to the fire-side. Martial, a grand authority on Spanish hand-books, recommended " such

sized companions on a long journey.'' Quartos and
folios, said he, may be left at home in the book-case—

     " Scrinia da magnis, *ne manus una* capit.''

Here also keep the passport, that indescribable nuisance
and curse of continental travel, to which a free-born
Briton never can get reconciled, and is apt to neglect,
whereby he puts himself in the power of the worst and
most troublesome people on earth. Passports in Spain
now in some degree supply the Inquisition, and have
been embittered by vexatious forms borrowed from
bureaucratic France.

Having thus disposed of these matters on the front
bow of his saddle, to which we always added a *bota*—
the pocket-pistol of Hudibras—one word on this *Bota*,
which is as necessary to the rider as a saddle to his
horse. This article, so Asiatic and Spanish, is at once
the bottle and the glass of the people of the Peninsula
when on the road, and is perfectly unlike the vitreous
crockery and pewter utensils of Great Britain. A
Spanish woman would as soon think of going to church
without her fan, or a Spanish man to a fair without
his knife, as a traveller without his *bota*. Ours, the
faithful, long-tried comforter of many a dry road, and
honoured now like a relic, is hung up a votive offering
to the Iberian Bacchus, as the mariners in Horace suspended their damp garments to the deity who had delivered them from the dangers of water. Its skin, now
shrivelled with age and with fruitless longings for wine,
is still redolent of the ruby fluid, whether the generous
Valdepeñas or the rich *vino de Toro*: and refreshing to
our nostrils is even an occasional smell at its red-stained
orifice. There the racy wine-perfume lingers, and
brings water into the mouth, it may be into the eye-
lid. What a dream of Spanish odours, good, bad, and
indifferent, is awakened by its well-known *borracha!*
—what recollections, breathing the aroma of the balmy
south, crowd in; of aromatic wastes, of leagues of
thyme, whence Flora sends forth advertisements to her
tiny bee-customer; of churches, all incense; of the
goats and monks, long-bearded and odoriferous; of
cities whose steam of garlic, ollas, oil, and tobacco

rises up to the heavens, mingled with the thousand and
one other continental sweets which assail a man's nose,
whether he lands at Calais or Cadiz! There hangs our
smelling-bottle *bota*, now a pleasure of memory; it has
had its day, and is never again to be filled in torrid,
thirsty Spain, nor emptied, which is better.

This *Bota*, from whence the terms *Butt* of sherry,
bouteille, and bottle are derived, is the most ancient
Oriental leathern bottle alluded to in Job xxxii. 19,
"My belly ready to burst like new bottles;" and in the
parable, Matt. ix. 17, about the old ones, the force and
point of which is entirely lost by our word *bottle*, which
being made of glass, is not liable to become useless by
age like one made of leather. Such a "bottle of
water" was the last among the few things which Abra-
ham gave to Hagar, when he turned out the mother of
the Arabians, whose descendants brought its usage into
Spain. The shape is like that of a large pear or shot-
pouch, and it contains from two to five quarts. The
narrow neck is mounted with a turned wooden cup,
from which the contents are drunk. The way to use it
is thus—grasp the neck with the left hand and bring
the rim of the cup to the mouth, then gradually raise
the bag with the other hand till the wine, in obedience
to hydrostatic laws, rises to its level, and keeps always
full in the cup without trouble to the mouth. The
gravity with which this is done, the long, slow, sustained, Sancho-like devotion of the thirsty Spaniards
when offered a drink out of another man's *bota*, is very
edifying, and is as deep as the sigh of delight and
gratitude with which, when unable to imbibe more, the
precious skin is returned. No drop of the divine contents is wasted, except by some newly-arrived bungler,
who, by lifting up the bottom first, inundates his chin.
The hole in the cup is made tight by a wooden spigot,
which again is perforated and stopped with a small
peg. Those who do not want to take a copious draught
do not pull out the spigot, but merely the little peg of
it; the wine then flows out in a thin thread. The Cata-
lonians and Aragonese generally drink in this way;
they never touch the vessel with their lips, but hold it

up at a distance above, and pilot the stream into their mouths, or rather under-jaws. It is much easier for those who have had no practice to pour the wine into their necks than into their mouths, but their drinking-bottles are made with a long narrow spout, and are called " *Porrones*."

The *Bota* must not be confounded with the *Borracha or Cuero*, the wine-skin of Spain, which is the *entire*, and answers the purpose of the barrel elsewhere. The *bota* is the retail receptacle, the *cuero* is the wholesale one. It is the genuine pig's skin, the adoration of which disputes in the Peninsula with the cigar, the dollar, and even the worship of the Virgin. The shops of the makers are to be seen in most Spanish towns; in them long lines of the unclean animal's blown-out hides are strung up like sheep carcases in our butchers' shambles. The tanned and manufactured article preserves the form of the pig, feet and all, with the exception of one : the skin is turned inside out, so that the hairy coat lines the interior, which, moreover, is carefully pitched like a ship's bottom, to prevent leaking; hence the peculiar flavour, which partakes of resin and the hide, which is called the *borracha*, and is peculiar to most Spanish wines, sherry excepted, which being made by foreigners, is kept in foreign casks, as we shall presently show when we touch on " good sherris sack." A drunken man, who is rarer in Spain than in England, is called a *borracho;* the term is not complimentary. These *cueros*, when filled, are suspended in *ventas* and elsewhere, and thus economise cellarage, cooperage, and bottling; and such were the bigbellied monsters which Don Quixote attacked.

As the *bota* is always near every Spaniard's mouth who can get at one, all classes being ever ready, like Sancho, to give " a thousand kisses," not only to his own legitimate *bota*, but to that of his neighbour, which is coveted more than wife : therefore no prudent traveller will ever journey an inch in Spain without getting one, and when he has, will never keep it empty, especially when he falls in with good wine. Every man's Spanish attendant will always find out, by instinct,

where the best wine is to be had; good wine neither
needs bush, herald, nor crier; in these matters, our
experience of them tallies with their proverb, " mas
vale vino *maldito*, que no agua *bendita*," " cursed bad
wine is better than holy water;" at the same time, in
their various scale of comparisons, there is good wine,
better wine, and best wine, but no such thing as bad
wine; of good wine, the Spaniards are almost as good
judges as of good water; they rarely mix them, because
they say that it is spoiling two good things. Vino *Moro*,
or Moorish wine, is by no means indicative of unclean-
ness, or other heretical imperfections implied generally
by that epithet; it simply means, that it is pure from
never having been baptized with water, for which the
Asturians, who keep small chandlers' shops, are so infamous, that they are said, from inveterate habit, to
adulterate even water; *aguan el agua*.

It is a great mistake to suppose, because Spaniards
are seldom seen drunk, and because when on a journey
they drink as much water as their beasts, that they have
any Oriental dislike to wine; the rule is " *Agua como
buey, y vino como Rey*," " to drink water like an ox,
and wine like a king." The extent of the *given* quantity of wine which they will always swallow, rather suggests that their habitual temperance may in some degree
be connected more with their poverty than with their
will. The way to many an honest breast lies through
the belly in this classical land, where the tutelar of
butlers still keeps the key of their cellars and hearts—
aperit præcordia Bacchus : nor is their Oriental blessing unconnected with some " savoury food " previously
administered. And independently of the very obvious
reasons which good wine does and ought to afford for
its own consumption, the irritating nature of Spanish
cookery provides a never-failing inducement. The constant use of the savoury class of condiments and of
pepper is very heating, " *la pimienta escalienta*." A
salt-fish, ham and sausage diet creates thirst; a good
rasher of bacon calls loudly for a corresponding long
and strong pull at the " *bota*," " *a torresno de tocino,
buen golpe de vino*."

This digression on *botas* will be pardoned by all who, having ridden in Spain, know the absolute necessity of them. The traveller will of course remember the advice given by the rogue of *Ventero* to Don Quixote to take shirts and money with him. " Put money in thy purse," said also honest Iago, for an empty one is a beggarly companion in the Peninsula as elsewhere. There is no getting to Rome or to Santiago if the pilgrim's scrip be scanty, or his mule lame : *Camino de Roma, ni mula coja ni Bolsa floja.*

Practically it may be said, that there is no paper money in Spain. Notes may be taken in some of the larger cities, but in the provinces the value of a man in office's promise to pay on paper, is not considered by the shrewd natives to be actually equal to cash ; while they will readily give these notes to foreigners, they prefer for their own use the old-fashioned representatives of wealth, gold and silver, towards the smallest fraction of which they have the largest possible veneration. Accounts are usually kept in *reales de vellon* of royal bullion ; and these are subdivided into *maravedis*, the ancient coin of the Peninsula : there are minor fractions even of farthings, consisting in material of infinitesimal bits of any metals, melted church bells, old cannon, etc., with names and values unknown in our happy land, where not much is to be got for a mite ; in Spain, where cheapness of earth-produce is commensurate with poverty, anything, even to an old button, goes for a *maravedi*, and we have found that in changing a dollar by way of experiment into small coppers in the market at Seville, among the multitudinous specimens of Spanish mints of all periods, Moorish and even Roman coins were to be met with, and still current.

The dollar, or *Duro*, of Spain is well known all over the world, being the form under which silver has been generally exported from the Spanish colonies of South America. It is the Italian " Colonato," so called because the arms of Spain are supported between the two pillars of Hercules. The coinage is slovenly : it is the weight of the metal, not the form, which is looked to

by the Spaniard, who, like the Turk, is not so clever
a workman or mechanist as devout worshipper of
bullion. Ferdinand VII. continued for a long while to
strike money with his father's head, having only had
the lettering altered : thus early Trajans exhibit the
head of Nero. When the Cortes entered Madrid after
the Duke's victory at Salamanca, they patriotically prohibited the currency of all coins bearing the head of
the intrusive Joseph; yet his dollars being chiefly made
out of stolen church plate, gilt and ungilt, were, although those of an usurper, intrinsically worth more
than the *legitimate* duro : this was a too severe test for
the loyalty of those whose real king and god is cash.
Such a decree was worthy of senators who were busier
employed in expelling French tropes from their dictionary than French troops from their country. The
wiser Chinese take Ferdinand's and Joseph's dollars
alike, calling them both " devil's head " money. These
bad prejudices against good coin have now given way
to the march of intellect; nay, the five-franc piece with
Louis-Philippe's clever head on it bids fair to oust the
pillared *Duro*. The silver of the mines of Murcia is
exported to France, where it is coined, and sent back in
the manufactured shape. France thus gains a handsome per centage, and habituates the people to her
image of power, which comes recommended to them
in the most acceptable likeness of current coin.

In Spain cash, ambrosial cash, rules the court, the
camp, the grove; hence the extraordinary credit of
three millions recently required for the secret service
expenses of the Tuileries, and official enthusiasm and
unanimity secured thereby in the Montpensier purchase.
The whole decalogue is condensed at Madrid into one
commandment, Love God as represented on earth not by
his vicar the Pope, but by his lord-lieutenant, Don Ducat.

" El *primero* es amar Don *Dinero*,
    Dios es omnipotente, Don *Dinero* es su lugarteniente."

Thus grandees and men in Spanish offices, both governmental and printing ones, have preferred the other day
five-franc pieces to the ribbons of the Legion of *honor;*

nor, considering the swindlers on whom this badge of Austerlitz has been prostituted, were these worthy Castilians much out in their calculations, if there be any truth in the catechism of Falstaff.

The *gold coinage* is magnificent, and worthy of the country and period from which Europe was supplied with the precious metals. The largest piece, the ounce, "*onza*," is worth sixteen dollars, or about 3*l*. 6*s*.; and while it puts to shame the diminutive Napoleons of France and sovereigns of England, tells the tale of Spain's former wealth, and contrasts strangely with her present poverty and scarcity of specie : these large coins have however been so *sweated*, not by the sun, but by Jews, foreign and domestic, so clipped worse than Spanish mules or French poodles, that they seldom retain their proper weight and value. They are accordingly looked upon every where with suspicion; a shopkeeper, in a big town, brings out his scales like Shylock, while in a village shrugs, *ajos*, and negative expressions are your change; nor, even if the natives are satisfied that they are not light, can sixteen dollars be often met with, nor do those who have so much ready money by them ever wish that the fact should be generally known. Spaniards, like the Orientals, have a dread of being supposed to have money in their possession; it exposes them to be plundered by robbers of all kinds, professional or legal; by the " *alcalde*," or village authority, and the " *escribano*," the attorney, to say nothing of Señor Mon's tax-gatherer; for the quota of contributions, many of which are apportioned among the inhabitants themselves of each district, falls heaviest on those who have, or are supposed to have, the most ready money.

The lower classes of Spaniards, like the Orientals, are generally avaricious. They see that wealth is safety and power, where everything is venal; the feeling of insecurity makes them eager to invest what they have in a small and easily concealed bulk, " *en lo que no habla*," " in that which does not tell tales." Consequently, and in self-defence, they are much addicted to hoarding. The idea of finding hidden treasures, which prevails in Spain as in the East, is based on some grounds; for in every country which has been much exposed to foreign invasions, civil wars, and domestic misrule, where there were no safe modes of investment, in moments of danger property was converted into gold or jewels and concealed with singular ingenuity. The mistrust which Spaniards entertain of each other often extends, when cash is in the case, even to the nearest relations, to wife and children. Many a treasure is thus lost from the accidental death of the hider, who, dying without a sign, carries his secret to the grave, adding thereby to the sincere grief of his widow and heir. One of the old vulgar superstitions in Spain is an idea that those who were born on a Good Friday, the day of mourning, were gifted with a power of seeing into the earth and of discovering hidden treasures. One place of concealment has always been under the bodies in graves; the hiders have trusted to the dead to defend what the quick could not: this accounts for the universal desecration of tombs and churchyards during Bonaparte's invasion. The Gauls growled like gowls amid the churchyards; they despoiled the mouldering corpses of the last pledge left by weeping affection; or, as Burke observed of their domestic doings, they unplumbed the dead to make missiles of destruction against the living. These hordes, in their hurried flight before the advancing Duke, also hid much of their ill-gotten gains, which to this day are hunted after. Who has forgotten Borrow's graphic picture of the treasure-seeking Mol? At this very moment the authorities of San Sebastian are narrowly superintending the diggings of an old Frenchwoman, to whom some dying thief at home has revealed the secret of a buried kettle full of gold ounces.

Having provided the "*Spanish*," those metallic sinews of war, which also make the mare go in peace, a prudent master, if he intends to be really the master, will hold the purse himself, and, moreover, will keep a sharp eye on it, for the jingle of coin dispels even a Spanish siesta, and causes many a sleepless day to every listener, from the beggar to the queen mother.

CHAPTER X

Don Quixote's first thought, after having determined to ride forth into Spain, was to get a horse; his second was to secure a squire; and as the narrative of his journey is still an excellent guide-book for modern travellers, his example is not to be slighted. A good Sancho Panza will on the whole be found to be a more constant comfort to a knight-errant than even a Dulcinea. To secure a really good servant is of the utmost consequence to all who make out-of-the-way excursions in the Peninsula; for, as in the East, he becomes often not only cook, but interpreter and companion to his master. It is therefore of great importance to get a person with whom a man can ramble over these wild scenes. The so doing ends, on the part of the attendant, in an almost canine friendship; and the Spaniard, when the tour is done, is broken-hearted, and ready to leave his home, horse, ass, and wife, to follow his master, like a dog, to the world's-end. Nine times out of ten it is the master's fault if he has bad servants: *tel maître tel valet. Al amo imprudente, el mozo negligente.* He must begin at once, and exact the performance of their duty; the only way to get them to do anything is, as the Duke said, to " frighten them," to " take a decided line." It is very difficult to make them see the importance of detail and of doing exactly what they are told, which they will always endeavour to shirk when they can; their task must be clearly pointed out to them at starting, and the earliest and smallest infractions, either in commission or omission, at once and seriously noticed, the moral victory is soon gained. The example of the masters, if they be active and orderly, is the best lesson to servants; *mucho sabe el rato, pero mas el gato;* the rats are well enough, but the cats are better. Achilles, Patroclus, and the Homeric heroes, were their own cooks; and many a man who, like Lord Blayney, may not be a hero, will be none the worse for following the epical example, in a Spanish venta: at all events a good servant, who is up to his work, and will work, is indeed a jewel; and on these, as on other occasions, he deserves to be well treated. Those who make themselves honey are eaten by flies—*quien se hace miel, le comen las moscas;* while no rat ever ventures to jest with the cat's son; *con hijo de gato, no se burlan los ratones.* The great thing is to make them get up early, and learn the value of time, which the groom cannot tie with his halter, *tiempo y hora, no se ata con soga:* while a cook who oversleeps himself not only misses his mass, but his meat, *quien se levanta tarde, ni oye misa, ni compra carne.* If (which is soon found out) the servants seem not likely to answer, the sooner they are changed the better; it is loss of time and soap, and he who is good for nothing in his own village will not be worth more either in Seville or elsewhere, so says the proverb.

The principal defects of Spanish servants and of the lower classes of Spaniards are much the same, and faults of race. As a mass, they are apt to indulge in habits of procrastination, waste, improvidence, and untidiness. They are unmechanical and obstinate, easily beaten by difficulties, which their first feeling is to raise, and their next to succumb to; they give the thing up at once. They have no idea indeed of grappling with anything that requires much trouble, or of doing anything as it ought to be done, or even of doing the same thing in the same way—accident and the impulse of the moment set them going. They are very unmechanical, obstinate, and prejudiced; ignorant of their own ignorance and incurious as Orientals; partly from pride, self-opinion, and idleness, they seldom will ask questions for information from others, which implies an inferiority of knowledge, and still more seldom will take an answer, unless it be such a one as they desire; their own wishes, opinions, and wants are their guides, and self the centre of their gravity, not those of their employers. As a Spaniard's *yes,* when you beg a favour, generally means *no,* so they cannot or will not understand that your *no* is really a negative when they come

petitioning to be idle; at the same time a great change
for the better comes over them when they are taken
out of the city on a rambling tour. The nomad life
excites them into active serviceable fellows; in fact the
uncertain harum-scarum nomad existence is exactly
what suits these descendants of the Arab; they cannot
bear the steady sustained routine of a well-managed
household; they abhor confinement; hence the difficulty
of getting Spaniards to garrison fortresses or to man
ships of war, from whence there is no escape.

As for what we call a well-appointed servants' hall,
the case is hopeless in Spanish field or city, and is
equally so whether the life be above or below stairs.
In the house of the middle or highest classes this is
particularly shown in everything that regards gastronomics, which are the tests and touchstones of good
service. In truth, the Spaniard, accustomed to his own
desultory, free and easy, impromptu, scrambling style
of dining, is constrained by the order and discipline,
the pomp and ceremony, and serious importance of a
well-regulated dinner, and their observance of forms
extends only to persons, not to things : even the grandee
has only a thin European polish spread over his Gotho-
Bedouin dining table; he lives and eats surrounded by
an humble clique, in his huge ill-furnished barrack-
house, without any elegance, luxury, or even comfort,
according to sound transpyrenean notions : few indeed
are the kitchens which possess a *cordon bleu*, and fewer
are the masters who really like an orthodox *entrée*, one
unpolluted with the heresies of garlic and red pepper :
again, whenever their cookery attempts to be foreign,
as in their other imitations, it ends in being a flavourless
copy; but few things are ever done in Spain in *real
style*, which implies forethought and expense; everything is a make-shift; the noble master *reposes* his
affairs on an unjust steward, and dozes away life on
this bed of roses, somnolescent over business and awake
only to intrigue; his numerous ill-conditioned, ill-
appointed servants have no idea of discipline or subor-
dination; you never can calculate on their laying even
the table-cloth, as they prefer idling in the church or

market to doing their duty, and would rather starve, dance, and sleep out of place and independently, than feast and earn their wages by fair work; nor has the employer any redress, for if he dismisses them he will only get just such another set, or even worse.

In our own Spanish household, the instant dinner and siesta were over, the cook with his kitchen-man, the valet with the footman invariably stripped off their working apparel—liveries are almost unheard of— donned their comical velvet embroidered hats, their sky-blue waistcoats, and scarlet sashes, and were off with a guitar to some scene of song and love-making, leaving their master alone in his glory to moralize on the uncertainty of human concerns and the faithlessness of mankind.

What can't be cured must be endured. To resume, therefore, the character of these Spanish servants; they are very loquacious, and highly credulous, as often is the case with those given to romancing, which they, and especially the Andalucians, are to a large degree; and, in fact, it is the only remaining romance in Spain, as far as the natives are concerned. As they have an especial good opinion of themselves, they are touchy, sensitive, jealous, and thin-skinned, and easily affronted whenever their imperfections are pointed out; their disposition is very sanguine and inflammable; they are always hoping that what they eagerly desire will come to pass without any great exertion on their parts; they love to stand still with their arms folded, while other men put their shoulders to the wheel. Their lively imagination is very apt to carry them away into extremes for good or evil, when they act on the moment like children, and having gratified the humour of the impulse relapse into their ordinary tranquillity, which is that of a slumbering volcano. On the other hand, they are full of excellent and redeeming good qualities; they are free from caprice, are hardy, patient, cheerful, good-homoured, sharp-witted, and intelligent : they are honest, faithful, and trustworthy; sober, and unaddicted to mean, vulgar vices; they have a bold, manly bearing, and will follow well wherever they are well led,

being the raw material of as good soldiers as are in
the world; they are loyal and religious at heart, and
full of natural tact, mother-wit, and innate good manners. In general, a firm, quiet, courteous, and somewhat reserved manner is the most effective. Whenever
duties are to be performed, let them see that you are
not to be trifled with. The coolness of a determined
Englishman's manner, when in earnest, is what few
foreigners can withstand. Grimace and gesticulation,
sound and fury, bluster, petulance, and impertinence
fume and fret in vain against it, as the sprays and foam
of the " French lake " do against the unmoved and
immoveable rock of Gibraltar. An Englishman, without being over-familiar, may venture on a far greater
degree of unbending in his intercourse with his Spanish
dependents than he can dare to do with those he has in
England. It is the custom of the country; they are
used to it, and their heads are not turned by it, nor
do they ever forget their relative positions. The
Spaniards treat their servants very much like the ancient
Romans or the modern Moors; they are more their
vernæ, their domestic slaves : it is the absolute authority
of the father combined with the kindness. Servants do
not often change their masters in Spain : their relation and duties are so clearly defined, that the latter
runs no risk of compromising himself or his dignity by
his familiarity, which can be laid down or taken up at
his own pleasure; whereas the scorn, contempt, and
distance with which the said courteous Don would treat
a roturier who presumed to be intimate, baffle description. In England no man dares to be intimate with his
footman; for supposing even such absurd fancy entered
his brain, his footman is his equal in the eye of man-
made law, God having created them utterly unequal in
all his gifts, whether of rank, wealth, form, or intellect. Conventional barriers accordingly must be erected
in self-defence : and social barriers are more difficult to
be passed than walls of brass, more impossible to be
repealed than the whole statutes at large. No master
in Spain, and still less a foreigner, should ever descend
to personal abuse, sneers, or violence. A blow is never

to be washed out except in blood, and Spanish revenge descends to the third and fourth generation; and whatever these backward Spaniards have to learn from foreigners, it is not the duty of revenge, nor how to perform it. There should be no threatenings in vain, but whenever the opportunity occurs for punishment, let it be done quietly and effectively, and the fault once punished should not be needlessly ripped up again; Spaniards are sufficiently unforgiving, and hoarders-up of unrevenged grievances require to be reminded. A kind and uniform behaviour, a showing consideration to them, in a manner which implies that you are accustomed to it, and expect it to be shown to you, keeps most things in their right places. Temper and patience are the great requisites in the master, especially when he speaks the language imperfectly. He must not think Spaniards stupid because they cannot guess the meaning of his unknown tongue. Nothing again is gained by fidgeting and overdoing, and however early you may get up, daybreak will not take place the sooner: *no por mucho madrugar, amanece mas temprano*. Let well alone: be not zealous overmuch: be occasionally both blind and deaf: shut the door, and the devil passes by: keep honey in mouth and an eye to your cash: *miel en boca y guarda la bolsa*. Still how much less expenditure is necessary in Spain than in performing the commonest excursion in England!—and yet many who submit to their own countrymen's extortions are furious at what they imagine is an especial cheating of them, *quasi* Englishmen, abroad: this outrageous economy, with which some are afflicted, is penny wise and pound foolish: pay, pay therefore with both hands. The traveller must remember that he gains caste, gets brevet rank in Spain—that he is taken for a grandee incog., and ranks with their nobility; he must pay for these luxuries: how small after all will be the additional per centage on his general expenditure, and how well bestowed is the excess, in keeping the temper good, and the capability of enjoying unruffled a tour, which only is performed once in a life! No wise man who goes into Spain for amusement will plunge into this guerrilla, this constant petty warfare, about sixpences. Let the traveller be true to himself; hold his tongue; avoid bad company, *quien hace su cama con perros, se levanta con pulgas*, those who sleep with dogs get up with fleas; and make room for bulls and fools, *al loco y toro da le corro*, and he may see Spain agreeably, and, as Catullus said to Veranius, who made the tour many centuries ago, may on his return amuse his friends and " old mother :"—

> " Visam te incolumem, audiamque Iberum
> Narrantem loca, facta, nationes,
> Sicut tuus est mos."

which may be thus Englished :—

> May you come back safe, and tell
> Of Spanish men, their things and places,
> Of Spanish ladies' eyes and faces,
> In your own way, and so well.

Two masters should take two servants, and both should be Spaniards : all others, unless they speak the language perfectly, are nuisances. A Gallegan or Asturian makes the best groom, an *Andaluz* the best cook and personal attendant. Sometimes a person may be picked up who has some knowledge of languages, and who is accustomed to accompany strangers through Spain as a sort of courier. These accomplishments are vary rare, and the moral qualities of the possessor often diminish in proportion as his intellect has marched; he has learnt more foreign tricks than words, and sea-port towns are not the best schools for honesty. Of these nondescripts the Hispano-Anglo, who generally has deserted from Gibraltar, is the best, because he will work, hold his tongue, and fight : a monkey would be a less inconvenience than a chattering Ibero-Gallo; one who has forgotten his national accomplishments—cooking and hairdressing, and learnt very few Spanish things, such as good temper and endurance. Whichever of the two is the sharpest should lead the way, and leave the other to bring up the rear. They should be mounted on good mules, and be provided with large panniers. One should act as the cook and valet, the other as the groom of the party; and the

utensils peculiar to each department should be carried
by each professor. Where only one servant is employed, one side of the pannier should be dedicated to
the commissariat, and the other to the luggage; in that
case the master should have a flying portmanteau,
which should be sent by means of *cosarios*, and precede
him from great town to great town, as a magazine,
wardrobe, or general supply to fall back on. The servants should each have their own saddle-bag and
leathern bottle, which, since the days of Sancho Panza,
are part and parcel of a faithful squire, and when all
are carried on an ass are quite patriarchal. "*Iba
Sancho Panza sobre su jumento, como un patriarca con
sus alforjas y bota.*"

The servants will each in their line look after their
own affairs; the groom will take with him the things
of the stable, and a small provision of corn, in order
that a feed may never be wanting, on an unexpected
emergency; he will always ascertain beforehand through
what sort of a country each day's journey is to be
made, and make preparations accordingly. The valet
will view his masters in the same light as the groom
does his beasts; and he will purvey and keep in readiness all that appertains to their comfort, always remem-
bering a moskito net—we shall presently say a word
on the fly-plague of the Peninsula—with nails to knock
into the walls to hang it up by, not forgetting a hammer and gimlet; common articles enough, but which
are never to be got at the moment and place where
they are the most wanted. He will also carry a small
canteen, the smaller and more ordinary the better, as
anything out of the common way attracts attention,
and suggests, first, the coveting other men's goods,
and so on to assaults, batteries, robberies, and other
inconveniences, which have been exploded on our roads;
although F. Moryson took care to caution our ancestors
" to be warie on this head, since theeves have their
spies commonly in all innes, to enquire into the condition of travellers." The manufactures of Spain are so
rude and valueless that what appears to us to be the
most ordinary appears to them to be the most excellent,

as they have never seen anything so good. The lower orders, who eat with their fingers, think everything is gold which glitters, *todo es oro lo que reluce;* as, after all, it is what is *on* the plate that is the rub, let no wise man have such smart forks and knives as to tempt cut-throats to turn them to unnatural purposes. However, avoid all superfluous luggage, especially prejudices and foregone conclusions, for " *en largo camino paja pesa,*" a straw is heavy on a long journey, and the last feather breaks the horse's back. A store of cigars, however, must always be excepted; take plenty and give them freely; it always opens a conversation well with a Spaniard, to offer him one of these little delicate marks of attention. Good snuff is acceptable to the curates and to monks (though there are none just now). English needles, thread, and pairs of scissors take no room, and are all keys to the good graces of the fair sex. There is a charm about a present, *backshish,* in most European as well as Oriental countries, and still more if it is given with tact, and at the proper time; Spaniards, if unable to make any equivalent return, will always try to repay by civilities and attentions.

Every one must determine for himself whether he prefers the assistance of this servant in the kitchen or at the toilet; since it is not easy for mortal man to dress a master *and* a dinner, and both well at the same time, let alone two masters. A cook who runs after two hares at onces catches neither. No prudent traveller on these, or on any occasions, should let another do for him what he can do for himself, and a man who waits upon himself is sure to be well waited on. If, however, a valet be absolutely necessary, the groom clearly is best left in his own chamber, the stable; he will have enough to do to curry and valet his four animals, which he knows to be good for their health, though he never scrapes off the cutaneous stucco by which his own illote carcass is Roman cemented. From long experience we have found that if the rider will get into the habit of carrying all the things requisite for his own dressing in a small separate bag, and employ the hour while the cook is getting the supper under

way, it is wonderful how comfortably he will proceed
to his puchero.

The cook should take with him a stewing-pan, and a
pot or kettle for boiling water; he need not lumber himself with much batterie de cuisine; it is not much needed
in the imperfect gastronomy of the Peninsula, where
men eat like the beasts which perish; all sort of artillery
is rather rare in Spanish kitchen or fortress; an hidalgo
would as soon think of having a voltaic battery in his
sitting-room as a copper one in his cuisine; most classes
are equally satisfied with the Oriental earthenware *ollas*,
pucheros, or pipkins, which are everywhere to be found,
and have some peculiar sympathy with the Spanish
cuisine, since a stew—be it even of a cat—never eats so
well when made in a metal vessel; the great thing is to
bring the raw materials,—first catch your hare. Those
who have meat and money will always get a neighbour
to lend them a pot. A *venta* is a place where the rich
are sent empty away, and where the poor hungry are not
filled; the whole duty of the man-cook, therefore, is to
be always thinking of his commissariat; he need not
trouble himself about his master's appetite, that will
seldom fail,—nay, often be a misfortune; a good appetite is not a good *per se*,[1] for it, even when the best,
becomes a bore when there is nothing to eat; his *capucho*
or mule hamper must be his travelling larder, cellar, and
store-room; he will victual himself according to the
route, and the distances from one great town to another,
and will always take care to start with a good provision:
indeed to attend to the commissariat is, it cannot be too
often repeated, the whole duty of a man-cook in hungry
Spain, where food has ever been *the* difficulty; a little
foresight gives small trouble and ensures great comfort,
while perils by sea and perils by land are doubled when
the stomach is empty, whereas, as Sancho Panza wisely
told his ass, all sorrows are alleviated by eating bread:
todos los duelos, con pan son buenos, and the shrewd
squire, who seldom is wrong, was right both in the

[1] When George IV. once complained that he had *lost* his royal
appetite, "What a scrape, sir, a *poor* man would be in if he
found it!" said his Rochester companion.

matter of bread and the moral : the former is admirable.
The central table-lands of Spain are perhaps the finest
wheat-growing districts in the world ; however rude and
imperfect the cultivation—for the peasant does but
scratch the earth, and seldom manures—the life-conferring sun comes to his assistance ; the returns are prodigious, and the quality superexcellent ; yet the growers,
miserable in the midst of plenty, vegetate in cabins composed of baked mud, or in holes burrowed among the
friable hillocks, in an utter ignorance of furniture, and
absolute necessaries. The want of roads, canals, and
means of transport prevents their exportation of produce,
which from its bulk is difficult of carriage in a country
where grain is removed for the most part on four-footed
beasts of burden, after the oriental and patriarchal
fashion of Jacob, when he sent to the granaries of Egypt.
Accordingly, although there are neither sliding scales nor
corn laws, and subsistence is cheap and abundant, the
population decreases in number and increases in wretch-
edness ; what boots it if corn be low-priced, if wages be
still lower, as they then everywhere are, and must be?

The finest bread in Spain is called *pan de candeal*,
which is eaten by men in office and others in easy circumstances, as it was by the clergy. The worst bread is the
pan de municion, and forms the fare of the Spanish
soldier, which, being sable as a hat, coarse and hard as
a brickbat, would just do to sop in the black broth of
the Spartan military ; indeed, the expression *de municion*
is synonymous in the Peninsula with badness of quality,
and the secondary meaning is taken from the perfection
of badness which is perceptible in everything connected
with Spanish ammunition, from the knapsack to the
citadel. Such bread and water, and both hardly earned,
are the rations of the poor patient Spanish private ; nor
can he when before the enemy reckon always on even
that, unless it be supplied from an ally's commissariat.

Perhaps the best bread in Spain is made at Alcalá de
Guadaira, near Seville, of which it is the oven, and hence
the town is called the Alcalá of bakers. There bread
may truly be said to be the soul of its existence, and
samples abound everywhere : *roscas*, or circular-formed

rusks, are hung up like garlands, and *hogazas*, loaves, placed on tables outside the houses. It is, indeed, as Spaniards say, *Pan de Dios*—the "angels' bread of Esdras." All classes here gain their bread by making it, and the water-mills and mule-mills are never still; women and children are busy picking out earthy particles from the grain, which get mixed from the common mode of threshing on a floor in the open air, which is at once Biblical and Homeric. At the outside of the villages, in corn-growing districts, a smooth open "threshing-floor" is prepared, with a hard surface, like a fives court : it is called the *era*, and is the precise Roman *area*. The sheaves of corn are spread out on it, and four horses yoked most classically to a low crate or harrow, composed of planks armed with flints, etc., which is called a *trillo*: on this the driver is seated, who urges the beasts round and round over the crushed heap. Thus the grain is shaken out of the ears and the straw triturated; the latter becomes food for horses, as the former does for men. When the heap is sufficiently bruised, it is removed and winnowed by being thrown up into the air; the light winds carry off the chaff, while the heavy corn falls to the ground. The whole operation is truly picturesque and singular. The scene is a crowded one, as many cultivators contribute to the mass and share in the labour; their wives and children cluster around, clad in strange dresses of varied colours. They are sometimes sheltered from the god of fire under boughs, reeds, and awnings, run up as if for the painter, and falling of themselves into pictures, as the lower classes of Spaniards and Italians always do. They are either eating and drinking, singing or dancing, for a guitar is never wanting. Meanwhile the fierce horses dash over the prostrate sheaves, and realise the splendid simile of Homer, who likens to them the fiery steeds of Achilles when driven over Trojan bodies. These out-of-door threshings take place of course when the weather is dry, and generally under a most terrific heat. The work is often continued at nightfall by torch-light. During the day the half-clad dusky reapers defy the sun and his rage, rejoicing rather in the heat like salamanders; it is true that their devotions to the porous water-jar are unremitting, nor is a swill at a good passenger's *bota* ever rejected; all is life and action; busy hands and feet, flashing eyes, and eager screams; the light yellow chaff, which in the sun's rays glitters like gold dust, envelops them in a halo, which by night, when partially revealed by the fires and mingled with the torch glare, is almost supernatural, as the phantom figures, now dark in shadows, now crimsoned by the fire flash, flit to and fro in the vaporous mist. The scene never fails to rivet and enchant the stranger, who, coming from the pale north and the commonplace in-door flail, seizes at once all the novelty of such doings. Eye and ear, open and awake, become inlets of new sensations of attention and admiration, and convey to heart and mind the poetry, local colour, movement, grouping, action, and attitude. But while the cold-blooded native of leaden skies is full of fire and enthusiasm, his Spanish companion, bred and born under unshorn beams, is chilly as an icicle, indifferent as an Arab: he passes on the other side, not only not admiring, but positively ashamed; he only sees the barbarity, antiquity, and imperfect process; he is sighing for some patent machine made in Birmingham, to be put up in a closed barn after the models approved of by the Royal Agricultural Society in Cavendish Square; his bowels yearn for the appliances of civilisation by which " bread stuffs " are more scientifically manipulated and manufactured, minus the poetry.

To return, however, to dry bread, after this new digression, and all those who have ever been in Spain, or have ever written on Spanish things, must feel how difficult it is to keep regularly on the road without turning aside at every moment, now to cull a wild flower, now to pick up a sparkling spar. This corn, so beaten, is very carefully ground, and in La Mancha in those charming windmills, which, perched on eminences to catch the air, look to this day, with their outstretched arms, like Quixotic giants; the flour is passed through several hoppers, in order to secure its fineness. The dough is most carefully kneaded, worked, and re-worked, as is done by our biscuit-makers; hence the close-grained, caky, somewhat heavy consistency of the crumb, whereas, according to Pliny, the Romans esteemed Spanish bread on account of its lightness.

The Spanish loaf has not that mysterious sympathy with butter and cheese as it has in our verdurous Old England, probably because in these torrid regions pasture is rare, butter bad, and cheese worse, albeit they suited the iron digestion of Sancho, who knew of nothing better : none, however, who have ever tasted Stilton or Parmesan will join in his eulogies of Castilian *queso,* the poorness of which will be estimated by the distinguished consideration in which a round cannon-ball Dutch cheese is held throughout the Peninsula. The traveller, nevertheless, should take one of them, for bad is here the best, in many other things besides these : he will always carry some good loaves with it, for in the damper mountain districts the daily bread of the natives is made of rye, Indian corn, and the inferior cerealia. Bread is the staff of the Spanish traveller's life, who, having added raw garlic, not salt, to it, then journeys on with security, *con pan y ajo crudo se anda seguro.* Again, a loaf never weighs one down, nor is ever in the way ; as Æsop, the prototype of Sancho, well knew. *La hogaza no embaraza.*

Having secured his bread, the cook in preparing supper should make enough for the next day's lunch, *las once,* the eleven o'clock meal, as the Spaniards translate *meridie,* twelve or mid-day, whence the correct word for luncheon is derived, *merienda merendar.* Wherever good dishes are cut up there are good leavings, " *donde buenas ollas quebran, buenos cascos quedan;*" and nothing can be more Cervantic than the occasional al fresco halt, when no better place of accommodation is to be met with. As the sun gets high, and man and beast hungry and weary, wherever a tempting shady spot with running water occurs, the party draws aside from the high road, like Don Quixote and Sancho Panza ; a retired and concealed place is chosen, the luggage is removed from the animals, the hampers which lard the lean soil are unpacked, the table-cloth is spread on the grass, the *botas* are laid in the water to cool their contents ; then out with the provision, cold partridge or turkey, sliced ham or *chorizo*—simple cates, but which are eaten with an appetite and relish for which aldermen would pay hundreds. They are followed, should grapes be wanting, with a soothing cigar, and a sweet slumber on earth's freshest, softest lap. In such wild banquets Spain surpasses the Boulevards. Alas! that such hours should be bright and winged as sunbeams! Such is Peninsular country fare. The *olla*, on which the rider may restore exhausted nature, is only to be studied in larger towns; and dining, of which this is the foundation in Spain, is such a great resource to travellers, and Spanish cookery, again, is so Oriental, classical, and singular, let alone its vital importance, that the subject will properly demand a chapter to itself.

CHAPTER XI

IT would exhaust a couple of Colonial numbers at least to discuss properly the merits and digest Spanish cookery. All that can be now done is to skim the subject, which is indeed fat and unctuous. Those meats and drinks will be briefly noticed which are of daily occurrence, and those dishes described which we have often helped to make, and oftener helped to eat, in the most larderless *ventas* and hungriest districts of the Peninsula, and which provident wayfarers may make and eat again, and, as we pray, with no worse appetite.

To be a good cook, which few Spaniards are, a man must not only understand his master's taste, but be able to make something out of nothing; just as a clever French *artiste* converts an old shoe into an épigramme d'agneau, or a Parisian milliner dresses up two deal boards into a fine live *Madame*, whose only fault is the appearance of too much embonpoint. Genuine and legitimate Spanish dishes are excellent in their way, for no man nor man-cook ever is ridiculous when he does not attempt to be what he is not. The *au naturel* may occasionally be somewhat plain, but seldom makes one sick; at all events it would be as hopeless to make a Spaniard understand real French cookery as to endeavour to explain to a député the meaning of our constitution or parliament. The ruin of Spanish cooks is their futile attempts to imitate foreign ones: just as their silly grandees murder the glorious Castilian tongue, by substituting what they fancy is pure Parisian, which they speak *comme des vaches Espagnoles. Dis moi ce que tu manges et je te dirai ce que tu es* is "un mot profond" of the great equity judge, Brillat Savarin, who also discovered that "*Les destinées des nations dépendent de la manière dont elles se nourrissent;*" since which General Foy has attributed all the *accidental* victories of the British to rum and beef. And this great fact much enhances our serious respect for punch, and our true love for the *ros-bif* of old England, of which, by the way, very little will be got in the Peninsula, where bulls are bred for baiting, and oxen for the plough, not the spit.

The national cookery of Spain is for the most part Oriental; and the ruling principle of its preparation is *stewing;* for, from a scarcity of fuel, roasting is almost unknown; their notion of which is putting meat into a pan, setting it in hot ashes, and then covering the lid with burning embers. The pot, or *olla*, has accordingly become a synonyme for the dinner of Spaniards, just as beefsteaks or frogs are vulgarly supposed to constitute the whole bill of fare of two other mighty nations. Wherever meats are bad and thin, the sauce is very important; it is based in Spain on oil, garlic, saffron, and red peppers. In hot countries, where beasts are lean, oil supplies the place of fat, as garlic does the want of flavour, while a stimulating condiment excites or curries up the coats of a languid stomach. It has been said of our heretical countrymen that we have but one form of sauce—melted butter—and a hundred different forms of religion, whereas in orthodox Spain there is but one of each, and, as with religion, so to change this sauce would be little short of heresy. As to colour, it carries that rich burnt umber, raw sienna tint, which Murillo imitated so well; and no wonder, since he made his particular brown from baked olla bones, whence it was extracted, as is done to this day by those Spanish painters who indulge in meat. This brown *negro de hueso* colour is the livery of tawny Spain, where all is brown from the *Sierra Morena* to duskier man. Of such hue is his cloak, his terra-cotta house, his wife, his ox, his ass, and everything that is his. This sauce has not only the same colour, but the same flavour everywhere; hence the difficulty of making out the material of which any dish is composed. Not Mrs. Glass herself could tell, by taste at least, whether the ingredients of the cauldron be hare or cat, cow or calf, the aforesaid ox or ass. It puzzles even the acumen of a Frenchman; for it is still the great boast of the town of Olvera that they served up some donkeys as rations to a Buonapartist detachment. All this is very Oriental. Isaac could not distinguish tame kid from wild venison, so perplexing was the disguise of the savoury sauce; and yet his senses of smell and touch were keen, and his suspicions of unfair cooking were awakened. A prudent diner, therefore, except when forced to become his own cook, will never look too closely into the things of the kitchen if he wishes to live a quiet life; for *quien las cosas mucho apura, no vive vida segura.*

All who ride or run through the Peninsula, will read thirst in the arid plains, and hunger in the soil-denuded hills, where those who ask for bread will receive stones. The knife and fork question has troubled every warrior in Spain, from Henri IV. down to Wellington; " subsistence is the great difficulty always found " is the text of a third of the Duke's wonderful despatches. This scarcity of food is implied in the very name of Spain, Σπανια, which means poverty and destitution, as well as in the term *Bisoños*, wanters, which long has been a synonyme for Spanish soldiers, who are always, as the Duke described them, " hors de combat," "always *wanting* in everything at the critical moment." Hunger and thirst have ever been, and are, the best defenders of the Peninsula against the invader. On sierra and steppe these gaunt sentinels keep watch and ward, and, on the scarecrow principle, protect this paradise, as they do the infernal regions of Virgil—

> " Malesuada fames et turpis egestas
> Horribiles visu."

A riding tour through Spain has already been likened to serving a campaign; and it was a saying of the Grand Condé, " If you want to know what want is, carry on a war in Spain." Yet, notwithstanding the thousands of miles which we have ridden, never have we yet felt that dire necessity, which has been kept at a respectable distance by a constant unremitting attention to the proverb, A man forewarned is forearmed. *Hombre prevenido nunca fu vencido*, there is nothing like precaution and *provision*. " If you mean to dine," writes the all-providing Duke to Lord Hill from Moraleja, " *you had better bring your things*, as I shall have nothing with me;"—the ancient Bursal fashion holds good on Spanish roads :—

> " Regula Bursalis est omni tempore talis,
> Prandia fer tecum, si vis comedere mecum."

A man who is prepared, is never beaten or starved; therefore, as the valorous Dalgetty has it, a prudent man will always victual himself in Spain with vivers for three days at least, and his cook, like Sancho Panza, should have nothing else in his head, but thoughts how to convey the most eatables into his ambulant larder.

He must set forth from every tolerable-sized town with an ample supply of tea, sugar, coffee, brandy, good oil, wine, salt, to say nothing of solids. The having something ready gives him leisure to forage and make ulterior preparations. Those who have a *corps de réserve* to fall back upon—say a cold turkey and a ham—can always convert any spot in the desert into an oasis ; at the same time the connection between body and soul may be kept up by trusting to *venta* luck, of which more anon; it offers, however, but a miserable existence to persons of judgment. And even when this precaution of provision be not required, there are never wanting in Spain the poor and hungry, to whom the taste of meat is almost unknown, and to whom these crumbs that fall from the rich man's table are indeed a feast; the relish and gratitude with which these fragments are devoured do as much good to the heart of the donor as to the stomach of the donees, for the best medicines of the poor are to be found in the cellars, kitchens, and hampers of the rich. All servants should be careful of their traps and stores, which are liable to be pilfered and plundered in *ventas,* where the élite of society is not always assembled: the luggage should be well corded, for the devil is always a gleaning, *ata al saco, ya espiga el diablo.*

Formerly all travellers of rank carried a silver olla with a key, the *guardacena,* the *save* supper. This ingenious contrivance has furnished matter for many a pleasantry in picaresque tales and farces. Madame Daunoy gives us the history of what befel the good Archbishop of Burgos and his orthodox olla.

There is nothing in life like making a good start; thus the party arrives safely at the first resting-place. The cook must never appear to have anything when he arrives at an inn; he must get from others all he can, and much is to be had for asking and crying, as even a Spanish Infante knows—the child that does not cry is not suckled, *quien no llora, no mama;* the artiste must never fall back on his own reservoirs except in cases of absolute need; during the day he must open his eyes and ears and must pick up everything eatable, and where he can and when he can. By keeping a sharp look-out and going quietly to work the cook may catch the hen and her chickens too. All is fish that comes into the net, and, like Buonaparte and his marshals, nothing should be too great for his ambition, nothing too small for his rapacity. Of course he will pay for his collections, which the aforesaid gentry did not: thus fruit, onions, salads, which, as they must be bought somewhere, had better be secured whenever they turn up. The peasants, who are sad poachers, will constantly hail travellers from the fields with offers of partridges, rabbits, melons, hares, which always jump up in this pays de l'imprévu when you least expect it: *Salta la liebre cuando menos uno piensa.*

Notwithstanding Don Quixote thought that it augured bad luck to meet with a hare on entering a village, let not a bold traveller be scared, but forthwith stew the omen; a hare, as in the time of Martial, is considered by Spaniards to be the glory of edible quadrupeds, and to this day no old stager ever takes a rabbit when he can get a hare, *á perro viejo echale liebre y no conejo*. In default, however, of catching one, rabbits may always be bagged. Spain abounds with them to such a degree, that ancient naturalists thought the animal indigenous, and went so far as to derive the name Spain from *Sephan*, the rabbit, which the Phœnicians found here for the first time. Be that as it may, the long-eared timid creature appears on the early Iberian coins, as it will long do on her wide wastes and tables. By the bye, a ready stewed rabbit or hare is to be eschewed as suspicious in a *venta:* at the same time, if the consumer does not find out that it is a cat, there is no great harm done—ignorance is bliss; let him not know it, he is not robbed at all. It is a pity to dispel his gastronomic delusion, as it is the knowledge of the cheat that kills, and not the cat. Pol ! me occidistis, amici. The cook therefore should ascertain beforehand what are the bonâ fide ingredients of every dish that he sets before his lord.

In going into the kitchens of the Peninsula, precedence must on every account be given to the *olla :* this word means at once a species of prepared food, and the earthenware utensil in which it is dressed, just as our term *dish* is applicable to the platter and to what is served on it. Into this *olla* it may be affirmed that the whole culinary genius of Spain is condensed, as the mighty Jinn was into a gallipot, according to the Arabian Night tales. The lively and gastronomic French, who are decidedly the leaders of European civilisation in the kitchen, deride the barbarous practices of the Gotho-Iberians, as being darker than Erebus and more ascetic than æsthetic; to credit their authors, a Peninsular breakfast consists of a teaspoonful of chocolate, a dinner, of a knob of garlic soaked in water, and a supper, of a paper cigarette; and according to their *parfait cuisinier*, the *olla* is made of two cigars boiled in three gallons of water—but this is a calumny, a mere invention devised by the enemy.

The *olla* is only well made in Andalucia, and there alone in careful, well-appointed houses; it is called a *puchero* in the rest of Spain, where it is but a poor affair, made of dry beef, or rather cow, boiled with *garbanzos* or chick peas, and a few sausages. These *garbanzos* are the vegetable, the potato of the land; and their use argues a low state of horticultural knowledge. The taste for them was introduced by the Carthaginians— the *puls punica*, which (like the *fides punica*, an especial ingredient in all Spanish governments and finance) afforded such merriment to Plautus, that he introduced the chick-pea eating Pœnus, pultiphagonides, speaking Punic, just as Shakespeare did the toasted-cheese eating Welshman talking Welsh. These garbanzos require much soaking, being otherwise hard as bullets; indeed, a lively Frenchman, after what he calls an apology for a dinner, compared them, in his empty stomach, as he was jumbled away in the dilly, to peas rattling in a child's drum.

The veritable *olla*—the ancient time-honoured *olla podrida*, or pot pourri—the epithet is now obsolete—is difficult to be made: a tolerable one is never to be eaten out of Spain, since it requires many Spanish things to concoct it, and much care; the cook must throw his whole soul into the pan, or rather pot; it may be made in one, but two are better. They must be of earthenware; for, like the French *pot au feu*, the dish is good for nothing when made in an iron or copper vessel; take therefore two, and put them on their separate stoves with water. Place into No. 1, *Garbanzos*, which have been placed to soak over-night. Add a good piece of beef, a chicken, a large piece of bacon; let it boil once and quickly; then let it simmer: it requires four or five hours to be well done. Meanwhile place into No. 2, with water, whatever vegetables are to be had: lettuces, cabbage, a slice of gourd, of beef, carrots, beans, celery, endive, onions and garlic, long peppers. These must be previously well washed and cut, as if they were destined to make a salad; then add red sausages, or "*chorizos;*"

half a salted pig's face, which should have been soaked over-night. When all is sufficiently boiled, strain off the water, and throw it away. Remember constantly to skim the scum of both saucepans. When all this is sufficiently dressed, take a large dish, lay in the bottom the vegetables, the beef in the centre, flanked by the bacon, chicken, and pig's face. The sausages should be arranged around, en couronne; pour over some of the soup of No. 1, and serve hot, as Horace did: " Uncta satis—ponuntur oluscula lardo." No violets come up to the perfume which a coming olla casts before it; the mouth-watering bystanders sigh, as they see and smell the rich freight steaming away from them.

This is the olla *en grande*, such as Don Quixote says was eaten only by canons and presidents of colleges; like turtle soup, it is so rich and satisfactory that it is a dinner of itself. A worthy dignitary of Seville, in the good old times, before reform and appropriation had put out the churches' kitchen fire, and whose daily pot-luck was transcendental, told us, as a wrinkle, that he on feast-days used turkeys instead of chickens, and added two sharp Ronda apples, and three sweet potatoes of Malaga. His advice is worth attention : he was a good Roman Catholic canon, who believed everything, absolved everything, drank everything, ate everything, and digested everything. In fact, as a general rule, anything that is good in itself is good for an *olla*, provided, as old Spanish books always conclude, that it contains nothing contrary to the holy mother church, to orthodoxy, and to good manners—" *que no contiene cosa que se oponga á nuestra madre Iglesia, y santa fé catolica, y buenas costumbres.*" Such an olla as this is not to be got on the road, but may be made to restore exhausted nature when halting in the cities. Of course, every olla must everywhere be made according to what can be got. In private families the contents of No. 1, the soup, is served up with bread, in a tureen, and the frugal table decked with the separate contents of the olla in separate platters; the remains coldly serve, or are warmed up, for supper.

The vegetables and bacon are absolute necessaries;

without the former an olla has neither grace nor sustenance; *la olla sin verdura, ni tiene gracia ni hartura,* while the latter is as essential in this stew as a text from Saint Augustine is in a sermon :

> *No hay olla sin tocino,*
> *Ni sermon sin Agustino.*

Bacon throughout the length and breadth of the Peninsula is more honoured than this, or than any one of all the fathers of the Church of Rome; the hunger after the flesh of the pig is equalled only by the thirst for the contents of what is put afterwards into his skin; and with reason, for the pork of Spain has always been, and is, unequalled in flavour; the bacon is fat and flavoured, the sausages delicious, and the hams transcendently superlative, to use the very expression of Diodorus Siculus, a man of great taste, learning, and judgment. Of all the things of Spain, no one need feel ashamed to plead guilty to a predilection and preference to the pig. A few particulars may be therefore pardoned.

In Spain pigs are more numerous even than asses, since they pervade the provinces. As those of Estremadura, the *Ham*pshire of the Peninsula, are the most esteemed, they alone will be now noticed. That province, although so little visited by Spaniards or strangers, is full of interest to the antiquarian and naturalist; and many are the rides at different periods which we have made through its tangled ilex groves, and over its depopulated and aromatic wastes. A granary under Roman and Moor, its very existence seems to be all but forgotten by the Madrid government, who have abandoned it to *feræ naturæ*, to wandering sheep, locusts, and swine. The entomology of Estremadura is endless, and perfectly uninvestigated—de minimis non curat Hispanus; but the heavens and earth teem with the minute creation; there nature is most busy and prolific, where man is most idle and unproductive; and in these lonely wastes, where no human voice disturbs the silence, the balmy air resounds with the buzzing hum of multitudinous insects, which career about on their business of love or food without settlements or kitchens, rejoicing in the fine weather which is the joy of their tiny souls, and short-lived pleasant existence. Sheep, pigs, locusts, and doves are the only living things which the traveller will see for hours and hours. Now and then a man occurs, just to prove how rare his species is here.

Vast districts of this unreclaimed province are covered with woods of oak, beech, and chestnut; but these park-like scenes have no charm for native eyes; blind to the picturesque, they only are thinking of the number of pigs which can be fattened on the mast and acorns, which are sweeter and larger than those of our oaks. The acorns are still called *bellota*, the Arabic *bollot—belot* being the Scriptural term for the tree and the gland, which, with water, formed the original diet of the aboriginal Iberian, as well as of his pig; when dry, the acorns were ground, say the classical authors, into bread, and, when fresh, they were served up as the second course. And in our time ladies of high rank at Madrid constantly ate them at the opera and elsewhere; they were the presents sent by Sancho Panza's wife to the Duchess, and formed the text on which Don Quixote preached so eloquently to the goatherds, on the joys and innocence of the golden age and pastoral happiness, in which they constituted the foundation of the kitchen.

The pigs during the greater part of the year are left to support nature as they can, and in gauntness resemble those greyhound-looking animals which pass for porkers in France. When the acorns are ripe and fall from the trees, the greedy animals are turned out in legions from the villages, which more correctly may be termed coalitions of pigsties. They return from the woods at night, of their own accord, and without a swine's general. On entering the hamlet, all set off at a full gallop, like a legion possessed with devils, in a handicap for home, into which each single pig turns, never making a mistake. We have more than once been caught in one of these pig-deluges, and nearly carried away horse and all, as befell Don Quixote, when really swept away by the "far-spread and grunting drove." In his own home each truant is welcomed like a prodigal son or a domestic father. These pigs are the pets of the peasants; they are brought up with their children, and partake, as in Ireland, in the domestic discomfort of their cabins; they are universally respected, and justly, for it is this animal who pays the "rint;" in fact, are the citizens, as at Sorrento, and Estremenian man is quite a secondary formation, and created to tend herds of these swine, who lead the happy life of former Toledan dignitaries, with the additional advantage of becoming more valuable when dead.

It is astonishing how rapidly they thrive on their sweet food; indeed it is the whole duty of a good pig—animal *propter convivia natum*—to get as fat and as soon as he can, and then die for the good of his country. It may be observed for the information of our farmers, that those pigs which are dedicated to St. Anthony, on whom a sow was in constant attendance, as a dove was on Venus, get the soonest fat; therefore in Spain young porkers are sprinkled with holy water on his day, but those of other saints are less propitious, for the killing takes place about the 10th and 11th of November, or, as Spaniards date it, *por el St. Andres*, on the day of St. Andrew, or on that of St. Martin; hence the proverb "every man and pig has his St. Martin or his fatal hour, *á cada puerco su San Martin.*"

The death of a fat pig is as great an event in Spanish families, who generally fatten up one, as the birth of a baby; nor can the fact be kept secret, so audible is his announcement. It is considered a delicate attention on the part of the proprietor to celebrate the auspicious event by sending a portion of the chitterlings to intimate friends. The Spaniard's proudest boast is that his blood is pure, that he is not descended from pork-eschewing Jew or Moor—a fact which the pig genus, could it reason, would deeply deplore. The Spaniard doubtless has been so great a consumer of pig, from grounds religious, as well as gastronomic. The eating or not eating the flesh of an animal deemed unclean by the impure infidel, became a test of orthodoxy, and at once of correct faith as well as of good taste; and good bacon, as has been just observed, is wedded to sound doctrine and St. Augustine. The Spanish name *Tocino* is derived from the Arabic *Tachim*, which signifies fat.

The Spaniards however, although tremendous consumers of the pig, whether in the salted form or in the skin, have to the full the Oriental abhorrence to the unclean animal in the *abstract*. *Muy puerco* is their last expression for all that is most dirty, nasty, or disgusting. *Muy cochina* never is forgiven, if applied to woman, as it is equivalent to the Italian *Vacca*, and to the canine feminine compliment bandied among our fair sex at Billingsgate; nor does the epithet imply moral purity or chastity; indeed in Castilian euphuism the unclean animal was never to be named except in a periphrasis, or with an apology, which is a singular remnant of the Moorish influence on Spanish manners. *Haluf* or swine is still the Moslem's most obnoxious term for the Christians, and is applied to this day by the ungrateful Algerines to their French bakers and benefactors, nay even to the "*illustre Bugeaud.*"

The capital of the Estremenian pig-districts is *Montanches*—mons anguis—and doubtless the hilly spot where the Duke of Arcos fed and cured " ces petits jambons vermeils," which the Duc de St. Simon ate and admired so much; " ces jambons ont un parfum si admirable, un goût si relevé et si vivifiant, qu'on en est surpris : il est impossible de rien manger si exquis." His Grace of Arcos used to shut up the pigs in places abounding in vipers, on which they fattened. Neither the pigs, dukes, nor their toadeaters seem to have been poisoned by these exquisite vipers. According to Jonas Barrington, the finest Irish pigs were those that fed on dead rebels : one Papist porker, the Enniscorthy boar, was sent as a show, for having eaten a Protestant parson : he was put to death and dishonoured by not being made bacon of.

Naturalists have remarked that the rattlesnakes in America retire before their consuming enemy, the pig, who is thus the *gastador* or pioneer of the new world's civilisation, just as Pizarro, who was suckled by a sow, and tended swine in his youth, was its conqueror. Be that as it may, Montanches is illustrious in pork, in which

the burgesses go the whole hog, whether in the rich red
sausage, the *chorizo*, or in the savoury piquant *embu-
chados*, which are akin to the *mortadelle* of Bologna,
only less hard, and usually boiled before eating, though
good also raw; they consist of the choice bits of the pig
seasoned with condiments, with which, as if by retribu-
tion, the paunch of the voracious animal is filled; the
ruling passion strong in death. We strongly recommend *Juan Valiente*, who recently was the alcalde of
the town, to the lover of delicious hams; each *jamon*
averages about 12 lb. ; they are sold at the rate of $7\frac{1}{2}$
reales, about 18d., for the *libra carnicera*, which weighs
32 of our ounces. The duties in England are now very
trifling; we have for many years had an annual supply
of these delicacies, through the favour of a kind friend
at the *Puerto*. The fat of these *jamones*, whence our
word ham and gammon, when they are boiled, looks
like melted topazes, and the flavour defies language,
although we have dined on one this very day, in order
to secure accuracy and undeniable prose, like Lope de
Vega, who, according to his biographer, Dr. Montal-
van, never could write poetry unless inspired by a
rasher; " Toda es cosa vil," said he, " á donde falta un
pernil " (in which word we recognise the precise *perna*
whereby Horace was restored) :—

> Therefore all writing is a sham,
> Where there is wanting Spanish ham.

Those of Gallicia and Catalonia are also celebrated,
but are not to be compared for a moment with those of
Montanches, which are fit to set before an emperor.
Their only rivals are the sweet hams of the *Alpujarras*,
which are made at *Trevelez*, a pig-hamlet situated under
the snowy mountains on the opposite side of Granada,
to which also we have made a pilgrimage. They are
called *dulces* or sweet, because scarcely any salt is used
in the curing; the ham is placed in a weak pickle for
eight days, and is then hung up in the snow; it can
only be done at this place, where the exact temperature
necessary is certain. Those of our readers who are
curious in Spanish eatables will find excellent garbanzos,
chorizos, red pepper, chocolate and Valencian sweet-

meats, etc. at Figul's, a most worthy Catalan, whose shop is at No. 10, Woburn Buildings, St. Pancras, London; the locality is scarcely less visited than Montanches, but the penny-post penetrates into this terra incognita.

So much space has been filled with these meritorious bacons and hams, that we must be brief with our remaining bill of fare. For a *pisto* or meat omelette take eggs, which are to be got almost everywhere: see that they are fresh by being pellucid; beat these *huevos trasparentes* well up; chop up onions and whatever savoury herbs you have with you; add small slices of any meat out of your hamper, cold turkey, ham, etc.; beat it all up together and fry it quickly. Most Spaniards have a peculiar knack in making these *tortillas, revueltas de huevos,* which to fastidious stomachs are, as in most parts of the Continent, a sure resource to fall back upon.

The *Guisado,* or stew, like the olla, can only be really done in a Spanish pipkin, and of those which we import, the Andalucian ones draw flavour out the best. This dish is always well done by every cook in every venta, barring that they are apt to put in bad oil, and too much garlic, pepper, and saffron. Superintend it, therefore, yourself, and take hare, partridge, rabbit, chicken, or whatever you may have foraged on the road; it is capital also with pheasant, as we proved only yesterday; cut it up, save the blood, the liver, and the giblets; do not wash the pieces, but dry them in a cloth; fry them with onions in a tea-cup of oil till browned; take an olla, put in these bits with the oil, equal portions of wine and water, but stock is better than water; claret answers well, Valdepeñas better; add a bit of bacon, onions, garlic, salt, pepper, *pimientos,* a bunch of thyme or herbs; let it simmer, carefully skimming it; half an hour before serving add the giblets; when done, which can be tested by feeling with a fork, serve hot. The stew should be constantly stirred with a *wooden* spoon, and grease, the ruin of all cookery, carefully skimmed off as it rises to the surface. When made with proper care and with a good salad, it forms a supper for a cardinal, or for Santiago himself.

Another excellent but very difficult dish is the *pollo con arroz,* or the chicken and rice.   It is eaten in perfection in Valencia, and therefore is often called *Pollo Valenciano.* Cut a good fowl into pieces, wipe it clean, but do not put it into water; take a saucepan, put in a wine-glass of fine oil, heat the oil well, put in a bit of bread; let it fry, stirring it about with a *wooden* spoon; when the bread is browned take it out and throw it away : put in two cloves of garlic, taking care that it does not burn, as, if it does, it will turn bitter; stir the garlic till it is fried; put in the chicken, keep stirring it about while it fries, then put in a little salt and stir again; whenever a sound of cracking is heard, stir it again; when the chicken is well browned or gilded, *dorado,* which will take from five to ten minutes, *stirring constantly,* put in chopped onions, three or four chopped red or green chilis, and stir about; if once the contents catch the pan, the dish is spoiled; then add tomatos, divided into quarters, and parsley; take two teacupsful of rice, mix all well up together; add *hot* stock enough to cover the whole over; let it boil *once,* and then set it aside to simmer until the rice becomes tender and done. The great art consists in having the rice turned out granulated and separate, not in a pudding state, which is sure to be the case if a cover be ever put over the dish, which condenses the steam.

It may be objected, that these dishes, if so curious in the cooking, are not likely to be well done in the rude kitchens of a *venta;* but practice makes perfect, and the whole mind and intellect of the artist is concentrated on one object, and not frittered away by a multiplicity of dishes, the rock on which many cooks founder, where more dinners are sacrificed to the eye and ostentation. One dish and one thing at a time is the golden rule of Bacon; many are the anxious moments that we have spent over the rim of a Spanish pipkin, watching, life set on the cast, the wizen she-mummy, whose mind, body, and spoon were absorbed in a single mess : Well, my mother, *que tal?* what sort of a stew is it? Let me smell and taste the *salsa.* Good, good; it promises much. *Vamos, Señora*—go on, my lady, thy spoon once more—how, indeed, can oil, wine, and nutritive juices amalgamate without frequent stirring? Well, very well it is. Now again, daughter of my soul, thy fork. *Asi, asi;* thus, thus. *Per Bacco,* by Bacchus, tender it is—may heaven repay thee! Indeed, from this tenderness of the meat arises ease of digestion; here, pot and fire do half the work of the poor stomach, which too often in inns elsewhere is overtaxed, like its owner, and condemned to hard labour and a brickbat beef-steak.

Poached eggs are at all events within the grasp of the meanest culinary capacity. They are called *Huevos estrellados*, starred eggs. When fat bacon is wedded to them, the dish is called *Huevos con magras*; not that *magras* here means thin as to condition, but rather as to slicing; and these slices, again, are positively thick ones when compared to those triumphs of close shaving which are carved at Vauxhall. To make this dish, with or without the bacon, take eggs; the contents of the shell are to be emptied into a pan filled with hot oil or lard, *manteca de puerco,* pig's butter: it must be remembered, although Strabo mentions as a singular fact that the Iberians made use of butter instead of oil, that now it is just the reverse; a century ago butter was only sold by the apothecaries, as a sort of ointment, and it used to be iniquitous. Spaniards generally used either Irish or Flemish salted butter, and from long habit thought fresh butter quite insipid; indeed, they have no objection to its being a trifle or so rancid, just as some aldermen like high venison. In the present age of progress the Queen Christina has a fancy dairy at Madrid, where she makes a few pounds of fresh butter, of which a small portion is or was sold, at five shillings the pound, to foreign ambassadors for their breakfast. Recently more attention has been paid to the dairy in the Swiss-like provinces of the north-west. The Spaniards, like the heroes in the Iliad, seldom boil their food (eggs excepted), at least not in water; for frying, after all, is but boiling in oil.

Travellers should be cautioned against the captivating name of *manteca Valenciana.* This Valencian butter

Salad

is composed (for the cow has nothing to do with it) of equal portions of garlic and hogs' lard pounded together in a mortar; it is then spread on bread, just as we do arsenic to destroy vermin. It, however, agrees well with the peasants, as does the soup of their neighbours the Catalans, which is made of bread and garlic in equal portions fried in oil and diluted with hot water. This mess is called *sopa de gato,* probably from making cats, not Catalans, sick.

One thing, however, is truly delicious in Spain—the salad, to compound which, says the Spanish proverb, four persons are wanted : a spendthrift for oil, a miser for vinegar, a counsellor for salt, and a madman to stir it all up. N.B.—Get the biggest bowl you can, in order that this latter operation may be thoroughly performed. The salad is the glory of every French dinner, and the disgrace of most in England, even in good houses, and from two simple causes; first, from the putting in eggs, mustard, and other heretical ingredients, and, secondly, from making it long before it is wanted to be eaten, whereby the green materials, which should be crisp and fresh, become sodden and leathery. Prepare, therefore, your salad in separate vessels, and never mix the sauce with the herbs until the instant that you are ready to transfer the refreshing result to your plate. Take lettuce, or whatever salad is to be got; do not cut it with a steel knife, which turns the edges of the wounds black, and communicates an evil flavour; let the leaf be torn from the stem, which throw away, as it is hard and bitter; wash the mass in many waters, and rinse it in napkins till dry; take a small bowl, put in equal quantities of vinegar and water, a teaspoonful of pepper and salt, and four times as much oil as vinegar and water, mix the same well together; prepare in a plate whatever fine herbs can be got, especially tarragon and chervil, which must be chopped small. Pour the sauce over the salad, powder it with these herbs, and lose no time in eating. For making a much worse salad than this, a foreign artiste in London used some years ago to charge a guinea.

Any remarks on Spanish salads would be incomplete

without some account of *gazpacho,* that vegetable soup,
or floating salad, which during the summer forms the
food of the bulk of the people in the torrid portions of
Spain.   This dish is of Arabic origin, as its name,
"soaked bread," implies.   This most ancient Oriental
Roman and Moorish refection is composed of onions,
garlic, cucumbers, chilis, all chopped up very small and
mixed with crumbs of bread, and then put into a bowl
of oil, vinegar, and fresh water.   Reapers and agricultural labourers could never stand the sun's fire without this cooling acetous diet.   This was the οξυκρατος of
the Greeks, the *posca,* potable food, meat and drink,
potus et esca, which formed part of the rations of the
Roman soldiers, and which Adrian (a Spaniard) delighted
to share with them, and into which Boaz at meal-time
invited Ruth to dip her morsel.   Dr. Buchanan found
some Syrian Christians who still called it *ail, ail, Hil
Hila,* for which our Saviour was supposed to have called
on the Cross, when those who understood that dialect
gave it him from the vessel which was full of it for the
guard.   In Andalucia, during the summer, a bowl of
gazpacho is commonly ready in every house of an evening, and is partaken of by every person who comes in.
It is not easily digested by strangers, who do not require it quite so much as the natives, whose souls are
more parched and dried up, and who perspires less.   The
components, oil, vinegar, and bread, are all that is given
out to the lower class of labourers by farmers who
profess to feed them; two cow's horns, the most primitive form of bottle and cup, are constantly seen suspended on each side of their carts, and contain this provision, with which they compound their *migas :* this
consists of crumbs of bread fried in oil, with pepper and
garlic; nor can a stronger proof be given of the common poverty of their fare than the common expression,
"*buenas migas hay,*" there *are good crumbs,* being
equivalent to capital eating.   In very cold weather the
mess is warmed, and then is called *gazpacho caliente.*
Oh ! dura messorum ilia—oh ! the iron mess digesting
stomachs of ploughmen.

CHAPTER XII

IN dipping into Spanish liquids we shall not mix wine with water, but keep them separate, as most Spaniards do; the latter is entitled to rank first, by those who prefer the opinion of Pindar, who held water to be the best of things, to that of Anacreon, who was not member of any temperance society. The profound regard for water of a Spaniard is quite Oriental; at the same time, as his blood is partly Gothic and partly Arab, his allegiance is equally mixed and divided; thus, if he adores the juice of flints like a Moslem, he venerates the juice of the grape like a German.

Water is the blood of the earth, and the purificator of the body in tropical regions and in creeds which, being regulated by latitudes, enforce frequent ablution; loud are the praises of Arab writers of wells and waterbrooks, and great is their fountain and pool worship, the dipping in which, if their miraculous cases are to be credited, effects more and greater cures than those worked by hydropathists at Grafenberg; a Spaniard's idea of a paradise on earth, of a " garden," is a wellwatered district; irrigation is fertility and wealth, and therefore, as in the East, wells, brooks, and watercourses have been a constant source of bickering; nay the very word *rivality* has been derived from these quarrel and law-suit engendering rivers, as the name given to the well for which the men of Gerah and Isaac differed, was called *esek* from the contention.

The flow of waters cannot be mistaken; the most dreary sterility edges the most luxuriant plenty, the most hopeless barrenness borders on the richest vegetation; the line of demarcation is perceived from afar, dividing the tawny desert from the verdurous garden. The Moors who came from the East were fully sensible of the value of this element; they collected the best springs with the greatest care, they dammed up narrow gorges into reservoirs, they constructed pools and underground cisterns, stemmed valleys with aqueducts that poured in

rivers, and in a word exercised a magic influence over
this element, which they guided and wielded at their
will; their system of irrigation was far too perfect to
be improved by Spaniard, or even destroyed. In those
favoured districts where their artificial contrivances
remain, Flora still smiles and Ceres rejoices with Pomona; wherever the ravages of war or the neglect of
man have ruined them, the garden has relapsed into the
desert, and plains once overflowing with corn, gladness,
and population, have shrunk into sad and silent deserts.

The fountains of Spain, especially in the hotter and
more Moorish districts, are numerous; they cannot fail
to strike and please the stranger, whether they be situated in the public walk, garden, market-place, or private
dwelling. Their mode of supply is simple: a river
which flows down from the hills is diverted at a certain
height from its source, and is carried in an artificial
canal, which retains the original elevation, into a reser-
voir placed above the town which is to be served; as
the waters rise to their level, the force, body, and alti-
tude of some of the columns thrown up are very great.
In our cold country, where, except at Charing Cross,
the stream is conveyed underground and unseen, all
this gush of waters, of dropping diamonds in the bright
sun, which cools the air and gladdens the sight and ear,
is unknown. Again there is a waste of the " article,"
which would shock a Chelsea Waterworks Director,
and induce the rate collector to refer to the fines as
per Act of Parliament. The fondest wish of those
Spaniards who wear long-tailed coats, is to imitate those
gentry; they are ashamed of the patriarchal uncivilised
system of their ancestors—much prefer the economical
lead pipe to all this extravagant and gratuitous splash-
ing—they love a turncock better than the most Oriental
Rebecca who comes down to draw water. The fountains in Spain as in the East are the meeting and greet-
ing places of womankind; here they flock, old and
young, infants and grandmothers. It is a sight to drive
a water-colour painter crazy, such is the colour, costume, and groupings, such is the clatter of tongues and
crockery; such is the life and action; now trip along a

bevy of damsel Hebes with upright forms and chamois
step light yet true; more graceful than opera-dancers,
they come laughing and carolling along, poising on
their heads pitchers modelled after the antique, and
after everything which a Sèvres jug is not. It would
seem that to draw water is a difficult operation, so long
are they lingering near the sweet fountain's rim. It
indeed is their al fresco rout, their tertulia; here for
awhile the hand of woman labour ceases, and the urn
stands still; here more than even after church mass, do
the young discuss their dress and lovers, the middle-
aged and mothers descant on babies and housekeeping;
all talk, and generally at once; but gossip refresheth
the daughters of Eve, whether in gilded boudoir or near
mossy fountain, whose water, if a dash of scandal be
added, becomes sweeter than eau sucrée.

The Iberians were decided water-drinkers, and this
trait of their manners, which are modified by climate
that changes not, still exists as the sun that regulates:
the vinous Greek Athenæus was amazed that even rich
Spaniards should prefer water to wine; and to this day
they are if possible curious about the latter's quality;
they will just drink the wine that grows the nearest,
while they look about and enquire for the best water;
thus even our cook Francisco, who certainly had one
of the best places in Seville, and who although a good
artiste was a better rascal—qualities not incompatible—
preferred to sacrifice his interests rather than go to
Granada, because this man of the fire had heard that
the water there was bad.

The mother of the Arabs was tormented with thirst,
which her Hispano-Moro children have inherited; in
fact in the dog-days, of which here there are packs,
unless the mortal clay be frequently wetted it would
crumble to bits like that of a figure modeller. Fire and
water are the elements of Spain, whether at an *auto de
fé* or in a church-stoop; with a cigar in his mouth a
Spaniard smokes like Vesuvius, and is as dry, combustible, and inflammatory; and properly to understand
the truth of Solomon's remark, that cold water is to a
thirsty soul as refreshing as good news, one must have

experienced what thirst is in the exposed plains of the calcined Castiles, where *coup de soleil* is rife, and a gentleman on horseback's brains seem to be melting like Don Quixote's when Sancho put the curds into his helmet.   It is just the country to send a patient to, who is troubled with hydrophobia.   "Those rayes," to use the words of old Howell, "that do but warm you in England, do roast you here; those beams that irradiate onely, and gild your honey-suckled fields, do here scorch and parch the chinky gaping soyle, and put too many wrinkles upon the face of your common mother."

Then, when the heavens and earth are on fire, and the sun drinks up rivers at one draught, when one burnt sienna tone pervades the tawny ground, and the green herb is shrivelled up into black gunpowder, and the rare pale ashy olive-trees are blanched into the livery of the desert; then, when the heat and harshness make even the salamander muleteers swear doubly as they toil along like demons in an ignited salitrose dust—then, indeed, will an Englishman discover that he is made of the same material, only drier, and learn to estimate water; but a good thirst is too serious an evil, too bordering on suffering, to be made, like an appetite, a matter of congratulation; for when all fluids evaporate, and the blood thickens into currant jelly, and the nerves tighten up into the catgut of an overstrung fiddle, getting attuned to the porcupinal irritability of the tension of the mind, how the parched soul sighs for the comfort of a Scotch mist, and fondly turns back to the uvula-relaxing damps of Devon!—then, in the blackhole-like thirst of the wilderness, every mummy hag rushing from a reed hut, with a porous cup of brackish water, is changed by the mirage into a Hebe, bearing the nectar of the immortals; then how one longs for the most wretched *Venta,* which heat and thirst convert into the Clarendon, since in it at least will be found water and shade, and an escape from the god of fire!   Well may Spanish historians boast, that his orb at the creation first shone over Toledo, and never since has set on the dominions of the great king, who, as we are assured by Señor Berni, "has the sun for his hat,"—*tiene al sol*

por su sombrero; but humbler mortals who are not
grandees of this solar system, and to whom a *coup de
soleil* is neither a joke nor a metaphor, should stow
away non-conductors of heat in the crown of their
beavers. Thus Apollo himself preserved us. And oh!
ye our fair readers, who chance to run such risks, and
value complexion, take for heaven's sake a parasol and
an *Alcarraza.*

This clay utensil—as its Arabic name *al Karaset* implies—is a porous refrigeratory vessel, in which water
when placed in a current of hot air becomes chilled by
evaporation; it is to be seen hung up on poles dangling
from branches, suspended to waggons—in short, is part
and parcel of a Spanish scene in hot weather and localities; every *posada* has rows of them at the entrance,
and the first thing every one does on entering, before
wishing even the hostess Good morning, or asking permission, is to take a full draught : all classes are learned
on the subject, and although on the whole they cannot
be accused of teetotalism, they are loud in their praises
of the pure fluid. The common form of praise is *agua
muy rica*—very rich water. According to their proverbs, good water should have neither taste, smell, nor
colour, " *ni sabor, olor, ni color,*" which neither makes
men sick nor in debt, nor women widows, " *que no
enferma, no adeuda, no enviuda;*" and besides being
cheaper than wine, beer, or brandy, it does not
brutalise the consumer, nor deprive him of his common
sense or good manners.

As Spaniards at all times are as dry as the desert or a
sponge, selling water is a very active business; on
every alameda and prado shrill voices of the sellers of
drinks and mouth combustibles—*vendedores de combustibles de boca*—are heard crying, " Fire, fire, *can-
dela*—Water; who wants water?"—*agua; quien quiere
agua?* which, as these Orientals generally exaggerate,
is described as *mas fresca que la nieve,* or colder than
snow; and near them little Murillo-like urchins run
about with lighted ropes like artillerymen for the convenience of smokers, that is, for every ninety and nine
males out of a hundred; while water-carriers, or rather

retail pedestrian aqueducts, follow thirst like fire-
engines; the *Aguador* carries on his back, like his col-
league in the East, a porous water-jar, with a little
cock by which it is drawn out; he is usually provided
with a small tin box strapped to his waist, and in which
he stows away his glasses, brushes, and some light
azucarillos—panales, which are made of sugar and
white of egg, which Spaniards dip and dissolve in their
drink. In the town, at particular stations water-
mongers in wholesale have a shed, with ranges of jars,
glasses, oranges, lemons, &c., and a bench or two on
which the drinkers "untire themselves." In winter
these are provided with an *añafe* or portable stove, which
keeps a supply of hot water, to take the chill off the
cold, for Spaniards, from a sort of dropsical habit, drink
like fishes all the year round. Ferdinand the Catholic,
on seeing a peasant drowned in a river, observed, "that
he had never before seen a Spaniard who had had
enough water."

At the same time it must be remembered that this
fluid is applied with greater prodigality in washing their
inside than their outside. Indeed, a classical author
remarks that the Spaniards only learnt the use of *hot*
water, as applicable to the toilette, from the Romans
after the second Punic war. Their baths and *thermæ*
were destroyed by the Goths, because they tended to
encourage effeminacy; and those of the Moors were prohibited by the Gotho-Spaniards partly from similar
reasons, but more from a religious hydrophobia. Ablutions and lustral purifications formed an article of faith
with the Jew and Moslem, with whom "cleanliness is
godliness." The mendicant Spanish monks, according to their practice of setting up a directly antagonist
principle, considered physical dirt as the test of moral
purity and true faith; and by dining and sleeping from
year's end to year's end in the same unchanged woollen
frock, arrived at the height of their ambition, according
to their view of the odour of sanctity, insomuch that
Ximenez, who was himself a shirtless Franciscan, induced Ferdinand and Isabella, at the conquest of
Granada, to close and abolish the Moorish baths. They

forbade not only the Christians but the Moors from using anything but holy water. Fire, not water, became the grand element of inquisitorial purification.

The fair sex was warned by monks, who practised what they preached, that they should remember the cases of Susanna, Bathsheba, and La Cava, whose fatal bathing under the royal palace at Toledo led to the downfall of the Gothic monarchy. Their aqueous anathemas extended not only to public, but to minutely private washings, regarding which Sanchez instructs the Spanish confessor to question his fair penitents, and not to absolve the over-washed. Many instances could be produced of the practical working of this enjoined rule; for instance, Isabella, the favourite daughter of Philip II., his eye, as he called her, made a solemn vow never to change her shift until Ostend was taken. The siege lasted three years, three months, and thirteen days. The royal garment acquired a tawny colour, which was called *Isabel* by the courtiers, in compliment to the pious princess. Again, Southey relates that the devout Saint Eufraxia entered into a convent of 130 nuns, not one of whom had ever washed her feet, and the very mention of a bath was an abomination. These obedient daughters to their Capuchin confessors were what Gil de Avila termed a sweet garden of flowers, perfumed by the good smell and reputation of sanctity, "*ameno jardin de flores, olorosas por el buen odor y fama de santidad.*" Justice to the land of Castile soap requires us to observe that latterly, since the suppression of monks, both sexes, and the fair especially, have departed from the strict observance of the religious duties of their excellent grandmothers. Warm baths are now pretty generally established in the larger towns. At the same time, the interiors of bedrooms, whether in inns or private houses, as well by the striking absence of glass and china utensils, which to English notions are absolute necessaries, as by the presence of French pie-dish basins, and duodecimo jugs, indicate that this " little damned spot " on the average Spanish hand, has not yet been quite rubbed out.

However hot the day, dusty the road, or long the

journey, it has never been our fate to see a Spanish
attendant use a single drop of water as a detergent,
or, as polite writers say, "perform his ablutions;" the
constant habit of bathing and complete washing is undoubtedly one reason why the French and other conti-
nentals consider our soap-loving countrymen to be
cracked.   Under the Spanish Goths the Hemerobap-
tistæ, or people who washed their persons once a day,
were set down as heretics.   The Duke of Frias, when
a few years ago on a fortnight's visit to an English
lady, never once troubled his basins and jugs; he simply
rubbed his face occasionally with the white of an egg,
which, as Madame Daunoy records, was the only ablution of the Spanish ladies in the time of Philip IV.;
but these details of the dressing-room are foreign to
the use made in Spain of liquids in kitchen and parlour.

One word on chocolate, which is to a Spaniard what
tea is to a Briton—coffee to a Gaul.   It is to be had
almost everywhere, and is always excellent; the best is
made by the nuns, who are great confectioners and
compounders of sweetmeats, sugarplums and orange-
flowers, water and comfits,

> " Et tous ces mets sucrés en pâte, ou bien liquides,
> Dont estomacs dévots furent toujours avides."

It was long a disputed point whether chocolate did or
did not break fast theologically, just as happened with
coffee among the rigid Moslems.   But since the learned
Escobar decided that *liquidum non rumpit jejunium,* a
liquid does not break fast, it has become the universal
breakfast of Spain.   It is made just liquid enough to
come within the benefit of clergy, that is, a spoon will
almost stand up in it; only a small cup is taken, *una
jicara,* a Mexican word for the cocoa-nuts of which they
were first made, generally with a bit of toasted bread or
biscuit: as these *jicaras* have seldom any handles, they
were used by the rich (as coffee-cups are among the
Orientals) enclosed in little filigree cases of silver or
gold; some of these are very beautiful, made in the
form of a tulip or lotus leaf, on a saucer of mother-o'-
pearl.   The flower is so contrived that, by a spring

underneath, on raising the saucer, the leaves fall back
and disclose the cup to the lips, while, when put down,
they re-close over it, and form a protection against the
flies. A glass of water should always be drunk after
this chocolate, since the aqueous chasse neutralizes the
bilious propensities of this breakfast of the gods, as
Linnæus called chocolate. Tea and coffee have sup-
planted chocolate in England and France; it is in Spain
alone that we are carried back to the breakfasts of Be-
linda and of the wits at Button's; in Spain exist, unchanged, the fans, the game of ombre, *tresillo,* and the
coche de colleras, the coach and six, and other social
usages of the age of Pope and the " Spectator."

Cold liquids in the hot dry summers of Spain are
necessaries, not luxuries; snow and iced drinks are sold
in the streets at prices so low as to be within the reach
of the poorest classes; the rich refrigerate themselves
with *agraz.* This, the Moorish *Hacaraz,* is the most
delicious and most refreshing drink ever devised by
thirsty mortal; it is the *new* pleasure for which Xerxes
wished in vain, and beats the " hock and soda water,"
the " *hoc erat in votis* " of Byron, and sherry cobler
itself. It is made of pounded unripe grapes, clarified
sugar, and water; it is strained till it becomes of the
palest straw-coloured amber, and well iced. It is particularly well made in Andalucia, and it is worth going
there in the dog-days, if only to drink it—it cools a
man's body and soul. At Madrid an agreeable drink
is sold in the streets; it is called *Michi Michi,* from the
Valencian *Mitj e Mitj,* " half and half," and is as unlike the heavy wet mixture of London, as a coal-porter
is to a pretty fair Valenciana. It is made of equal portions of barley-water and orgeat of *Chufa*s, and is
highly iced. The Spaniards, among other cooling
fruits, eat their strawberries mixed with sugar and the
juice of oranges, which will be found a more agreeable
addition than the wine used by the French, or the cream
of the English,—the one heats, and the other, whenever it is to be had, makes a man bilious in Spain.
Spanish ices, *helados,* are apt to be too sweet, nor is
the sugar well refined; the ices, when frozen very hard

and in small forms, either representing fruits or shells, are called *quesos,* cheeses.

Another favourite drink is a weak bottled beer mixed with iced lemonade. Spaniards, however, are no great drinkers of beer, notwithstanding that their ancestors drank more of it than wine, which was not then either so plentiful or universal as at the present; this substitute of grapeless countries passed from the Egyptians and Carthaginians into Spain, where it was excellent, and kept well. The vinous Roman soldiers derided the beer-drinking Iberians, just as the French did the English *before* the battle of Agincourt. "Can sodden water—barley-broth—decoct their cold blood to such valiant heat?" Polybius sneers at the magnificence of a Spanish king, because his home was furnished with silver and gold vases full of beer, of barley-wine. The genuine Goths, as happens everywhere to this day, were great swillers of ale and beer, heady and stupifying mixtures, according to Aristotle. Their archbishop, St. Isidore, distinguished between *celia ceria,* the ale, and *cerbisia,* beer, whence the present word *cerbeza* is derived. Spanish beer, like many other Spanish matters, has now become small. Strong English beer is rare and dear; among one of the infinite ingenious absurdities of Spanish customs' law, English beer in barrels used to be prohibited, as were English bottles if empty—but prohibited beer, in prohibited bottles, was admissible, on the principle that two fiscal negatives made an exchequer affirmative.

CHAPTER XIII

THE wines of Spain deserve a chapter to themselves. Sherry indeed is not less popular among us than Murillo, in spite of the numbers of bad copies of the one, which are passed off for undoubted originals, and butts of the other, which are sold neat as imported. The Spaniard himself is neither curious in port, nor particular in Madeira; he prefers quantity to quality, and loves flavour much less than he hates trouble; a cellar in a private house, of rare fine or foreign wines, is perhaps a greater curiosity than a library of ditto books; an hidalgo with twenty names simply sends out before his frugal meal for a quart of wine to the nearest shop, as a small burgess does in the City for a pint of porter. Local in everything, the Spaniard takes the goods that the gods provide him, just as they come to hand; he drinks the wine that grows in the nearest vineyards, and if there are none, then regales himself with the water from the least distant spring. It is so in everything; he adds the smallest possible exertion of his own to the bounties of nature; his object is to obtain the largest produce for the smallest labour; he allows a life-conferring sun and a fertile soil to create for him the raw material, which he exports, being perfectly contented that the foreigner should return it to him when re-created by art and industry; thus his wool, barilla, hides, and cork-bark, are imported by him back again in the form of cloth, glass, leather, and bungs.

The most celebrated and perfect wines of the Peninsula are port and sherry, which owe their excellence to foreign, not to native skill, the principal growers and makers being Europeans, and their system altogether un-Spanish; nothing can be more rude, antique, and unscientific, than the wine-making in those localities where no stranger has ever settled. But Spain is a land bottled up for antiquarians, and it must be confessed that the national process is very picturesque and classical; no Ariadne revel of Titian is more glittering or animated, no bas-relief more classical in which sacrifices are celebrated

> " To Bacchus, who first from out the purple grape
> Crushed the sweet poison of misused wine."

Often have we ridden through villages redolent with vinous aroma, and inundated with the blood of the berry, until the very mud was encarnadined; what a busy scene! Donkeys laden with panniers of the ripe fruit,

damsels bending under heavy baskets, men with red-
dened legs and arms, joyous and jovial as satyrs, hurry
jostling on to the rude and dirty vat, into which the fruit
is thrown indiscriminately, the black-coloured with the
white ones, the ripe bunches with the sour, the sound
berries with those decayed; no pains are taken, no selection is made; the filth and negligence are commensurate
with this carelessness; the husks are either trampled
under naked feet or pressed out under a rude beam; in
both cases every refining operation is left to the fermentation of nature, for there is a divinity that shapes
our ends, rough hew them how we may.

The wines of Spain, under a latitude where a fine
season is a certainty, might rival those of France, and
still more those of the Rhine, where a good vintage is
the exception, not the rule. Their varieties are infinite,
since few districts, unless those that are very elevated,
are without their local produce, the names, colours, and
flavours of which are equally numerous and varied.
The thirsty traveller, after a long day's ride under a
burning sun, when seated quietly down to a smoking
peppery dish, is enchanted with the cool draught of these
vins du pays, which are brought fresh to him from the
skins or amphora jars; he longs to transport the apparently divine nectar to his own home, and wonders that
"the trade" should have overlooked such delicious
wine. Those who have tried the experiment will find a
sad change for the worse come over the spirit of their
dream, when the long-expected importation greets their
papillatory organs in London. There the illusion is dispelled; there to a cloyed fastidious taste, to a judgment
bewildered and frittered away by variety of the best
vintages, how flat, stale, and unprofitable does this
much-fancied beverage appear! The truth is, that its
merit consists in the thirst and drinking vein of the
traveller, rather than in the wine itself. Those therefore of our readers whose cellars are only stocked with
choice Bordeaux, Xerez, and Champagne, may sustain
with resignation the absence of other sorts of Spanish
grape juice. If an exception is to be made, let it be only
in favour of Valdepeñas and Manzanilla.

The local wines may therefore be tossed off rapidly. The Navarrese drink their Peralta, the Basques their Chacolet, which is a poor vin ordinaire and inferior to our good cider. The Arragonese are supplied from the vineyards of Cariñena; the Catalans, from those of Sidges and Benicarló; the former is a rich sweet wine, with a peculiar aromatic flavour; the latter is the well-known black strap, which is exported largely to Bordeaux to enrich clarets for our vitiated taste, and as it is rich red, and full flavoured, much comes to England to concoct what is denominated curious old port by those who sell it. The fiery and acrid brandy which is made from this Benicarló is sent to the Bay of Cadiz to the tune of 1000 butts a year to doctor up worse sherry.

The central provinces of Spain consume but little of these; Leon has a wine of its own which grows chiefly near Zamora and Toro, and it is much drunk at the neighbouring and learned university of Salamanca, where, as it is strong and heady, it promotes prejudice, as port is said to do elsewhere. Madrid is supplied with wines grown at Tarancon, Arganda, and other places in its immediate vicinity, and those of the latter are frequently substituted for the celebrated Valdepeñas of La Mancha, which was mother's milk to Sancha Panza and his two eminent progenitors; they differed, as their worthy descendant informed the Knight of the Wood, on the merits of a cask; one of them just dipped his tongue into the wine, and affirmed that it had a taste of iron; the other merely applied his nose to the bung-hole, and was positive that it smacked of leather; in due time when the barrel was emptied, a key tied to a thong confirmed the degustatory acumen of these connoisseurs.

The red blood of this " valley of stones " issues with such abundance, that quantities of old wine are often thrown away, for the want of skins, jars, and casks into which to place the new. From the scarcity of fuel in these denuded plains, the prunings of the vine are sometimes as valuable as the grapes. Even at Valdepeñas, with Madrid for its customer, the wine continues to be made in an unscientific, careless manner. Before the French invasion, a Dutchman, named Muller, had begun to improve the system, and better prices were obtained; whereupon the lower classes, in 1808, broke open his cellars, pillaged them, and nearly killed him because he made wine dearer. It is made of a Burgundy grape which has been transplanted and transported from the stinted suns of fickle France, to the certain and glorious summers of La Mancha. The genuine wine is rich, full-bodied, and high-coloured. It will keep pretty well, and improves for four or five years, nay, longer. To be really enjoyed it must be drunk on the spot; the curious in wine should go down into one of the *cuevas* or cave-cellars, and have a goblet of the ruby fluid drawn from the big-bellied jar. The wine, when taken to distant places, is almost always adulterated; and at Madrid with a decoction of log-wood, which makes it almost poisonous, acting upon the nerves and muscular system.

The best vineyards and *bodegas* or cellars are those which did belong to Don Carlos, and those which do belong to the Marques de Santa Cruz. One anecdote will do the work of pages in setting forth the habitual indifference of Spaniards, and the way things are managed for them. This very nobleman, who certainly was one of the most distinguished among the grandees in rank and talent, was dining one day with a foreign ambassador at Madrid, who was a decided admirer of Valdepeñas, as all judicious men must be, and who took great pains to procure it quite pure by sending down trusty persons and sound casks. The Marques at the first glass exclaimed, " What capital wine ! where do you manage to buy it in Madrid ?"   " I send for it," was the reply, " to your *administrador* at Valdepeñas, Anglice unjust steward, and shall be very happy to get you some."

The wine is worth on the spot about 5*l.* the pipe, but the land carriage is expensive, and it is apt, when conveyed in skins, to be tapped and watered by the muleteers, besides imbibing the disagreeable smack of the pitched pigskin. The only way to secure a pure, unadulterated, legitimate article, is to send up *double* quarter sherry casks; the wine is then put into one, and that again is protected by an outer cask, which acts as a preventive guard, against gimlets, straws, and other ingenious contrivances for extracting the vinous contents, and for introducing an aqueous substitute. It must then be conveyed either on mules or in waggons to Cadiz and Santander. It is always as well to send for two casks, as *accidents* in this *pays de l'imprévu* constantly happen where wine and women are in the case. The importer will receive the most satisfactory certificates signed and sealed on paper, first duly stamped, in which the alcalde, the muleteer, the guardia, and all who have shared in the booty, will minutely describe and prove the *accident*, be it an upset, a breaking of casks, or what not. Very little pure Valdepeñas ever reaches England; the numerous vendors' bold assertions to the contrary notwithstanding. As sherry is a subject of more general interest, it will be treated with somewhat more detail.

CHAPTER XIV

SHERRY, a wine which requires more explanation than many of its consumers imagine, is grown in a limited nook of the Peninsula, on the south-western corner of sunny Andalucia, which occupies a range of country of which the town of Xerez is the capital and centre. The wine-producing districts extend over a space which is included—consult a map—within a boundary drawn from the towns of Puerto de Sa. Maria, Rota, San Lucar, Tribujena, Lebrija, Arcos, and to the Puerto again. The finest vintages lie in the immediate vicinity of Xerez, which has given therefore its name to the general produce. The wine, however, becomes inferior in proportion as the vineyards get more distant from this central point.

Although some authors—who, to show their learning, hunt for Greek etymologies in every word—have derived sherry from Ξηρος, dry, to have done so from the

Persian Schiraz would scarcely have been more far-fetched. *Sherris sack*, the term used by Falstaff, no mean authority in this matter, is the precise *seco de Xerez*, the term by which the wine is known to this day in its own country; the epithet *seco*, or dry—the *seck* of old English authors, and the *sec* of French ones—being used in contradistinction to the *sweet* malvoisies and muscadels, which are also made of the same grape. The wine, it is said, was first introduced into England about the time of Henry VII., whose close alliance with Ferdinand and Isabella was cemented by the marriage of his son with their daughter. It became still more popular among us under Elizabeth, when those who sailed under Essex sacked Cadiz in 1596, and brought home the fashion of good " sherris sack, from whence," as Sir John says, " comes valour." The visit to Spain of Charles I. contributed to keeping up among his countrymen this taste for the drinks of the Peninsula, which extended into the provinces, as we find Howell writing from York, in 1645, for " a barrell or two of oysters, which shall be well eaten," as he assures his friend, " with a cup of the best sherry, to which this town is altogether addicted." During the wars of the succession, and those fatal quarrels with England occasioned by the French alliance and family compact of Charles III., our consumption of sherries was much diminished, and the culture of the vine and the wine-making was neglected and deteriorated. It was restored at the end of last century by the family of Gordon, whose houses at Xerez and the Puerto most deservedly rank among the first in the country. The improved quality of the wines was their own recommendation; but as fashion influences everything, their vogue was finally established by Lord Holland, who, on his return from Spain, introduced superlative sherry at his undeniable table.

The quality of the wine depends on the grape and the soil, which has been examined and analysed by competent chemists. Omitting minute and uninteresting particulars, the first class and the best is termed the *Albariza;* this whitish soil is composed of clay mixed

with carbonate of lime and silex. The second sort is
called *Barras*, and consists of sandy quartz, mixed with
lime and oxide of iron. The third is the *Arenas*, being,
as the name indicates, little better than sand, and is by
far the most widely extended, especially about San
Lucar, Rota, and the back of Arcos; it is the most productive, although the wine is generally coarse, thin, and
ill-flavoured, and seldom improves after the third year :
it forms the substratum of those inferior sherries which
are largely exported to the discredit of the real article.
The fourth class of soil is limited in extent, and is the
Bugeo, or dark-brown loamy sand which occurs on the
sides of rivulets and hillocks. The wine grown on it is
poor and weak; yet all the inferior produces of these
different districts are sold as sherry wines, to the great
detriment of those really produced near Xerez itself,
which do not amount to a fifth of the quantity exported.

The varieties of the grape are far greater than those
of the soil on which they are grown. Of more than a
hundred different kinds, those called *Listan* and *Palo-
mina Blanca* are the best. The increased demand for
sherry, where the producing surface is limited, has led
to the extirpation of many vines of an inferior kind,
which have been replaced by new ones whose produce is
of a larger and better quality. The *Pedro Ximenez*, or
delicious sweet-tasted grape which is so celebrated, came
originally from Madeira, and was planted on the Rhine,
from whence about two centuries ago one Peter Simon
brought it to Malaga, since when it has extended over
the south of Spain. It is of this grape that the rich and
luscious sweet wine called *Pajarete* is made; a name
which some have erroneously derived from *Pajaros*, the
birds, who are wont to pick the ripest berries; but it
was so called from the wine having been originally only
made at Paxarete, a small spot near Xerez : it is now
prepared everywhere, and thus the grapes are dried in
the sun until they almost become raisins, and the syrop
quite inspissated, after that they are pressed, and a
little fine old wine and brandy is added. This wine is
extremely costly, as it is much used in the rearing and
maturation of young sherry wines.

There is an excellent account of all the vines of Andalucia by Rojas Clemente. This able naturalist disgraced himself by being a base toady of the wretched minion Godoy, and by French partisanship, which is high treason to his own country. Accordingly, to please his masters, he " contrasts the frank generosity, the vivacity, and genial cordiality of the Xerezanos, with the sombre stupidity and ferocious egotism of the insolent people on the banks of the Thames," by whom he had just before been most hospitably welcomed. This worthy gentleman wrote, however, within sight of Trafalgar, and while a certain untoward event was rankling in his and his estimable patron's bosom.

The vines are cultivated with the greatest care, and demand unceasing attention, from the first planting to their final decay. They generally fruit about the fifth year, and continue in full and excellent bearing for about thirty-five years more, when the produce begins to diminish both in quantity and in quality. The best wines are produced from the slowest ripening grapes ; the vines are delicate, have a true bacchic hydrophobia, or antipathy to water—are easily affected and injured by bad smells and rank weeds. The vine-dresser enjoys little rest ; at one time the soil must be trenched and kept clean, then the vines must be pruned, and tied to the stakes, to which they are trained very low ; anon insects must be destroyed ; and at last the fruit has to be gathered and crushed. It is a life of constant care, labour, and expense.

The highest qualities of flavour depend on the grape and soil, and as the favoured spots are limited, and the struggle and competition for their acquisition great, the prices paid are always high, and occasionally extravagantly so ; the proprietors of vineyards are very numerous, and the surface is split and partitioned into infinite petty ownerships. Even the *Pago de Macharnudo*, the finest of all, the Clos le Vougeot, the Johannisberg of Xerez, is much subdivided ; it consists of 1200 *aranzadas*, one of which may be taken as equivalent to our acre, being, however, that quantity of land which can be ploughed with a pair of bullocks in a day—of these

1200, 460 belong to the great house of Pedro Domecq, and their mean produce may be taken at 1895 butts, of which some 350 only will run very fine. Among the next most renowned *pagos*, or wine districts, may be cited Carrascal, Los Tercios, Barbiana *alta y baja*, Añina, San Julian, Mochiele, Carraola, Cruz del Husillo, which lie in the immediate *termino* or boundary of Xerez; their produce always ensures high prices in the market. Many of these vineyards are fenced with canes, the *arundo donax*, or with aloes, whose stiff-pointed leaves form palisadoes that would defy a regiment of dragoons, and are called by the natives the devil's tooth-picks; in addition, the *capataz del campo*, or country bailiff, is provided, like a keeper, with large and ferocious dogs, who would tear an intruder to pieces. The fruit when nearly mature is especially watched; for, according to the proverb, it requires much vigilance to take care of ripe grapes and maidens—*Niñas y vinas, son mal de guardar.*

When the period of the vintage arrives, the cares of the proprietors and the labours of the cultivators and makers increase. The bunches are picked and spread out for some days on mattings; the unripe grapes, which have less substance and spirit, are separated, and are exposed longer to the sun, by which they improve. If the berries be over-ripe, then the saccharine prevails, and there is a deficiency of tartaric acid. The selected grapes are sprinkled with lime, by which the watery and acetous particles are absorbed and corrected. A nice hand is requisite in this powdering, which, by the way, is an ancient African custom, in order to avoid the imputation of Falstaff, "There is lime in this sack." The treading out the fruit is generally done by night, because it is then cooler, and in order to avoid as much as possible the plague of wasps, by whom the half-naked operators are liable to be stung. On the larger vineyards there is generally a jumble of buildings, which contain every requisite for making the wine, as well as cellars into which the must or pressed grape juice is left to pass the stages of fermentation, and where it remains until the following spring before it is removed from the

lees. When the new wine is racked off, all the produce
of the same vineyard and vintage is housed together,
and called a *partido* or lot.

The vintage, which is the all-absorbing, all-engrossing
moment of the year, occupies about a fortnight, and is
earlier in the Rota districts than at Xerez, where it
commences about the 20th of September; into these brief
moments the hearts, bodies, and souls of men are condensed; even Venus, the queen of neighbouring Cadiz,
and who during the other three hundred and fifty-one
days of the year, allies herself willingly to Bacchus, is
now forgotten. Nobles and commoners, merchants and
priests, talk of nothing but wine, which then and there
monopolises man, and is to Xerez what the water is at
Grand Cairo, where the rising of the Nile is at once a
pleasure and a profit. When the vintage is concluded,
the custom-house officers take note in their respective
districts of the quantity produced on each vineyard, to
whom it is sold, and where it is taken to; nor can it be
resold or removed afterwards, without a permit and a
charge of a four per cent. ad valorem duty. It need not
be said, that in a land where public officers are inadequately paid, where official honesty and principle are
all but unknown, a bribe is all-sufficient; false returns
are regularly made, and every trick resorted to to facilitate trade, and transfer revenue into the pockets of the
collectors, rather than into the Queen's treasury; thus
are defeated the vexations and extortions of commerce-
hampering excise, to hate which seems to be a second
nature in man all over the world, Commissioners excepted. In the first year a decided difference takes place
in these new wines; some become *bastos* or coarse,
others sour and others good; those only which exhibit
great delicacy, body, and flavour are called *finos* or fine;
in a lot of one hundred butts, rarely more than ten to
fifteen can be calculated as deserving this epithet, and
it is to the high price paid for these by the *almacenistas*
or storers of wines, that the growers look for remuneration; the qualities of the wines usually produced in each
particular *termino* or district do not vary much; they
have their regular character and prices among the trade,

by whom they are perfectly understood and exactly valued.

These singular changes in the juice of grapes grown on the same vineyard, invariably take place, although no satisfactory reason has been yet assigned; the chemical processes of nature have hitherto defied the investigations of man, and in nothing more than in the elaboration of that lusus naturæ vel Bacchi, that variety of flavour which goes by the name of *amontillado;* this has been given to it from its resemblance in dryness and quality to the wines of *Montilla*, near Cordova : the latter, be it observed, are scarcely known in England at all, nor indeed in Spain, except in their own immediate neighbourhood, where they supply the local consumption. This *amontillado*, when the genuine product of nature, is very valuable, as it is used in correcting young Sherry wines, which are running over sweet; it is very scarce, since out of a hundred butts of *vino fino*, not more than five will possess its properties. Much of the wine which is sold in London as pure *amontillado*, is a fictitious preparation, and made up for the British market.

All sherries are a matured mixture of grape juice; champagne itself is a manufactured wine; nor does it much matter, provided a palatable and wholesome beverage be produced. In all the leading and respectable houses, the wine is prepared from grapes grown in the district, nor is there the slightest mystery made in explaining the artificial processes which are adopted; the rearing, educating, and finishing, as it were, of these wines, is a work of many years, and is generally intrusted to the *Capataz*, the chief butler, or head man, who very often becomes the real master; this important personage is seldom raised in Andalucia, or in any wine-growing districts of Spain; he generally is by birth an Asturian, or a native of the mountains contiguous to Santander, from whence the chandlers and grocers, hence called *Los Montañeses*, are supplied throughout the Peninsula. These Highlanders are celebrated for the length of their pedigrees, and the tasting properties of their tongues; we have more than once in Estrema-

dura and Leon fallen in with flights of these ragged
gentry, wending, Scotch-like, to the south in search of
fortune; few had shoes or shirts, yet almost every one
carried his family parchment in a tin case, wherein his
descent from Tubal—respectable, although doubtful—
was proven to be as evident as the sun is at noon day.

These gentleman of good birth and better taste seldom smoke, as the narcotic stupifying weed deadens
papillatory delicacy. Now as few wine-masters in Spain
would give up the cigar to gain millions, the *Capataz*
soon becomes the sole possessor of the secrets of the
cellar; and as no merchants possess vineyards of their
own sufficient to supply their demand, the purchases of
new wines must be made by this confidential servant,
who is thus enabled to cheat both the grower and his
own employer, since he will only buy of those who give
him the largest commission. Many contrive by these
long and faithful services to amass great wealth; thus
Juan Sanchez the *Capataz of the late* Petro Domecq,
died recently worth 300,000*l*. Towards his latter end,
having been visited by his confessor and some qualms
of conscience, he bequeathed his fortune to pious and
charitable uses, but the bulk was forthwith secured by
his attorneys and priests, whose charity began at home.

As the chancellor is the keeper of the Queen's conscience, so the *Capataz* is the keeper of the *bodega* or
the wine-store, which is very peculiar, and the grand lion
of Xerez. The rich and populous town, when seen from
afar, rising in its vine-clad knoll, is characterised by
these huge erections, that look like the pent-houses
under which men-of-war are built at Chatham. These
temples of Bacchus resemble cathedrals in size and lofti-
ness, and their divisions, like Spanish chapels, bear the
names of the saints to whom they are dedicated, and
few tutelar deities have more numerous or more devout
worshippers; but Romanism mixes itself up in everything of Spain, and fixes its mark alikt on salt-pans and
mine-shafts, as on boats and *bodegas*. These huge
repositories are all above ground, and are the antithesis
of our under-ground cellars. The wines of Xerez are
thus found to ripen both better and quicker, as one

year in a *bodega* inspires them with more life than do ten years of burial. As these wines are more capricious in the development of their character than young ladies at a boarding-school, the greatest care is taken in the selection of eligible and healthy situations for their education; the neighbourhood of all offensive drains or effluvia is carefully avoided, since these nuisances are sure to affect the delicately organised fluids, although they fail to damage the noses of those to whose charge they are committed; and strange to say, in this land of contradictions, Cologne itself is scarcely more renowned for its twenty and odd bad smells ascertained by Coleridge, than is this same tortuous, dirty, and old-fashioned Xerez. Here, as in the Rhenish city, all the sweets are bottled up for exportation, all the stinks kept for home consumption. The new *bodegas* are consequently erected in the newer portions of the town, in dry and open places; connected with them are offices and workshops, in which everything bearing upon the wine trade is manufactured, even to the barrels that are made of American oak staves. The interior of the *bodega* is kept deliciously cool; the glare outside is carefully excluded, while a free circulation of air is admitted; an even temperature is very essential, and one at an average of 60 degrees is the best of all. There are more than a thousand *bodegas* registered at the custom-house for the Xerez district; the largest only belong to the first-rate firms, and mostly to Europeans, that is, to English and Frenchmen. A heavy capital is required, much patience and forethought, qualities which do not grow on these or on any hills of Spain. This necessity will be better understood when it is said, that some of these stores contain from one to four thousand butts, and that few really fine sherries are sent out of them until ten or twelve years old. Supposing, therefore, that each butt averages in value only 25*l.*, it is evident how much time and investment of wealth is necessary.

Sherry wine, when mature and perfect, is made up from many butts. The " entire," indeed, is the result of Xerez grapes, but of many different ages, vintages, and varieties of flavour. The contents of one barrel serve to correct another until the proposed standard aggregate is produced; and to such a certainty has this uniform admixture been reduced, that houses are enabled to supply for any number of years exactly that particular colour, flavour, body, etc., which particular customers demand. This wine improves very much with age, gets softer and more aromatic, and gains both body and aroma, in which its young wines are deficient. Indeed, so great is the change in all respects, that one scarcely can believe them ever to have been the same: the baby differs not more from the man, nor the oak from the acorn.

That *Capataz* has attained the object of his fondest wishes, who has observed in his compositions the poetical principles of Horace, the *callida junctura*, the *omne tulit punctum qui miscuit utile dulci;* this happy and skilful junction of the sweet and solid, should unite fulness of body, an oily, nutty flavour and *bouquet*, dryness, absence from acidity, strength, durability, and spirituosity. Very little brandy is necessary, as the vivifying power of the unstinted sun of Andalucia imparts sufficient alcohol, which ranges from 20 to 23 per cent. in fine sherries, and only reaches about 12 in clarets and champagnes. Fine pure sherry is of a rich brown colour, but in order to flatter the conventional tastes of some English, "pale old sherry" must be had, and colour is chemically discharged at the expense of delicate aroma. Another absurd deference to British prejudice, is the sending sherries to the East Indies, because such a trip is found sometimes to benefit the wines of Madeira. This is not only expensive but positively injurious to the juice of Xerez, as the wine returns diminished in quantity, turbid, sharp, and deteriorated in flavour, while from the constant fermentation it becomes thinner in body and more spirituous. The real secret of procuring good sherry is to pay the best price for it at the best house, and then to keep the purchase for many years in a good cellar before it is drunk.

To return to the *Capataz*. This head master passes this life of probation in tasting. He goes the regular round of his butts, ascertaining the qualities, merits, and demerits of each pupil, which he notes by certain marks or hieroglyphics. He corrects faults as he goes along, making a memorandum also of the date and remedy applied, and thus at his next visit he is enabled to report good progress, or lament the contrary. The new wines, after the fermentation is past, are commonly enriched with an *arrope*, or sort of syrup, which is found very much to encourage them. There are extensive manufactories of this cordial at San Lucar, and wherever the *arenas*, or sandy soil, prevails. The must, or new grape juice, before fermentation has commenced, is boiled slowly down to the fifth of its bulk. It must simmer, and requires great care in the skimming and not being burnt. Of this, when dissolved, the *vino de color*, the *madre vino*, or mother wine, is made, by which the younger ones are nourished as by mother's milk. When old, this balsamic ingredient becomes strong, perfumed as an essence, and very precious, and is worth from three to five hundred guineas a butt; indeed it scarcely ever will be sold at all. All the principal *bodegas* have certain huge and time-honoured casks which contain this divine ichor, which inspires ordinary wines with generous and heroic virtues; hence possibly their dedication of their tuns not to saints and saintesses, but to Wellingtons and Nelsons. It is from these reservoirs that distinguished visitors are allowed just a sip. Such a compliment was paid to Ferdinand VII. by Pedro Domecq, and the cask to this day bears the royal name of its assayer. Whatever quantity is taken out of one of these for the benefit of younger wines, is replaced by a similar quantity drawn from the next oldest cask in the cellar.

After a year or two trial of the new wines, it is ascertained how they will eventually turn out; if they go wrong, they are expelled from the seminary, and shipped off to the leathern-tongued consumers of Hamburgh or Quebec, at about 15*l.* per butt. All the various forms, stages, and steps of education are readily explained in the great establishments, among which the first are those of Domecq and John David Gordon, and nothing can exceed the cordial hospitality of these princely merchants; whoever comes provided with a letter of introduction is carried off bodily, bags, baggage, and all, to

their houses, which, considering the iniquity of Xerezan
inns, is a satisfactory move. Then and there the guest
is initiated into the secrets of trade, and is handed over
to the *Capataz*, who delivers an explanatory lecture on
vinology, which is illustrated, like those of Faraday, by
experiments : tasting sherry at Xerez has, as Señor
Clemente would say, very little in common with the commonplace customs of the London Docks. Here the
swarthy professor, dressed somewhat like Figaro in the
Barber of Seville, is followed by sundry jacketed and
sandalled Ganymedes, who bear glasses on waiters ; the
lecturer is armed with a long stick, to the end of which
is tied a bit of hollow cane, which he dips into each butt ;
the subject is begun at the beginning, and each step in
advance is explained to the listening party with the
gravity of a judicious foreman of a jury : the sample is
handed round and tasted by all, who, if they are wise,
will follow the example of their leader (on whom wine
has no more effect than on a glass), by never swallowing
the sips, but only permitting the tongue to agitate it in
the mouth, until the exact flavour is mastered ; every
cask is tried, from the young wine to the middle-aged,
from the mature to the golden ancient. Those who are
not stupified by the fumes, cannot fail to come out
vastly edified. The student should hold hard during the
first trials, for the best wine is reserved until the last.
He ascends, if he does not tumble off, a vinous ladder of
excellence. It would be better to reverse the order of the
course, and commence with the finest sorts while the
palate is fresh and the judgment unclouded. The thirster
after knowledge must not drink too deeply now, but remember the second ordeal to which he will afterwards
be exposed at the hospitable table of the proprietor,
whose joy and pride it is to produce fine wine and plenty
of it, when his friends meet around his mahogany.

What a grateful offering is then made to the jovial
god, by whom the merchant lives, and by whom the
deity is now set from his glassy prison free ! What a
drawing of popping corks, half consumed by time !—
what a brushing away of venerable cobwebs from flasks
binned apart while George the Third was king ! The

delight of the worthy Amphitryon on producing a fresh
bottle, exceeds that of a prolific mother when she blesses
her husband with a new baby. He handles the darling
decanter, as if he dearly loved the contents, which indeed
are of his own making ; how the clean glasses are held
up to the light to see the bright transparent liquid
sparkle and phosphoresce within; how the intelligent
nose is passed slowly over the mantling surface, redolent
with fragrancy; how the climax of rapture is reached
when the godlike nectar is raised to the blushing lips !

The wine suffices in itself for sensual gratification and
for intellectual conversation : all the guests have an
opinion; what gentleman, indeed, cannot judge on a
horse or a bottle? When differences arise, as they will
in matters of taste, and where bottles circulate freely,
the master-host *decides*—

> " Tells all the names, lays down the law,
> Que ça est bon ; ah, goûtez ça."

There is to him a combination of pleasure and profit
in these genial banquets, these noctes cœnæque Deum.
Many a good connection is thus formed, when an English gentleman, who now, perhaps for the first time,
tastes pure and genuine sherry. A good dinner naturally promotes good humour with mankind in general,
and with the donor in particular. A given quantity of
the present god opens both heart and purse-strings,
until the tongue on which the magic flavour lingers,
murmurs gratefully out, " Send me a butt of *amontillado pasado,* and another of *seco reanejo,* and draw for
the cash at sight."

An important point will now arise, what is the price?
That ever is the question and the rub. Pure genuine
sherry, from ten to twelve years old, is worth from 50
to 80 guineas per butt, in the *bodega,* and when freight,
insurance, duty, and charges are added, will stand the
importer from 100 to 130 guineas in his cellar. A butt
will run from 108 to 112 gallons, and the duty is 5s. 6d.
per gallon. Such a butt will bottle about 52 dozen.
The reader will now appreciate the bargains of those
" pale " and " golden sherries " advertised in the Eng-

lish newspapers at 36s. the dozen, bottles included. They are *maris expers,* although much indebted to French brandy, Sicilian Marsala, Cape wine, Devonshire cider, and Thames water.

The growth of wine amounts to some 400,000 or 500,000 *arrobas* annually. The arroba is a Moorish name, and a dry measure, although used for liquids; it contains a quarter of a hundredweight; 30 arrobas go to a *bota,* or butt, of which from 8000 to 10,000 of really fine are annually exported: but the quantities of so-called sherries, "neat as imported," in the manufacture of which San Lucar is fully occupied, is prodigious, and is increasing every year. To give an idea of the extent of the growing traffic, in 1842 25,096 butts were exported from these districts, and 29,313 in 1843; while in 1845 there were exported 18,135 butts from Xerez alone, and 14,037 from the Puerto, making the enormous aggregate of 32,172 butts. Now as the vineyards remain precisely the same, probably some portion of these additional barrels may not be quite the genuine produce of the Xerez grape: in truth, the ruin of sherry wines has commenced, from the numbers of second-rate houses that have sprung up, which look to quantity, not quality. Many thousand butts of bad Niebla wine are thus palmed off on the enlightened British public after being well brandied and doctored; thus a conventional notion of sherry is formed, to the ruin of the real thing; for even respectable houses are forced to fabricate their wines so as to suit the depraved taste of their consumers, as is done with pure clarets at Bordeaux, which are charged with Hermitages and Benicarló. Thus delicate idiosyncratic flavour is lost, while headache and dyspepsia are imported; but there is a fashion in wines as in physicians. Formerly Madeira was the vinous panacea, until the increased demand induced disreputable traders to deteriorate the article, which in the reaction became dishonoured. Then sherry was resorted to as a more honest and wholesome beverage. Now its period of decline is hastening from the same causes, and the average produce is becoming inferior, to end in disrepute, and possibly in a return to the wines of Madeira, whose makers have learnt a lesson in the stern school of adversity.

Be that as it may, the people at large of Spain are scarcely acquainted with the taste of sherry wine, beyond the immediate vicinity in which it is made; and more of it is swallowed at Gibraltar at the messes, than in either Madrid, Toledo, or Salamanca. Sherry is a foreign wine, and made and drunk by foreigners; nor do the generality of Spaniards like its strong flavour, and still less its high price, although some now affect its use, because, from its great vogue in England, it argues civilisation to adopt it. This use obtains only in the capital and richer seaports; thus at inland Granada, not 150 miles from Xerez, sherry would hardly be to be had, were it not for the demand created by our travelling countrymen, and even then it is sold per bottle, and as a liqueur. At Seville, which is quite close to Xerez, in the best houses, one glass only is handed round, just as only one glass of Greek wine was in the house of the father of even Lucullus among the ancient Romans, or as among the modern ones is still done with Malaga or Vino de Cypro; this single glass is drunk as a *chasse*, and being considered to aid digestion, is called the *golpe medico,* the coup de médecin; it is equivalent, in that hot country, to the thimbleful of Curaçoa or Cognac, by which coffee is wound up in colder England and France.

In Andalucia it was no less easy for the Moor to encourage the use of water as a beverage, than to prohibit that of wine, which, if endued with strength, which sherry is, must destroy health when taken largely and habitually, as is occasionally found out at Gibraltar. Hence the natives of Xerez themselves infinitely prefer a light wine called Manzanilla, which is made near San Lucar, and is at once much weaker and cheaper than sherry. The grape from whence it is produced grows on a poor and sandy soil. The vintage is very early, as the fruit is gathered before it is quite ripe. The wine is of a delicate pale straw colour, and is extremely wholesome; it strengthens the stomach, without heating or inebriating, like sherry. All classes are passionately fond of it, since the want of alcohol enables them to drink more of it than of stronger beverages, while the dry quality acts as a tonic during the relaxing heats. It may be compared to the ancient Lesbian, which Horace quaffed so plentifully in the cool shade, and then described as never doing harm. The men employed in the sherry wine vaults, and who have therefore that drink at their command, seldom touch it, but invariably, when their work is done, go to the neighbouring shop to refresh themselves with a glass of " innocent " Manzanilla. Among their betters, clubs are formed solely to drink it, and with iced water and a cigar it transports the consumer into a Moslem's dream of paradise. It tastes better from the cask than out of the bottle, and improves as the cask gets low.

The origin of the name has been disputed; some who prefer sound to sense derive it from *Manzana,* an apple, which had it been cider might have passed; others connect it with the distant town of *Mansanilla* on the opposite side of the river, where it is neither made nor drunk. The real etymology is to be found in its striking resemblance to the bitter flavour of the flowers of camomile (*manzanilla*), which are used by our doctors to make a medicinal tea, and by those of Spain for fomentations. This flavour in the wine is so marked as to be at first quite disagreeable to strangers. If its eulogistic consumers are to be believed, the wine surpasses the tea in hygæian qualities : none, say they, who drink it are ever troubled with gravel, stone, or gout. Certainly, it is eminently free from acidity. The very best Manzanilla is to be had in London of Messrs. Gorman, No. 16, Mark Lane. Since " *Drink it, ye dyspeptics*," was enjoined last year in the " Handbook," the importation of this wine to England, which previously did not exceed ten butts, has in twelve short months overpassed two hundred; a compliment delicate as it is practical, which is acknowledged by the author —a drinker thereof—with most profound gratitude.

By the way, the real thing to eat with Manzanilla is the *alpistera*. Make it thus :—To one pound of fine flour (mind that it is dry) add half a pound of double-refined, well-sifted, pounded white sugar, the yolks and whites of four very fresh eggs, well beaten together; work the mixture up into a paste; roll it out very thin; divide it into squares about half the size of this page; cut it into strips, so that the paste should look like a hand with fingers, then dislocate the strips, and dip them in hot melted fine lard, until of a delicate pale brown; the more the strips are curled up and twisted the better; the *alpistera* should look like bunches of ribbons; powder them over with fine white sugar. They are then as pretty as nice. It is not easy to make them well; but the gods grant no excellence to mortals without much labour and thought. So Venus the goddess of grace was allied to hard-working Vulcan, who toiled and pondered at his fire, as every cook who has an aspiring soul has ever done.

CHAPTER XV

HAVING thus, and we hope satisfactorily, discussed the eatables and drinkables of Spain, attention must naturally be next directed to those houses on the roads and in the towns, where these comforts to the hungry and weary public are to be had, or are not to be had, as sometimes will happen in this land of " the unexpected;" the Peninsular inns, with few exceptions, have long been divided into the bad, the worse, and the worst; and as the latter are still the most numerous and national, as well as the worst, they will be gone into the last. In few countries will the rambler agree oftener with dear Dr. Johnson's speech to his squire Boswell, " Sir, there is nothing which has been contrived by man, by which so much happiness is produced, as by a good tavern." Spain offers many negative arguments of the truth of our great moralist and eater's reflection; the inns in general are fuller of entertainment for the mind than the body, and even when the

newest, and the best in the country, are indifferent if
compared to those which Englishmen are accustomed to
at home, and have created on those high roads of the
Continent, which they most frequent.   Here few gentlemen will say with Falstaff, "Shall I not take mine
ease in mine inn?" Badness of roads and discomforts
of *ventas* cannot well escape the notice of those who
travel on horseback and slowly, since they must dwell
on and in them; whereas a rail whisks the passenger
past such nuisances, with comet-like rapidity, and all
things that are soon out of sight are quicker out of
mind; nevertheless, let no aspiring writer be deterred
from quitting the highways for the byeways of the
Peninsula. "There is, Sir," as Johnson again said to
Boswell, "a good deal of Spain that has not been
perambulated. I would have you go thither; a man of
inferior talents to yours, may furnish us with useful
observations on that country."

Why the public accommodations should be second-
rate is soon explained. Nature and the natives have
long combined to isolate still more their Peninsula,
which already is moated round by the unsocial sea, and
is barricadoed by almost impassable mountains. The
Inquisition all but reduced Spanish man to the condition of a monk in a wall-enclosed convent, by standing sentinel, and keeping watch and ward against the
foreigner and his perilous novelties;[1] Spain thus un-

[1] The very word *Novelty* has become in common parlance
synonymous with danger change, by the fear of which all
Spaniards are perplexed; as in religion it is a heresy. Bitter
experience has taught all classes that every change, every promise of a new era of blessing and prosperity has ended in a
failure, and that matters have got worse: hence they not only
bear the evils to which they are accustomed, rather than try a
speculative amelioration, but actually prefer a bad state of
things, of which they know the worst, to the possibility of an
untried good. *Mas vale el mal conocido, que el bien por conocer.*
"How is my lady the wife of your grace?" says a Spanish
gentleman to his friend. "*Como está mi Señora la Esposa de
Usted?*" "She goes on without Novelty"—"*Sigue sin Novedad,*" is the reply, if the fair one be much the same. "*Vaya
Usted con Dios, y que no haya Novedad!*" "Go with God, your
grace! and may nothing new happen," says another, on starting
his friend off on a journey.

visited and unvisiting, became arranged for Spaniards
only, and has scarcely required conveniences which are
more suited to the curious wants of other Europeans
and strangers who here are neither liked, wished for,
nor even thought of, by natives who seldom travel
except on compulsion and never for amusement; why
indeed should they? since Spain is paradise, and each
man's own parish in his eyes is the central spot of its
glory. When the noble and rich visited the provinces,
they were lodged in their own or in their friends' houses,
just as the clergy and monks were received into convents. The great bulk of the Peninsular family, not
being overburdened with cash or fastidiousness, have
long been and are inured to infinite inconveniences and
negations; they live at home in an abundance of privations, and expect when abroad to be worse off; and
they well know that comfort never lodges at a Spanish
inn; as in the East, they cannot conceive that any
travelling should be unattended by hardships, which
they endure with Oriental resignation, as *cosas de
España,* or things of Spain which have always been so,
and for which there is no remedy but patient resignation; the bliss of ignorance, and the not knowing of
anything better, is everywhere the grand secret of
absence of discontent; while to those whose everyday life
is a feast, every thing that does not come up to their
conventional ideas becomes a failure, but to those whose
daily bread is dry and scanty, whose drink is water,
every thing beyond prison-fare appears to be luxury.

In Spain there has been little demand for those
accommodations which have been introduced on the
Continent by our nomade countrymen, who carry their
tea, towels, carpets, comforts and civilisation with
them; to travel at all for mere pleasure is quite a
modern invention, and being an expensive affair, is the
most indulged in by the English, because they can best
afford it, but as Spain lies out of their hackneyed
routes, the inns still retain much the same state of
primitive dirt and discomfort, which most of those
on the Continent presented. until repolished by our hints
and guineas.

In the Peninsula, where intellect does not post in a
Britannic britzcka and four, the inns, and especially
those of the country and inferior order, continue much
as they were in the time of the Romans, and probably
long before them; nay those in the very vicinity of
Madrid, "the only court on earth," are as classically
wretched, as the hostelry at Aricia, near the Eternal
City, was in the days of Horace. The Spanish inns,
indeed, on the bye-roads and remoter districts, are such
as render it almost unadvisable for any English lady to
venture to face them, unless predetermined to go
through roughing it, in a way of which none who have
only travelled in England can form the remotest idea :
at the same time they may be and have been endured
by even the sick and delicate. To youth, and to all
men in enjoyment of good health, temper, patience,
and the blessing of foresight, neither a dinner nor a
bed will ever be wanting, to both of which hunger and
fatigue will give a zest beyond the reach of art; and
fortunately for travellers, all the Continent over, and
particularly in Spain, bread and salt, as in the days of
Horace, will be found to appease the wayfarer's bark-
ing stomach, nor will he who after that sleeps soundly
be bitten by fleas, "*quien duerme bien, no le pican las
pulgas.*" The pleasures of travelling in this wild land
are cheaply purchased by these trifling inconveniences,
which may always be much lessened by *provision* in
brain and basket; the expeditions teem with incident,
adventure, and novelty; every day and evening present
a comedy of real life, and offer means of obtaining insight into human nature, and form in after-life a perpetual fund of interesting recollections : all that was
charming will be then remembered, and the disagreeable, if not forgotten, will be disarmed of its sting,
nay, even as having been in a battle, will become a
pleasant thing to recollect and to talk, may be twaddle,
about. Let not the traveller expect to find too much ;
if he reckons on finding nothing he will seldom be disappointed; so let him not look for five feet in a cat,
"*no busces cinco pies al gato.*" Spain, as the East,
is not to be enjoyed by the over-fastidious in the fleshly

comforts : there, those who over analyse, who peep too
much behind the culinary or domestic curtains, must
not expect to pass a tranquil existence.

First and foremost among these refuges for the destitute comes the *fonda,* the hotel. This, as the name
implies, is a foreign thing, and was imported from
Venice, which in its time was the Paris of Europe, the
leader of sensual civilisation, and the sink of every lie
and iniquity. Its *fondacco,* in the same manner, served
as a model for the Turkish *fondack.* The *fonda* is only
to be found in the largest towns and principal sea-ports,
where the presence of foreigners creates a demand and
supports the establishment. To it frequently is attached a café, or " *botilleriá,*" a bottlery and a place for
the sale of liqueurs, with a " *neveria,*" a snowery where
ices and cakes are supplied. Men only, not horses, are
taken in at a *fonda ;* but there is generally a keeper of
a stable or of a minor inn in the vicinity, to which the
traveller's animals are consigned. The *fonda* is tolerably furnished in reference to the common articles with
which the sober unindulgent natives are contented : the
traveller in his comparisons must never forget that
Spain is not England, which too few ever can get out
of their heads. Spain is Spain, a truism which cannot
be too often repeated ; and in its being Spain consists
its originality, its raciness, its novelty, its idiosyncrasy,
its best charm and interest, although the natives do
not know it, and are every day, by a foolish aping of
European civilisation, paring away attractions, and
getting commonplace, unlike themselves, and still more
unlike their Gotho-Moro and most picturesque fathers
and mothers. Monks, as we said in our preface, are
gone, mantillas are going, the shadow of cotton *versus*
corn has already darkened the sunny city of Figaro, and
the end of all Spanish things is coming. *Ay! de mi
España!*

Thus in Spain, and especially in the hotter provinces,
it is heat and not cold which is the enemy : what we
call furniture—carpets, rugs, curtains, and so forth—
would be a positive nuisance, would keep out the cool,
and harbour plagues of vermin beyond endurance. The

walls of the apartments are frequently, though simply, whitewashed : the uneven brick floors are covered in winter with a matting made of the "*esparto,*" rush, and called an "*estera,*" as was done in our king's palaces in the days of Elizabeth : a low iron or wooden truckle bedstead, with coarse but clean sheets and clothes, a few hard chairs, perhaps a stiff-backed, most uncomfortable sofa, and rickety table or so, complete the scanty inventory. The charges are moderate; about two dollars, or 8*s*. 6*d*., per head a-day, includes lodging, breakfast, dinner, and supper. Servants, if Spanish, are usually charged half; English servants, whom no wise person would take on the Continent, are nowhere more useless, or greater incumbrances, than in this hungry, thirsty, tealess, beerless, beefless land : they give more trouble, require more food and attention, and are ten times more discontented than their masters, who have poetry in their souls; an æsthetic love of travel, for its own sake, more than counterbalances with them the want of material gross comforts, about which their pudding-headed four-full-meals-a-day attendants are only thinking. Charges are higher at Madrid, and Barcelona, a great commercial city, where the hotels are appointed more European-like, in accommodation and prices. Those who remain any time in a large town bargain with the innkeeper, or go into a boarding-house, "*casa de pupilos,*" or "*de huespedes,*" where they have the best opportunity of learning the Spanish language, and of obtaining an idea of national manners and habits. This system is very common. The houses may be known externally by a white paper ticket attached to the *extremity* of one of the windows or balconies. This position must be noted; for if the paper be placed in the *middle* of the balcony, the signal means only that lodgings are here to be let. Their charges are very reasonable.

Since the death of Ferdinand VII. marvellous improvements have taken place in some *fondas*. In the changes and chances of the multitudinous revolutions, all parties ruled in their rotation, and then either killed or banished their opponents. Thus royalists, liberals,

patriots, moderates, etc., each in their turn, have been
expatriated; and as the wheel of fortune and politics
went round, many have returned to their beloved Spain
from bitter exile in France and England. These travellers, in many cases, were sent abroad for the public
good, since they were thus enabled to discover that
some things were better managed on the other side of
the water and Pyrenees. Then and there suspicion
crossed their minds, although they seldom will admit it
to a foreigner, that Spain was not altogether the
richest, wisest, strongest, and first of nations, but
that she might take a hint or two in a few trifles,
among which perhaps the accommodations for man and
beast might be included. The ingress, again, of
foreigners by the facilities offered to travellers by the
increased novelties of steamers, mails, and diligences
necessarily called for more waiters and inns. Every
day, therefore, the fermentation occasioned by the
foreign leaven is going on; and if the national *musto,*
or grape-juice, be not over-drugged with French
brandy, something decent in smell and taste may yet
be produced.

In the sea-ports and large towns on the Madrid roads
the twilight of café and cuisine civilisation is breaking
from La belle France. Monastic darkness is dispelled,
and the age of convents is giving way to that of
kitchens, while the large spaces and ample accommodations of the suppressed monasteries suggest an easy
transition into " first-rate establishments," in which the
occupants will probably pay more and pray less. News,
indeed, have just arrived from Malaga, that certain
ultra-civilised hotels are actually rising, to be defrayed
by companies and engineered by English, who seem to
be as essential in regulating these novelties on the Continent as in the matters of railroads and steamboats.
Rooms are to be papered, brick floors to be exchanged
for boards, carpets to be laid down, fireplaces to be
made, and bells are to be hung, incredible as it may
appear to all who remember Spain as it was. They
will ring the knell of nationality; and we shall be much
mistaken if the grim old Cid, when the first one is

pulled at Burgos, does not answer it himself by knocking the innovator down. Nay, more, for wonders never cease; vague rumours are abroad that secret and solitary closets are contemplated, in which, by some magical mechanism, sudden waters are to gush forth; but this report, like others, *viâ* Madrid and Paris telegraph, requires confirmation. Assuredly, the spirit of the Holy Inquisition, which still hovers over orthodox Spain, will long ward off these English heresies, which are rejected as too bad even by free-thinking France.

The genuine Spanish town inn is called the *posada,* as being meant to mean, a house of *repose* after the pains of travel. Strictly speaking, the keeper is only bound to provide lodging, salt, and the power of cooking whatever the traveller brings with him or can procure out of doors; and in this it differs from the *fonda,* in which meats and drinks are furnished. The *posada* ought only to be compared to its type, the *khan* of the East, and never to the inn of Europe. If foreigners, and especially Englishmen, would bear this in mind, they would save themselves a great deal of time, trouble, and disappointment, and not expose themselves by their loss of temper on the spot, or in their note-books. No Spaniard is ever put out at meeting with neither attention nor accommodation, although he maddens in a moment on other occasions at the slightest personal affront, for his blood boils without fire. He takes these things coolly, which colder-blooded foreigners seldom do. The native, like the Oriental, does not expect to find anything, and accordingly is never surprised at only getting what he brings with him. His surprise is reserved for those rare occasions when he finds anything actually ready, which he considers to be a godsend. As most travellers carry their provisions with them, the uncertainty of demand would prevent mine host from filling his larder with perishable commodities; and formerly, owing to absurd local privileges, he very often was not permitted to sell objects of consumption to travellers, because the lords or proprietors of the town or village had set up other shops, little monopolies of their own. These inconveniences sound worse on paper

than in practice; for whenever laws are decidedly
opposed to common sense and the public benefit, they
are neutralised in practice; the means to elude them are
soon discovered, and the innkeeper, if he has not the
things by him himself, knows where to get them. On
starting next day a sum is charged for lodging, service,
and dressing the food: this is called *el ruido de casa,*
an indemnification to mine host for the *noise,* the dis-
turbance, that the traveller is supposed to have created,
which is the old Italian *incommodo de la casa,* the rout-
ing and inconveniencing of the house; and no word can
be better chosen to express the varied and never-ceas-
ing din of mules, muleteers, songs, dancing, and laughing, the dust, the *row,* which Spaniards, men as well
as beats, kick up. The English traveller, who will have
to pay the most in purse and sleep for his *noise,* will
often be the only quiet person in the house, and might
claim indemnification for the injury done to his
acoustic organs, on the principle of the Turkish soldier
who forces his entertainer to pay him teeth-money, to
compensate for the damage done to his molars and
incisors from masticating indifferent rations.

Akin to the *posada* is the "*parador,*" a word probably derived from Waradah, Arabicè, "a halting-
place;" it is a huge caravansary for the reception of
waggons, carts, and beasts of burden; these large
establishments are often placed outside the town to
avoid the heavy duties and vexatious examinations at
the gates, where dues on all articles of consumption
are levied both for municipal and government purposes.
They are the old *sisa,* a word derived from the Hebrew
Sisah, to take a sixth part, and are now called *el dere-
cho de puertas*, the gate-due; and have always been as
unpopular as the similar *octroi* of France; and as they
are generally farmed out, they are exacted from the
peasantry with great severity and incivility. There is
perhaps no single grievance among the many, in the
mistaken system of Spanish political and fiscal economy,
which tends to create and keep alive, by its daily retail
worry and often wholesale injustice, so great a feeling
of discontent and ill-will towards authority as this does;

it obstructs both commerce and travellers. The officers are, however, seldom either strict or uncivil to the higher classes, and if courteously addressed by the stranger, and told that he is an English gentleman, the official *Cerberi* open the gates and let him pass unmolested, and still more if quieted by the Virgilian sop of a bribe. The laws in Spain are indeed strict on paper, but those who administer them, whenever it suits their private interest, that is ninety-nine times out of a hundred, evade and defeat them; they obey the letter, but do not perform the spirit, " *se obedece, pero no se cumple;*" indeed, the lower classes of officials in particular are so inadequately paid that they are compelled to eke out a livelihood by taking bribes and little presents, which, as *Backshish* in the East, may always be offered, and will always be accepted, as a matter of compliment. The *idea* of a bribe must be concealed; it shocks their dignity, their sense of honour, their " *pundonor;*" if, however, the money be given to the head person as something for his people to drink, the delicate attention is sacked by the chief, properly appreciated, and works its due effect.

Another term, almost equivalent to the " posada," is the " *meson,*" which is rather applicable to the inns of the rural and smaller towns, to the " *hosterias,*" than to those of the greater. The " *mesonero,*" like the Spanish " *ventera,*" has a bad reputation. It is always as well to stipulate something about prices beforehand. The proverb says, " *Por un ladron, pierden ciento en el meson*"—" *Ventera hermosa, mal para la bolsa.*" " For every one who is robbed on the road, a hundred are in the inn."—"The fairer the hostess, the fouler the reckoning." It is among these innkeepers that the real and worst robbers of Spain are to be met with, since these classes of worthies are everywhere only thinking how much they can with decency overcharge in their bills. This is but fair, for nobody would be an innkeeper if it were not for the profit. The trade of innkeeping is among those which are considered derogatory in Spain, where so many Hindoo notions of caste, self-respect, purity of blood, etc., exist. The harbouring strangers for gain is opposed to every ancient and Oriental law of sacred hospitality. Now no Spaniard, if he can help it, likes to degrade himself; this accounts for the number of *fondas* in towns being kept by Frenchmen, Italians, Catalans, Biscayans, who are all *foreigners* in the eye of the Castilian, and disliked and held cheap; accordingly the innkeeper in Don Quixote protests that he is a *Christian,* although a *ventero,* nay, a genuine old one— *Cristiano viejo rancio;* an old Christian being the common term used to distinguish the genuine stock from those renegade Jews and Moors who, rather than leave Spain, became *pseudo-Christians* and publicans.

The country *Parador, Meson, Posada,* and *Venta,* call it how you will, is the Roman stabulum, whose original intention was the housing of cattle, while the accommodation of travellers was secondary, and so it is in Spain to this day. The accommodation for the *beast* is excellent; cool roomy stables, ample mangers, a never-failing supply of fodder and water, every comfort and luxury which the animal is capable of enjoying, is ready on the spot; as regards *man,* it is just the reverse; he must forage abroad for anything he may want. Only a small part of the barn is allotted him, and then he is lodged among the brutes below, or among the trusses and sacks of their food in the lofts above. He finds, in spite of all this, that if he asks the owner what he has got, he will be told that "there is everything," *hay de todo*, just as the rogue of a *ventero* informed Sancho Panza, that his empty larder contained all the birds of the air, all the beasts of the earth, all the fishes of the sea,—a Spanish magnificence of promise, which, when reduced to plain English, too often means, as in that case, there is everything that you have brought with you. This especially occurs in the *venta*s of the out-of-the-way and rarely-visited districts, which, however empty their larders, are full of the spirit of Don Quixote to the brim; and the everyday occurrences in them are so strange, and one's life is so dramatic, that there is much difficulty in "realising," as the Americans say; all is so like being in a dream or at a play, that one scarcely can believe it to be actually taking place, and true. The man of the note-book and the artist almost forget that there is nothing to eat; meanwhile all this food for the mind and portfolio, all this local colour and oddness, is lost upon your Spanish companion, if he be one of the better classes : he is ashamed, where you are enchanted; he blushes at the sad want of civilisation, clean table-cloth, and beef-steaks, and perhaps he is right : at all events, while you are raving about the Goths, Moors, and this lifting up the curtain of two thousand years ago, he is thinking of Mivart's; and when you quote Martial, he and the ventero set you down as talking nonsense, and stark staring mad; nay, a Spanish gentleman is often affronted, and suspects, from the impossibility to him, that such things can be objects of real admiration, that you are laughing at him in your sleeve, and considering his country as Roman, African, or in a word, as un-European, which is what he particularly dislikes and resents.

These *ventas* have from time immemorial been the subject of jests and pleasantries to Spanish and foreign wits. Quevedo and Cervantes indulge in endless diatribes against the roguery of the masters, and the misery of the accommodations, while Gongora compares them to Noah's ark; and in truth they do contain a variety of animals, from the big to the *small,* and more than a pair, of more than one kind of the latter. The word *venta* is derived from the Latin *vendendo,* on the lucus a *non* lucendo principle of etymology, because provisions are *not* sold in it to travellers : old Covarrubias explains this mode of dealing as consisting " especially in *selling* a cat for a hare," which indeed was and is so usual a venta practice, that *venderlo à uno gato por liebre* has become in common Spanish parlance to be equivalent to *doing* or taking one in. The natives do not dislike the feline tribe when well stewed : no cat was safe in the Alhambra, the galley-slaves bagged her in a second. This *venta* trait of Iberian gastronomy did not escape the compiler of Gil Blas.

Be that as it may, a *venta,* strictly speaking, is an isolated country inn, or house of reception on the road, and, if it be not one of physical entertainment, it is at least one of moral, and accordingly figures in prominent characters in all the personal narratives and travels in Spain; it sharpens the wit of both hungry cooks and lively authors, and ingenii largitor *venter* is as old as Juvenal. Many of these *ventas* have been built on a large scale by the noblemen or convent brethren to whom the village or adjoining territory belonged, and some have at a distance quite the air of a gentleman's mansion. Their walls, towers, and often elegant elevations glitter in the sun, gay and promising, while all within is dark, dirty, and dilapidated, and no better than a whitened sepulchre. The ground floor is a sort of common room for men and beasts; the portion appropriated to the stables is often arched over, and is very imperfectly lighted to keep it cool, so that even by day the eye has some difficulty at first in making out the details. The ranges of mangers are fixed round the walls, and the harness of the different animals suspended on the pillars which support the arches; a wide door, always open to the road, leads into this great stable; a small space in the interior is generally left unincumbered, into which the traveller enters on foot or on horseback; no one greets him; no obsequious landlord, bustling waiter, or simpering chambermaid takes any notice of his arrival: the *ventero* sits in the sun smoking, while his wife continues her uninterrupted *chasse* for "small deer" in the thick covers of her daughters' hair; nor does the guest pay much attention to them; he proceeds to a gibbous water-jar, which is always set up in a visible place, dips in with the ladle, or takes from the shelf in the wall an *alcarraza* of cold water; refreshes his baked clay, refills it, and replaces it in its hole on the *taller,* which resembles the decanter stands in a butler's pantry: he then proceeds, unaided by ostler or boots, to select a stall for his beast,—unsaddles and unloads, and in due time applies to the *ventero* for fodder; the difference of whose cool reception contrasts with the eager welcome which

awaits the traveller at bedtime : his arrival is a godsend to the creeping tribe, who, like the *ventero,* have
no regular larder ; it is not upstairs that he eats, but
where *he* is eaten like Polonius ; the walls are frequently
stained with the marks of nocturnal combats, of those
internecine, truly Spanish *guerrillas,* which are waged
without an Elliot treaty, against enemies who, if not
exterminated, murder sleep. Were these fleas and
French ladybirds unanimous, they would eat up a Goliath ;
but fortunately, like other Spaniards, they never act
together, and are consequently conquered and slaughtered in detail ; hence the proverbial expression for great
mortality among men, *mueren como chinches.*

Having first provided for the wants and comforts of
his beast, for " the master's eye fattens the horse," the
traveller begins to think of himself. One, and the
greater side of the building, is destined to the cattle,
the other to their owners. Immediately opposite the
public entrance is the staircase that leads to the upper
part of the building, which is dedicated to the lodg-
ment of fodder, fowls, vermin, and the better class of
travellers. The arrangement of the larger class of
posadas and *ventas* is laid out on the plan of a convent,
and is well calculated to lodge the greatest number of
inmates in the smallest space. The ingress and egress
are facilitated by a long corridor, into which the doors
of the separate rooms open ; these are called " *cuar-
tos,*" whence our word " quarters " may be derived.
There is seldom any furniture in them ; whatever is
wanted, is or is not to be had of the host from some
lock-up store. A rigid puritan will be much distressed
for the lack of any artificial contrivance to hold water ;
the best toilette on these occasions is a river's bank,
but rivers in unvisited interiors of the Castiles are often
rarer even than water-basins. It is, however, no use
to draw nets in streams where there are no fish, nor
to expect to find conveniences which no one else ever
asks for, and those articles which seem to the foreigner
to be of the commonest and daily necessity, are unknown to the natives. However, as there are no carpets to be spoiled, and cold water retains its properties

although brought up in a horse-bucket or in the cook's brass cauldron, ablutions, as the albums express it, can be performed. What a school, after all, a *venta* is to the slaves of comforts, and without how many absolute essentials do they manage to get on, and happily! What lessons are taught of good-humoured patience, and that British sailor characteristic of making the best of every occurrence, and deeming any port a good one in a storm! Complaint is of no use; if you tell the landlord that his wine is more sour than his vinegar, he will gravely reply, " *Señor,* that cannot be, for both came out of the same cask."

The portion of the ground-floor which is divided by the public entrance from the stables, is dedicated to the kitchen and accommodation of the travellers. The kitchen consists of a huge open range, generally on the floor, the *ollas* pots and culinary vessels being placed against the fire arranged in circles, as described by Martial, " multâ villica quem coronat *ollâ,*" who, as a good Spaniard would do to this day, after thirty-five years' absence at Rome, writes, after his return to Spain, to his friend Juvenal a full account of the real comforts that he once more enjoys in his best-beloved patria, and which remind us of the domestic details in the opening chapter of Don Quixote. These rows of pipkins are kept up by round stones called " *sesos,*" *brains;* above is a high, wide chimney, which is armed with ironwork for suspending pots of a large size; sometimes there are a few stoves of masonry, but more frequently they are only the portable ones of the East. Around the blackened walls are arranged pots and pipkins, gridirons and frying-pans, which hang in rows, like tadpoles of all sizes, to accommodate large or small parties, and the more the better; it is a good sign, " *en casa llena, pronto se guisa cena.*" Supper is then sooner ready.

The vicinity of the kitchen fire being the warmest spot, and the nearest to the flesh-pot, is the *querencia,* the favourite " resort " of the muleteers and travelling bagsmen, especially when cold, wet, and hungry. The first come are the best served, says the proverb, in the matters of soup and love. The earliest arrivals take the cosiest corner seats near the fire, and secure the promptest non-attendance; for the better class of guests there is sometimes a "private apartment," or the boudoir of the *ventera*, which is made over to those who bring courtesy in their mouths, and seem to have cash in their pockets; but these out-of-the-way curiosities of comfort do not always suit either author or artist, and the social kitchen is preferable to solitary state. When a stranger enters into it, if he salutes the company, " My lords and knights, do not let your graces molest yourselves," or courteously indicates his desire to treat them with respect, they will assuredly more than return the compliment, and as good breeding is instinctive in the Spaniard, will rise and insist on his taking the best and highest seat. Greater, indeed, is their reward and satisfaction, if they discover that the invited one can talk to them in their own lingo, and understands their feelings by circulating *his* cigars and wine *bota* among them.

At the side of the kitchen is a den of a room, into which the *ventero* keeps stowed away that stock of raw materials which forms the foundation of the national cuisine, and in which garlic plays the first fiddle. The very name, like that of monk, is enough to give offence to most English. The evil consists, however, in the abuse, not in the use : from the quantity eaten in all southern countries, where it is considered to be fragrant, palatable, stomachic, and invigorating, we must assume that it is suited by nature to local tastes and constitutions. Wherever any particular herb grows, there lives the ass who is to eat it. " *Donde crece la escoba, nace el asno que la roya.*" Nor is garlic necessarily either a poison or a source of baseness; for Henry IV. was no sooner born, than his lips were rubbed with a clove of it by his grandfather, after the revered old custom of Bearn.

Bread, wine, and raw garlic, says the proverb, make a young man go briskly, *Pan, vino, y ajo crudo, hacen andar al mozo agudo.* The better classes turn up their noses at this odoriferous delicacy of the lower classes, which was forbidden per statute by Alonzo XI. to his

knights of *La Banda;* and Don Quixote cautions Sancho
Panza to be moderate in this food, as not becoming to
a governor : with even such personages however it is a
struggle, and one of the greatest sacrifices to the altar
of civilisation and *les convenances.* To give Spanish
garlic its due, it must be said that, when administered
by a judicious hand (for, like prussic acid, all depends
on the quantity), it is far milder than the English.
Spanish garlic and onions degenerate after three years'
planting when transplanted into England. They gain
in pungency and smell, just as English foxhounds, when
drafted into Spain, lose their strength and scent in the
third generation. A clove of garlic is called *un diente*,
a tooth. Those who dislike the piquant vegetable must
place a sentinel over the cook of the venta while she is
putting into her cauldron the ingredients of his supper,
or Avicenna will not save him; for if God sends meats,
and here they are a godsend, the evil one provides the
cooks of the venta, who certainly do bedevil many
things.

Thrice happy, then, the man blessed with a provident
servant who has foraged on the road, and comes prepared with cates on which no Castilian Canidia has
breathed; while they are stewing he may, if he be a
poet, rival those sonnets made in Don Quixote on
Sancho's ass, saddle-bags, and sapient attention to their
provend, " *su cuerda providencia.* " The odour and
good tidings of the arrival of unusual delicacies soon
spread far and wide in the village, and generally attract
the *Cura,* who loves to hear something new, and does
not dislike savoury food : the quality of a Spaniard's
temperance, like that of his mercy, is strained; his
poverty and not his will consents to more and other
fastings than to those enjoined by the church; hunger,
the sauce of Saint Bernard, is one of the few wants
which is not experienced in a Spanish venta. Our
practice in one was to invite the curate, by begging
him to bless the pot-luck, to which he did ample justice,
and more than repaid for its visible diminution by good-
fellowship, local information, and the credit reflected on
the stranger in the eyes of the natives, by beholding

him thus patronised by their pastor and master. It is
not to be denied in the case of a stew of partridges, that
deep sighs and exclamations *que rico!* "how rich!"
escape the envious lips of his hungry flock when they
behold and whiff the odoriferous dish as it smokes past
them like a railway locomotive.

Nor, it must be said, was all this hospitality on one
side; it has more than once befallen us in the rude *ventas*
of the Salamanca district, that the silver-haired *cura,*
whose living barely furnished the means whereby to
live, on hearing the simple fact that an Englishman was
arrived, has come down to offer his house and fare.
Such, or indeed any Spaniard's invitation is not to be
accepted by those who value liberty of action or time;
seat rather the good man at the head of the *venta* board,
and regale him with your best cigar, he will tell you of
El gran Lor—the great Lord—the Cid of England; he
will recount the Duke's victories, and dwell on the good
faith, mercy, and justice of our brave soldiers, as he
will execrate the cruelty, rapacity, and perfidy of those
who fled before their gleaming bayonets.

But, to return to first arrival at *ventas*, whether
saddle-bag or stomach be empty or full, the *ventero*
when you enter remains unmoved and imperturbable, as if
he never had had an appetite, or had lost it, or had dined.
Not that his genus ever are seen eating except when
invited to a guest's stew; air, the economical ration of
the chameleon, seems to be his habitual sustenance, and
still more as to his wife and womankind, who never will sit
and eat even with the stranger; nay, in humbler Spanish
families they seem to dine with the cat in some corner,
and on scraps; this is a remnant of the Roman and
Moorish treatment of women as inferiors. Their lord
and husband, the innkeeper, cannot conceive why
foreigners on their arrival are always so impatient, and
is equally surprised at their inordinate appetite; an
English landlord's first question "Will you not like to
take some refreshment?" is the very last which he would
think of putting; sometimes by giving him a cigar, by
coaxing his wife, flattering his daughter, and caressing
Maritornes, you may get a couple of his *pollos* or fowls,

which run about the ground-floor, picking up anything, and ready to be picked up themselves and dressed.

All the operations of cookery and eating, of killing, sousing in boiling water, plucking, et cætera, all preparatory as well as final, go on in this open kitchen. They are carried out by the ventera and her daughters or maids, or by some crabbed, smoke-dried, shrivelled old she-cat, that is, or at least is called, the "*tia*," "my aunt," and who is the subject of the good-humoured remarks of the courteous and hungry traveller before dinner, and of his full stomach jests afterwards. The assembled parties crowd round the fire, watching and assisting each at their own savoury messes, "*Un ojo á la sarten, y otro á la gata*"—"One eye to the pan, the other to the real cat," whose very existence in a *venta*, and among the pots, is a miracle; by the way, the naturalist will observe that their ears and tails are almost always cropped close to the stumps. All and each of the travellers, when their respective stews are ready, form clusters and groups round the frying-pan, which is moved from the fire hot and smoking, and placed on a low table or block of wood before them, or the unctuous contents are emptied into a huge earthen reddish dish, which in form and colour is the precise *paropsis*, the food platter, described by Martial and by other ancient authors. Chairs are a luxury; the lower classes sit on the ground as in the East, or on low stools, and fall to in a most Oriental manner, with an un-European ignorance of forks;[1] for which they substitute a short wooden or horn spoon, or dip their bread into the dish, or fish up morsels with their long pointed knives. They eat copiously, but with gravity—with appetite, but without greediness; for none of any nation, as a mass, are better bred or mannered than the lower classes of Spaniards.

[1] Forks are an Italian invention : old Coryate, who introduced this "neatnesse" into Somersetshire, about 1600, was called *furcifer* by his friends. Alexander Barclay thus describes the previous English mode of eating, which sounds very *ventaish*, although worse mannered :—

"If the dishe be pleasaunt, eyther flesche or fische,
Ten hands at once swarm in the dish."

They are very pressing in their invitations whenever any eating is going on. No Spaniard or Spaniards, however humble their class or fare, ever allow any one to come near or pass them when eating, without inviting him to partake. "*Guste usted comer?*" "Will your grace be pleased to dine?" No traveller should ever omit to go through this courtesy whenever any Spaniards, high or low, approach him when at any meal, especially if taking it out of doors, which often happens in these journeyings; nor is it altogether an empty form; all classes consider it a compliment if a stranger, and especially an Englishman, will condescend to share their dinner. In the smaller towns, those invited by the English will often partake, even the better classes, and who have already dined; they think it civil to accept, and rude to refuse the invitation, and have no objection to eating any given *good* thing, which is the exception to their ordinary frugal habits : all this is quite Arabian. The Spaniards seldom accept the invitation at once; they expect to be urged by an obsequious host, in order to appear to do a gentle violence to their stomachs by eating to oblige *him*. The angels declined Lot's offered hospitalities until they were " pressed *greatly*." Travellers in Spain must not forget this still existing Oriental trait; for if they do not greatly press their offer, they are understood as meaning it to be a mere empty compliment. We have known Spaniards who have called with an intention of staying dinner, go away, because this ceremony was not gone through according to their punctilious notions, to which our off-hand manners are diametrically opposed. Hospitality in a hungry inn-less land becomes, as in the East, a sacred duty; if a man eats all the provender by himself, he cannot expect to have many friends. Generally speaking, the offer is not accepted; it is always declined with the same courtesy which prompts the invitation. "*Muchas gracias, buen provecho le haga á usted,*" " Many thanks—much good may it do your grace," an answer which is analogous to the *prosit* of Italian peasants after eating or sneezing. These customs, both of inviting and declining, tally exactly, and even to the expressions used among the Arabs to this day. Every passer-by is invited by Orientals—"*Bismillah ya see-dee*," which means both a grace and invitation—" In the name of God, sir, (*i.e.*) will you dine with us?" or "*Tafud'-dal*," "Do me the favour to partake of this repast." Those who decline reply, "*Heneê an*," "May it benefit."

Supper, which, as with the ancients, is their principal meal, is seasoned with copious draughts of the wine of the country, drunk out of a jug or *bota* which we have already described, for glasses do not abound; after it is done, cigars are lighted, the rude seats are drawn closer to the fire, stories are told, principally on robber or love events, the latter of which are by far the truest. Jokes are given and taken; laughter, inextinguishable as that of Homer's gods, forms the chorus of conversation, especially after good eating or drinking, to which it is the best dessert. In due time songs are sung, a guitar is strummed, for some black-whiskered Figaro is sure to have heard of the " arrival," and steals down from the pure love of harmony and charms of a cigar; then flock in peasants of both sexes, dancing is set on foot, the fatigues of the day are forgotten, and the catching sympathy of mirth extending to all, is prolonged until far into the night; during which, as they take a long siesta in the day, all are as wakeful as owls, and worse caterwaulers than cats; to describe the scene baffles the art of pen or pencil. The roars, the dust, the want of everything in these low-classed ventas, are emblems of the nothingness of Spanish life—a jest. One by one the company drops off; the better classes go upstairs, the humbler and vast majority make up their bed on the ground, near their animals, and like them, full of food and free from care, fall instantly asleep in spite of the noise and discomfort by which they are surrounded. This counterfeit of death is more equalising, as Don Quixote says, than death itself, for an honest Spanish muleteer stretched on his hard pallet sleeps sounder than many an uneasy trickster head that wears another's crown. "Sleep," says Sancho, "covers one over like a cloak," and a cloak or its cognate mantle forms the best part of their wardrobe by day, and their bed furniture by night. The earth is now, as it was to the Iberians, the national bed; nay, the Spanish word which expresses that commodity, *cama*, is derived from the Greek καμαι. Thus they are lodged on the ground floor, and thereby escape the three classes of little animals which, like the inseparable Graces, are always to be found in fine climates in the wholesale, and in Spanish *ventas* in the retail. Their pillow is composed either of their pack-saddles or saddle-bags; their sleep is short, but profound. Long before daylight all are in motion; "they *take up* their bed," the animals are fed, harnessed, and laden, and the heaviest sleepers awakened: there is little morning toilette, no time or soap is lost by biped or quadruped in the processes of grooming or lavation: both carry their wardrobes on their back, and trust to the shower and the sun to cleanse and bleach; their moderate accounts are paid, salutations or execrations (generally the latter), according to the length of the bills, pass between them and their landlords, and another day of toil begins. Our faithful and trustworthy squire seldom failed for a couple of hours after leaving the *venta* to pour forth an eloquent stream of oaths, invectives, and lamentations at the dearness of inns, the rascality of their keepers in general, and of the host of the preceding night in particular, although probably a couple of dollars had cleared the account for a couple of men and animals, and he himself had divided the extra-extortion with the honest *ventero*.

These Spanish venta scenes vary every day and night, as a new set of actors make their first and last appearance before the traveller: of one thing there can be no mistake, he has got out of England, and the present year of our Lord. Their undeniable smack of antiquity gives them a relish, a *borracha*, which is unknown in Great Britain, where all is fused and modernised down to last Saturday night; here alone can you see and study those manners and events which must have occurred on the same sites when Hannibal and Scipio were last there, as it would be very easy to work out from the classical authors. We would just suggest a comparison between the arrangement of the Spanish country *venta* with that of the Roman inn now uncovered at the entrance of Pompeii, and its exact counterpart, the modern " *osteria*," in the same district of Naples. In the Museo Borbonico will be found types of most of the utensils now used in Spain, while the Oriental and most ancient style of cuisine is equally easy to be identified with the notices left us in the cookery books of antiquity. The same may be said of the tambourines, castanets, songs, and dances,—in a word, of everything; and, indeed, when all are hushed in sleep, and stretched like corpses amid their beasts, the Valencians especially, in their sandals and kilts, in their mantas, and in and on their rush-baskets and mattings, we feel that Strabo must have beheld the old Iberians exactly in the same costume and position, when he told us what we see now to be true, το πλεον εν σαγοις, εν όις περ και στιβαδοκοιτουσι.

The " *ventorillo* " is a lower class of *venta*—for there is a deeper bathos; it is the German *kneipe* or hedge alehouse, and is often nothing more than a mere hut, run up with reeds or branches of trees by the road-side, at which water, bad wine, and brandy, " *aguardiente*," toothwater, are to be sold. The latter is always detestable, raw, and disflavoured with aniseed, and turns white in water like Eau de Cologne, not that the natives ever expose it to such a trial. These " *ventorillos* " are at best suspicious places, and the haunts of the spies of regular robbers, or of skulking footpads when there are any, who lurk inside with the proprietress; she herself generally might sit as a model for Hecate, or for one of the witches in Shakespeare over their cauldron; her attendant imps are, however, sufficiently interesting personages to form a chapter by themselves.

CHAPTER XVI

An *olla* without bacon would scarcely be less insipid than a volume on Spain without banditti; the stimulant is not less necessary for the established taste of the

home-market, than brandy is for pale sherries neat as
imported. In the meantime, while the timid hesitate to
put their heads into this supposed den of thieves as much
as into a house that is haunted, those who are not scared
by shadows, and do not share in the fears of cockney
critics and delicate writers in satin-paper albums, but
adventure boldly into the hornet's nest, come back in a
firm belief in the non-existence of the robber genus. In
Spain, that *pays de l'imprévu*, this unexpected absence
of personages who render roads uncomfortable, is one
of the many and not disagreeable surprises, which await
those who prefer to judge of a country by going there
themselves, rather than to put implicit faith in the foregone conclusions and stereotyped prejudices of those
who have not, although they do sit in judgment on those
who have, and decide " without a view." This very
summer, some dozen and more friends of ours have made
tours in various parts of the Peninsula, driving and
riding unarmed and unescorted through localities of former suspicion, without having the good luck of meeting
even with the ghost of a departed robber; in truth and
fact, we cannot but remember that such things as monks
and banditti were, although they must be spoken of
rather in the past than in the present tense.

The actual security of the Spanish highways is due to
the *Moderados*, as the French party and imitators of the
juste milieu are called, and at the head of whom may be
placed *Señor Martinez de la Rosa*. He, indeed, is a
moderate in poetry as well as politics, and a rare speci-
men of that sublime of mediocrity which, according to
Horace, neither men, gods, nor booksellers can tolerate;
his reputation as an author and statesman—alas! poor
Cervantes and Cisneros—proves too truly the present
effeteness of Spain. Her pen and her sword are blunted,
her laurels are sear, and her womb is barren; but,
among the blind, he who has one eye is king.

This dramatist, in the May of 1833, was summoned
from his exile at Granada to Madrid by the suspicious
Calomarde. The mail in which he travelled was stopped
by robbers about ten o'clock of a wet night near Almu-
radiel;—the *guard*, at the first notice, throwing himself

on his belly, with his face in the mud, in imitation of the postillions, who pay great respect to the gentlemen of the road. The passengers consisted of himself, a German artist, and an English friend of ours now in London, and who, having given up his well-garnished purse at once with great good-humour, was most courteously treated by the well-satisfied recipients: not so the Deutscher, on whom they were about to do personal violence in revenge for a scanty scrip, had not his profession been explained by our friend, by whose interference he was let off. Meanwhile, the *Don* was hiding his watch in the carriage lining, which he cut open, and was concealing his few dollars, the existence of which when questioned he stoutly denied. They, however, re-appeared under threats of the bastinado, which were all but inflicted. The passengers were then permitted to depart in peace, the leader of their spoilers having first shaken hands with our informant, and wished him a pleasant journey: "May your grace go with God and without novelty;" adding, "You are a *caballero*, a gentleman, as all the English are; the German is a *pobrecito*, a poor devil; the Spaniard is an *embustero*, a regular swindler." This latter gentleman, thus hardly delineated by his Lavater countryman, has since more than gotten back his cash, having risen to be prime minister to Christina, and humble and devoted servant of Louis-Philippe, *cosas de España.*

Possibly this little incident may have facilitated the introduction of the mounted guards, who are now stationed in towns, and by whom the roads are regularly patrolled; they are called *guardias civiles*, and have replaced the ancient "brotherhood" of Ferdinand and Isabella. As they have been dressed and modelled after the fashion of the transpyrenean gendarmerie, the Spaniards, who never lose a chance of a happy nickname, or of a fling at the things of their neighbour, whom they do not love, term them, either *Polizontes* or *Polizones*, words with which they have enriched their phraseology, and that represent the French *polissons*, scoundrels, or they call them *Hijos de Luis-Philipe,* "sons of Louis-Philippe;" for they are ill-bred enough, in spite of the Montpensier marriage, and the Nelsonic achievements of Monsieur de Joinville, to consider the words as synonymes.

The number of these rogues, French king's sons, civil guards, call them as you will, exceeds five thousand. During the recent Machiavelianisms of their putative father, they have been quite as much employed in the towns as on the highway, and for political purposes rather than those of pure police, having been used to keep down the expression of indignant public opinion, and, instead of catching thieves, in upholding those first-rate criminals, foreign and domestic, who are now robbing poor Spain of her gold and liberties; but so it has always been. Indeed, when we first arrived in the Peninsula, and naturally made inquiries about banditti, according to all sensible Spaniards, it was not on the road that they were most likely to be found, but in the confessional boxes, the lawyers' offices, and still more in the *bureaux* of government; and even in England some think that purses are exposed to more danger in Chancery Lane and Stone Buildings, than in the worst cross-road, or the most rocky mountain pass in the Peninsula.

It will be long, however, before this " great fact " is believed within the sound of Bow-bells, where many of those who provide the reading public with correct information, dislike having to eat their own words, and to have their settled opinions shaken or contradicted. Nor is it pleasant at a certain time of life to go again to school, as one does when studying Niebuhr's Roman History, and then to find that the alphabet must be re-begun, since all that was thought to be right is in fact wrong. Distant Spain is ever looked at through a telescope which either magnifies richness and goodness, from which half at least must be deducted according to the proverb, *de los dineros y bondad, se ha de quitar la mitad*, or darkens its dangers and difficulties through a discoloured medium. A bad name given to a dog or country is very adhesive; and the many will repeat each other in cuckoo-note. " Il y a des choses," says Montesquieu, " que tout le monde dit, parcequ'elles ont été dites une fois;" thus one silly sheep makes many, who will follow their leader; *ovejas y bobas, donde va una, van todas*. So in the end error becomes stamped with current authority, and is received, until the false, imaginary picture is alone esteemed, and the true, original portrait scouted as a cheat.

It has so long and annually been considered permissible, when writing about romantic Spain, to take leave of common sense, to ascend on stilts, and converse in the Cambyses vein, that those who descend to humble prose, and confine themselves to commonplace matter-of-fact, are considered not only to be inæsthetic, unpoetical, and unimaginative, but deficient in truth and power of observation. The genius of the land, when speaking of itself and its things, is prone to say the thing which is not; and it must be admitted that the locality lends itself often and readily to misconceptions. The leagues and leagues of lonely hills and wastes, over which beasts of prey roam, and above which vultures sulkily rising part the light air with heavy wing, are easily peopled, by those who are in a prepared train of mind, with equally rapacious bipeds of Plato's unfeathered species. Rocky passes, contrived as it were on purpose for ambuscades, tangled glens overrun with underwood, in spite of the prodigality of beauty which arrests the artist, suggest the lair of snakes and robbers. Nor is the feeling diminished by meeting the frequent crosses set up on classically piled heaps, which mark the grave of some murdered man, whose simple, touching epitaph tells the name of the departed, the date of the treacherous stab, and entreats the passenger, who is as he was, and may be in an instant as he is, to pray for his unannealed soul. A shadow of death hovers over such spots, and throws the stranger on his own thoughts, which, from early associations, are somewhat in unison with the scene. Nor is the welcome of the outstretched arms of these crosses over-hearty, albeit they are sometimes hung with flowers, which mock the dead. Nor are all sermons more eloquent than these silent stones, on which such brief emblems are fixed. The Spaniards, from long habit, are less affected by them than foreigners, being all accustomed to behold crosses and bleeding crucifixes

in churches and out; they moreover well know that by
far the greater proportion of these memorials have been
raised to record murders, which have not been perpetrated by robbers, but are the results of sudden quarrel
or of long brooded-over revenge, and that wine and
women, nine times out of ten, are at the bottom of the
calamity. Nevertheless, it makes a stout English heart
uncomfortable, although it is of little use to be afraid
when one is in for it, and on the spot. Then there is
no better chance of escape, than to brave the peril and
to ride on. Turn, therefore, dear reader, a deaf ear to
the tales of local terror which will be told in every out-
of-the-way village by the credulous, timid inhabitants.
You, as we have often been, will be congratulated on
having passed such and such a wood, and will be
assured that you will infallibly be robbed at such and
such a spot a few leagues onward. We have always
found that this ignis fatuus, like the horizon, has re-
ceded as we advanced; the dangerous spot is either a
little behind or a little before the actual place—it van-
ishes, as most difficulties do, when boldly approached
and grappled with.

At the same time these sorts of places and events
admit of much fine writing when people get safely back
again, to say nothing of the dignity and heroic elevation
which may be thus obtained by such an exhibition of
valour during the long vacation. Peaked hats, hair-
breadth escapes from long knives and mustachios, lying
down for an hour on your stomach with your mouth in
the mud, are little interludes so diametrically opposed
to civilisation, and the humdrum unpicturesque routine
of free Britons who pay way and police rates, that they
form almost irresistible topics to the pen of a ready
writer. And such exciting incidents are sure to take,
and to affect the public at home, who, moreover, are
much pleased by the perusal of *authentic* accounts from
Spain itself, and the best and latest intelligence, which
tally with their own preconceived ideas of the land.
Hence those authors are the most popular who put the
self-love of their reader in best humour with his own
stock of knowledge. And this accounts for the fre-

quency, in Peninsular sketches, personal narratives, and so forth, of robberies which are certainly oftener to be met with in their pages than on the plains of the Peninsula. The writers know that a bandit adventure is as much expected in the journals of such travels as in one of Mrs. Ratcliffe's romances; such fleeting books are chiefly made by "*striking events;*" accordingly, the authors string together all the floating traditional horrors which they can scrape together on Spanish roads, and thus feed and keep up the notion entertained in many counties of England, that the whole Peninsula is peopled with banditti. If such were the case society could not exist, and the very fact, of almost all of the reporters having themselves escaped by a miracle, might lead to the inference that most other persons escape likewise : a blot is not a blot till it is hit.

Our ingenious neighbours, strange to say in so gallant a people, have a still more decided bandittiphobia. According to what the badauds of Paris are told in print, every rash individual, before he takes his place in the dilly for Spain, ought by all means to make his will, as was done four hundred years ago at starting on a pilgrimage to Jerusalem; possibly this may be predicated in the spirit of French diplomacy, which always has a concealed arrière pensée, and it may be bruited abroad, on the principle with which illicit distillers and coinforgers give out that certain localities are haunted, in order to scare away others, and thus preserve for themselves a quiet possession. Perhaps the superabundance of l'esprit Français may give colour and substance to forms insignificant in themselves, as a painter lost in a brown study over a coal fire converts cinders into castles, monsters, and other creatures of his lively imagination ; or it may be, as conscience makes cowards of all, that these gentlemen really see a bandit in every bush of Spain, and expect from behind every rock an avenging minister of retaliation, in whose pocket is a list of the church plate, Murillos, etc. which were found missing after their countrymen's invasion. Be that as it may, even so clever a man as Monsieur Quinet, a real Dr. Syntax, fills pages of his recent *Vacances* with his

continual trepidations, although, from having arrived
at his journey's end without any sort of accident, albeit
not without every kind of fear, it might have crossed
him, that the bugbears existed only in his own head,
and he might have concealed, in his pleasant pages, a
frame of mind the exhibition of which, in England at
least, inspires neither interest nor respect; an over-care
of self is not over-heroic.

It must be also admitted that the respectability and
character of many a Spaniard is liable to be misunderstood, when he sets forth on any of his travels, except
in a public wheel conveyance; as we said in our ninth
chapter, he assumes the national costume of the road,
and leaves his wife and long-tailed coat behind him.
Now as most Spaniards are muffled up and clad after
the approved melodrame fashion of robbers, they may
be mistaken for them in reality; indeed they are generally sallow, have fierce black eyes, uncombed hair, and
on these occasions neglect the daily use of towels and
razors; a long beard gives, and not in Spain alone, a
ferocious ruffian-like look, which is not diminished when
gun and knife are added to match faces à la Brutus.
Again, these worthies thus equipped, have sometimes
a trick of staring rather fixedly from under their
slouched hat at the passing stranger, whose, to them,
outlandish costume excites curiosity and suspicion;
naturally therefore some difficulty does exist in distinguishing the merino from the wolf, when both are dis-
guised in the same clothing—a *zamarra* sheepskin to
wit. A private Spanish gentleman, who, in his native
town, would be the model of a peaceable and inoffensive
burgess, or a respectable haberdasher, has, when on his
commercial tour, altogether the appearance of the Bravo
of Venice, and such-like heroes, by whom children are
frightened at a minor theatre. In consequence of the
difficulty of outliving what has been learnt in the nursery, many of our countrymen have, with the best intentions, set down the bulk of the population of the Peninsula as one gang of robbers—they have exaggerated
their numbers like Falstaff's men of buckram; the said
imagined Rinaldo Rinaldinis being probably in a still

greater state of alarm from having on their part taken
our said countrymen for robbers, and this mutual mis-
understanding continues, until both explain their slight
mistake of each other's character and intention.
Although we never fell into the error of thus mistaking
Spanish peaceable traders for privateers and men-of-
war, yet that injustice has been done by them to us;
possibly this compliment may have been paid to our
careful observation of the bearing and garb of their
great Rob Roy himself and in his own country, which,
to one about to undertake, in those days, long and solitary rides over the Peninsula, was an unspeakable
advantage.

But even in those perilous times, robberies were the
exception, not the rule, in spite of the full, whole, and
exact particulars of natives as well as strangers; the
accounts were equally exaggerated by both parties;
in fact, the subject is the standing dish, the common
topic of the lower classes of travellers, when talking
and smoking round the venta fires, and forms the
natural and agreeable religio loci, the associations connected with wild and cut-throat localities. Though
these narrators' pleasure is mingled with fear and pain,
they delight in such histories as children do in goblin
tales. Their Oriental amplification is inferior only to
their credulity, its twin sister, and they end in believing
their own lies. Whenever a robbery really does take place,
the report spreads far and wide, and gains in detail and
atrocity, for no muleteer's story or sailor's yarn loses
in the telling. The same dire event,—names, dates,
and localities only varied,—is served up, as a monkish
miracle in the mediæval ages was, at many other places,
and thus becomes infinitely multiplied. It is talked of
for months all over the country, while the thousands
of daily passengers who journey on unhurt are never
mentioned. It is like the lottery, in which the great
prize alone attracts attention, not the infinite majority
of blanks. These robber-tales reach the cities, and are
often believed by most respectable people, who pass
their lives without stirring a league beyond the walls.
They sympathise with all who are compelled to expose

themselves to the great pains and perils, the travail
of travel, and they endeavour with the most good-
natured intentions to dissuade rash adventurers from
facing them, by stating as facts, the apprehensions of
their own credulity and imagination.

The muleteers, *venteros,* and masses of common
Spaniards see in the anxious faces of timid strangers,
that their audience is in the listening and believing vein,
and as they are garrulous and egotists by nature, they
seize on a theme on which they alone hold forth; they
are pleased at being considered an authority, and with
the superiority which conveying information gives, and
the power of inspiring fear confers; their mother-wit,
in which few nations surpass them, soon discovers the
sort of information which " our correspondent " is in
want of, and as words here cost nothing, the gulping
gobemouche is plentifully supplied with the required
article.   These reports are in due time set up in type,
and are believed because in print; thus the tricks played
on poor Mr. Inglis and his note-book were the laughter
of the whole Peninsula, grave authorities caught the
generous infection, until Mr. Mark's robber-jokes at
Malaga were booked and swallowed as if he had been
an apostle instead of a consul.

As it was our fate to have wandered up and down
the Peninsula when Ferdinand VII. was king of the
Spains, and Jose Maria, at whose name old men and
women there tremble yet, was autocrat of Andalucia,
the moment was propitious for studying the philosophy
of Spanish banditti, and our speculations were much
benefited by a fortunate acquaintance with the redoubtable chief himself, from whom, as well as from many
of his intelligent followers, we received much kindness
and valuable information, which is acknowledged with
thankfulness.

Historically speaking, Spain has never enjoyed a good
character in this matter of the highway; it had but an
indifferent reputation in the days of antiquity, but then,
as now, it was generally the accusation of foreigners.
The Romans, who had no business to invade it, were
harassed by the native guerrilleros, those undisciplined

bands who waged the " little war," which Iberia always
did. Worried by these unmilitary voltigeurs, they
called all Spaniards who resisted them "*latrones;*" just
as the French invaders, from the same reasons, called
them *ladrones* or brigands, because they had no uniform; as if the wearing a schako given by a plundering
marshal, could convert a pillager into an honest man,
or the want of it could change into a thief, a noble
patriot who was defending his own property and
country; but l'habit ne fait pas le moine, say the French,
and *aunque la mona se viste de seda, mona se queda,*
although a monkey dresses in silk, monkey it remains,
rejoin the Spaniards.

Armed men are in fact the weed of the soil of Spain,
in peace or war; to have their hand against all mankind
seems to be an instinct in every descendant of Ishmael,
and particularly among this Quixotic branch, whose
knight-errants, reformers on horseback, have not un-
frequently been robbers in the guise of gentlemen.
During the war against Buonaparte, the Peninsula
swarmed with insurgents, many of whom were inspired, by a sense of loyalty, with indignation at their
outraged religion, and with a deep-rooted national
loathing of the *gabacho,* and good service did these
Minas and Co. do to the cause of their lawful king;
but others used patriotic professions as specious cloaks
to cover their instinctive passion for a lawless and free-
booting career, and before the liberation of the country
was effected, had become formidable to all parties alike.
The Duke of Wellington, with his characteristic saga-
city, foresaw, at his victorious conclusion of the
struggle, how difficult it would be to weed out " this
strange fruit borne on a tree grafted by patriotism."
The transition from murdering a Frenchman, to plundering a stranger, appeared a simple process to these
patriotic scions, whose numbers were swelled with all
who were, or who considered themselves to be, ill used
—with all who could not dig, and were ashamed to beg.
The evil was diminished during the latter years of the
reign of Ferdinand VII., when the old hands began to
die off, and an advance in social improvement was un-

questionably general, before which these lawless occupations gave way, as surely as wild animals of prey do before improved cultivation. These evils, that are abated by internal quiet and the continued exertions of the authorities, increase with troubled times, which, as the tempest calls forth the stormy petrel, rouse into dangerous action the worst portions of society, and create a sort of civil cachexia, as we now see in Ireland.

Another source was, not to say is, Gibraltar, that hotbed of contraband, that nursery of the smuggler, the *prima materia* of a robber and murderer. The financial ignorance of the Spanish government calls him in, to correct the errors of Chancellors of Exchequers :— "trovata la legge, trovato l'inganno." The fiscal regulations are so ingeniously absurd, complicated, and vexatious, that the honest, legitimate merchant is as much embarrassed as the irregular trader is favoured. The operation of excessive duties on objects which people must, and therefore will have, is as strikingly exemplified in the case of tobacco in Andalucia, as it is in that, and many other articles on the Kent and Sussex coasts : in both countries the fiscal scourge leads to breaches of the peace, injury to the fair dealer, and loss to the revenue : it renders idle, predatory and ferocious, a peasantry which, under a wiser system, and if not exposed to overpowering temptation, might become virtuous and industrious. In Spain the evasion of such laws is only considered as cheating those who cheat the people ; the villagers are heart and soul in favour of the smuggler, as they are of the poacher in England ; all their prejudices are on his side. Some of the mountain curates, whose flocks are all in that line, deal with the crime in their sermons as a conventional, not a moral, one ; and, like other people, decorate their mantelpieces with a painted clay figure of the sinner in his full *majo* dress. The smuggler himself, so far from feeling degraded, enjoys the reputation which attends success in personal adventure, among a people proud of individual prowess ; he is the hero of the Spanish stage, and comes on equipped in full costume, with his blunder-

buss, to sing the well-known "*Yo! que soy contra-
brandista! yo ho!*" to the delight of all listeners from
the Straits to the Bidasoa, custom-house officers not
excepted.

The *prestige* of such a theatrical exhibition, like the
"Robbers" of Schiller, is enough to make all the
students of Salamanca take to the high-road. The contrabandista is the Turpin, the Macheath of reality, and
those heroes of the old ballads and theatres of England, who have disappeared more in consequence of
enclosures, rapid conveyances, and macadamisation (for
there is nothing so hateful to a highwayman as gas and
a turnpike), than from fear of the prison or the halter.
The writings of Smollett, the recollections of many now
alive of the dangers of Hounslow Heath and Finchley
Common, recall scenes of life and manners from which
we have not long emerged, and which have still more
recently been corrected in Spain. The contrabandista
in his real character is welcome in every village; he is
the newspaper and channel of intelligence; he brings
tea and gossip for the curate, money and cigars for the
attorney, ribands and cottons for the women; he is
magnificently dressed, which has a great charm for all
Moro-Iberian eyes; he is bold and resolute—"none but
the brave deserve the fair;" a good rider and shot;
he knows every inch of the intricate country, wood or
water, hill or dale; in a word, he is admirably educated
for the high-road—for what Froissart, speaking of the
celebrated Amerigot Tetenoire, calls "a fayre and
godlie life." And the transition from plundering the
king's revenue, to taking one of his subjects' purse on
the highway, is easy.

Many circumstances combined to make this freeboot-
ing career popular among the lower classes. The delight of power, the exhibition of daring and valour, the
temptation of sudden wealth, always so attractive to
half-civilised nations, who prefer the rich spoil won by
the bravery of an hour, to that of the drudgery of years;
the gorgeous apparel, the lavish expenditure, the song,
the wassail, the smiles of the fair, and all the joyous
life of liberty, freemasonry, and good fellowship,

operated with irresistible force on a warlike, energetic, and imaginative population.

This smuggling was the origin of Jose Maria's career, who rose to the highest rank and honours of his profession, as did *Napoléon le Grand* and "Jonathan Wild the Great," and principally, as Fielding says of his hero, by a power of doing mischief, and a principle of considering honesty to be a corruption of *honosty,* the qualities of an ass (ονος). But it is a great mistake to suppose that there always are men fitted to be captains of formidable gangs; nature is chary in the production of such specimens of dangerous grandeur, and as ages may elapse before the world is cursed with another Alaric, Buonaparte, or Wild, so years may pass before Spain witnesses again another Jose Maria.

The *Ladron en grande,* the robber on a great scale, is the grandee of the first class in his order; he is the captain of a regularly-organised band of followers, from eight to fourteen in number, well armed and mounted, and entirely under command and discipline. These are very formidable; and as they seldom attack any travellers except with overwhelming forces, and under circumstances of ambuscade and surprise, where every thing is in their favour, resistance is generally useless, and can only lead to fatal accidents. Never, for the sake of a sac de nuit, risk being sent to Erebus; submit, therefore, at once and with good grace to the summons, which will take no denial, of "*abajo,*" down, "*boca á tierra,*" mouth to the earth. Those who have a score or so of dollars, four or five pounds, the loss of which will ruin no man, are very rarely ill-used; a frank, confident, and good-humoured surrender not only prevents any bad treatment, but secures even civility during the disagreeable operation; pistols and sabres are, after all, a poor defence compared to civil words, as Mr. Cribb used to say. The Spaniard, by nature high-bred and a "*caballero,*" responds to any appeal to qualities of which he thinks his nation has reason to be proud; he respects coolness of manner, in which bold men, although robbers, sympathise. Why should a man, because he loses a few dollars, lose also his presence of

mind or temper, or perhaps life? Nor are these grandees of the system without a certain magnanimity, as
Cervantes knew right well. Witness his graphic
account of Roque Guinart, whose conduct to his
victims and behaviour to his comrades tallied, to our
certain knowledge, with that observed by Jose Maria,
and was perfectly analogous to the similar traits of
character exhibited by the Italian bandit Ghino de
Tacco, the immortalised by Dante, as well as by our
Robin Hood and Diana's foresters. Being strong,
they could afford to be generous and merciful.

Notwithstanding these moral securities, if only by
way of making assurance doubly sure, an Englishman
will do well when travelling in exposed districts to be
provided with a decent bag of dollars, which makes a
handsome purse, feels heavy in the hand, and is that
sort of amount which the Spanish brigand thinks a
native of our proverbially rich country ought to have
with him on his travels. He has a remarkable tact in
estimating from the look of an individual, his equipage,
etc., how much ready money it is befitting his condition for him to have about him; if the sum should not
be enough, he resents severely his being robbed of the
regular perquisite to which he considers himself entitled
by the long-established usage of the high-road. The
person unprovided altogether with cash is generally
made a severe example of, pour encourager les autres,
either by being well beaten or stripped to the skin, after
the fashion of the thieves of old, near Jericho. The
traveller should have a watch of some kind—one with
a gaudy gilt chain and seals is the best suited; not to
have one exposes him to more indignities than a
scantily-filled purse. The money may have been spent,
but the absence of a watch can only be accounted for by
a premeditated intention of not being robbed of it, which
the " ladron " considers as a most unjustifiable attempt
to defraud him of his right.

The Spanish " ladrones " are generally armed with a
blunderbuss, that hangs at their high-peaked saddles,
which are covered with a white or blue fleece, emblem-
atical enough of shearing propensities; therefore, per-

haps, the order of the golden fleece has been given to certain foreigners, in reward for having eased Spain of her independence and Murillos. Their dress is for the most part very rich, and in the highest style of the fancy; hence they are the envy and models of the lower classes, being arrayed after the fashion of the smuggler, or the bull-fighter, or in a word, the " *majo* " or dandy of Andalucia, which is the home and head-quarters of all those who aspire to the elegant accomplishments and professions just alluded to. The next class of robbers —omitting some minor distinctions, such as the " *salteadores*," or two or three persons who lie in ambuscade and *jump out* on the unprepared traveller—is the " *ratero*," " the rat." He is not brought regularly up to the profession and organised, but takes to it on a sudden, and for the special occasion which, according to the proverb, makes a thief, *La ocasion hace el ladron;* and having committed his petty larceny, returns to his pristine occupation or avocation.

The " *raterillo*," or small rat, is a skulking footpad, who seldom attacks any but single and unprotected passengers, who, if they get robbed, have no one to blame but themselves; for no man is justified in exposing Spaniards to the temptation of doing a little something in that line. The shepherd with his sheep, the ploughman at his plough, the vine-dresser amid his grapes, all have their gun, ostensibly for their individual protection, which furnishes means of assault and battery against those who have no other defence but their legs and virtue. These self-same extemporaneous thieves are, however, remarkably civil to armed and prepared travellers; to them they touch their hats, and exclaim, " Good day to you, my lord knight," and " May your grace go with God," with all that innocent simplicity which is observable in pastorals, opera-ballets, and other equally correct representations of rural life. These rats are held in as profound contempt by the higher classes of the profession, as political ones used to be, before parties were betrayed by turncoats, who, with tails and without, deserted to the enemies' camp. The *ladron en grande* looks down on this sneaking competitor as a regular M.D. and member of the College of Physicians does on a quack, who presumes to take fees and kill without a licence. However despicable, these rats are very dangerous; lacking the generous feeling which the possession of power and united force bestows, they have the cowardice and cruelty of weakness : hence they frequently murder their victim, because dead men tell no tales.

The distinction between these higher and lower classes of rogues will be better understood by comparing the Napoleon of war, with the Napoleon of peace. The Corsican was the *ladron en grande;* he warred against mankind, he led his armed followers to pillage and plunder, he made his den the receiving house of the stolen goods of the Continent : but he did it openly and manfully by his own right hand and good sword; and valour and audacity are qualities too high and rare not to command admiration—qualified, indeed, when so misapplied. Louis-Philippe is a *ratero,* who, skulking under disguise of amity and good faith, works out in the dark, and by cunning, his ends of avarice and ambition; who, acting on the artful dodger (no) principle, while kissing the Queen, picks her pocket of a crown.

It must be stated for the purposes of history that at the time when Spain was, or was said to be, overrun with rats and robbers, there was, as Spaniards have it, a remedy for everything except death; and as the evils were notorious, it was natural that means of prevention should likewise exist. If the state of things had been so bad as exaggerated report would infer, it would have been impossible that any travelling or traffic could have been managed in the Peninsula. The mails and diligences, being protected by government, were seldom attacked, and those who travelled by other methods, and had proper recommendations, seldom failed in being provided by the authorities with a sufficient escort. A regular body of men was organised for that purpose; they were called " *Miguelites,*" from, it is said, one Miguel de Prats, an armed satellite of the famous or infamous Cæsar Borgia. In Catalonia they are called " *Mozos de la Escuadra,*" " Lads of the

squadron, land marines;" they are the modern "*Her-
mandad*," the brotherhood which formed the old
Spanish rural armed police. Composed of picked and
most active young men, they served on foot, under the
orders of the military powers; they were dressed in a
sort of half uniform and half *majo* costume. Their
gaiters were black instead of yellow, and their jackets
of blue trimmed with red. They were well armed with
a short gun and a belt round the waist in which the
ammunition was placed, a much more convenient contrivance than our cartouche-box; they had a sword, a
cord for securing prisoners, and a single pistol, which
was stuck in their sashes, at their backs. This corps
was on a perfect par with the robbers, from whom some
of them were chosen; indeed, the common condition of
the "*indulto*," or pardon to robbers, is to enlist, and
extirpate their former associates—set a thief to catch
a thief; both the honest and renegade *Miguelites* hunted
"*la mala gente*," as gamekeepers do poachers. The
robbers feared and respected them; an escort of ten or
twelve *Miguelites* might brave any number of banditti,
who never or rarely attack where resistance is to be
anticipated; and in travelling through suspected spots
these escorts showed singular skill in taking every precaution, by throwing out skirmishers in front and at the
sides. They covered in their progress a large space of
ground, taking care never to keep above two together,
nor more distant from each other than gun-shot; rules
which all travellers will do well to remember, and to
enforce on all occasions of suspicion. The rare instances in which Englishmen, especially officers of the
garrison of Gibraltar, have been robbed, have arisen
from a neglect of this precaution; when the whole party
ride together they may be all caught at once, as in a
casting-net.

It may be remarked that Spanish robbers are very
shy in attacking armed English travellers, and particularly if they appear on their guard. The robbers
dislike fighting, and the more as they do so at a disadvantage, from having a halter round their necks, and
they hate danger, from knowing what it is; they have

no chivalrous courage, nor any more abstract notions of fair play than a Turk or a tiger, who are too un-civilised to throw away a chance; accordingly, they sel-dom join issue where the defendants seem pugnacious, which is likely to be the case with Englishmen. They also peculiarly dislike English guns and gunpowder, which, in fact, both as arms and ammunition, are in-finitely superior to those of Spain. Though three or four Englishmen had nothing to fear, yet where there were ladies it was better to be provided with an escort of *Miguelites*. These men have a keen and accurate eye, and were always on the look-out for prints of horses and other signs, which, escaping the notice of super-ficial observers, indicated to their practised observa-tions the presence of danger. They were indefatigable, keeping up with a carriage day and night, braving heat and cold, hunger and thirst. As they were maintained at the expense of the government, they were not, strictly speaking, entitled to any remuneration from those travellers whom they were directed to escort; it was, however, usual to give to each man a couple of *pesetas* a-day, and a dollar to their leader. The trifling addi-tion of a few cigars, a " *bota* " or two of wine, some rice and dried cod-fish for their evening meal, was well bestowed; exercise sharpened their appetites; and they were always proud to drink to their master's long life and purse, and protect both.

Those, whether natives or foreigners, who could not obtain or afford the expense of an escort to themselves, availed themselves of the opportunity of joining com-pany with some party who had one. It is wonderful how soon the fact of an escort being granted was known, and how the number of travellers increased, who were anxious to take advantage of the convoy. As all go armed, the united allied forces became more for-midable as the number increased, and the danger be-came less. If no one happened to be travelling with an escort, then travellers waited for the passage of troops, for the government's sending money, tobacco, or any-thing else which required protection. If none of these opportunities offered, all who were about to travel joined company. This habit of forming caravans is very Oriental, and has become quite national in Spain, insomuch that it is almost impossible to travel alone, as others will join; weaker and smaller parties will unite with all stronger and larger companies whom they meet going the same road, whether the latter like it or not. The muleteers are most social and gregarious amongst each other, and will often endeavour to derange their employer's line of route, in order to fall in with that of their chance-met comrades. The caravan, like a snow-ball, increases in bulk as it rolls on; it is often pretty considerable at the very outset, for, even before starting, the muleteers and proprietors of carriages, being well known to each other, communicate mutually the number of travellers which each has got.

Travelling in out-of-the-way districts in a " coche de colleras," and especially if accompanied with a baggage-waggon, exposes the party to be robbed. When the caravan arrives in the small villages it attracts imme-diate notice, and if it gets wind that the travellers are foreigners, they are supposed to be laden with gold and booty. Such an arrival is a rare event; the news spreads like wildfire, and collects all the " mala gente," the bad set of idlers and loiterers, who act as spies, and convey intelligence to their confederates; again, the bulk of the equipage, the noise and clatter of men and mules, is seen and heard from afar, by robbers if there be any, who lurk in hiding-places or eminences, and are well provided with telescopes, besides with longer and sharper noses, which, as Gil Blas says, smell coin in travellers' pockets, while the slow pace and impossibility of flight renders such a party an easy prey to well-mounted horsemen.

This condition of affairs, these dangers real or imaginary, and these precautions, existed principally in journeys by cross roads, or through provinces rarely visited, and unprovided with public carriages; if, how-ever, such districts were reputed the worst, they often had the advantage of being freer from regular bands, for where there are few passengers, why should there be robbers, who like spiders place their nets where the supply of flies is sure?—and little do the humbler masses of Spain care either for robbers or revolutionists; they have nothing to lose, and are beneath the notice of pickpockets or pseudo-patriots. Their rags are their safeguard, a fine climate clothes them, a fertile soil feeds them; they doze away in the happy want and poverty, ever the best protections in Spain, or strum their guitars and sing staves in praise of empty purses. The better provided have to look out for themselves; indeed, whenever the law is insufficient men take it into their own hands, either to protect themselves or their property, or to administer wild justice, and obtain satisfaction for wrongs, which in plain Spanish is called revenge. An Irish landlord arms his servants and raises walls round his " demesne "— an English squire employs watchers and keepers to preserve his pheasants—so in suspected localities a Spanish hidalgo protects his person by hiring armed peasants; they are called " *escopeteros*," people with guns—a definition which is applicable to most Spaniards. When out of town this custom of going armed, and early acquaintance with the use of the gun, is the principal reason why, on the shortest notice, bodies of men, whom the Spaniards call soldiers, are got together; every field furnishes the raw material—a man with a musket. Baggage, commissariat, pay, rations, uniform, and discipline, which are European rather than Oriental, are more likely to be found in most other armies than in those of Spain. These things account for the facility with which the Spanish nation flies so magnanimously to arms, and after bush-fighting and buccaneering expeditions, disappears at once after a reverse; " every man to his own home," as of old in the East, and that, with or without proclamation. These " *escopeteros*," occasionally robbers themselves, live either by robbery or by the prevention of it; for there is some honour among thieves; " *entre lobos no se come*," " wolves don't eat each other " unless very hard up indeed. These fellows naturally endeavour to alarm travellers with over-exaggerated accounts of danger, ogres and antres vast, in order that their ser-

vices may be engaged; their inventions are often believed by swallowers of camels, who note down as facts,
these tricks upon travellers got up for the occasion,
by people who are making long noses at them, behind
their backs; but these longer lies are among the accidents of long journeys, " *en luengas vias, luengas
mentiras.*"

As we are now writing history, it may be added that
great men like Jose Maria often granted passports.
This true trooper of the Deloraine breed was untram-
melled with the fetters of spelling. Although he could
barely write his name, he could *rubricate* [1] as well as
any other Spaniard in command, or Ferdinand VII.
himself. " His mark " was a protection to all who
would pay him black mail. It was authenticated with
such a portentous griffonage as would have done credit
to Ali Pacha. An intimate friend of ours, a merry
gastronomic dignitary of Seville, who was going to the
baths of Caratraca, to recover from over-indulgence in
rich ollas and valdepeñas, and had no wish, like the
gouty abbot of Boccaccio, to be put on robber regimen,
procured a pass from Jose Maria, and took one of his
gang as a travelling escort, who sat on the coach-box,
and whom he described to us as his " *santito,*" his little
guardian angel.

While on the subject of this spiritual and supernatural protection, it may be added that firm faith was
placed in the wearing a relic, a medal of the Virgin,
her rosary or scapulary. Thus the Duchess of Abrantes
this very autumn hung the *Virgen del Pilar* round the
neck of her favourite bull-fighter, who escaped in con-

---

[1] The kings of Spain seldom use any other royal signature,
except the ancient Gothic *rubica,* or mark. This monogram is
something like a Runic knot. Spaniards exercise much ingenuity in these intricate flourishes, which they tack on to their
names, as a collateral security of authenticity. It is said that a
rubrica without a name is of more value than a name without
a rubrica. Sancho Panza tells Don Quixote that his rubrica
alone is worth, not one, but three hundred jackasses. Those
who cannot write rubricate; " *No saber firmar,*"—not to know
how to sign one's name,—is jokingly held in Spain to be one of
the attributes of grandeeship.

sequence. Few Spanish soldiers go into battle without such a preservative in their *petos,* or stuffed waddings, which is supposed to turn bullets, and to divert fire, like a lightning conductor, which probably it does, as so few are ever killed. In the more romantic days of Spain no duel or tournament could be fought without a declaration from the combatants, that they had no relic, no *engaño* or cheat, about their persons. Our friend Jose Maria attributed his constant escapes to an image of the Virgin of Grief of Cordova, which never quitted his shaggy breast. Indeed, the native districts of the lower classes in Spain may be generally known by their religious ornaments. These talismanic amulets are selected from the saint or relic most honoured, and esteemed most efficacious, in their immediate vicinity. Thus the " Santo Rostro," or Holy Countenance of Jaen, is worn all over the kingdom of Granada, as the Cross of Caravaca is over Murcia; the rosary of the Virgin is common to all Spain. The following miraculous proof of its saving virtues was frequently painted in the convents :—A robber was shot by a traveller and buried; his comrades, some time afterwards passing by, heard his voice,—" this fellow in the cellarage;"— they opened the grave and found him alive and unhurt, for when he was killed, he had happened to have a rosary round his neck, and Saint Dominick (its inventor) was enabled to intercede with the Virgin in his behalf. This reliance on the Virgin is by no means confined to Spain, since the Italian banditti always wear a small silver heart of the Madonna, and this mixture of ferocity and superstition is one of the most terrific features of their character. Saint Nicholas, however, the English " Old Nick," is in all countries the patron of schoolboys, thieves, or, as Shakespeare calls them, " Saint Nicholas's clerks." " Keep thy neck for the hangman, for I know thou worshippest St. Nicholas as a man of falsehood may;" and like him, Santu Diavolu, Santu Diavoluni, Holy Devil, is the appropriate saint of the Sicilian bandit.

San Dimas, the " good thief," is a great saint in Andalucia, where his disciples are said to be numerous.

A celebrated carving by Montañes, in Seville, is called
" *El Cristo, del buen ladron,*"—" the Christ, *of* the
good thief;" thus making the Saviour a subordinate
person.   Spanish robbers have always been remarkably
good Roman Catholics.   In the Rinconete y Cortadillo,
the Lurker and Cutpurse of Cervantes, whose Moni-
podio must have furnished Fagin to Boz, a box is placed
before the Virgin, to which each robber contributes, and
one remarks that he " robs for the service of God, and
for all honest fellows."   Their mountain confessors of
the Friar Tuck order, animated by a pious love for
dollars when expended in expiatory masses, consider
the payment to them of good doubloons such a laudable restitution, such a sincere repentance, as to entitle
the contrite culprit to ample absolution, plenary indulgence, and full benefit of clergy.   Notwithstanding this,
these ungrateful " good thieves " have been known to
rob their spiritual pastors and masters, when they catch
them on the high road.

To return to the saving merit of these talismans.   We
ourselves suspended to our sheepskin jacket one of the
silver medals of Santiago, which are sold to pilgrims at
Compostella, and arrived back again to Seville from
the long excursion, safe and sound and unpillaged except by *venteros* and our faithful squire—an auspicious
event, which was entirely attributed by the aforesaid
dignitary to the intervention vouchsafed by the patron
of the Spains to all who wore his order, which thus
protects the bearer as a badge does a Thames water-
man from a press-gang.

An account of the judicial death of one of the gang
of Jose Maria, which we witnessed, will be an appropriate conclusion to these remarks, and an act of justice
towards our fair readers for this detail of breaches of
the peace, and the bad company into which they have
been introduced.   Jose de Roxas, commonly called (for
they generally have some nickname) *El Veneno,*
" Poison," from his viper-like qualities, was surprised
by some troops: he made a desperate resistance, and
when brought to the ground by a ball in his leg, killed
the soldier who rushed forward to secure him.   He

proposed when in prison to deliver up his comrades if
his own life were guaranteed to him. The offer was
accepted, and he was sent out with a sufficient force;
and such was the terror of his name, that they sur-
rendered themselves, *not however to him,* and were
pardoned. Veneno was then tried for his previous
offences, found guilty, and condemned : he pleaded that
he had indirectly accomplished the object for which his
life was promised him, but in vain; for such trials in
Spain are a mere form, to give an air of legality to a
predetermined sentence :—the authorities adhered to the
killing letter of their agreement, and

> " Kept the word of promise to the ear,
> But broke it to the hope."

As Veneno was without friends or money, wherewith
Gines Passamonte anointed the palm of justice and got
free, the sentence was of course to be carried into
effect. The courts of law and the prisons of Seville are
situated near the Plaça San Francisco, which has always
been the site of public executions. On the day previous
nothing indicates the scene which will take place on the
following morning; everything connected with this ceremony of death is viewed with horror by Spaniards, not
from that abstract abhorrence of shedding blood which
among other nations induces the lower orders to detest
the completer of judicial sentences, as the smaller
feathered tribes do the larger birds of prey, but from
ancient Oriental prejudices of pollution, and because
all actually employed in the operation are accounted
infamous, and lose their caste, and purity of blood.
Even the gloomy scaffolding is erected in the night by
unseen, unknown hands, and rises from the earth like
a fungus work of darkness, to make the day hideous
and shock the awakening eye of Seville. When the
criminal is of noble blood the platform, which in ordinary cases is composed of mere carpenter's work, is
covered with black baize. The operation of hanging,
among so unmechanical a people, with no improved
patent invisible drop, used to be conducted in a cruel
and clumsy manner. The wretched culprits were

dragged up the steps of the ladder by the executioner, who then mounted on their shoulders and threw himself off with his victims, and, while both swung backwards and forwards in the air, was busied, with spider-like fingers, in fumbling about the neck of the sufferers, until being satisfied that life was extinct he let himself down to the ground by the bodies. Execution by hanging was, however, graciously abolished by Ferdinand VII., the beloved; this father of his people determined that the future death for civil offences should be strangulation, —a mode of removing to a better world those of his children who deserved it, which is certainly more in accordance with the Oriental bowstring.

Veneno was placed, as is usual, the day before his execution, " *en capilla* " in a chapel or cell set apart for the condemned, where the last comforts of religion are administered. This was a small room in the prison, and the most melancholy in that dwelling of woe, for such indeed, as Cervantes from sad experience knew, and described a Spanish prison to be, it still is. An iron grating formed the partition of the corridor, which led to the chamber. This passage was crowded with members of a charitable brotherhood, who were collecting alms from the visitors, to be expended in masses for the eternal repose of the soul of the criminal. There were groups of officers, and of portly Franciscan friars smoking their cigars and looking carefully from time to time into the amount of the contributions, which were to benefit their bodies, quite as much as the soul of the condemned. The levity of those assembled without formed, meantime, a heartless contrast with the gloom and horror of the melancholy interior. A small door opened into the cell, over which might well be inscribed the awful words of Dante—

" Lasciate ogni speranza, voi ch' entrate !"

At the head of this room was placed a table, with a crucifix, an image of the Virgin, and two wax tapers, near which stood a silent sentinel with a drawn sword; another soldier was stationed at the door, with a fixed bayonet. In a corner of this darkened apartment was

the pallet of Veneno; he was lying curled up like a
snake, with a striped coverlet (the Spanish *manta*)
drawn closely over his mouth, leaving visible only a
head of matted locks, a glistening dark eye, rolling rest-
lessly out of the white socket. On being approached he
sprung up and seated himself on a stool : he was almost
naked; a chaplet of beads hung across his exposed
breast, and contrasted with the iron chains around his
limbs :—Superstition had riveted her fetters at his birth,
and the Law her manacles at his death.   The expression
of his face, though low and vulgar, was one which once
seen is not easily forgotten,—a slouching look of more
than ordinary guilt : his sallow complexion appeared
more cadaverous in the uncertain light, and was heightened by a black, unshorn beard, growing vigorously on
a half-dead countenance. He appeared to be reconciled to his fate, and repeated a few sentences, the
teaching of the monks, as by rote : his situation was
probably more painful to the spectator than to himself
—an indifference to death, arising rather from an ignorance of its dreadful import, than from high moral courage : he was the Bernardine of Shakespeare, " a man
that apprehends death no more dreadfully than a
drunken sleep, careless, reckless, and fearless of what's
past, present, and to come, insensible of mortality, and
desperately mortal."

Next morning the triple tiers of the old balconies, roofs,
and whole area of the Moorish and most picturesque
square were crowded by the lower orders; the men
wrapped up in their cloaks—(it was a December morning)—the women in their mantillas, many with young
children in their arms, brought in the beginning of life to
witness its conclusion. The better classes not only
absent themselves from these executions, but avoid any
allusion to the subject as derogatory to European civilisation; the humbler ranks, who hold the conventions of
society very cheap, give loose to their morbid curiosity
to behold scenes of terror, which operates powerfully on
the women, who seem impelled irresistibly to witness
sights the most repugnant to their nature, and to behold
sufferings which they would most dread to undergo;
they, like children, are the great lovers of the horrible,

whether in a tale or in dreadful reality; to the men it was as a tragedy, where the last scene is death—death which rivets the attention of all, who sooner or later must enact the same sad part.[1] They desire to see how the criminal will conduct himself; they sympathise with him if he displays coolness and courage, and despise him on the least symptom of unmanliness. An open square was then formed about the scaffold by lines of soldiers drawn up, into which the officers and clergy were admitted. As the fatal hour drew nigh, the increasing impatience of the multitude began to vent itself in complaints of how slowly the time passed—that time was of no value to them, but of such precious import to him, whose very moments were numbered.

When at length the cathedral clock tolled out the fatal hour, a universal stir of tiptoe expectation took place, a pushing forward to get the best situations. Still ten minutes had to elapse, for the clock of the tribunal is purposely set so much later than that of the cathedral, in order to afford the utmost possible chance of a reprieve. When that clock too had rung out its knell, all eyes were turned to the prison-door, from whence the miserable man came forth, attended by some Franciscans. He had chosen that order to assist at his dying moments, a privilege always left to the criminal. He was clad in a coarse yellow baize gown, the colour which denotes the crime of murder, and is appropriated always to Judas Iscariot in Spanish paintings. He walked slowly on his last journey, half supported by those around him, and stopping often, ostensibly to kiss the crucifix held before him by a friar, but rather to prolong existence—sweet life!—even yet a moment. When he arrived reluctantly at the scaffold, he knelt down on the steps, the threshold of death;—the reverend attendants covered him over with their blue robes—his dying confession was listened to unseen. He then mounted the platform attended by a single friar; addressed the crowd in broken sentences, with a gasping breath—told them that he died repentant, that he was justly punished, and that he forgave his executioner. " Mio delito me mata, y no *ese hombre*,"

[1] " Chacun fuit à le voir naître, chacun court à le voir mourir !"
—*Montaigne.*

—my offence puts me to death, and not *this fellow;* as
" Ese hombre " is a contemptuous expression, and implies insult, the ruling feeling of the Spaniard was displayed in death against the degraded functionary. The
criminal then exclaimed, " *Viva la fé! viva la religion!
viva el rey! viva el nombre de Jesus!*" All of which met
no echo from those who heard him. His dying cry was
" *Viva la Virgen Santisima!*" at these words the devotion to the goddess of Spain burst forth in one general
acclamation, " *Viva la Santisima!*" So strong is their
feeling towards the Virgin, and so lukewarm their comparative indifference towards their king, their faith, and
their Saviour! Meanwhile the executioner, a young
man dressed in black, was busied in the preparations
for death. The fatal instrument is simple : the culprit
is placed on a rude seat; his back leans against a strong
upright post, to which an iron collar is attached, en-
closing his neck, and so contrived as to be drawn home
to the post by turning a powerful screw. The executioner
bound so tightly the naked legs and arms of Veneno,
that they swelled and became black—a precaution not
unwise, as the father of this functionary had been killed
in the act of executing a struggling criminal. The priest
who attended Veneno was a bloated, corpulent man,
more occupied in shading the sun from his own face,
than in his ghostly office; the robber sat with a writhing
look of agony, grinding his clenched teeth. When all
was ready, the executioner took the lever of the screw in
both hands, gathered himself up for a strong muscular
effort, and, at the moment of a preconcerted signal, drew
the iron collar tight, while an attendant flung a black
handkerchief over the face—a convulsive pressure of the
hands and a heaving of the chest were the only visible
signs of the passing of the robber's spirit. After a pause
of a few moments, the executioner cautiously peeped
under the handkerchief, and after having given another
turn to the screw, lifted it off, folded it up, carefully
put it into his pocket, and then proceeded to light a
cigar

——— " with that air of satisfaction
Which good men wear who've done a virtuous action."

The face of the dead man was slightly convulsed, the mouth open, the eye-balls turned into their sockets from the wrench. A black bier, with two lanterns fixed on staves, and a crucifix, was now set down before the scaffold—also a small table and a dish, into which alms were again collected, to be paid to the priests who sang masses for his soul. The mob having discussed his crimes, abused the authorities and judges, and criticised the manner of the new executioner (it was his maiden effort), began slowly to disperse, to the great content of the neighbouring silversmiths, who ventured to open their closed shutters, having hitherto placed more confidence in bolts and bars, than in the moral example presented to the spectators. The body remained on the scaffold till the afternoon; it was then thrown into a scavenger's cart, and led by the "*pregonero*," the common crier, beyond the jurisdiction of the city, to a square platform called "*La mesa del Rey*," the king's table, where the bodies of the executed are quartered and cut up—"a pretty dish to set before a king." Here the carcass was hewed and hacked into pieces by the bungling executioner and his attendants, with that inimitable defiance of anatomy for which they and Spanish surgeons are equally renowned—

> " Le gambe di lui gettaron in una fossa;
> Il Diavol ebbe l'alma, i lupi l'ossa."

> " The legs of the robber were thrown in a hole,
> The wolves got his bones, the devil his soul."

CHAPTER XVII

The transition from the Spanish *ventero* to the *ladron* was easy, nor is that from the robbers to the doctors of Spain difficult; the former at least offer a polite alternative, they demand " your money or your life," while the latter in most cases take both; yet these able practi-

tioners, from being less picturesque in costume, and
more undramatic in operations, do not enjoy so brilliant
a European reputation as the bandits. Again, while our
critical monitors cry thieves on every road of the Peninsula, no friendly warning is given against the *Sangrado*,
whose aspect is more deadly than the *coup de soleil* of a
Castilian sun : woe waits the wayfarer who falls into his
hands; the patient cannot be too quick in ordering the
measure to be taken of his coffin, or, as Spaniards say,
of his tombstone, which last article is shadowed out by
the first feeling of the invalid's pulse—*tomar el pulso,
es prognosticar al enfermo la loza.* It was probably
from a knowledge of this contingent remainder, that
Monsieur Orfila went, or was sent, from Paris to Madrid,
about the time of the Montpensier marriage with the
Infanta, in the hopes of rescuing her elder and reigning
sister, the "innocent" Isabel, from the fatal native
lancets—a well-meant interference of the foreigner, by
the way, which the Spanish faculty resented and rejected
to a man; nor were the guarded suggestions of this
eminent *toxicologiste*, or investigator of poisons, with
regard to the administration of medicines and dispen-
saries, received so thankfully as they deserved.

However magnificently endowed in former times were
the hospitals and almshouses of Spain, the provision now
made for poor and ailing humanity is very inadequate.
The revenues were first embezzled by the managers, and
since have almost been swept away. Trustees for pious
and charitable uses are defenceless against armed
avarice and appropriation in office; and being *corporate*
bodies, they want the sacredness of *private* interests,
which every one is anxious to defend. Hence the greedy
minion Godoy began the spoliation, by seizing the funds,
and giving in lieu government securities, which of course
turned out to be worthless. Then ensued the French
invasion, and the confiscation of military despots. Civil
war has done the rest; and now that the convents are
suppressed, the deficiency is more evident, for in the
remoter country districts the monks bestowed relief to
the poor, and provided medicines for the sick. With
few exceptions, the hospitals, the *Casas de Misericordia,*

or houses for the destitute, are far from being well conducted in Spain, while those destined for lunatics, and
for exposed children, notwithstanding recent improvements, do little credit to science and humanity.

The base, brutal, and bloody *Sangrados* of Spain have
long been the butts of foreign and domestic novelists,
who spoke many a true word in their jests. The common
expression of the people in regard to the busy mortality
of their patients, is, that they die like bugs, *mueren
como chinches*. This recklessness of life, this inatten-
tion to human suffering, and backwardness in curative
science, is very Oriental; for, however science may have
set westward from the East, the arts of medicine and
surgery have not. There, as in Spain, they have long
been subordinate, and the professors held to be of a low
caste—a fatal bar in the Peninsula, where the point of
personal honour is so nice, and men will die rather than
submit to conventional degradations. The surgeon of
the Spanish Moors was frequently a despised and de-
tested Jew, which would create a traditionary loathing
of the calling. The physician was of somewhat a higher
caste; but he, like the botanist and chemist, was rather
to be met with among the Infidels than the Christians.
Thus Sancho the Fat was obliged to go in person to
Cordova in search of good advice. And still in Spain, as
in the East, all whose profession is to put living creatures to death, are socially almost excommunicated;
the butcher, the bullfighter, and public executioner for
example. Here the soldier who sabres, takes the highest
rank, and he who cures, the lowest; here the M.D.'s,
whom the infallible Pope consults and the autocrat king
obeys, are admitted only into the *sick* rooms of good
company, which, when in rude health, shuts on them the
door of their saloons; but the excluded take their revenge on those who morally cut them, and all Spaniards
are very dangerous with the knife, and more particularly
if surgeons. Madrid is indeed the court of death, and
the necrology of the Escorial furnishes the surest evidence of this fact in the premature decease of royalty,
which may be expected to have the best advice and aid,
both medical and theologico-therapeutical, that the

capital can afford; but brief is the royal span, especially in the case of females and *infantes,* and the *result* is undeniable in these statistics of death; the cause lies between the climate and the doctor, who, as they aid the other, may fairly be left to settle the question of relative excellence between each other.

The Spanish medical man is shunned, not only from ancient prejudices, and because he is dangerous like a rattle-snake, but from jealousies that churchmen entertain against a rival profession, which, if well received, might come in for some share of the legacies and power-conferring secrets, which are obtained easily at death-beds, when mind and body are deprived of strength. Again, a Spanish surgeon and a Spanish confessor take different views of a patient; one only wishes, or ought to wish, to preserve him in this world, the other in the next,—neither probably in their hearts having much opinion of the remedies adopted by each other : the spiritual practice changes not, for novelty itself, a heresy in religion, is not favourably beheld in anything else. Thus the universities, governed by ecclesiastics, persuaded the poor bigot Philip III. to pass a law prohibiting the study of any *new* system of medicine, and *requiring* Galen, Hippocrates, and Avicenna. Dons and men for whom the sun still continued to stand still, scouted the exact sciences and experimental philosophy as dangerous innovations, which, they said, made every medical man a Tiberius, who, because he was fond of mathematics where strict demonstration is necessary, was rather negligent in his religious respect for the gods and goddesses of the Pantheon; and so, in 1830, they scared the timid Ferdinand VII. (whose resemblance to Tiberius had nothing to do with Euclid) by telling him that the schools of medicine created materialists, heretics, citizen-kings, chartists, barricadoers, and revolutionists. Thereupon the beloved monarch shut up the lecture rooms forthwith, opening, it is true, by way of compensation, a tauromachian university;—men indeed might be mangled, but bulls were to be mercifully put out of their misery, secundum artem, and with the honours of science.

This low social position is very classical: the physicians of Rome, chiefly *liberti*, freed slaves, were only made citizens by Cæsar, who wished to *conciliate* these ministers of the fatal sisters when the capital was wanting in population after extreme emigrations—an act of favour which may cut two ways; thus Adrian VI. (tutor to the Spanish Charles V.) approved of there being 500 medical practitioners in the Eternal City, because otherwise "the *multitude* of living beings would eat each other up." However, when his turn came to be diminished, the grateful people serenaded his surgeon, as the "deliverer of the country." In our days, there was only one medical man admitted by the Seville *sangre su*, the best or noblest set (whose blood is held to be blue, of which more anon) when in rude and antiphlebotomical health; and every stranger was informed apologetically by the exclusive Amphitryons that the M.D. was *de casa conocida*, or born of a good family; thus his social introduction was owing to personal, not professional qualifications. And while adventurers of every kind are betitled, the most prodigal dispenser of Spanish honours never dreams of making his doctor even a *titulado*, a rank somewhat higher than a pair de France, and lower than a medical baronetage in England. This aristocratical ban has confined doctors much to each other's society, which, as they never take each other's physic, is neither unpleasant nor dangerous. At Seville the medical *tertulia*, club or meeting, was appropriately held at the apothecary's shop of *Campelos*, and a sable *junta* or consultation it was, of birds of bad omen, who croaked over the general health with which the city was afflicted, praying, like Sangrado in 'Gil Blas,' that by the blessing of Providence much sickness might speedily ensue. The crowded or deserted state of this rookery was the surest evidence of the hygeian condition of the fair capital of Bætica, and one which, when we lived there, we have often anxiously inspected; for, whatever be the pleasantries of those in insolent health, when sickness brings in the doctor, all joking is at an end; then he is made much of even in Spain, from a choice of evils, and for fear of the confessor and undertaker.

The poor in no countries have much predilection for
the hospital; and in Spain, in addition to pride, which
everywhere keeps many silly sick out of admirably-con-
ducted asylums, here a well-grounded fear deters the
patient, who prefers to die a *natural* death. Again, from
their being poor, the necessity of their living at all, is
less evident to the managers than to the sufferers; as,
say the Malthusians, there is no place vacant at Nature's
table d'hôte to those who cannot pay, so bed and board
are not pressed on Spanish applicants, by the hospital
committee; an admitted patient's death saves trouble
and expense, neither of which are popular in a land
where cash is scarce, and a love for hard work not prevalent, where a sound man is worth little, and a sick one
still less; nor is every doctor always popular for working
cures, as could be exemplified in sundry cases of Spanish
wives and heirs in general; therefore in the hospitals of
the Peninsula, if only half die, it is thought great luck :
the dead, moreover, tell no tales, and the living sing
praises for their miraculous escape. *El medico lleva la
plata, pero Dios es que sana!*—God works the cure, the
doctor sacks the fee ! Meanwhile the sextons are busy
and merry, as those in Hamlet, and as indeed all grave-
diggers are, when they have a job on hand that will be
paid for; deeply do they dig into the silent earth, that
bourn from whence no travellers return to blab. They
sing and jest, while dust is heaped on dust, and the
corpus delicti covered, and with it the blunders of the
medico; thus all parties, the deceased excepted, are well
satisfied; the man with the lancet is content that disagreeable evidence should be put out of sight, the fellow-
labourer with the spade is thankful that constant means
of living should be afforded to him; and when the funeral
is over, both carry out the proverbial practice of Peninsular survivors : *Los muertos en la huesa, y los vivos
á la mesa*, the dead in their grave, the quick to their
dinner.

But at no period were Spaniards careful even of their
own lives, and much less of those of others, being a
people of untender bowels. Familiarity with pain blunts
much of the finer feelings of persons employed even in

our hospitals, for those who live by the dead have only
an undertaker's sympathy for the living, and are as dull
to the poetry of innocent health, as Mr. Giblet is to a
sportive house-fed lamb. Matters are not improved in
Spain, where the wounds, blood, and slaughterings of
the pastime bull-fight, the *mueran* or death mob-cries,
and *pasele por las armas*, the shoot him on the spot, the
Draco and Durango decrees, and practices of all in
power, educate all sexes to indifference to blood; thus
the fatal knife-stab or surgeon's cut are viewed as *cosas
de España* and things of course. The philosophy of the
general indifference to life in Spain, which almost
amounts to Oriental fatalism, in the number of executions and general resignation to bloodshed, arises partly
from life among the many being at best but a struggle
for existence; thus in setting it in the cast, the player
only stakes coppers, and when one is removed, there is
somewhat less difficulty for survivors; hence every one
is for himself and for to-day; après moi le déluge, *el
ultimo mono se ahoga*, the last monkey is drowned, or
as we say, the devil takes the hindmost.

The neglect of well-supported, well-regulated hospitals, has recoiled on the Spaniards. The rising profession are deprived of the advantages of *walking* them,
and thus beholding every nice difficulty solved by experienced masters. Recently some efforts have been made
in large towns, especially on the coasts, to introduce
reforms and foreign ameliorations; but official jobbing
and ignorant routine are still among the diseases that are
not cured in Spain. In 1811, when the English army
was at Cadiz, a physician, named Villarino, urged by
some of our indignant surgeons, brought the disgraceful
condition of Spanish hospitals before the Cortes. A
commission was appointed, and their sad report, still
extant, details how the funds, food, wine, etc., destined
for the patients were consumed by the managers and
their subalterns. The results were such as might be
expected; the authorities held together, and persecuted
Villarino as a *revolucionario*, or reformer, and succeeded
in disgracing him. The superintendent of this establishment was the notorious Lozano de Torres, who starved

the English army after Talavera, and was " a thief and
a liar," in the words of the Duke. The Regency, after
this very exposure of his hospital, promoted him to the
civil government of Old Castile; and Ferdinand VII.,
in 1817, made him Minister of Justice.

As buildings, the hospitals are generally very large;
but the space is as thinly tenanted as the unpeopled
wastes of Spain. In England wards are wanting for
patients—in Spain, patients for wards. The names of
some of the greatest hospitals are happily chosen; that
of Seville, for instance, is called *La Sangre*, the blood,
or *Las Cinco Llagas*, the five bleeding wounds of our
Saviour, which are sculptured over the portal like
bunches of grapes. Blood is an ominous name for this
house and home of *Sangrado*, where the lancet, like the
Spanish knife, gives no quarter. In instruments of life
and death, this establishment resembled a Spanish
arsenal, being wanting in everything at the critical moment; its dispensary, as in the shop of Shakespeare's
apothecary, presented a beggarly account of empty pill-
boxes, while as to a visiting Brodie, the part of that
Hamlet was left out. The grand hospital at Madrid is
called *el general*, the General, and the medical assistance
is akin to the military co-operation of such Spanish
generals as Lapeña and Venegas, who in the moment of
need left Graham at Barrosa, and the Duke at Talavera,
without a shadow of aid. There is nothing new in
this, if the old proverb tells truth, *socorros de España,
o tarde o nunca;* Spanish succours arrive late or never.
In cases of battle, war, and sudden death as in peace,
the professional men, military or medical, are apt to
assist in the meaning of the French word *assister*, which
signifies to be present without taking any part in what
is going on. And this applies, where knocks on the head
are concerned, not to the medical men only, but to the
universal Spanish nation; when any one is stabbed in the
streets, he will infallibly bleed to death, unless the
authorities arrive in time to pick him up, and to bind up
his wounds : every one else—Englishmen excepted, we
describe things witnessed—passes on the other side; not
from any fear at the sight of blood, nor abhorrence of

murder, but from the dread which every Spaniard feels
at the very idea of getting entangled in the meshes of
La Justicia, whose ministers lay hold of all who interfere
or are near the body as principals or witnesses, and
Spanish justice, if once it gets a man into its fangs,
never lets him go until drained of his last farthing.

The schools and hospitals, especially in the inland
remote cities, are very deficient in all improved mechanical appliances and modern discoveries, and the few
which are to be met with are mostly of French and
second-rate manufacture. It is much the same with their
medical treatises and technical works; all is a copy, and
a bad one; it has been found to be much easier to translate and borrow, than to invent; therefore, as in modern
art and literature, there is little originality in Spanish
medicine. It is chiefly a veneering of other men's ideas,
or an adaptation of ancient and Moorish science. Most
of their terms of medicinal art, as well as of drugs,
jalea, elixir, jarave, rob, sorbete, julepe, etc., are purely
Arabic, and indicate the sources from whence the knowledge was obtained, for there is no surer historical test
than language of the origin from whence the knowledge
of the science was derived with its phraseology; and
whenever Spaniards depart from the daring ways of their
ancestors, it is to adopt a timid French system. The
few additions to their medical libraries are translations
from their neighbours, just as the scanty materia medica
in their apothecaries' shops is rendered more dangerous
and ineffective by quack nostrums from Paris. It is a
serious misfortune to sanative science in the Peninsula,
that all that is known of the works of thoughtful, careful
Germany, of practical, decided England, is passed
through the unfair, inaccurate alembic of French translation; thus the original becomes doubly deteriorated,
and the sacred cosmopolitan cause of truth and fact is
too often sacrificed to the Gallic mania of suppressing
both, for the honour of their own country. Can it be
wondered, therefore, that the acquaintance of the
Spanish faculty with modern works, inventions, and
operations is very limited, or that their text-books and
authorities should too often be still Galen, Celsus, Hip-

pocrates, and Boerhaave? The names of Hunter, Har-
vey, and Astley Cooper, are scarcely more known among
their M.D.'s than the last discoveries of Herschel; the
light of such distant planets has not had time to arrive.

To this day the *Colegio de San Carlos*, or the College
of Surgeons at Madrid, relies much on teaching the obstetric art by means of wax preparations; but learning
a trade on paper is not confined in Spain to medical
students; the great naval school at Seville is dedicated
to San Telmo, who, uniting in himself the attributes of
the ancient Castor and Pollux, appears in storms at the
mast-head in the form of lights to rescue seamen. Hence,
whenever it comes on to blow, the pious crews of Spanish
crafts fall on their knees, and depend on this marine
Hercules, instead of taking in sail, and putting the
helm up. Our tars, who love the sea *propter se*, for
better for worse, having no San Telmo to help them in
foul weather (although the somewhat irreverent gunner
of the Victory did call him of Trafalgar Saint Nelson),
go to work and perform the miracle themselves—*aide
toi, et le ciel t'aidera.* In our time, the middies in this
college were taught navigation in a room, from a small
model of a three-decker placed on a large table; and thus
at least they were not exposed to sea-sickness. The
Infant Antonio, Lord High Admiral of Spain, was walking in the Retiro gardens near the pond, when it was
proposed to cross in a boat; he declined, saying, "Since
I sailed from Naples to Spain I have never ventured on
water." But, in this and some other matters, things
are managed differently on the Thames and the Bætis.
Thus, near Greenwich Hospital, a floating frigate, large
as life, is the school of young chips of old blocks, who
every day behold in the veterans of Cape St. Vincent
and Trafalgar living examples of having "done their
duty." The evidence of former victories thus becomes
a guarantee for the realisation of their young hopes, and
the future is assured by the past.

Next to the barracks, prisons, arsenals, and fortresses
of Spain, the establishments for suffering mortality are
the least worth seeing, and are the most to be avoided
by wise travellers, who can indulge in much better speci-

mens at home. This assertion will be better understood
by a sketch or two taken on the spot a few years ago.
The so-called asylums for lunatics are termed in Spanish
hospitales de *locos*, a word derived from the Arabic,
locao, mad; they, like the cognate Morastans (μωρος) of
Cairo, were generally so mismanaged, that the directors
appeared to be only desirous of obtaining admission
themselves. Insanity seemed to derange both the intel-
lects of the patients and to harden the bowels of their
attendants, while the usual misappropriation of the
scanty funds produced a truly reckless, makeshift,
wretched result. There was no attempt at *classification*,
which indeed is no thing of Spain. The inmates were
crowded together,—the monomaniac, the insane, the
raving mad,—in one confusion of dirt and misery, where
they howled at each other, chained like wild beasts, and
were treated even worse than criminals, for the passions
of the most outrageous were infuriated by the savage
lash. There was not even a curtain to conceal the sad
necessities of these human beings, then reduced to
animals : everything was public even unto death, whose
last groan was mingled with the frantic laugh of the
surviving spectators. In some rare cases the bodies of
those whose minds are a void, were confined in solitary
cells, with no other companions save affliction. Of
these, many, when first sent there by friends and relations to be put out of the way, were *not* mad, soon indeed
to become so, as solitude, sorrow, and the iron entered
their brain. These establishments, which the natives
ought to hide in shame, were usually among the first
lions which they forced on the stranger, and especially
on the Englishman, since, holding our worthy countrymen to be all *locos*, they naturally imagined that they
would be quite at home among the inmates.

They, in common with many others on the Continent,
entertain a notion that all Britons bold have a bee in their
bonnet; they think so on many, and perhaps not always
unreasonable, grounds. They see them preferring English ways, sayings, and doings, to their own, which of
itself appears to a Spaniard, as to a Frenchman, to be
downright insanity. Then our countrymen tell the truth

in bulletins, use towels, and remove superfluous hairs daily. And letting alone other minor exhibitions of eccentricity, are not the natives of England, Scotland, and Ireland guilty of three actions, any one of which would qualify for Bedlam if the Lord Chancellor were to issue a writ *de lunatico inquirendo?*—have they not bled for Spain, in purse and person, on the battlefield, on the railroad, in the Stock Exchange?—

"Oh tribus Antyceris caput insanabile!"

To return, however, to Spanish madmen and their hospitals, the sight was a sad one, and alike disgraceful to the sane, and degrading to the insane native. The wild maniacs implored a "loan" from the foreigner, for from their own countrymen they had received a stone. A sort of madness is indeed seldom wanting to the frantic energy and intense eagerness of all Spanish mendicants; and here, albeit the reasoning faculties were gone, the national propensity to beg and borrow survived the wreck of intellect, and in fact it was and is the indestructible "common sense" of the country.

There was generally some particular patient whose aggravated misery made him or her the especial object of cruel curiosity. Thus, at Toledo, in 1843, the *keepers* (fit wild beast term) always conducted strangers to the cage or den of the wife of a celebrated Captain-General and first-rate fusilier of Catalonia, an officer superior in power to our Lord-Lieutenant of Ireland. She was permitted to wallow in naked filth, and be made a public show. The Moors, at least, do not confine their harmless female maniacs, who wander naked through the streets, while the men are honoured as saints, whose minds are supposed to be wandering in heaven. The old Iberian doctors, according to Pliny, professed to cure madness with the herb *vettonica*, and hydrophobia with decoction of the *cynorrhodon* or dog-rose-water, as being doubly unpalateable to the rabid canine species. The modern Spaniards seemed only to desire, by ignorance and ill-usage, to darken any lucid interval into one raving uniformity.

The foundling hospitals were, when we last examined

them, scarcely better managed than the lunatic asylums; they are called *casas de espositos*, houses of the exposed —or *la Cuna*, the cradle, as if they were the cradle, not the coffin, of miserable infants. Most large cities in Spain have one of these receptacles; the principal being in the Levitical towns, and the natural fruit of a rich celibate clergy, both regular and secular. The *Cuna* in our time might have been defined as a place where innocents were massacred, and natural children deserted by their unnatural parents were provided for by being slowly starved. These hospitals were first founded at Milan in 787, by a priest named Datheus. That of Seville, which we will describe, was established by the clergy of the cathedral, and was managed by twelve directors, six lay and six clerical; few, however, attended or contributed save in subjects. The hospital is situate in the *Calle de la Cuna;* near an aperture left for charitable donations, is a marble tablet with this verse from the Psalms, inscribed in Latin, "When my father and mother forsake me, then the Lord will take me in."

A wicket door is pierced in the wall, which opens on being tapped to admit the sinless children of sin; and a nurse sits up at night to receive those exposed by parents who hide their guilt in darkness.

> " Toi que l'amour fit par un crime,
>   Et que l'amour défait par un crime à son tour,
>   Funeste ouvrage de l'amour,
>   De l'amour funeste victime."

Some of the babies are already dying, and are put in here in order to avoid the expense of a funeral; others are almost naked, while a few are well supplied with linen and necessaries. These latter are the offspring of the better classes, by whom a temporary concealment is desired. With such the most affecting letters are left, praying the nurse to take more than usual care of a child which will surely be one day reclaimed, and a mark or ornament is usually fastened to the infant, in order that it may be identified hereafter, if called for, and such were the precise customs in antiquity. Every particular regarding every exposed babe is registered in a book, which is a sad record of human crime and remorse.

Those children which are afterwards reclaimed, pay about sixpence for every day during which the hospital has maintained them; but little attention is paid to the appeals for particular care, or to the promise of redemption, for Spaniards seldom trust each other. Unless some name is sent with it, the child is baptized with one given by the matron, and it usually is that of the saint of the day of its admission. The number was very great, and increasing with increasing poverty, while the funds destined to support the charges decreased from the same cause. There is a certain and great influx nine months after the Holy week and Christmas, when the whole city, male and female, pass the night in kneeling to relics and images, etc.; accordingly nine months afterwards, in January and November, the daily numbers often exceed the usual average by fifteen to twenty.

There is always a supply of wet nurses at the *Cuna,* but they are generally such as from bad character cannot obtain situations in private families; the usual allotment was three children to one nurse. Sometimes, when a respectable woman is looking out for a place as wet-nurse, and is anxious not to lose her breast of milk, she goes, in the meanwhile, to the *Cuna,* when the poor child who draws it off plumps up a little, and then, when the supply is withdrawn, withers and dies. The appointed nurses dole out their milk, not according to the wants of the infants, but to make it do for their number. Some few are farmed out to poor mothers who have lost their own babe; they receive about eight shillings a month, and these are the children which have the best chance of surviving, for no woman who has been a mother, and has given suck, will willingly, when left alone, let an infant die. The nurses of the *Cuna* were familiar with starvation, and even if their milk of human kindness were not dried up or soured, they have not the means of satisfying their hungry number. The proportion who died was frightful; it was indeed an organised system of infanticide. Death is a mercy to the child, and a saving to the establishment; a grown-up man's life never was worth much in Spain, much less that of a deserted baby. The exposure of children to immediate death by the Greeks and Romans, was a trifle less cruel than the protracted dying in these Spanish charnel-houses. This *Cuna,* when last we visited it, was managed by an inferior priest, who, a true Spanish unjust steward, misapplied the funds. He became rich, like Gil Blas's overseer at Valladolid, by taking care of the property of the poor and fatherless; his well-garnished quarters and portly self were in strange contrast with the condition of his wasted charges. Of these, the sick and dying were separated from the healthy; the former were placed in a large rcom, once the saloon of state, whose gilded roof and fair proportions mocked the present misery. The infants were laid in rows on dirty mattresses along on the floor, and were left unheeded and unattended. Their large heads, shrivelled necks, hollow eyes, and wax wan figures, were shadowed with coming death. Called into existence by no wish or fault of their own, their brief span was run out ere begun, while their mother was far away exclaiming, "When I have sufficiently wept for his birth, I will weep for his death."

Those who were more healthy lay paired in cradles arranged along a vast room; but famine was in their cheeks, need starved in their eyes, and their shrill cry pained the ear on passing the threshold; from their being underfed, they were restless and ever moaning. Their existence had indeed begun with a sob, with *El primer sollozo de la Cuna,* the first sigh of the cradle, as Rioja says, but all cry when entering the world, while many leave it with smiles. Some, the newly exposed, just parted from their mother's breast, having sucked their last farewell, looked plump and rosy; they slept soundly, blind to the future, and happily unconscious of their fate.

About one in twelve survived to idle about the hospital, ill clad, ill fed, and worse taught. The boys were destined for the army, the girls for domestic service, nay, for worse, if public report did not wrong their guardian priest. They grew up to be selfish and unaffectionate; having never known what kindness was, their young hearts closed ere they opened; "the world

was not their friend, nor the world's law." It was on
their heads that the barber learned to shave, and on
them were visited the sins of their parents; having had
none to care for them, none to love, they revenged themselves by hating mankind. Their occupation consisted
in speculating on who their parents may be, and
whether they should some day be reclaimed and become
rich. A few occasionally are adopted by benevolent and
childless persons, who, visiting the *Cuna*, take a fancy
to an interesting infant; but the child is liable ever
after to be given up to its parents, should they reclaim
it. Townshend mentions an Oriental custom at Barcelona, where the girls when marriageable were
paraded in procession through the streets, and any
desirous of taking a wife was at liberty to select his
object by "throwing his handkerchief." This Spanish
custom still prevails at Naples.

Such was the *Cuna* of Seville when we last beheld it.
It is now, as we have recently heard with much pleasure,
admirably conducted, having been taken in charge by
some benevolent ladies, who here as elsewhere are the
best nurses and guardians of man in his first or second
infancy, not to say of every intermediate stage.

Our readers will concur in deeming that wight unfortunate who falls ill in Spain, as, whatever be his
original complaint, it is too often followed by secondary
and worse symptoms, in the shape of the native doctor;
and if the judgment passed by Spaniards on that member of society be true, Esculapius cannot save the invalid from the crows; the faculty even at Madrid are
little in advance of their provincial colleagues, nay,
often they are more destructive, since, being practitioners in the only court, the heaven on earth, they are
in proportion superior to the medical men of the rest
of the world, of whom of course they can learn nothing.
They are, however, at least a century behind their
brother professors of England. An unreasonable idea of
self-excellence arises both in nations and in individuals,
from having no knowledge of the relative merits of
others, and from having few grounds or materials
whereon to raise comparison; it exists therefore the

strongest among the most uninformed and those who mix the least in the world. Thus in spite of manifold deficiencies, some of which will be detailed, the self-esteem of these medical men exceeds, if possible, that of the military; both have killed their "ten thousands." They hold themselves to be the first *sabreurs,* physicians, and surgeons on earth, and the best qualified to wield the shears of the Parcæ. It would be a waste of time to try to dispel this fatal delusion; the well-intentioned monitor would simply be set down as malevolent, envious, and an ass; for they think their ignorance the perfection of human skill. Few foreigners can ever hope to succeed among them, nor can any native who may have studied abroad, easily introduce a better system: his elder brethren would make common cause against him as an innovator; he would be summoned to no consultations, the most lucrative branch of practice, while the confessors would poison the ears of the women (who govern the men) with cautions against the danger to their souls, of having their bodies cured by a Jew, a heretic, or a foreigner, for the terms are almost convertible.

Meanwhile, as in courts of justice and other matters in Spain, all sounds admirably on *paper*—the forms, regulations, and system are perfect in theory. Colleges of physicians and surgeons superintend the science, the professors are members of infinite learned societies, lectures are delivered, examinations are conducted, and certificates duly signed and sealed, are given. The young *Galenista* is furnished with a licence to kill, but what is wanting from beginning to end, to practitioner and patient, is *life.* The medical men know, nevertheless, every aphorism of the ancients by rote, and *discourse* as eloquently and plausibly on any case as do their ministers in Cortes. Both write capital theories and opinions extemporaneously. Their splendid language supplies words which seem to have cost thought. What is deficient is that clinical and best of education where the case is brought before the student with the corollary of skilful treatment: *accidental* deaths are consequently more common than cures.

Dissection again is even now repulsive to their
Oriental prejudices; the pupils learn rather by plates,
diagrams, models, preparations, and skeletons, than
from anatomical experiments on a subject. As among
the ancients and in the East to this day an idea is prevalent among the masses in Spain, that the touch of a
dead body pollutes; nor is the objection raised by the
clergy, that it savours of impiety to mutilate a form
made in the image of God, yet exploded. It will be
remembered by our medical readers, if we have any,
that Vesalius, the father of modern anatomy, when at
Madrid was demanded by the Inquisition from Philip
II., to be burnt for having performed an operation.
The king sent him to expiate his sin by a pilgrimage to
the Holy Land; he was shipwrecked, and died of starvation at Zante.

Can it be wondered at, with such a theoretical education, that practice should continue to be antiquated,
classical, and Oriental, and necessarily very limited? In
difficult cases of compound fracture, gun-shot wounds,
the doctors give the patient up almost at once, although
they continue to meet and take fees, until death relieves
him of his complicated sufferings. In chronic cases and
slighter fractures they are less dangerous; for as their
pottering remedies do neither good nor harm, the
struggle for life and death is left to nature, who sometimes works the cure. In acute diseases and inflamma-
tions they seldom succeed; for however fond of the
lancet, they only nibble with the case, and are scared
at the bold decided practice of Englishmen, whereat
they shrug up shoulders, invoke saints, and descant
learnedly on the impossibility of treating complaints
under the bright sun and warm air of Catholic Spain,
after the formulæ of cold, damp, and foggy, heretical
England.

Most Spaniards who can afford it have their family
or bolster doctor, the *Medico de Cabecera,* and their
confessor. This pair take care of the bodies and souls
of the whole house, bring them gossip, share their
puchero, purse, and tobacco. They rule the husband
through the women and the nursery, nor do they allow

their exclusive privileges to be infringed on. Etiquette
is the life of a Spaniard, and often his death, since every
one has heard (the Spaniards swear it is all a French lie)
that Philip III. was killed, rather than violate a form.
He was seated too near the fire, and, although burning, of course as king of Spain the impropriety of
moving himself never entered his head, and when he
requested one of his attendants to do so, none, in the
absence of the proper officer whose duty it was to
superintend the royal chair, ventured to take that improper liberty.   In case of sudden emergencies among
her Catholic Majesty's subjects, unless the family
doctor be present, any other one, even if called in, generally declines acting until the regular Esculapius
arrives.   An English medical friend of ours saved a
Spaniard's life by chancing to arrive when the patient,
in an apoplectic fit, was foaming at the mouth and
wrestling with death; all this time a strange doctor was
sitting quietly in the next room smoking his cigar at
the *brasero,* the chafing-dish, with the women of the
family.   Our friend instantly took 30 ounces from the
sufferer's arm, not one of the Spanish party even moving from their seats. Thus Apollo preserved him ! The
same medical gentleman happened to accidentally call
on a person who had an inflammation in the cornea of
the eye : on questioning he found that many consultations had been previously held, at which no determination was come to until at the last, when sea-bathing
was prescribed, with a course of asses' milk and Chiclana snake-broth; our heretical friend, who lacked the
true faith, just touched the diseased part with caustic.
When this application was reported at the next consultation, the native doctors all crossed themselves with
horror and amazement, which was increased when the
patient recovered in a week.

As a general rule at the first visit, they look as wise
as possible, shake their heads before the women, and
always magnify the complaint, which is a safe proceeding all over the world, since all physicians can either
cure or kill the patient; in the first event they get
greater credit and reward, while in the other alternative,

the disease, having been beyond the reach of art, bears
the blame. The *medicos* exhibit considerable ingenuity
in prolonging an apparent necessity for a continuance of
their visits. A common interest induces them to pull
together—a rare exception in Spain—and play into each
other's hands. The family doctor, whenever appear-
ances will in anywise justify him, becomes alarmed, and
requires a consultation, a *Junta*. What any Spanish
Junta is in affairs of peace or war need not be explained;
and these are like the rest, they either do nothing, or
what they do do, is done badly. At these meetings
from three to seven *Medicos de apelacion,* consulting
physicians, attend, or more, according to the patient's
purse: each goes to the sick man, feels his pulse, asks
him some questions, and then retires to the next room
to consult, generally allowing the invalid the benefit of
hearing what passes. The *Protomedico,* or senior,
takes the chair; and while all are lighting their cigars,
the family doctor opens the case, by stating the birth,
parentage, and history of the patient, his constitution,
the complaint, and the medicines hitherto prescribed.
The senior next rises, and gives his opinion, often speaking for half an hour; the others follow in their rotation,
and then the *Protomedico,* like a judge, sums up, going
over each opinion with comments: the usual termination
is either to confirm the previous treatment, or make
some insignificant alteration: the only certain thing is
to appoint another consultation for the next day, for
which the fees are heavy, each taking from three to five
dollars. The consultation often lasts many hours, and
becomes at last a chronic complaint.

It must be said, in justice to these able practitioners,
that as a body they are careful in their dress: external
appearance, not to say finery in apparel, raises in the
eyes of the many, a profession which here is of uncertain social standing. On the same principle how careful is the costume, how brilliant are the shirt-studs of
foreign fiddlers when in England! The worthy Andalucian doctor of our Spanish family, and an efficient
one, as two of his patients now at rest could testify,
never paid a visit except when gaily attired. So the

Matador, when he enters the arena to kill the bull, is clad as a first-rate dandy *majo.* This attention to person arises partly from the Moro-Ibero love of ostentation, and partly from sound Galenic principles and a high sense of professional duty. The ancient authorities enforced on the practitioner an attention to everything which created cheerful impressions, in order that he might arrive at the patient's pillow like a messenger of good tidings, and as a minister of health, not of death. They held that a grave costume might suggest unpleasant associations to the sick man. Raven-coloured undertaker tights, and a funereal, cadaverous look to match, are harbingers of blue devils and black crape, which no man, even when in blessed health, contemplates with comfort; while the effect of such a *facies hippocratica* staring in the face of a poor devil whose life is despaired of, must be fatal.

The prescriptions of these well-dressed gentlemen are somewhat more old-fashioned than their coats. Their grand recipe in the first instance is to do nothing beyond taking the fee and leaving nature alone, or, as the set phrase has it, *dejar á la naturaleza.* The young and those whose constitutions are strong and whose complaints are weak, do well under the healing influence of their kind nurse Nature, and recover through her vis medicatrix, which, if not obstructed by art, everywhere works wonderful cures. The *Sangrado* will say that a Spanish man or woman is more marvellously made than a clock, inasmuch as his or her machinery has a power in itself to regulate its own motions, and to repair accidents; and therefore the watchmaker who is called in, need not be in a hurry to take it to pieces when a little oiling and cleaning may set all to rights. The remedies, when the proper time for their application arrives, are simple, and are sought for rather among the vegetables of the earth's surface than from the minerals in its bowels. The external recipes consist chiefly of papers smeared with lard, applied to the abdomen, sinapisms and mustard poultices to the feet, fomentations of marsh-mallows or camomile flowers, and the aid of the curate. The internal remedies, the

tisanes, the *Leches de Almendras, de Burras,* decoc-
tions of rice, and so forth, succeed each other in such
regular order, that the patient scholar has nothing to
do but repeat the medical passages in Horace's
'Satires.' In no country, however, can all the sick be
always expected to recover even then, since "*Para todo
hay remedio, sino para la muerte*"—"There is a
remedy for everything except death." If by chance
the patient dies, the doctor and the disease bear the
blame. Perhaps the old Iberian custom was the safest;
then the sick were exposed outside their doors, and the
advice of casual passengers was asked, whose prescriptions were quite as likely to answer as images, relics,
snake-soup, or milk of almonds or asses :—

> "And, doctor, do you really think
> That asses' milk I ought to drink?
> It cured yourself, I grant, is true,
> But then 'twas mother's milk to you."

Nor, if the doctors knew how to prescribe them, are
the nicer and most efficacious remedies, the preparations of modern chemical science, to be procured in any
except the very largest towns; although, as in Romeo's
apothecary, "the needy" shelves are filled with empty
boxes "to make a show." The trade of a druggist is
anything but free, and the numbers are limited; none
may open a *Botica* without a strict examination and
licence; although, of course, this is to be had for money.
None may sell any potent medicine, except according
to the prescription of some *local* medical man; everything is a monopoly. The commonest drugs are often
either wanting or grossly adulterated, but, as in their
arsenals and larders, no dispenser will admit such destitution; *hay de todo,* I have everything, swears he, and
gallantly makes up the prescription simply by substituting other ingredients; and as the correct ones nine times
out of ten are harmless, no great injury is sustained.
There is nothing new in this, for Quevedo, in his *Zahur-
das de Pluton,* or Satan's Pigsties, introduces a yellow-
faced bilious judge scourging Spanish apothecaries for
doing exactly the same, "Hence your shops," quoth

he, for he both preached and flogged, " are arsenals of death, whose ministers here get their pills (balls rather) which banish souls from the earth;" but these and other things have been long done with impunity, as Pliny said, no physician was ever hung for murder. One advantage of general distrust in drugs and doctors is, that the great masses of the people think very little about them or their complaints : thus they escape all fancied and imaginary complaints, which, if indulged in, become chronic, and more difficult to cure than those afflicting the body—for who can minister to a mind diseased?   Again, from this want of confidence in remedies, very little physic at all is taken; owing to this limited demand, druggists' shops are as rare in Spain as those of booksellers.   No red, green, or blue bottles illuminate the streets at night, and there are more of these radiant orbs in the Fore street of the capital of the west of England, than in the whole capital of the Spains, albeit with a population six times greater.   It is true that, at Madrid, feeding on plum-pudding, diluted with sour cider and clotted cream, is not habitual.

Many of the prescriptions of Spain are local, and consist of some particular spring, some herb, some animal, or some particular air, or place, or bath, is recommended, which, however, is said to be very dangerous, unless some resident local *medico* be first consulted. One example is as good as a thousand : near Cadiz is Chiclana, to which the faculty invariably transport those patients whom they cannot cure, that is, about ninety-five in the hundred; so in chronic complaints sea-bathing there, is prescribed, with a course of asses' milk; and if that fail, then a broth made of a long harmless snake, which abounds in the aromatic wastes near *Barrosa*. We have forgotten the generic name of this valuable reptile of Esculapius, one of which our naturalists should take alive, and either breed from it in the Regent's Park, or at least investigate his comparative anatomy with those exquisite vipers which make, as we have shown, such delicious pork at Montanches.

We cannot refrain from giving one more prescription. Many of the murders in Spain should rather be called homicides, being free from malice prepense, and caused by the *readiness* of the national *cuchillo*, with which all the lower classes are armed like wasps; it is thus always at hand, when the blood is most on fire, and before any refrigeratory process commences. Thus, where an unarmed Englishman *closes* his fist, a Spaniard opens his knife. This rascally instrument becomes fatal in jealous broils, when the lower classes light their anger at the torch of the Furies, and prefer using, to speaking daggers. Then the thrust goes home; and however unskilled the regular *Sangrados* may be in anatomy and handling the scalpel, the universal people know exactly how to manage their knife and where to plant its blow; nor is there any mistake, for the wound, although not so deep as a well, nor so wide as a church door, " 'twill serve." It is usually given after the treacherous fashion of their Oriental and Iberian ancestors, and if possible by a stab behind, and " under the fifth rib;" and " one blow " is enough. The blade, like the cognate Arkansas or Bowie knife of the Yankees, will " rip up a man right away," or drill him until a surgeon can see through his body. The number killed on great religious and other festivals, exceeds those of most Spanish battles in the field, although the occurrence is scarcely noticed in the newspapers, so much is it a matter of course; but crimes which call forth a second edition and double sheet in our papers, are slurred over on the Continent, for foreigners conceal what we most display.

In minor cases of flirtation, where capital punishment is not called for, the offending party just gashes the cheek of the peccant one, and suiting the word to the action observes, " *ya estas senalaā;*" " Now you are marked." This is precisely *winkel quarte,* the gash in the cheek, which is the only salve for the touchy honour of a German student, when called *ein dummer junge,* a stupid youth : —

> " Und ist die quart gesessen
> So ist der touche vergessen."

Again, " *Mira que te pego, mira que te mato,*" " Mind
I don't strike thee—mind I don't kill thee;" are playful
fondling expressions of a *Maja* to a *Majo*. When this
particular gash is only threatened, the Seville phrase
was, " *Mira que te pinto un jabeque;*" " Take care that
I don't draw you a xebeck " (the sharp Mediterranean
felucca). " They jest at wounds who never felt a scar,"
but whenever this *jabeque* has really been inflicted, the
patient, ashamed of the stigma, and not having the
face to show himself or herself, is naturally anxious to
recover a good character and skin, which only one
cosmetic, one sovereign panacea, can effect. This in
Philip IV.'s time was cat's grease, which then removed
such superfluous marks; while Don Quixote considered
the oil of Apariccio to be the only cure for scratches
inflicted by female or feline claws.

In process of time, as science advanced, this was
superseded by *Unto del hombre*, or man's grease. Our
estimable friend Don Nicolas Molero, a surgeon in high
practice at Seville, assured us that previously to the
French invasion he had often prepared this cataleptic
specific, which used to be sold for its weight in gold,
until, having been adulterated by unprincipled empirics,
it fell into disrepute. The receipt of the balsam of
Fierabras has puzzled the modern commentators of Don
Quixote, but the kindness of Don Nicolas furnished us
with the ingredients of this *pommade divine,* or rather
mortale. " Take a man in full health who has been
just killed, the fresher the better, pare off the fat round
the heart, melt it over a slow fire, clarify, and put it
away in a cool place for use." The multitudinous
church ceremonies and holidays in Spain, which bring
crowds together, combined with the sun, wine, and
women, have always ensured a supply of fine subjects.

In Spain, as elsewhere, the doctor mania is an expensive amusement, which the poor and more numerous class, especially in rural localities, seldom indulge
in. Like their mules, they are rarely ill, and they only
take to their beds to die. They have, it is true, a
parish doctor, to whom certain districts are apportioned; when he in his turn succumbs to death, or **is**

otherwise removed, the vacancy is usually announced in the newspapers, and a new functionary is often advertised for. His trifling salary is made up of payments in money and in kind, so much in corn and so much in cash; the leading principle is cheapness, and, as in our new poor-law, that proficient is preferred, who will contract to do for the greatest number at the smallest charge. His constituents decline sometimes to place full confidence in his skill or alacrity; they oftener do consult the barber, the quack, or *curandero;* for there is generally in orthodox Spain some charlatan wherever sword, rosary, pen, or lancet is to be wielded. The nostrums, charms, relics, incantations, etc., to which recourse is had, when not mediæval, are scarcely Christian; but the spiritual pharmacopœia of this land of Figaro is far too important to form the tail-piece of any chapter.

CHAPTER XVIII

THE Reverend Dr. Fernando Castillo, an esteemed Spanish author and teacher, remarks, in his luminous Life of St. Domenick, that Spain has been so bountifully provided by heaven with fine climate, soil, and extra number of saints, that his countrymen are prone to be idle and to neglect such rare advantages. Certainly they may not dig and delve so deeply as is done in lands less favoured, but the reproach of omitting to call on Hercules to do their work, or of not making the most of Santiago in any bodily dilemma, is a somewhat too severe reproach: nowhere in case of sickness have the saving virtues of relics, and the adjurations of holy monks, been more implicitly relied on.

As our learned readers well know, the medical practice of the ancients was, as that of the Orientals still is, more peculiar than scientific. When disease was thought to be a divine punishment for sin, it was held

to be wicked to resist by calling in human aid : thus
Asa was blamed, and thus Moslems and Spaniards
resign themselves to their fate, distrusting, and very
properly, their medical men : " Am I a god, to kill or
make alive?" In the large towns, in these days of
progress, some patients may " suffer a recovery " according to European practice; but in the country and
remote villages,—and we speak from repeated personal
experience,—the good old reliance on relics and charms
is far from exploded; and however Dr. Sangrado and
Philip III., whose decrees on medical matters yet adorn
the Spanish statutes at large, deplore the introduction
of perplexing chemistry, mineral therapeuticals still
remain a considerable dead letter, as the church has
transferred the efficacy of faith from spiritual to tem-
poral concerns, and gun-shot wounds. Even Ponz, the
Lysons of Spain, and before the Inquisition was
abolished, ventured to express surprise at the number
of images ascribed to St. Luke, who, says he, was not
a sculptor, but a physician, whence possibly their sanative influence. The old Iberians were great herbalist
doctors; thus those who had a certain plant in their
houses, were protected, as a blessed palm branch now
wards off lightning. They had also a drink made of a
hundred herbs, and hence called *centum herbæ, a bebida
de cien herbas,* which, like Morison's vegetable pills,
cured every possible disease, and was so palatable that
it was drunk at banquets, which modern physic is not;
moreover, according to Pliny, they cured the gout with
flour, and relieved elongated uvulas by hanging purslain
round the patient's throat. So now the *curas y curan-
deros,* country curates and quacks, furnish charms and
incantations, just as Ulysses stopped his bleeding by
cantation : a medal of Santiago cures the ague, a handkerchief of the Virgin the ophthalmia, a bone of San
Magin answers all the purposes of mercury, a scrap of
San Frutos supplied at Segovia the loss of common
sense; the Virgin of Oña destroyed worms in royal
Infantes, and her sash at Tortosa delivers royal Infantas. Every Murcian peasant believes that no disease
can affect him or his cattle, if he touches them with the

cross of Caravaca, which angels brought from heaven and placed on a red cow. When we were last at Manresa, the worthy man who showed the cave in which Loyola the founder of the Jesuists did penance for a year, increased an honest livelihood by the sale of its pulverised stones, that were swallowed by the faithful in cases in which an English doctor would prescribe Dover's or James's powders. Every province, not to say parish, has its own tutelar saint and relic, which are much honoured and resorted to in their local jurisdiction, and very little thought of out of it, their power to cure having been apparently granted to them by Santiago, as a commission to commit is by Queen Victoria to a magistrate, whose authority does not extend beyond the county bounds. Zaragoza was admirably provided: a portion of the liver of Santa Engracia was anciently resorted to, in cases where blue pill would be beneficial; the oil of her lamps, which never smoked the ceilings, cured *lamparones,* or tumours in the neck, while that which burnt before the *Virgen del Pilar,* or the image of the Virgin which came down from heaven on a pillar, restored lost legs; Cardinal de Retz mentions in his Memoirs having seen a man whose wooden substitutes became needless when the originals grew again on being rubbed with it; and this portent was long celebrated by the Dean and Chapter, as well it deserved, by an especial holiday, for Macassar oil cannot do much more. This graven image is at this moment the object of popular adoration, and disputes even with the worship of tobacco and money: countless are the mendicants, the halt, blind, and the lame, who cluster around her shrine, as the equally afflicted ancients, with whom physicians were in vain, did around that of Minerva; and it must be confessed that the cures worked are almost incredible.

It may be said that all this is a raking up of remnants of mediæval superstition and darkness, and it is probable that the medical men in Madrid and the larger towns, and especially those who have studied at Paris, do not place implicit confidence in these spiritual, nor indeed in any other purely Spanish remedies; but their tried medicinal properties are set forth at length in scores of Spanish county and other histories which we have the felicity to possess, all of which have passed the scrutinising ordeal of clerical censors, and have been approved of as containing nothing contrary to the creed of the Church of Rome or good customs; nor can it be permitted that a church which professes to be always one, the same, and the only true one, should at its own convenience "turn its back on itself," and deny its own drugs and doctrines.   Nothing is set down here which was not perfectly notorious under the reign of Ferdinand VII.; and whatever the doctors of physic or theology may now disbelieve in Spain, more reliance is still placed, in the rural districts, where foreign civilisation has not penetrated, on miracles than on medicines.

We have often and often seen little children in the streets dressed like Franciscan monks—Cupids in cowls —whose pious parents had vowed to clothe them in the robes of this order, provided its sainted founder preserved their darlings during measles or dentition.   Nothing was more common than that women, nay, ladies in good society, should appear for a year in a particular religious dress, called *el habito,* or with some religious badge on their sleeves in token of similar deliverance. One instance in our time amused all the tertulias of Seville, who maliciously attributed the sudden relief which a fair high-born unmarried invalid experienced from an apparent dropsical complaint to causes not altogether supernatural; *Pues, Don Ricardo,* "and so, Master Richard," would her friends of the same age and rank often say, "you are a stranger; go and ask dearest *Esperanza* why she wears the Virgin of Carmel; come back and let us know her story, and we will tell you the real truth." *Vaya! vaya! Don Ricardo, usted es muy majadero,*—"Go to, Master Richard, your Grace is an immense bore," replied the penitent, if she suspected the authors and motive of the embassy.

The pious in antiquity raised temples to Minerva medica or Esculapius, as Spaniards do altars to *Na. Señora de los Remedios,* our Lady of the Remedies, and to San Roque, whose intervention renders " sound as a roach," a proverb devised in his honour by our ancestors, who, before the Reformation, trusted likewise to him; and both thought, if Cicero is to be credited, that these tutelars did *at least* as much as the doctor. Alas! for the patient credulity of mankind, which still gulps down such medicinal quackery as all this, and which long will continue to do so even were one of the dead to rise from the grave, to deprecate the absurd treatment by which he and so many have been sacrificed.

However, by way of compensation, the saving the *soul* has been made just as primary a consideration in Spain as the curing the *body* has been in England. These relics, charms, and amulets represent our patent medicines; and the wonder is how any one in Great Britain can be condemned to death in this world, or how any one in the Peninsula can be doomed to perdition in the next : possibly the penances are in neither case quite specific. Be that as it may, how numerous and well-appointed are the churches and convents there, compared to the hospitals; how amply provided the relic-magazine with bones and spells, when compared to the anatomical museums and chemists' shops; again, what a flock of holy practitioners come forth *after* a Spaniard has been stabbed, starved, or executed, not one of whom would have stirred a step to save an army of his countrymen when alive; and what coppers are now collected to pay masses to get his soul out of purgatory!

Beware, nevertheless, gentle Protestant reader, of dying in Spain, except in Cadiz or Malaga, where, if you are curious in Christian burial, there is snug lying for heretics; and for your life avoid being even sick at Madrid, since if once handed over to the faculty make thy last testament forthwith, as, if the judgment passed on their own doctors by Spaniards be true, Esculapius cannot save thee from the crows : avoid the Spanish doctors therefore like mad dogs, and throw their physic after them.

The masses and many in Spain have their own tute-

lars and refuges for the destitute; the kings and queens
—whom God preserve!—have their own especial
patroness by prerogative, in the image of the Virgin of
Atocha at Madrid, which they and the rest of the royal
family visit every Sunday in the year when in royal
health.   No sooner was the sovereign taken danger-
ously ill, and the court physicians at a loss what to do,
as sometimes is the case even in Madrid, than the image
used to be brought to his bedside; witness the case
of Philip III., thus described by Bassampierre in his
dispatch:—'' Les médecins en désespèrent depuis ce
matin que l'on a commencé à user des *remèdes spirituels,*
et faire transporter au palais *l'image* de N.D. de
Athoche.''   The patient died three days after the image
was sent for.

   Although neither priest nor physician might credit the
sanative properties of rags and relics, they gladly called
them in, for if the case then went wrong, how could
mortal man be expected to succeed when the supernatural remedy had failed?   All inquests in awkward
cases are hushed up by ascribing the death to the visit-
ation of God.   Again, if a relic does not always cure it
rarely kills, as calomel has been known to do.   This
interruptive principle, one distinct from human remedies,
is admitted by the church in the prayers for sick persons; and where faith is sincere, even relics must offer
a powerful moral medical cordial, by acting on the
imagination, and giving confidence to the patient.   This
chance is denied to the poor Protestant, nay, even to a
newly-converted tractarian, for truly, to believe in the
efficacy of a monkish bone, the lesson must have been
learnt in the nursery.   Their substitute in Lutheran
lands, in partibus infidelium, is found in laudanum, news,
and gossip; the latter being the grand specific by which
Sir Henry kept scores of dowagers alive, to the despair
of joointure-paying sons, from marquises down to
baronets; and how much real comfort is conveyed by
the gentle whisper, '' Your ladyship cannot conceive
what an interest his or her Royal Highness the ——
takes in your ladyship's convalescence!''   The *form* of
the moral restorative will vary according to climate,

creeds, manners, etc. ; it is to the *substance* alone that
the philosophical physician will look. That chord must
be touched, be it what it may, to which the pulse of
the patient will respond; nor, provided he is recovered,
do the means much signify.

One word only on Spanish midwifery. There is a dislike to male accoucheurs, and the midwife, or *comadre,*
generally brings the Spaniard into the world by the
efforts of nature and the aid of *manteca de puerco,* or
hog's lard, a launching appropriate enough to a babe,
who, if it survives to years of discretion, will assuredly
love bacon. The newly-born is then wrapped up, like an
Egyptian mummy, and is carefully protected from fresh
air, soap, and water; an amulet is then hung round its
neck to disarm the evil eye, or some badge of the Virgin
is to ensure good luck : thus the young idea is taught
from the cradle, what errors are to be avoided and what
safeguards are to be clung to, lessons which are seldom
forgotten in after-life. Without entering further into
baby details, the scanty population of the Peninsula may
in some measure be thus accounted for. Parturition also
is frequently fatal; in ordinary cases the midwife does
very well, but when a difficulty arises she loses her head
and patient. It is in these trying moments, as in the
critical operations of the kitchen, that a male artiste is
preferable.

The Queens and Infantas of Spain have additional
advantages. The palladium of the city of Tortosa is the
cinta [1] or girdle, which the Virgin, accompanied by St.
Peter and St. Paul, brought herself from heaven to a
priest of the cathedral in 1178; an event in honour of
which a mass is still said every second Sunday in
October. The gracious gift was declared authentic in
1617, by Paul V., and to justify his infallibility it works
every sort of miracle, especially in obstetric cases; it is
also brought out to defend the town on all occasions of
public calamity, but failed in the case of Suchet's attack.
This girdle, more wonderful than the cestus of Venus,
was conveyed in 1822, by Ferdinand VII.'s command, in

---

[1] Hallarse en *Cinta* is the Spanish equivalent for our " being
in the family way."

solemn procession to Aranjuez, in order to facilitate the
accouchement of the two Infantas, and as Lucina when
duly invoked favoured women in travail, so their Royal
Highnesses were happily delivered, and one of the babes
then born, is the husband of Isabel II.   For humbler
Castilian women, when pregnant, a spiritual remedy was
provided by the canons of Toledo, who took the liveliest
interest in many of the cases.   The grand entrance to
the cathedral had thirteen steps, and all females who
ascended and descended them ensured an early and easy
time of it.   No wonder therefore, when these steps were
reduced to the number of seven, that the greatest possible
opposition should have been made by the fair sex, married
and unmarried.   All these things of Spain are rather
Oriental; and to this day the Barbary Moors have a
cannon at Tangiers by which a Christian ship was sunk,
and across this their women sit to obtain an easy
delivery.   In all ages and countries where the science of
midwifery has made small progress, it is natural that
some spiritual assistance should be contrived for perils
of such inevitable recurrence as childbirth.   The panacea
in Italy was the girdle of St. Margaret, which became
the type of this *Cinta* of Tortosa, and it was resorted to
by the monks in all cases of difficult parturition.   It was
supposed to benefit the sex, because when the devil
wished to eat up St. Margaret, the Virgin bound him
with her sash, and he became tame as a lamb.   This
sash brought forth sashes also, and in the 17th century
had multiplied so exceedingly, that a traveller affirmed
" if all were joined together, they would reach all down
Cheapside;" but the natural history of relics is too well
known to be enlarged upon.

Any account of Spanish doctors without a death, would
be dull as a blank day with fox-hounds, although the
medical man, differing from the sportsman, dislikes being
in at it.   He, the moment the fatal sisters three are
running into their game, slips out, and leaves the last
act to the clergyman : hence the Spanish saying," When
the priest begins, the physician ends."   It is related in
the history of Don Quixote, that no sooner did the barber
feel the poor knight's wrist, than he advised him to

attend to his soul and send for his confessor; and now, when a Castilian hidalgo takes to his bed, his friends pursue much the same course, nor does the catastrophe often differ. Lord Bacon, great in wise saws and instances, prayed that his death might come from Spain, because then it would be long on the journey; but he was not aware that the gentleman in black formed an exception to the proverbial procrastination and dilatoriness of their fellow countrymen. As patients are soon dispatched, the law [1] of the land subjects every physician to a fine of ten thousand maravedis, who fails after his first visit to prescribe confession; the chief object in sickness being, as the preamble states, to cure the soul; and so it is in Italy, where Gregory XVI. issued in 1845 three decrees; one to forbid railroads, another to prohibit scientific meetings, and a third to order all medical men to cease to attend invalids who had not sent for the priest and communicated after the third visit. In Spain, the first question asked in our time of the sick man was, not whether he truly repented of his sins, but whether he had got the Bull; and if the reply was in the negative, or his old nurse had omitted to send out and buy one, the last sacraments were denied to the dying wretch.

One word on this wonderful Bull, that disarms death of its sting, and which, although few of our readers may ever have heard of it, plays a far more important part in the Peninsula than the quadruped does in the arena. Fastings are nowhere more strictly enjoined than here, where Lent represents the Ramadan of the Moslem. The denials have been mitigated to those faithful who have good appetites, by the paternal indulgence of their holy father at Rome, who, in consideration that it was necessary to keep the Spanish crusaders in fighting condition in order more effectually to crush the infidel, conceded to Saint Ferdinand the permission that his army might eat meat rations during Lent, provided there were any, for, to the credit of Spanish commissariats in general, few troops fast more regularly and religiously. The auspicious day on which the arrival is proclaimed of this welcome bull that announces dinner, is celebrated by

[1] Recopilacion. Lib. iii. Tit. xvi. Ley 3.

bells merry as at a marriage feast; in the provincial cities mayors and corporations go to cathedral in what is called state, to the wonder of the mob and amusement of their betters at the resurrection of quiz coaches, the robes, maces, and obsolete trappings, by which these shadows of a former power and dignity hope to mark individual and collective insignificancy. A copy of this precious Bull cannot of course be had for nothing, and as it must be paid for, and in ready money, it forms one of the certain branches of public income. Although the proceeds ought to be expended on crusading purposes, Ferdinand VII., the Catholic King, and the only sovereign in possession of such a revenue, never contributed one mite towards the Christian Greeks in their recent struggle against the Turkish unbelievers.

These bulls, or rather paper-money notes, are prepared with the greatest precautions, and constituted one of the most profitable articles of Spanish manufacture; a maritime war with England was dreaded, not so much from regard to the fasting transatlantic souls, as from the fear of losing, as Dr. Robertson has shown, the sundry millions of dollars and silver dross remitted from America in exchange for these spiritual treasures. They were printed at Seville, at the Dominican convent, the *Porta cœli;* but Soult, who now it appears is turning devotee, burnt down this gate of heaven, with its passports, and the presses. The bulls are only good for the year during which they are issued; after twelve months they become stale and unprofitable. There is then, says Blanco White, and truly, for we have often seen it, " a prodigious hurry to obtain new ones by all those who wish well to their souls, and do not overlook the ease and comfort of their stomachs." A fresh one must be annually taken out, like a game-certificate, before Spaniards venture to sport with flesh or fowl, and they have reason to be thankful that it does not cost three pounds odd : for the sum of *dos reales*, or less than sixpence, man, woman, and child may obtain the benefit of clergy and cookery; but evil betides the uncertificated poacher, treadmills for life are a farce, perdition catches his soul. His certificate is demanded by the keeper of conscience when he is caught in the trap of sickness, and if without one, his conviction is certain; he cannot plead ignorance of the law, for a postscript and condition is affixed to all notices of jubilees, indulgences, and other purgatorial benefits, which are fixed on the church doors; and the language is as courteous and peremptory as in our popular assessed tax-paper—" Se *ha* de tener la bula:" you *must* have the bull; if you expect to derive any relief from these relaxations in purgatory, which all Spaniards most particularly do: hence the common phrase used by any one, when committing some little peccadillo in other matters, *tengo mi bula para todo*— I have got my bull, my licence to do any thing. The possession of this document acts on all fleshly comforts like soda on indigestion, indeed it neutralises everything except heresy. As it is cheap, a Protestant resident, albeit he may not quite believe in its saving effects, will do well to purchase one for the sake of the peace of mind of his weaker brethren, for in this religion of forms and outer observances, more horror is felt by rigid Spaniards, at seeing an Englishman eating meat during a fast, than if he had broken all the ten commandments. The sums levied from the nation for these bulls is very large, although they are diminished before finally paid into the exchequer; some of the honey gathered by so many bees will stick to their wings, and the place of chief commissioner of the Bula is a better thing than that in the Excise or Customs of unbelieving countries.

To return to the dying man: if he has the bull, the host is brought to him with great pomp; the procession is attended by crowds who bear crosses, lighted candles, bells and incense; and as the chamber is thrown open to the public, the ceremony is accompanied by multitudes of idlers. The spectacle is always imposing, as it must be, considering that the incarnate Deity is believed to be present. It is particularly striking on Easter Sunday, when the host is taken to all the sick who have been unable to communicate in the parish church. Then the priest walks either under a gorgeous canopy, or is mounted in the finest carriage in the town; and while all as he passes kneel to the wafer which he bears, he chuckles internally at his own reality of power over his prostrate subjects; the line of streets are gaily decorated as for the triumphal procession of a king : the windows are hung with velvets and tapestries, and the balconies filled with the fair sex arrayed in their best, who shower sweet flowers down on the procession just at the moment of its passage, and sweeter smiles during all the rest of the morning on their lovers below, whose more than divided adoration is engrossed by female divinities.

To die without confession and communicating is to a Spaniard the most poignant of calamities, as he cannot be saved while he is taught that there is in these acts a preserving virtue of their own, independent of any exertions on his part. The host is given when human hopes are at an end, and the heat, noise, confusion, and excitement, seldom fail to kill the already exhausted patient. Then, when life's idle business at a gasp is o'er, the body is laid out in a *capilla ardiente*, or an apartment prepared as a chapel, by taking out the furniture; where the family is rich, a room on the ground floor is selected, in which a regular altar is dressed up, and rows of large candles lighted placed around the body; the public is then allowed to enter, even in the case of the sovereign : thus we beheld Ferdinand VII. laid out dead and full dressed with his hat on his head, and his stick in his hand. This public exhibition is a sort of coroner's inquest; formerly, as we have often seen, the body was clad in a monk's dress, with the feet naked and the hands clasped over the breast; the sepulchral shadow then thrown over the dead and placid features by the cowl, seldom failed to raise a solemn undefinable feeling in the hearts of spectators, speaking, as it did, a language to the living which could not be misunderstood.

The woollen dresses of the mendicant orders were by far the most popular, from the idea that, when old, they had become too saturated with the odour of sanctity for the vile nostrils of the evil one; and as a tattered dress often brought more than half-a-dozen new ones, the sale of these old clothes was a benefit alike to the pious vendor and purchaser; those of St. Francis were preferred, because at his triennial visits to purgatory, he

knows his own, and takes them back with him to heaven;
hence Milton peopled his shadowy limbo with wolves in
sheep's clothing :—

> —— " who, to be sure of Paradise,
> Dying put on the robes of Dominick,
> Or in Franciscan think to pass unseen."

Women in our time were often laid out in nuns'
dresses, wearing also the scapulary of the Virgin of
Carmel, which she gave to Simon Stock, with the assurance that none who died with it on, should ever suffer
eternal torments. The general adoption of these grave
fashions induced an accurate foreigner to remark, that
no one ever died in Spain except nuns and monks. In
this hot country, burial goes hand in hand with death,
and it is absolutely necessary from the rapidity with
which putrefaction comes on. The last offices are performed in somewhat an indecent manner : formerly the
interment took place in churches, or in the yards near
them, a custom which from hygeian reasons is now prohibited. Public cemeteries, which give at least 4 per
cent. interest, have been erected outside the towns, in
which long lines of catacombs gape greedily for those
occupants who can pay for them, while a wide ditch is
opened every day for those who cannot. In this *campo
santo*, or holy field, death levels all ranks, which seems
hard on those great families who have built and endowed
chapels to secure a burial among their ancestors. They
however raised no objections to the change of law, nor
have ever much troubled themselves about the dilapidated
sepulchres and crumbling effigies of their " grandsires
cut in alabaster;" the real opposition arose from the
priests, who lost their fees, and thereupon assured their
flocks, that a future resurrection was anything but
certain to bodies committed into such new-fangled
depositories.

Be that as it may, the corpse in its slight coffin is
carried out, followed by the male relations, and is then
put into its niche without further form or prayer. Ladies
who die soon after marriage, and before the bridal hours
have danced their measure, are sometimes buried in their

wedding dresses, and covered with flowers, the dying injunctions of Shakespeare's Queen Catherine :—

> " When I am dead, good wench,
> Let me be used with honour ; strew me o'er
> With maiden flowers, that all the world may know
> I was a chaste wife to my grave."

At such funerals the coffin is opened in the catacomb, to gratify the indecent curiosity of the crowd ; the dress is next day discussed all over the town, and the *entierro* or funeral is pronounced to be *muy lucido* or very brilliant ; but life in Spain is a jest, and these things show it. The place assigned for children who die under seven years of age lies apart from that of the adults ; their early death is held in Spain to be rather a matter of congratulation than of grief, since those whom the gods love die young ; their epitaphs tell a mixed tale of joy and sorrow. *El parvulo fue arrebatado á la gloria*, the little one was snatched up into Paradise :—

> " There is beyond the sky a heaven of joy and love,
> And holy children, when they die, go to that world above."

Yet nature will not be put aside, and many a mother have we seen, loitering alone near the graves, adorning them with roses and plucking up weeds which have no business to grow there ; the little corpses are carried to the tomb by little children of the same age, clad in white, and are strewed with flowers short-lived as themselves, sweets to the sweet. The parents return home yearning after the lost child—its cradle is empty, its piteous moan is heard no more, its playthings remain where it left them, and recall the cruel gap which grief cannot fill up, although it

> " Stuffs out its vacant garments with its form."

The bodies of the lower orders, dressed in their ordinary attire, are borne to their long home by four men, as is described by Martial ; " no useless coffins enclose their breasts," they are carried forth as was the widow's son at Nain. And often have we seen the frightful death-tray standing upright at the doors of the humble dead, with a human outline marked on the wood by the death-damp of a hundred previous burdens. Such bodies are cast into the trench like those of dogs, and often naked, as the survivors or sextons strip them even of their rags. Those poorer still, who cannot afford to pay the trifling fee, sometimes during the night, suspend the bodies of their children in baskets, near the cemetery porch. We once beheld a cloaked Spaniard pacing mournfully in the burial-ground of Seville, who, when the public trench was opened, drew from beneath the folds the body of his dead child, cast it in and disappeared. Thus half the world lives without knowing how the other half dies.

In the upper ranks the etiquette of the funeral commences after the reality is over. The first necessary step is within three days to pay a visit of condolence to the family; this is called *para dar el pesame.* The relations are all assembled in the best room, and seated on chairs placed at the head, the women at one end and the men at another. When a condoling lady and gentleman enter, she proceeds to shake hands with all the other ladies one after another, and then seats herself in the next vacant chair; the gentleman bows to each of the men as he passes, who rise and return it, a grave dumb-show of profound affliction being kept up by all. On reaching the chief mourners, they are addressed by each condoler with this phrase, " *Acompaño á usted en su sentimiento;*" " I share in the affliction of your grace;" the company meanwhile remain silent as an assemblage of undertakers. After sitting among them the proper time, each retires with much the same form.

In a few days afterwards a printed letter is sent round in the name of all the surviving relations to announce the death to the friends of the family, and to beg the favour of attendance at the funeral service : these invitations are all headed with a cross (+), which is called *El Cristus.* Before the invasion of the enemy, who not only destroyed the walls of convents, but sapped religious belief also, very many books were printed, and private letters written, with this sign prefixed. In our time sundry medical men at Seville always headed with it their prescriptions, the Cardinal Archbishop having granted a certain number of years' release from purgatory to all who sanctified with this mark their recipes even of senna and rhubarb.   Under this cross, in the invitation, are placed the letters R. I. P. A., which signify " Requiescat in pace.   Amen."   At the appointed hour the mourners meet in the *casa mortuaria*, or the house of death, and proceed together to church.   All are dressed in full black, and before the progress of paletots and civilisation, wore no cloaks : this, as it rendered each man of them more uncomfortable than St. Bartholomew was without his skin, was considered an offering of genuine grief to the manes of the deceased. Uncloaking in Spain is, be it remembered, a mark of respect, and is equivalent to our taking off the hat. When the company arrives at church, they are received by the ministers, and the ceremony is very solemnly performed before a catafalque covered with a pall, which is placed before the altar, and is brilliantly lighted up with wax candles.   As soon as the service is concluded, all advance and bow to the chief mourners, who are seated apart, and thus the tragedy concludes.   Parents do not put on mourning for their children, which is a remnant of the patriarchal and Roman superiority of the head of the family, for whom, however, when dead, all the other members pay the most observant respect.   The forms and number of days of mourning are most nicely laid down, and are most rigidly observed, even by distant relations, who refrain from all kinds of amusements :—

> " None bear about the mockery of woe
>   To public dances or to private show."

We well remember the death of a kind and venerable Marquesa at Seville just before the carnival, whose chief grief at dying, was the thought of the number of young ladies who would thus be deprived of their balls and masquerades; many, anxious and obliging, were the inquiries sent after her health, and more even were the daily prayers offered up to the Virgin, for the prolongation of her precious existence, could it be only for a few weeks.

November drear, brings in other solemnities connected
with the dead, and in harmony with the fall of the sear
and yellow leaves, to which Homer compares the races
of mortal men. The night before the first of November—
our All Hallow-e'en—is kept in Spain as a vigil or wake;
it is the fated hour of love divinations and mysteries;
then anxious maidens used to sit at their balconies to
see the image of their destined husbands pass or not
pass by. November the first is dedicated to the sainted
dead, and November the second to all souls : it is termed
in Spanish *el dia de los difuntos*, the day of the dead,
and is most scrupulously observed by all who have lost
during the past year some friend, some relation—how
few have not ! The dawn is ushered in by mournful
bells, which recall the memory of those who cannot come
back at the summons ; the cemeteries are then visited ;
at Seville, long processions of sable-clad females, bearing chased lamps on staves, walk slowly round and
round, chaunting melancholy dirges, returning when it
gets dusk in a long line of glittering lights. The graves
during the day are visited by those who take a sad interest in their occupants, and lamps and flower garlands
are suspended as memorials of affection, and holy water
is sprinkled, every drop of which puts out some of the
fires of purgatory. These picturesque proceedings at
once resemble the *Eed es Segheer* of modern Cairo, the
feralia of the Romans, the Νεμεσια of the Greeks : here
are the flower offerings of Electra, the *funes assensi*,
the funeral torches of pagan mourners, which have
vainly been prohibited to Christian Spaniards by their
early Council of Illiberis. In Navarre, and in the north-
west of Spain, bread and wheat offerings called *robos*
are made, which are the doles or gifts offered for the
souls' rest of the deceased by the pious of ancient Rome.

As on this day the cemetery becomes the public attraction, it too often looks rather a joyous fashionable promenade, than a sad and religious performance. The
levity of mere strangers and the mob, contrasts strangely
with the sorrow of real mourners. But life in this world
presses on death, and the gay treads on the heels of
pathos ; the spot is crowded with mendicants, who

appeal to the order of the day, and importune every tender recollection, by begging for the sake of the lamented dead. Outside the dreary walls all is vitality and mirth; a noisy sale goes on of cakes, nuts, and sweetmeats, a crash of horses and carriages, a din and flow of bad language from those who look after them, which must vex the repose of the *benditas animas*, or the blessed souls in purgatory, for whom otherwise all classes of Spaniards manifest the fondest affection and interest.

Such is the manner in which the body of a most ortho-dox Catholic Castilian is committed to the earth; his soul, if it goes to purgatory, is considered and called blessed by anticipation, as the admittance into Paradise is certain, at the expiration of the term of penal trans-portation, that is, " when the foul crimes done in the days of nature are burnt and purged away," as the ghost in Hamlet says, who had not forgotten his Virgil. If the scholar objects to a Spanish clergyman, that the whole thing is Pagan, he will be told that he may go farther and fare worse. In the case of a true Roman Catholic, this term of hard labour may be much short-ened, since that can be done by masses, any number of which will be said, if first paid for. The vicar of St. Peter holds the keys, which always unlock the gate to those who offer the golden gift by which Charon was bribed by Æneas; thus, to a judicious rich man, nothing, supposing that he believes the Pope *versus* the Bible, is so easy as to get at once into Heaven; nor are the poor quite neglected, as any one may learn who will read the extraordinary number of days' redemption which may be obtained at every altar in Spain by the performance of the most trumpery routine. The only wonder is how any one of the faithful should ever fail to secure his delivery from this spiritual Botany Bay without going there at all, or, at least, only for the form's sake. It was calculated by an accurate and laborious German, that an active man, by spending three shillings in coach-hire, might obtain in an hour, by visiting different privi-leged altars during the Holy week, 29,639 years, nine months, thirteen days, three minutes and a half diminution of purgatorial punishment. This merciful reprieve was offered by Spanish priests in South America, on a grander style, on one commensurate with that colossal continent; for a single mass at the San Francisco in Mexico, the Pope and prelates granted 32,310 years, ten days, and six hours indulgence. As a means of raising money, says our Mexican authority, " I would not give this simple institution of masses for the benefit of souls, for the power of taxation possessed by any government; since no tax-gatherer is required; the payments are enforced by the best feelings, for who would not pay to get a parent's or friend's soul from the fire?" Purgatory has thus been a Golconda mine of gold to his Holiness, as even the poorest have a chance, since charitable persons can deliver blank souls by taking out a *habeas animam* writ, that is, by paying the priest for a mass. The especial days are marked in the almanac, and known to every waiter at the inn; moreover, notice is put on the church door, *Hoy se saca anima*, " this day you can get out a soul." They are generally left in their warm quarters in winter, and taken out in the spring.

Alas for poor Protestants, who, by non-payment of St. Peter's pence, have added an additional act of heresy, and the worst of all, the one which Rome never pardons. These defaulters can only hope to be saved by faith, and its fruits, good works; they must repent, must quit their long-cherished sins, and lead a new life; for them there is no rope of St. Francis to pull them out, if once in the pit; no rosary of St. Domenick to remove them, quick, presto, begone, from torment to happiness. Outside the pale of the Vatican, their souls have no chance, and inside the frontiers of Spain their bodies have scarcely a better prospect, should they die in that orthodox land. There the greatest liberal barely tolerates any burial at all of their black-blooded heretical carcasses, as no corn will grow near them. Until within a very few years at seaport towns, their bodies used to be put in a hole in the sands, and beyond low water mark; nay, even this concession to the infidel offended the semi-Moro fishermen, who true believers and persecutors feared that their soles might be

poisoned : not that either sailor or priest ever exhibited
any fear of taking British current coin, all cash that
comes into their nets being most Catholic, so says the
proverb, *El dinero es muy Catolico.*

Matters connected with the grave have been placed,
as regards Protestants, on a much more pleasant foot-
ing within these last few years ; and it may be a consolation to invalids, who are sent to Spain for change of
climate, and who are particular, to know, in case of
accidents, that Protestant burial-grounds are now permitted at Cadiz, Malaga, and in a few other places. The
history of the permission is curious, and has never, to
the best of our belief, been told. In the days of Philip
II. Lutherans were counted in many degrees worse than
dogs ; when caught alive, they were burnt by the holy
tribunal ; and when dead, were cast out on the dung-
hill. Even when our poltroon James I. sent, in 1622,
his ill-judged olive-bearing mission, by which Spain was
saved from utter humiliation, Mr. Hole, the secretary
of the ambassador, Lord Digby, having died at Santander, the body was not allowed to be buried at all ; it was
put into a shell, and sunk in the sea ; but no sooner was
his lordship gone, than " the fishermen," we quote from
Somers' tracts, " fearing that they should catch no fish
as long as the coffin of a heretic lay in their waters,"
fished it up, " and the corpse of our countryman and
brother was thrown above ground, to be devoured by
the fowls of the air." In the treaty of 1630, the 31st
Article provided for the disposal of the goods of those
Englishmen who might die in Spain, but not for their
bodies. " These," says a commentator of Rymer," must
be left stinking above ground, to the end that the dogs
may be sure to find them." When Mr. Washington,
page to Charles I., died at Madrid, at the time his
master was there, Howell, who was present, relates
that it was only as an especial favour to the suitor of
the Spanish Infanta that the body was allowed to be
interred in the garden of the embassy, under a fig-tree.
A few years afterwards, 1650, Ascham, the envoy of
Cromwell, was assassinated, and his corpse put, without
any rites, into a hole ; but the Protector was not a man

to be trifled with, and knew well how to deal with a Spanish government, always a craven and bully, from whom nothing ever is to be obtained by concession and gentleness, which is considered as weakness, while everything is to be extorted from its *fears*. He that very year *commanded* a treaty to be prepared for the proper burial of his subjects, to which the blustering Spaniard immediately assented. This provision was stipulated into the treaty of Charles II. in 1664, and was conceded and ratified again in 1667 to Sir Richard Fanshawe.

No step, however, appears to have been taken before 1796, when Lord Bute purchased a spot of ground for the burial of Englishmen outside the Alcalá-gate, at Madrid. During the war, when all Spain was a churchyard to our countrymen, this bit of land was taken possession of by a worthy Madrilenian, not for his place of sepulture, but for good and profitable cultivation. In 1831 Mr. Addington caused some researches to be made, and the original conveyance was found in the *Contaduria de Hypothecas*, the registry of deeds and mortgages which backward Spain possesses, and which advanced England does not. The intruder was ejected after some struggling on his part. Before Lord Bute's time the English had been buried at night and without ceremonies, in the garden of the convent *de los Recoletos ;* and, as Lord Bute's new bit of ground was extensive and valuable, the pious monks wished to give up the English corner in their garden, in exchange for it; but the transfer was prevented by the recent law which forbade all burial in cities. The field purchased by Lord Bute is now unenclosed and uncultivated; fortunately it has not been much wanted, only fifteen Protestants having died at Madrid during the last thirty years. In November, 1831, Ferdinand VII. finally settled this grave question by a decree, in which he granted permission for the erection of a Protestant burial-ground in all towns where a British consul or agent should reside, subject to most *degrading* conditions. The first cemetery set apart in Spain, in virtue of this gracious decree from a man replaced on his throne by the death of 30,000 Englishmen, was the work of Mr. Mark, our consul at

Malaga; he enclosed a spot of ground to the east of that city, and placed a tablet over the entrance, recording the royal permission, and above that a cross. Thus he appealed to the dominant feelings of Spaniards, to their loyalty and religion. The Malagenians were amazed when they beheld this emblem of Christianity raised over the last home of Lutheran dogs, and exclaimed, " So even these Jews make use of the cross !" The term Jew, it must be remembered, is the acme of Spanish loathing and vituperation. The first body interred in it was that of Mr. Boyd, who was shot by the bloody Moreno, with the poor dupe Torrijos and the rest of his rebel companions.

CHAPTER XIX

FEW who love Don Quixote, will deem any notice on the Peninsular surgeon complete in which the barber is not mentioned, even be it in a postcript. Although the names of both these learned professors have long been nearly synonymous in Spain, the barber is much to be preferred, inasmuch as his cuts are less dangerous, and his conversation is more agreeable. He with the curate formed the quiet society of the Knight of La Mancha, as the apothecary and vicar used to make that of most of our country squires of England. Let, therefore, every Adonis of France, now bearded as a pard although young, nay, let each and all of our fair readers, albeit equally exempt from the pains and penalties of daily shaving, make instantly, on reaching sunny Seville, a pilgrimage to the shrine of San Figaro. His shop— apocryphal it is to be feared as other legendary localities —lies near the cathedral, and is a no less established lion than the house of Dulcinea is at Toboso, or the prison tower of Gil Blas is at Segovia. Such is the magic power of genius. Cervantes and Le Sage have given form, fixture, and local habitation to the airy nothings

of their fancy's creations, while Mozart and Rossini, by
filling the world with melody, have bidden the banks of
the Guadalquivir re-echo to their sweet inventions.

To those even who have no music in their souls, the
movement from doctors to barbers is harmonious in a
land where beards were long honoured as the type of
valour and chivalry, and where shaving took the precedence of surgery; and even to this day, *la tiendo de
barbero*, the shop of the man of the razor, is better
supplied than many a Spanish hospital both with
patients and cutting instruments.   One word first on the
black whiskers of tawny Spain.   These *patillas*, as
they are now termed, must be distinguished from the
ancient mustachio, the *mostacho*, a very classical but
almost obsolete word, which the scholars of Salamanca
have derived from μυστάξ, the upper lip.   Their present
and usual name is *Bigote*, which is also of foreign
etymology, being the Spanish corruption of the German
oath *bey gott*, and formed under the following circumstances : for nicknames, which stick like burrs, often
survive the history of their origin.   The free-riding
followers of Charles V., who wore these tremendous
appendages of manhood, swore like troopers, and gave
themselves infinite airs, to the more infinite disgust of
their Spanish comrades, who have a tolerable good
opinion of themselves, and a first-rate hatred of all their
foreign allies.   These strange mustachios caught their
eyes, as the stranger sounds which proceeded from beneath them did their ears.   Having a quick sense of the
ridiculous, and a most Oriental and schoolboy knack at
a nickname, they thereupon gave the sound to the substance, and called the redoubtable garnish of hair, *bigotes*.   This process in the formation of phrases is
familiar to philologists, who know that an essential part
often is taken for the whole.   For example, a hat, in
common Spanish parlance, is equivalent to a grandee,
as with us the woolsack is to a Lord Chancellor.   It is
natural that unscholastic soldiers, when dealing with
languages which they do not understand, should fix on
their enemies, as a term of reproach, those words which,
from hearing used the most often, they imagine must

constitute the foundation of the hostile grammar. Thus
our troops called the Spaniards *los Carajos*, from their
terrible oaths and terrible runnings away. So the clever
French designated as *les godams*, those " stupid " fellows in red jackets who never could be made to know
when they were beaten, but continued to make use of
that significant phrase in reference to their victors, until
they politely showed them the shortest way home over
the Pyrenees.

The real Spanish mustachio, as worn by the real Don
Whiskerandoses, men with shorter cloaks and purses
than beards and rapiers, have long been cut off, like the
pig-tails of our monarchs and cabinet ministers. Yet
their merits are embalmed in metaphors more enduring
than that masterpiece in bronze with which Mr. Wyatt,
full of Phidias, has adorned King George's back and
Charing Cross. Thus *hombre de mucho bigote*, a man
of much moustache, means, in Spanish, a personage of
considerable pretension, a fine, liberal fellow, and anything, in short, but a bigot in wine, women, or theology.
The Spanish original realities, like the pig-tails of Great
Britain, have also been immortalised by fine art, and
inimitably painted by Velasquez. Under his life-conferring brush they required no twisting with hot irons.
Curling from very ire and martial instinct, they were
called *bigotes á la Fernandina*, and their rapid growth
was attributed to the eternal cannon smoke of the
enemy, into which nothing could prevent their valorous
wearers from poking their faces. This luxuriance has
diminished in these degenerate times, unless Napier's
' History of the Peninsular War ' be, as the Spaniards
say, written in a spirit of envy and jealousy against their
heroic armies, which alone trampled on the invincible
eagles of Austerlitz.

As among the Egyptian gods and priests, rank was
indicated by the cut of the beard, so in Spain the
military, civil and clerical shapes were carefully defined.
The Charley, or Imperial, as we term the little tuft in
the middle of the under lip, a word by the way which
is derivable either from our Charles or from his name-
sake emperor, was called in Spain *El perrillo* " the little

dog," the terminating tail being omitted, which however becoming in the animal and bronzes, shocked Castilian euphuism.

In the mediæval periods of Spain's greatness the beard and not the whisker was the real thing; and as among the Orientals and ancients, it was at once the mark of wisdom and of soldiership; to cut it off was an insult and injury scarcely less than decapitation; nay, this nicety of honour survived the grave. The seated corpse of the Cid, so tells his history, knocked down a Jew who ventured to take the dead lion by his beard, which, as all natural philosophers know, has an independent vitality, and grows whether its master be alive or dead, be willing or unwilling. When the insolent Gauls pulled these flowing ornaments of the aged Roman senators, they, who with unmoved dignity had seen Marshal Brennus steal their plate and pictures, could not brook that last and greatest outrage. In process of time and fashion the beards of Spain fell off, and being only worn by mendicant monks and he-goats, were considered ungentlemanlike, and were substituted among cavaliers by the Italian mostachio; the seat of Spanish honour was then placed under the nose, that sensitive sentinel. The renowned Duke of Alva being of course in want of money, once offered one of his bigotes as a pledge for a loan, and one only was considered to be a sufficient security by the Rothschilds of the day, who remembered the hair-breadth escape of their ancestor too well to laugh at anything connected with a hero's beard; *nous avons changé tout cela.* The united Hebrews of Paris and London would not now advance a stiver for every particular hair on the bodies of Narvaez and Espartero, not even if the moustache reglémentaire of Montpensier, and a bushel of Bourbon beards, warranted legitimate, were added.

The use of the *bigote* in Spain is legally confined to the military, most of whose generals—their name is legion—are tenderly chary of their Charlies, dreading razors no less than swords; when the Infante Don Carlos escaped from England, the only real difficulty was in getting him to cut off his moustache; he would almost sooner have lost his head, like his royal English *tocayo* or omonyme.   Elizabeth's gallant Drake, when he burnt Philip's fleet at Cadiz, simply called his Nelsonic touch "singeing the King of Spain's whiskers." Zurbano the other day thought it punishment enough for any Basque traitors to cut off their *bigotes*, and turn them loose, like rats without tails, *pour encourager les autres*. It is indeed a privation.   Thus Majaval, the pirate murderer, who by the glorious uncertainty of English law was not hanged at Exeter, offered his prison beard, when he reached Barcelona, to the delivering Virgin. Many Spanish civilians and shopkeepers, in imitation of the transpyrenean *Calicots,* men who wear moustachios on their lips in peace, and spectacles on their noses in war, so constantly let them grow, that Ferdinand VII. fulminated a royal decree, which was to cut them off from the face of the Peninsula, as the Porte is docking his true believers.   Such is the progress of young and beardless civilisation.   The attempt to shorten the cloaks of Madrid nearly cost Charles III. his crown, and this cropping mandate of his beloved grandson was obeyed as Spanish decrees generally are, for a month all but twenty-nine days.   These decrees, like solemn treaties, charters, stock-certificates, and so forth, being mostly used to light cigars; now-a-days that the Moro-Spaniard is aping the true Parisian polish, the national countenance is somewhat put out of face, to the serious sorrow and disparagement of poor Figaro.

As for his house and home none can fail finding it out; no cicerone is wanted, for the outside is distinguished from afar by the emblems of his time-honoured profession : first and foremost hangs a bright glittering metal Mambrino-helmet basin, with a neat semicircular opening cut out of the rim, into which the throat of the patient is let during the operation of lathering, which is always done with the hand and most copiously ; near it are suspended huge grinders, which in an English museum would pass for the teeth of elephants, and for those of Saint Christopher in Spanish churches, where comparative anatomy is scouted as heretical in the matter of relics; strange to say, and no Spanish theologian could ever satisfy us why, this saint is not the " especial advocate " against toothache ; here Santa Apollonia is the soothing patroness. Near these molars are displayed awful phlebotomical symbols, and rude representations of bloodlettings ; for in Spain, in church and out, painting does the work of printing to the many who can see, but cannot read. The barber's pole, with its painted bandage riband, the support by which the arm was kept extended, is wanting to the threshold of the Figaros of Spain, very much because bleeding is generally performed in the foot, in order that the equilibrium of the whole circulation may be maintained. The painting usually presents a female foot, which being an object, and not unreasonably, of great devotion in Spain, is selected by the artist ; tradition also influences the choice, for the dark sex were wont formerly to be bled regularly as calves are still, to obtain whiteness of flesh and fairness of complexion : as it was usual on each occasion that the lover should restore the exhausted patient by a present, the purses of gallants kept pace with the venous depletion of their mistresses. The *Sangrados* of Spain, professional as well as unprofessional, have long been addicted to the shedding of innocent blood ; indeed, no people in the world are more curious about the pedigree purity of their own blood, nor less particular about pouring it out like water, whether from their own veins or those of others. One word on this vital fluid with which unhappy Spain is too often watered during her intestine disorders.

If the Iberian anatomists did not discover its circulation, the heralds have " tricked " out its blazoning, as we do our admirals, with all the nicety of armorial colouring. *Blue blood, Sangre azul,* is the ichor of demigods which flows in the arteries of the grandees and highest nobility, each of whose pride is to be

> " A true Hidalgo, free from every stain
> Of Moor or Jewish blood,"

a boast which like some others of theirs wants confirmation, as it is in the power of one woman to taint the blood of Charlemagne ; and nature, which cannot be

written down by Debretts, has stamped on their countenances the marks of hybrid origin, and particularly
from these very and most abhorred stocks; it is from
this tint of celestial azure that the term *sangre su* is
given in Spain to the elect and best set of earth, the
haute volée, who soar above vulgar humanity. *Red*
blood flows in the veins of poor gentlemen and younger
brothers, and is just tolerated by all, except judicious
mothers, whose daughters are marriageable. *Blood,*
simple blood, is the puddle which paints the cheek of
the plebeian and roturier; it has, or ought to possess,
a perfect incompatibility with the better coloured fluid,
and an oil and vinegar property of non-amalgamation.
There is more difference, as Salario says, between such
bloods, than there is between red wine and Rhenish.
These and other dreams are, it is to be feared, the fond
metaphors of heralds. The rosy stream in mockery of
rouge croix and *blue* dragons flows inversely and per-
versely : in the arteries of the lusty muleteer it is the
lava blood of health and vigour; in the monkey marquis
and baboon baron it stagnates in the dull lethargy of
a blue collapse. Their noble ichor is virtually more
impoverished than their nominal rent-roll, since the
operation of transmission of wholesome blood from
young veins into a worn-out frame, which is so much
practised elsewhere, is too nice for the *Sangre su* and
Sangrados of Spain; the thin fluid is never enriched with
the calipash heiress of an alderman, nor is the decayed
genealogical stock renewed by the golden graft of a
banker's only daughter. The insignificant grandees of
Spain quietly permitted Christina to barter away their
country's liberties; but when her children by the base-
born Muñoz came betwixt them and their nobility, then
alone did they remonstrate. Indifferent to the degradation of the throne, they were tremblingly alive to the
punctilios of their own order. Those Peninsular ladies
who are blues, by blood not socks, are equally fastidious
in the serious matter of its admixture even by Hymen :
one of them, it is said, having chanced in a moment of
weakness to mingle her azure with something brownish,
alleged in excuse that she had done so for her charac-

ter's sake. "*Que disparate, mi Señora.*" "What nonsense, my lady!" was her fair confidante's reply; "ten bastards would have less discoloured your blood, than one legitimate child the issue of such a misalliance."

To stick, however, to our colours; *black blood* is the vile Stygean pitch which is found in the carcasses of Jews, Gentiles, Moors, Lutherans, and other combustible heretics, with whose bodies the holy tribunal made bonfires for the good of their souls. Nay, in the case of the Hebrew this black blood is also thought to stink, whence Jews were called by learned Latinists *putos, quia putant*; and certainly at Gibraltar an unsavoury odour seems to be gentilitious in the children of Israel, not however to unorthodox and unheraldic nostrils a jot more so, than in the believing Spanish monk. Recently the colour *black* has been assigned to the blood of political opponents, and a copious "*shedding of vile black blood*" has been the regular panacea of every military Sangrado. How extremes meet! Thus, this aristocracy of colour, in despotical old Spain, which lies in the veins, is placed on the skin in new republican America. Where is the free and easy Yankee would recognise a brother, in a black?

To return to Figaro. There is no mistaking his shop; for independently of the external manifestations of the fine arts practised within, his threshold is the lounge of all idlers, as well as of those who are anxious to relieve their chins of the thick stubble of a three days' growth. The house of the barber has, since the days of Solomon and Horace, been the mart of news and gossip,—of epigram and satire, as Pasquino the tailor's was at Rome. It is the club of the lower orders, who here take up a position, and listen, cloaked as Romans, to some reader of the official Gazette, which, with a cigar, indicates modern civilisation, and soothes him with empty vapour. Here, again, is the mint of scandal, and all who have lived intimately with Spaniards, know how invariably every one stabs his neighbour behind his back with words, the lower orders occasionally using knives sharper even than their tongues. Here, again,

resort gamblers, who, seated on the ground with cards
more begrimed than the earth, pursue their fierce game
as eager as if existence was at stake; for there is generally some well-known cock of the walk, a bully, or
guapo, who will come up and lay his hand on the cards,
and say, " No one shall play with any cards but with
mine "—*aqui no se juega sino con mis barajas.* If the
parties are cowed, they give him a halfpenny each. If,
however, one of the challenged be a spirited fellow, he
defies him—*Aqui no se cobra el barato sino con un puñal
de Albacete*—" You get no change here except out of
an Albacete knife." If the defiance be accepted, *Vamos alla* is the answer—" Let's go to it." There's an
end then of the cards, all flock to the more interesting
écarté; instances have occurred, where Greek meets
Greek, of their tying the two advanced feet together,
and yet remaining fencing with knife and cloak for a
quarter of an hour before the blow be dealt. The knife
is held firmly, the thumb is pressed straight on the blade,
and calculated either for the cut or thrust.

The term *Barato* strictly means the present which is
given to waiters who bring a new pack of cards. The
origin is Arabic, *Baara,* " a *voluntary* gift;" in the corruption of the *Baratero,* it has become an involuntary
one. Our legal term *Barratry* is derived from the
mediæval *Barrateria,* which signified cheating or foul
play. Cervantes well knew that *Baratar* in old Spanish
meant to exchange unfairly, to thimble-rig, to sell anything under its real value, and therefore gave the name
of *Barrateria* to Sancho's sham government. The
Baratero is quite a thing of Spain, where personal
prowess is cherished, and there is one in every regiment,
ship, prison, and even among galley-slaves.

The interior of the barber's shop is equally a *cosa de
España.* Her neighbour may boast to lead Europe in
hair-dressing and clipping poodles, but Figaro snaps
his fingers at her civilisation, and no cat's ears and tail
can be closer shaved than his one's are. The walls
of his operating room are neatly lathered with white-
wash: on a peg hangs his brown cloak and conical hat;
his shelves are decorated with clay-painted figures of

picturesque rascals, arrayed in all their Andalucian tog-gery—bandits, bull-fighters, and smugglers, who, espe-cially the latter, are more universally popular than all or any long-tail-coated chancellors of exchequers. The walls are enlivened with rude prints of fandango dancings, miracles, and bull-fights, in which the Spanish vulgar delight, as ours do in racing and ring notabilities. Nor is a portrait of his *querido*, his black-eyed sweetheart, often wanting. Near these, for religion mixes itself with everything of Spain, are images of the Virgin, patron saints, with stoups for holy water, and little cups in which lighted wicks burn floating on green oil; and formerly no bar-ber prepared for an operation, whether on veins, teeth, or beards, without first making the sign of a cross. Thus hallowed, his implements of art are duly arranged in order; his glass, soap, towels, and leather strap, and guitar, which indeed, with the razor, constitutes the genus barber. "These worthies," said Don Quixote, "are all either *guitarristas o copleros;* they are either makers of couplets, or accompany other songsters with catgut." Hence Quevedo, in his ' Pigsties of Satan,' punishes unrighteous Figaros, by hanging up near them a guitar, which tantalises their touch, and moves away when they wish to take it down.

Few Spaniards ever shave themselves: it is too mechanical, so they prefer, like the Orientals, a "razor that is hired," and as that must be paid for, scarcely any go to the expensive luxury of an every-day shave. Indeed, Don Quixote advised Sancho, when nominated a governor, to shave at least every other day if he wished to look like a gentleman. The peculiar sallow-ness of a Spaniard's face is heightened by the contrast of a sable bristle. Figaro himself is dressed much after the fashion in which he appears on transpyrenean stages; he, on true Galenic principles, takes care not to alarm his patients by a lugubrious costume. There is nothing black, or appertaining to the grave about him; he is all tags, tassels, colour, and embroidery, quips and quirks; he is never still; always in a bustle, he is lying and lathering, cutting chins and capers, here, there, and everywhere. *Figaro la, Figaro qua.* If he has a moment free from taking off beards and making paper cigars, he whips down his guitar and sings the last seguidilla; thus he drives away dull care, who hates the sound of merry music, and no wonder; the operator performs his professional duties much more skilfully than the rival surgeon, nor does he bungle at any little extraneous *amateur* commissions; and there are more real performances enacted by the barbers in Seville itself, than in a dozen European opera houses.

These Figaros, says their proverb, are either mad or garrulous, *Barberos, o locos, o parleros.* Hence, the Andalucian autocrat, Adrian, when asked how he liked to be shaved, replied " Silently." Humbler mortals must submit to let Figaro have his wicked way in talk; for when a man is fixed in his operating chair, with his jaws lathered, and his nose between a finger and a thumb, there is not much conversational fair play or reciprocity. The Spanish barber is said to learn to shave on the orphan's head, and nothing, according to one described by Martial, escaped except a single wary he-goat. The experiments tried on the veins and teeth of aching humanity, are sometimes ludicrous—at others serious, as we know to our cost, having been silly enough to leave behind in Spain two of our wise teeth as relics, tokens, and trophies of Figaro's unrelenting prowess. We cannot but remember such things were, and were dearer, than the pearls in Cleopatra's ears, which she melted in her gazpachos. " A mouth without molars," said Don Quixote to Sancho, " is worse than a mill without grinding-stones;" and the Don was right.

CHAPTER XX

Now that the most approved methods of travelling, living, and being buried in Spain have been touched on,

our kind readers will naturally inquire, what are the
peculiar attractions which should induce gentlemen and
ladies who take their ease at home, to adventure into
this land of roughing it, in which *rats* rather than hares
jump up when the least expected. "What to observe"
is a question easier asked than answered; who indeed
can cater for the multitudinous variety of fancies, the
differences by which Nature keeps all nature right?
Who shall decide when doctors disagree, as they always
do, on matters of taste, since every one has his own
way of viewing things, and his own hobby and predilection? Say not, however, with Smellfungus, that all is
a wilderness from Dan to Beersheba,—nor seek for
weeds where flowers grow. The search for the excellent is the high road to excellence, as not to appreciate
it when found is the surest test of mediocrity. The
refining effort and habit teaches the mind to think;
from long pondering on the beautiful world without,
snatches are caught of the beautiful world within, and
a glimpse is granted to the chosen few, of glories hidden
from the vulgar many. They indeed have eyes, but
see not; nay, scarcely do they behold the things of
external nature, until told what to look for, where to
find it, and how to observe it; then a new sense, a
second sight, is given. Happy, thrice happy those from
whose eyes the film has been removed, who instead of
a previous vague general and unintelligent stare, have
really learnt to *see!* To them a fountain of new delights,
pure and undefiled, welling up and overflowing, is
opened; in proportion as they comprehend the infinite
form, colour, and beauty with which Nature clothes her
every work, albeit her sweetest charms are only revealed to the initiated, reserved as the rich reward of
those who bow to her shrine with singleness of purpose, and turn to her worship with all their hearts,
souls, and understandings.

It was with these beneficent intentions that our good
friend John Murray first devised Handbooks; and next,
by writing them himself, taught others how to dip into
inkstands for red books, which tell man, woman, and
child what to observe, to the ruin of *laquais de place,*

and discomfiture of authors of single octavos and long
vacation excursions. Few gentlemen who publish the
notes of their Peninsular gallop much improve their
light diaries by discussing heavy handbook subjects;
skimming, like swallows, over the surface, and in pursuit of insects, they neither heed nor discern the gems
which lurk in the deeps below; they see indeed all the
scum and straws which float on the surface, and write
down on their tablets all that is rotten in the state of
Spain. Hence the sameness of some of their works;
one book and bandit reflects another, until writers and
readers are imprisoned in a vicious circle. Nothing
gives more pain to Spaniards than seeing volume after
volume written on themselves and their country by
foreigners, who have only rapidly glanced at one-half of
the subject, and that half the one of which they are
the most ashamed, and consider the least worth notice.
This constant prying into the nakedness of the land and
exposing it afterwards, has increased the dislike which
they entertain towards the *impertinente curioso* tribe:
they well know and deeply feel their country's decline;
but like poor gentlefolks, who have nothing but the
past to be proud of, they are anxious to keep these
family secrets concealed, even from themselves, and
still more from the observations of those who happen
to be their superiors, not in blood, but in worldly prosperity. This dread of being shown up sharpens their
inherent suspicions, when strangers wish to "observe,"
and examine into their ill-provided arsenals and institutions, just as Burns was scared even by the honest
antiquarian Grose; so they lump the good and the bad,
putting them down as book-making Paul Prys:—

> " If there's a hole in a' your coats,
>   I rede ye tent it ;
> A chiel's amang ye, taking notes,
>   And faith ! he'll prent it."

The less observed and said about these Spanish matters, these *cosas de España*—the present tatters in her
once proud flag, on which the sun never set—is, they
think, the soonest mended. These comments heal
slower than the knife-gash—" *Sanan cuchilladas, mas*

NO *malas palabras.*" Let no author imagine that the fairest observations that he can take and make of Spain as she is, setting down nought in malice, can ever please a Spaniard; his pride and self-esteem are as great as the self-conceit and low consequence of the American; both are morbidly sensitive and touchy; both are afflicted with the notion that all the world, who are never troubling their heads about them, are thinking of nothing else, and linked in one common conspiracy, based in envy, jealousy, or ignorance; "you don't understand us, I guess." Truth, except in the shape of a compliment, is the greatest of libels, and is howled against as a lie and forgery from the Straits to the Bidasoa; Napier's history, for example. The Spaniard, who is hardly accustomed to a free, or rather a licentious press, and the scavenger propensity with which, in England and America, it rakes into the sewers of private life and the gangrenes of public, is disgusted with details which he resents as a breach of hospitality in strangers. He considers, and justly, that it is no proof either of goodness of breeding, heart, or intellect, to be searching for blemishes rather than beauties, for toadstools rather than violets; he despises those curmudgeons who see motes rather than beams in the brightest eyes of Andalucia. The productions of strangers, and especially of those who ride and write the quickest, must savour of the pace and sources from whence they originate. Foreigners who are unacquainted with the language and good society of Spain are of necessity brought the most into contact with the lowest scenes and the worst class of people, thus road-scrapings and postillion information too often constitute the raw-head-and-bloody-bones material of their composition. All this may be very amusing to those who like these subjects, but they afford a poor criterion for descanting on whatever does the most honour to a country, or gives sound data for judging its real condition. How would we ourselves like that Spaniards should form their opinions of England and Englishmen from the Newgate calendars, the reports of cads, and the annals of beer-shops?

Various as are the objects worth observing in Spain, many of which are to be seen there only, it may be as well to mention what is *not* to be seen, for there is no such loss of time as finding this out oneself, after weary chace and wasted hour. Those who expect to meet with well-garnished arsenals, libraries, restaurants, charitable or literary institutions, canals, railroads, tunnels, suspension-bridges, steam-engines, omnibuses, manufactories, polytechnic galleries, pale-ale breweries, and similar appliances and appurtenances of a high state of political, social, and commercial civilisation, had better stay at home. In Spain there are no turnpike-trust meetings, no quarter-sessions, no courts of *justice*, according to the real meaning of that word, no treadmills, no boards of guardians, no chairmen, directors, masters-extraordinary of the court of chancery, no assistant poor-law commissioners. There are no anti-tobacco-teetotal-temperance-meetings, no auxiliary-missionary-propagating societies, nothing in the blanket and lying-in asylum line, nothing, in short, worth a revising-barrister of three years' standing's notice, unless he be partial to the study of the laws of bankruptcy. Spain is no country for the political economist, beyond affording an example of the decline of the wealth of nations, and offering a wide topic on errors to be avoided, as well as for experimental theories, plans of reform and amelioration. In Spain, Nature reigns; she has there lavished her utmost prodigality of soil and climate, which Spaniards have for the last four centuries been endeavouring to counteract by a culpable neglect of agricultural speeches and dinners, and a non-distribution of prizes for the biggest boars, asses, and labourers with largest families.

The landed proprietor of the Peninsula is little better than a weed of the soil; he has never observed, nor scarcely permitted others to observe, the vast capabilities which might and ought to be called into action. He seems to have put Spain into Chancery, such is the general dilapidation. The country is little better than a terra incognita, to naturalists, geologists, and all other branches of ists and ologists. Everywhere there, the material is as superabundant as native labourers and operatives are deficient. All these interesting branches of inquiry, healthful and agreeable, as being out-of-door pursuits, and bringing the amateur in close contact with nature, offer to embryo authors who are ambitious to *book something new,* a more worthy subject than the old story of dangers of bull-fights, bandits, and black eyes. Those who aspire to the romantic, the poetical, the sentimental, the artistical, the antiquarian, the classical, in short, to any of the sublime and beautiful lines, will find both in the past and present state of Spain, subjects enough in wandering with lead-pencil and note-book through this singular country, which hovers between Europe and Africa, between civilisation and barbarism; this land of the green valley and barren mountain, of the boundless plain and the broken sierra; those Elysian gardens of the vine, the olive, the orange, and the aloe; those trackless, vast, silent, uncultivated wastes, the heritage of the wild bee;—in flying from the dull uniformity, the polished monotony of Europe, to the racy freshness of that original, unchanged country, where antiquity treads on the heels of to-day, where Paganism disputes the very altar with Christianity, where indulgence and luxury contend with privation and poverty, where a want of all that is generous or merciful is blended with the most devoted heroic virtues, where the most cold-blooded cruelty is linked with the fiery passions of Africa, where ignorance and erudition stand in violent and striking contrast.

"There," says the Handbook, in a style which qualifies the author for the best bound and fairest edited album, "let the antiquarian pore over the stirring memorials of many thousand years, the vestiges of Phœnician enterprise, of Roman magnificence, of Moorish elegance, in that storehouse of ancient customs, that repository of all elsewhere long forgotten and passed by; there let him gaze upon those classical monuments, unequalled almost in Greece or Italy, and on those fairy Aladdin palaces, the creatures of Oriental gorgeousness and imagination, with which Spain alone can enchant the dull European; there let the man of

feeling dwell on the poetry of her envy-disarming decay,
fallen from her high estate, the dignity of a dethroned
monarch, borne with unrepining self-respect, the last
consolation of the innately noble, which no adversity
can take away; let the lover of art feed his eyes with
the mighty masterpieces of ideal Italian art, when
Raphael and Titian strove to decorate the palaces of
Charles, the great emperor of the age of Leo X. Let
him gaze on the living nature of Velazquez and Murillo,
whose paintings are truly to be seen in Spain alone; let
the artist sketch frowning forms of the castle, the pomp
and splendour of the cathedral, where God is worshipped in a manner as nearly befitting his glory as the
arts and wealth of finite man can reach. Let him dwell on
the Gothic gloom of the cloister, the feudal turret, the
vasty Escorial, the rock-built alcazar of imperial Toledo,
the sunny towers of stately Seville, the eternal snows
and lovely vega of Granada; let the geologist clamber
over mountains of marble, and metal-pregnant sierras;
let the botanist cull from the wild hothouse of nature
plants unknown, unnumbered, matchless in colour, and
breathing the aroma of the sweet south; let all, learned
and unlearned, listen to the song, the guitar, the castanet; or join in the light fandango and spirit-stirring
bull-fight; let all mingle with the gay, good-humoured,
temperate peasantry, free, manly, and independent, yet
courteous and respectful; let all live with the noble,
dignified, high-bred, self-respecting Spaniard; let all
share in their easy, courteous society; let all admire
their dark-eyed women, so frank and natural, to whom
the voice of all ages and nations has conceded the palm
of attraction, to whom Venus has bequeathed her magic
girdle of grace and fascination; let all—but enough on
starting on this expedition, "where," as Don Quixote
said, "there are opportunities, brother Sancho, of putting our hands into what are called adventures up to
our elbows."

Nor was the La Manchan hidalgo wrong in assigning
a somewhat adventurous character to the searchers in
Spain for useful and entertaining knowledge, since the
natives are fond, and with much reason, of comparing

themselves and their country to *tesoros escondidos*, to hidden treasures, to talents buried in napkins; but they are equally fond of turning round, and falling foul of any pains-taking foreigner who digs them up, as Le Sage did the soul of Pedro Garcias. Nothing throughout the length and breadth of the land creates greater suspicion or jealousy than a stranger's making drawings, or writing down notes in a book : whoever is observed *sacando planes,* " taking plans," *mapeando el pais,* " mapping the country,"—for such are the expressions of the simplest pencil sketch—is thought to be an engineer, a spy, and, at all events, to be about no good. The lower classes, like the Orientals, attach a vague mysterious notion to these, to them unintelligible, proceedings; whoever is seen at work is immediately reported to the civil and military authorities, and, in fact, in out-of-the-way places, whenever an unknown person arrives, from the rarity of the occurrence, he is the observed of all observers. Much the same occurs in the East, where Europeans are suspected of being emissaries of their governments, as neither they nor Spaniards can at all understand why any man should incur trouble and expense, which no native ever does, for the mere purpose of acquiring knowledge of foreign countries, or for his own private improvement or amusement. Again, whatever particular investigations or questions are made by foreigners, about things that to the native appear unworthy of observation, are magnified and misrepresented by the many, who, in every place, wish to curry favour with whoever is the governor or chief person, whether civil or military. The natives themselves attach little or no importance to views, ruins, geology, inscriptions, and so forth, which they see every day, and which they therefore conclude cannot be of any more, or ought not to be of more, interest to the stranger. They judge of him by themselves; few men ever draw in Spain, and those who do are considered to be professional, and employed by others.

One of the many fatal legacies left to Spain by the French, was an increased suspicion of men with the pencil and note-book. Previously to their invasion spies and agents were sent, who, under the guise of travellers, reconnoitred the land; and then, casting off the clothing of sheep, guided in the wolves to plunder and destruction. The aged prior of the Merced, at Seville, observed to us, when pointing out the empty frames and cases from whence the Messrs. Soult and Co. had " removed " the Murillos and sacred plate,—" *Lo creira usted*—Will your Grace believe it, I beheld among the *ladrones* a person who grinned at me when I recognised him, to whom, some time before the invaders' arrival, I had pointed out these very treasures. *Tonto de mi!* Oh! simpleton that I was, to take a *gabacho* for an honest man." Yet this worthy individual was decorated with the legion of honour of Buonaparte, whose " first note in his pocket-book " of agenda, *after* the conquest of England, was to " carry off the Warwick vase;" as Denon, who too had spoiled the Egyptians, told Sir E. Tomason. We English, whose shops, " bursting with opulence into the streets," have not yet been visited, although the temptation is held out by royal pamphleteers, can scarcely enter into the feelings of those whose homes are still reeking with blood, and blighted by poverty. The Castilian cat, who has been scalded, flies even from cold water.

Some excuse, therefore, may be alleged in favour of Spanish authorities, especially in rarely visited districts, when they behold a strange barbarian eye peeping and peering about. Their first impression, as in the East, is that he may be a Frank : hence the shaking, quaking, and ague which comes over them. At Seville, Granada, and places where foreign artists are somewhat more plentiful, the processes of drawing may be passed over with pity and contempt, but in lonely localities the star-gazing observer is himself the object of argus-eyed, official observation. He is, indeed, as unconscious of the portentous emotions and ill-omened fears which he is exciting, as was the innocent crow of the meanings attached to his movements by the Roman augurs, and few augurs of old ever rivalled the Spanish alcaldes of to-day in quick suspicion and perception of evil, especially where none is intended. Witness what actually occurred to three excellent friends of ours.

The readers of Borrow's inimitable ' Bible in Spain '

will remember his hair-breadth escape from being shot
for Don Carlos by the miraculous intervention of the
alcalde of Corcubion, who, if still alive, must be a
phœnix, and clearly worth observation, as he was a
reader of the "grand Baintham," or our illustrious
Jeremy Bentham, to whom the Spanish reformers sent
for a paper *constitution*, not having a very clear meaning of the word or thing, whether it was made of cotton
or parchment.   Another of the very best investigators
and writers on Spain, Lord Carnarvon, was nearly put
to death in the same districts for Don Miguel; Captain
Widdrington, also one of the kindest and most honourable of men, was once arrested on suspicion of being an
agent of Espartero; and we, our humble selves, have
had the felicity of being marched to a guard-house for
sketching a Roman ruin, and the honour of being taken,
either for Curius Dentatus, an alligator, or Julius
Cæsar,—as there is no absurdity, no inconceivable
ignorance, too great for the local Spanish "Dogberries," who rarely deviate into sense; when their fears
or suspicions are roused, they are as deaf alike to the
dictates of common reason or humanity as adders or
Berbers; and here, as in the East, even the best inten-
tioned may be taken up for spies, and have their beards,
at least, cut off, as was done to King David's envoyés.
All classes, in regard to strangers, generally get some
hostile notions into their heads, and then, instead of
fairly and reasonably endeavouring to arrive at the
truth, pervert every innocent word, and twist every
action, to suit their own preconceived nonsense, until
trifles become to their jealous minds proofs as strong
as Holy Writ.   In justice, however, it must be said,
that when these authorities are once satisfied that the
stranger is an Englishman, and that no harm is intended, no people can be more civil in offering assistance of every kind, especially the lower classes, who
gaze at the magical performance of drawing with wonder : the higher classes seldom take any notice, partly
from courtesy, and much from the *nil admirari* principle
of Orientals, which conceals both inferiority and ignorance, and shows good breeding.

The drawing any garrison-town or fortified place in Spain is now most strictly forbidden. The prevailing ignorance of everything connected with the arts of design is so great, that no distinction is made between the most regular plan and the merest artistical sketch : a drawing is with them a drawing, and punishable as such. A Spanish barrack, garrison, or citadel is therefore to be observed but little, and still less to be sketched. A gentleman, nay, a lady also, is liable, under any circumstances, when drawing, to be interrupted, and often is exposed to arrest and incivility. Indeed, whether an artist or not, it is as well not to exhibit any curiosity in regard to matters connected with military buildings ; nor will the loss be great, as they are seldom worth looking at. The troops in our time were in a most admired disorder. If they wore shoes they had no stockings ; if they had muskets, flints were not plentiful ; if powder was supplied, balls were scarce ; nothing, in short, was ever according to regulations. Nay, the buttons even on the officers' coats were never dressed in file : some had the numbers up, some down, some awry ; but uniformity is a thing of Europe, and not of the East. At this moment, when the church is starved, when widows' pensions are unpaid, when governmental bankruptcy walks the land, whose bones, marrow, and all are wasted to support the army, whose swords uphold the hated men in office, the bands of the Royal Guard, the Prætorian bands, do not keep tune, nor do the rank and file march in time. However painful these things to pipe-clay martinets, the artist loses much, by not being able to sketch such tumble-down forts and ragged garrisons, each *Bisoño* of which is more precious to painter eye than the officer in command at Windsor ; while his short-petticoated *querida* is more Murillo-like than a score of patronesses of Almack's.

The safest plan for those who want to observe, and to book what they observe, is to obtain a Spanish passport, with the object of their curiosity and inquiries clearly specified in it. There is seldom any difficulty at Madrid, if application be made through the English minister, in obtaining such a document ; indeed, when the applicant is well known, it is readily given by any of the provincial Captains-General. As it is couched in the Spanish language, it is understood by all, high and low; an advantage which is denied in Spain to those issued by our ambassadors, and even by the Foreign Office, who, to the *credit* of themselves and nation, give passes to Englishmen in the French language, whereby among Spaniards a suspicion arises that the bearer may be a Frenchman, which is not always pleasant. We preserve among rare Peninsular relics a passport granted by our kind patron the redoubtable Conde de España, and backed by the no less formidable Quesada and Sarsfield, in which it was enjoined, in choice, intelligible Castilian, to all and every minor rulers and governors, whether with the pen or sword, to aid and assist the bearer in his examination of the fine arts and antiquities of the Peninsula. These autocrats were more implicitly obeyed in their respective Lord Lieutenancies than Ferdinand himself; in fact, the pashas of the East are their exact types, each in their district being the heads of both civil and military tribunals; and as they not only administer, but suit the law according to the length of their own feet, they in fact make it and trample upon it, and all in any authority below them imitate their superiors as nearly as they dare. These things of Spain are managed with a gravity truly Oriental, both in the rulers and in the resignation of those ruled by them; these great men's passport and signature were obeyed by all minor authorities as implicitly as an Oriental firman; the very fact of a stranger having a Captain-General's passport, is soon known by everybody, and, to use an Oriental phrase, "makes his face to be whitened;" it acts as a letter of introduction, and is in truth the best one of all, since it is addressed to people in power in each village or town, who, true sheikhs, are looked up to by all below them with the same deference, as they themselves look up to all above them. The worth of a person recommended, is estimated by that of the person who recommends; *tal recomendacion tal recomendado.* To complete this thing of Oriental Spain, these three omnipotent despots, who defied laws human and divine, who made dice of their enemies' bones, and goblets of their skulls, have all since been assassinated, and sent to their account with all their sins on their heads. In limited monarchies ministers who go too far, lose their places, in Spain and Turkey their heads : the former, doubtless, are the most severely punished.

Those who wish to observe Spanish man, which, next to Spanish woman, forms the proper study of mankind, will find that one key to decipher this singular people is scarcely European, for this *Berberia Cristiana* is a neutral ground placed between the hat and the turban; many indeed of themselves contend that Africa begins even at the Pyrenees. Be that as it may, Spain, first civilised by the Phœnicians, and long possessed by the Moors, has indelibly retained the original impressions. Test her, therefore, and her males and females, by an Oriental standard, how analogous does much appear that is strange and repugnant, if compared with European usages. Take care, however, not to let either the ladies or gentlemen know the hidden processes of your mind, for nothing gives greater offence. The fair sex is willing, to prevent such a mistake, to lay aside even their becoming *mantillas*, as their hidalgos doff their stately Roman cloaks. These old clothes they offer up as sacrifices on the altar of civilisation, and to the mania of looking exactly like the rest of the world, in Hyde Park and the Elysian Fields.

Another remarkable Oriental trait is the general want of love for the beautiful in art, and the abundance of that Αφιλοκαλια with which the ancients reproached the genuine Iberians; this is exhibited in the general neglect and indifference shown towards Moorish works, which instead of destroying they ought rather to have protected under glasses, since such attractions are peculiar to the Peninsula. The *Alhambra*, the pearl and magnet of Granada, is in their estimation little better than a *casa de ratones*, or a rat's hole, which in truth they have endeavoured to make it by centuries of neglect; few natives even go there, or understand the all-absorbing interest, the concentrated devotion, which it excites in the stranger; so the Bedouin regards the ruins of Palmyra, insensible to present beauty, as to past poetry and romance. Sad is this non-appreciation of the Alhambra by the Spaniards, but such are Asiatics, with whom sufficient for the day is *their to-day;* who care neither for the past nor for the future, who think only for the present and themselves, and like them the masses of Spaniards, although not wearing turbans, lack the organs of veneration and admiration for anything beyond matters connected with the first person and the present tense. Again, the leaven of hatred against the Moor and his relics is not extinct; they resent almost as heretical the preference shown by foreigners to the works of infidels rather than to those of good Catholics; such preference again at once implies their inferiority, and convicts them of bad taste in their non-appreciation, and of Vandalism in labouring to mutilate, what the Moor laboured to adorn. The charming writings of Washington Irving, and the admiration of European pilgrims, have latterly shamed the authorities into a somewhat more conservative feeling towards the Alhambra; but even their benefits are questionable; they " repair and beautify " on the churchwarden principle, and there is no less danger in such " restorations " than in those fatal scourings of Murillo and Titian in the Madrid gallery, which are effacing the lines where beauty lingers. Even their tardy appreciation is somewhat interested : thus Mellado, in his late Guide, laments that there should be no account of the Alhambra, of which he speaks coldly, and suggests, as so many " English " visit it, that a descriptive work would be a *segura especulacion!* a safe speculation ! Thus the poetry of the Moorish Alhambra is coined into the Spanish prose of profitable shillings and sixpences.

Travellers however should not forget, that much which to them has the ravishing, enticing charms of novelty, is viewed by the dull sated eye of the native, with familiarity which breeds contempt; they are weary, oh fatal lassitude ! even of the beautiful : alas ! exclaimed the hermit on Monserrat, to the stranger who was ravished by exquisite views, then and there beheld by him for the first and last time, " all this has no attraction for me; twenty and nine are the years that I have seen this unchanged scene, every sunrise, every noon, every sunset." But *sordent domestica*, observes Pliny, nor are all things or persons honoured in their own homes as they ought to be, since the days that Mahomet the true prophet failed to persuade his wife and valet that his powers were supernatural. Can it be wondered that ruins and "old rubbish" should be held cheap among the Moro-Spaniards? or that their so-called "guides" should mislead and misdirect the stranger? It cannot well be avoided, since few of the writers ever travel in their own country, and fewer travel out of it; thus from their limited means of comparison, they cannot appreciate differences, nor tell what are the wants and wishes of a foreigner: accordingly, scenes, costumes, ruins, usages, ceremonies, etc., which they have known from childhood, are passed over without notice, although, from their passing newness to the stranger, they are exactly what he most desires to have pointed out and explained. Nay, the natives frequently despise or are ashamed of those very things, which most interest and charm the foreigner, for whose observation they select the modern rather than the old, offering especially their poor pale copies of Europe, in preference to their own rich, racy, and natural originals, doing this in nothing more than in the costume and dwellings of the lower classes, who happily are not yet afflicted with the disease of French polish: they indeed, when they dig up ancient coins, will rub off the precious rust of twice ten hundred years, in order to render them, as they imagine, more saleably attractive; but they fortunately spare themselves, insomuch that Charles III., on failing in one of his laudable attempts to improve and modernise them, compared his loving subjects to naughty children, who quarrel with their good nurse when she wants to wash them.

Again, no country in the world can vie with Spain, where the dry climate at least is conservative, with memorials of auld lang syne, with tower and turret, Prout-like houses and toppling balconies, so old that they seem only not to fall into the torrents and ravines

over which they hang. Here is every form and colour
of picturesque poverty; vines clamber up the irregulari-
ties, while below naiads dabble, washing their red and
yellow garments in the all-gilding glorious sun-beams.
What a picture it is to all but the native, who sees none
of the wonders of lights and shadows, reflections,
colours, and outlines; who, blind to all the beauties, is
keenly awake only to the degradation, the rags and
decay; he half suspects that your sketch and admiration
of a smuggler or bullfighter is an insult, and that you are
taking it, in order to show in England what Mons.
Guizot will never be forgiven for calling the " brutal "
things of Spain; accordingly, while you are sincerely
and with reason delighted with sashes and *Zamarras*,
he begs you to observe his ridiculous Boulevard-cut
coat: or when you sit down opposite to a half-ruined
Roman wall, some crumbling Moorish arch, or mediæval
Gothic shrine, he implores you to come away and draw
the last spick and span Royal Academical abortion,
coldly correct and classically dull, in order to carry
home a sample which may do credit to Spain, as ap-
proximating to the way things are managed at Charing
Cross.

Without implicitly following the advice of these
Spaniards of better intention than taste, no man of
research will undervalue any assistance by which his
objects are promoted, even should he be armed with a
captain-general's passport, and a red Murray. Meagre
is the oral information which is to be obtained from
Spaniards on the spot; these incurious semi-Orientals
look with jealousy on the foreigner, and either fence
with him in their answers, raise difficulties, or, being
highly imaginative, magnify or diminish everything as
best suits their own views and suspicions. The national
expressions " *Quien sabe? no se sabe,*"—" who knows?
I do not know," will often be the prelude to " *No se
puede,*"—" it can't be done."

These impediments and impossibilities are infinitely increased when the stranger has to do with men in office,
be it ever so humble; the first feeling of these Dogberries
is to suspect mischief and give refusals. " No," may be

assumed to be their natural answer; nor even if you
have a special order of permission, is admission by any
means certain. The keeper, who here as elsewhere, considers the objects committed to his care as his own
private property and source of perquisite, must be conciliated : often when you have toiled through the heat
and dust to some distant church, museum, library, or
what not, after much ringing and waiting, you will be
drily informed that it is shut, can't be seen, that it is
the wrong day, that you must call again to-morrow;
and if it be the right day, then you will be told that the
hour is wrong, that you are come too early, too late;
very likely the keeper's wife will inform you that he is
out, gone to mass, or market, or at his dinner, or at
his *siesta*, or if he is at home and awake, he will swear
that his wife has mislaid the key, " which she is always
doing." If all these and other excuses won't do, and
you persevere, you will be assured that there is nothing
worth seeing, or you will be asked why you want to see
it? As a general rule, no one should be deterred from
visiting anything, because a Spaniard of the upper
classes gives his opinion that the object is beneath
notice; he will try to convince you that Toledo, Cuenca,
and other places which cannot be matched in Christendom, are ugly, odious, old cities; he is ashamed of them
because the tortuous, narrow lanes do not run in rows
as straight as Pall Mall and the Rue de Rivoli. In fact
his only notion of a civilised town is a common-place
assemblage of rectangular wide streets, all built and
coloured uniformly, like a line of foot-soldiers, paved
with broad flags, and lighted with gas, on which
Spaniards can walk about dressed as Englishmen, and
Spanish women like those of France; all of which said
wonders a foreigner may behold far better nearer home;
nor is it much less a waste of time to go and see what
the said Spaniard considers to be a real lion, since the
object generally turns out to be some poor imitation, without form, angle, history, nationality, colour,
or expression, beyond that of utilitarian comfort
and common-place convenience—great advantages no
doubt both to contractors and political economists, but

death and destruction to men of the pencil and note-book.

The sound principles in Spanish sight-seeing are few and simple, but, if observed, they will generally prove successful; first, persevere; never be put back; never take an answer if it be in the negative; never lose temper or courteous manners; and lastly, let the tinkle of metal be heard at once; if the chief or great man be inexorable, find out privately who is the wretched sub who keeps the key, or the crone who sweeps the room; and then send a discreet messenger to say that you will pay to be admitted, without mentioning " nothing to nobody." Thus you will always obtain your view, even when an official order fails. On our first arrival at Madrid, when but young in these things of Spain, we were desirous of having daily permission to examine a royal gallery, which was only open to the public on certain days in the week. In our grave dilemma we consulted a sage and experienced diplomatist, and this was the oracular reply :—" Certainly, if you wish it, I will make a request to Señor Salmon " (the then Home Secretary), " and beg him to give you the proper order, as a personal favour to myself. By the way, how much longer shall you remain here?"—" From three to four weeks."—" Well, then, after you have been gone a good month, I shall get a courteous and verbose epistle from his Excellency, in which he will deeply regret that, on searching the arch-ives of his office, there was no instance of such a request having ever been granted, and that he is compelled most reluctantly to return a refusal, from the fear of a prece-dent being created. My advice to you is to give the porter a dollar, to be repeated whenever the door-hinges seem to be getting rusty and require oiling." The hint was taken, as was the bribe, and the prohibited portals expanded so regularly, that at last they knew the sound of our footsteps. Gold is the Spanish *sesame*. Thus Soult got into Badajoz, thus Louis Philippe put Espar-tero out, and Montpensier in. Gold, bright red gold, is the sovereign remedy which in Spain smooths all diffi-culties, nay, some in which even force has failed, as here the obstinate heads may be guided by a straw of bullion, but not driven by a bar of iron. The magic influence of a bribe pervades the land, where everything is venal, even to the scales of justice. Here men who have objects to gain begin to work from the bottom, not from the top, as we do in England. In order to ensure success, no step in the official ladder must be left unanointed. A wise and prudent suitor bribes from the porter to the premier, taking care not to forget the under-secretary, the over-secretary, the private secretary, all in their order, and to regulate the douceur according to each man's rank and influence. If you omit the porter, he will not deliver your card, or will say Señor Mon is out, or will tell you to call again *mañana*, the eternal to-morrow. If you forget the chief clerk, he will mislay your petition, or poison his master's ear. In matters of great and political importance, the sovereign, him or herself, must have a share; and thus it was that Calomarde continued so long to manage the beloved Ferdinand and his counsels. He was the minister who laid the greatest bribe at the royal feet. " Sire, by strict attention and honesty, I have just been enabled to economise 50,000*l.*, on the sums allotted to my department, which I have now the honour and felicity to place at your Majesty's disposal."—" Well done, my faithful and good minister, here is a cigar for you." This Calomarde, who began life as a foot-boy, smuggled through the Christinist swindle, by which Isabel now wears the crown of Don Carlos. The rogue was rewarded by being made *Conde de S*ᵃ*. Isabel*, a title which since has been conferred on Mons. Bresson's baby—a delicate compliment to his sire's labours in the transfer of the said crown to Louis Philippe—but Spaniards are full of dry humour.

In the East, the example and practice of the Sultan and Vizier is followed by every pacha, down to the lowest animal who wields the most petty authority; the disorder of the itching palm is endemic and epidemic, all, whether high and low, want, and must have money; all wish to get it without the disgrace of begging, and without the danger of highway robbery. Public poverty is the curse of the land, and all *empleados* or persons in office excuse themselves on dire necessity, the old plea of a certain gentleman, which has no law. Some allowance, therefore, may be made for the rapacity which, with very few exceptions, prevails; the regular salaries, always inadequate, are generally in arrear, and the public servants, poor devils, swear that they are forced to pay themselves by conniving at defrauding the government; this few scruple to do, as all know it to be an unjust one, and that it can afford it; indeed, as all are offenders alike, the guilt of the offence is scarcely admitted. Where robbing and jobbing are the universal order of the day, one rascal keeps another in countenance, as one goître does another in Switzerland. A man who does not feather his nest when in place, is not thought honest, but a fool; *es preciso, que cada uno comd de su oficio.* It is necessary, nay, a *duty*, as in the East, that all should live by their office; and as office is short and insecure, no time or means is neglected in making up a purse; thus poverty and their will alike and readily consent.

Take a case in point. We remember calling on a Spaniard who held the highest office in a chief city of Andalucia. As we came into his cabinet a cloaked personage was going out; the great man's table was covered with gold ounces, which he was shovelling complacently into a drawer, gloating on the glorious haul. "Many ounces, Excellency," said we. "Yes, my friend," was his reply—"*no quiero comer mas patatas,* —I do not intend to dine any more on potatoes." This gentleman, during the *Sistema*, or Riego constitution, had, with other loyalists, been turned out of office; and, having been put to the greatest hardships, was losing no time in taking prudent and laudable precautions to avert any similar calamity for the future. His practices were perfectly well known in the town, where people simply observed, "*Está atesorando*, he is laying up treasures," —as every one of them would most certainly have done, had they been in his fortunate position. Rich and honest Britons, therefore, should not judge too hardly of the sad shifts, the strange bed-fellows, with which want makes the less provided Spaniards acquainted. *Donde no hay abundancia, no hay observancia.* The empty sack cannot stand upright, nor was ever a sack made in Spain into which gain and honour could be stowed away together; *honra y provecho, no caben en un saco o techo;* here virtue itself succumbs to poverty, induced by more than half a century of misgovernment, let alone the ruin caused by Buonaparte's invasion, to which domestic troubles and civil wars have been added.

To return, however, to sight-seeing in Spain. Lucky was the traveller prepared even to bribe and pay, who ever in our time chanced to fall in with a librarian who knew what books he had, or with a priest who could tell what pictures were in his chapel; ask him for *the* painting by Murillo—a shoulder-shrug was his reply, or a curt "*no hay*," "there is none;" had you inquired for the "blessed Saint Thomas," then he might have pointed it out; the *subject*, not the artist, being all that was required for the service of the church. An incurious bliss of ignorance is no less grateful to the Spanish mind, than the *dolce far niente* or sweet indolent doing nothing is to the body. All that gives trouble, or "fashes," destroys the supreme height of felicity, which consists in avoiding exertion. A chapter might be filled with instances, which, had they not occurred to our humble selves, would seem caricature inventions. The not to be able to answer the commonest question, or to give any information as to matters of the most ordinary daily occurrence, is so prevalent, that we at first thought it must proceed from some fear of committal, some remnant of inquisitorial engendered reserve, rather than from bonâ fide careless and contented ignorance. The result, however, of much intercourse and experience arrived at, was, that few people are more communicative than the lower classes of Spaniards, especially to an Englishman, to whom they reveal private and family secrets : their want of knowledge applies rather to things than to persons.

If you called on a Spanish gentleman, and, finding him out, wished afterwards to write him a note, and inquired of his man or maid servant the number of the house ;—"I do not know, my lord," was the invariable answer, " I never was asked it before, I have never looked for it : let us go out and see. Ah ! it is number 36." Wishing once to send a parcel by the wagon from Merida to Madrid, " On what day, my lord," said I to the pot-bellied, black-whiskered *ventero,* " does your *galera* start for the Court?" " Every Wednesday," answered he; " and let not your grace be anxious "—" *Disparate*—nonsense," exclaimed his copper-skinned, bright-eyed wife, " why do you tell the English knight such lies? the wagon, my lord, sets out on Fridays." During the logomachy, or the few words which ensued between the well-matched pair, our good luck willed, that the *mayoral* or driver of the vehicle should come in, who forthwith informed us that the days of departure were Thursdays; and he was right. This occurred in the provinces; take, therefore, a parallel passage in the capital, the heart and brain of the Castiles. " *Señor, tenga Usted la bondad*—My lord," said I to a portly, pompous bureaucrat, who booked places in the dilly to Toledo,—" have the goodness, your grace, to secure me one for Monday, the 7th."—" I fear," replied he, politely, for the *negocio* had been prudently opened by my offering him a real Havannah, " that your lordship has made a mistake in the date. Monday is the 8th of the current month "—which it was not. Thinking to settle the matter, we handed to him, with a bow, the almanack of the year, which chanced to be in our pocket-book. " *Señor,*" said he, gravely, when he had duly examined it, " I knew that I was right; this one was printed at Seville,"—which it was— " and we are here at Madrid, which is *otra cosa,* that is, altogether another affair." In this solar difference and pre-eminence of the Court, it must be remembered, that the sun, at its creation, first shone over the neighbouring city, to which the dilly ran; and that even in the last century, it was held to be heresy at Salamanca, to say that it did not move round Spain. In sad truth, it has there stood still longer than in astronomical lectures or metaphors. Spain is no paradise for calculators; here, what ought to happen, and what would happen elsewhere according to Cocker and the doctrine of probabili-

ties, is exactly the event which is the least likely to come
to pass.   One arithmetical fact only can be reckoned
upon with tolerable certainty : let given events be represented by numbers; then two and two may at one time
make three, or possibly five at another; but the odds are
four to one against two and two ever making four;
another safe rule in Spanish official numbers; *e.g.* " five
thousand men killed and wounded "--" five thousand
dollars will be given," and so forth, is to deduct two
noughts, and sometimes even three, and read fifty to
five instead.

Well might even the keen-sighted, practical Duke say
it is difficult to understand the Spaniards exactly; there
neither men nor women, suns nor clocks go together;
there, as in a Dutch concert, all choose their own tune
and time, each performer in the orchestra endeavouring
to play the first fiddle.   All this is so much a matter of
course, that the natives, like the Irish, make a joke of
petty mistakes, blunders, unpunctualities, inconse-
quences, and pococurantisms, at which accurate Germans
and British men of business are driven frantic.   Made
up of contradictions, and dwelling in the *pays de l'imprévu*, where exception is the rule, where accident and
the impulse of the moment are the moving powers, the
happy-go-lucky natives, especially in their collective
capacity, act like women and children.   A spark, a trifle,
sets the impressionable masses in action, and none can
foresee the commonest event ; nor does any Spaniard ever
attempt to guess beyond *la situacion actual*, the actual
present, or to foretell what the morrow will bring ; that
he leaves to the foreigner, who does not understand him.
Paciencia y barajar is his motto ; and he waits *patiently*
to see what next will turn up after another *shuffle*.

There is one thing, however, which all know exactly,
one question which all can answer; and providentially
this refers to the grand object of every foreigner's observation—" When will the bull-fight be and begin?"
and this holds good, notwithstanding that there is a
proviso inserted in the notices, that it will come off on
such a day and hour, " if the weather permits."   Thus,
although these spectacles take place in summer, when

for months and months rain and clouds are matters of
history, the cautious authorities doubt the blessed sun
himself, and mistrust the certainty of his proceedings, as
much as if they were ir-regulated by a Castilian clock-
maker.

CHAPTER XXI

OUR honest John Bulls have long been more partial
to their Spanish namesakes, than even to those perpetrated by the Pope, or made in the Emerald Isle; to see
a bull-fight has been the emphatic object of enlightened
curiosity, since Peninsular sketches have been taken and
published by our travellers. No sooner had Charles the
First, when prince, lost his heart at Madrid, than his
royal father-in-law-that-was-to-be, regaled him and the
fair inspirer of his tender passion, with one of these
charming spectacles; an event which, as many men and
animals were butchered, was thought by the historiogra-
phers of the day to be one that posterity would not
willingly let die; their contemporary accounts will ever
form the gems of every tauromachian library that aspires
to be complete.

These sports, which recall the bloody games of the
Roman amphitheatre, are now only to be seen in Spain,
where the present clashes with the past, where at every
moment we stumble on some bone and relic of Biblical
and Roman antiquity; the close parallels, nay the identi-
ties, which are observable between these combats and
those of classical ages, both as regards the spectators
and actors, are omitted, as being more interesting to the
scholar than to the general reader; they were pointed
out by us some years ago in the Quarterly Review, No.
cxxiv. And as human nature changes not, men when
placed in given and similar circumstances, will without
any previous knowledge or intercommunication arrive
at nearly similar results; the gentle pastime of spearing

and killing bulls in public and single-handed was probably devised by the Moors, or rather by the Spanish Moors, for nothing of the kind has ever obtained in Africa either now or heretofore. The Moslem Arab, when transplanted into a Christian and European land, modified himself in many respects to the ways and usages of the people among whom he settled, just as his Oriental element was widely introduced among his Gotho-His-pano neighbours. Moorish Andalucia is still the head-quarters of the tauromachian art, and those who wish carefully to master this, the science of Spain *par excellence*, should commence their studies in the school of Ronda, and proceed thence to take the highest honours in the University of Seville, the Bullford of the Peninsula.

By the way, our boxing, baiting term bull-*fight* is a very lay and low translation of the time-honoured Castilian title, *Fiestas de Toros*, the feasts, festivals of bulls. The gods and goddesses of antiquity were conciliated by the sacrifice of hecatombs; the lowing tickled their divine ears, and the purple blood fed their eyes, no less than the roasted sirloins fattened the priests, while the grand spectacle and death delighted their dinnerless congregations. In Spain, the Church of Rome, never indifferent to its interests, instantly marshalled into its own service a ceremonial at once profitable and popular;[1] it consecrated butchery by wedding it to the altar, availing itself of this gentle handmaid, to obtain funds in order to raise convents; even in the last century Papal bulls were granted to mendicant orders, authorising them to celebrate a certain number of *Fiestas de Toros*, on condition of devoting the profit to finishing their church; and in order to swell the receipts at the doors, spiritual indulgences and soul releases from purgatory, the number of years being apportioned to the relative prices of the

---

[1] The love for killing oxen still prevails at Rome, where the ambition of the lower orders to be a butcher, is, like their white costume, a remnant of the honourable office of killing at the Pagan sacrifices. In Spain butchers are of the lowest caste, and cannot prove " purity of blood." Francis I. never forgave the " Becajo de Parigi " applied by Dante to *his* ancestor.

seats, were added as a bonus to all paid for places at a spectacle hallowed by a pious object. So at the *taurobolia* of antiquity, those who were sprinkled with bull blood were absolved from sin. Protestant ministers, who very properly fear and distrust papal bulls, replace them by bazaars and fancy fairs, whenever a fashionable chapel requires a new blue slate roofing. Again, when not devoted to religious purposes, every bull-fight aids the cause of charity; the profits form the chief income of the public hospitals, and thus furnish both funds and patients, as the venous circulation of the mob thirsting for gore, rises to blood heat under a sun of fire, and the subsequent mingling of sexes, opening of bottles and knives, occasion more deaths among the lords and ladies of the Spanish creation, than among the horned and hoofed victims of the amphitheatre.

It is a common but very great mistake, to suppose that bull-fights are as numerous in Spain as bandits; it is just the contrary, for this may there be considered the tip-top æsthetic treat, as the Italian Opera is in England, and both are rather expensive amusements; true it is that with us, only the salt of the earth patronises the performers of the Haymarket, while high and low, vulgar and exquisite, alike delight in those of the Spanish fields. Each bull-fight costs from 200*l.* to 300*l.*, and even more when got up out of Andalucia or Madrid, which alone can afford to support a standing company; in other cities the actors and animals have to be sent for express, and from great distances. Hence the representations occur like angels' visits, few and far between; they are reserved for the chief festivals of the church and crown, for the unfeigned devotion of the faithful on the holy days of local saints, and the Virgin; they are also given at the marriages and coronations of the sovereign, and thence are called Fiestas *reales*, *Royal* festivals—the ceremonial being then deprived of its religious character, although it is much increased in worldly and imposing importance. The sight is indeed one of surpassing pomp, etiquette, and magnificence, and has succeeded to the *Auto de Fé*, in offering to the most Catholic Queen and her subjects the greatest possible means of tasting

rapture, that the limited powers of mortal enjoyment
can experience in this world of shadows and sorrows.

They are only given at Madrid, and then are conducted
entirely after the ancient Spanish and Moorish customs,
of which such splendid descriptions remain in the ballad
romances.   They take place in the great square of the
capital, which is then converted into an arena.   The
windows of the quaint and lofty houses are arranged as
boxes, and hung with velvets and silks.   The royal
family is seated under a canopy of state in the balcony
of the central mansion.   There we beheld Ferdinand VII.
presiding at the solemn swearing of allegiance to his
daughter. He was then seated where Charles I. had sat
two centuries before; he was guarded by the unchanged
halberdiers, and was witnessing the unchanged spectacle.
On these royal occasions the bulls are assailed by gentlemen, dressed and armed as in good old Spanish times,
before the fatal Bourbon accession obliterated Castilian
costume, customs, and nationality.   The champions, clad
in the fashions of the Philips, and mounted on beauteous
barbs, the minions of their race, attack the fierce animal
with only a short spear, the immemorial weapon of the
Iberians.   The combatants must be hidalgos by birth,
and have each for a *padrino*, or godfather, a first-rate
grandee of Spain, who passes before royalty in a splendid
equipage and six, and is attended by bands of running
footmen, who are arrayed either as Greeks, Romans,
Moors, or fancy characters.   It is not easy to obtain
these *caballeros en plaza*, or poor knights, who are
willing to expose their lives to the imminent dangers,
albeit during the fight they have the benefit of experienced *toreros* to advise their actions and cover their
retreats.

In 1833 a gentle dame, without the privity of her
lord and husband, inscribed his name as one of the
champion volunteers.   In procuring him this agreeable
surprise, she, so it was said in Madrid, argued thus :
" Either *mi marido* will be killed—in that case I shall
get a new husband ; or he will survive, in which event
he will get a pension."   She failed in both of these
admirable calculations—such is the uncertainty of

human events. The terror of this poor *héros malgré lui*, on whom chivalry had been thrust, was absolutely ludicrous when exposed by his well-intentioned better-half, to the horns of this dilemma and bull. Any other horns, my dearest, but these! He was wounded at the first rush, did survive, and did not get a pension; for Ferdinand died soon after, and few pensions have been paid in the Peninsula, since the land has been blessed with a *charte*, constitution, liberty, and a representative government.

One anecdote, where another lady is in the case, may be new to our fair readers. We quote from an ancient authentic chronicler:—" It will not be amiss here to mention what fell out in the presence of Charles the First of Blessed Memory, who, while Prince of Wales, repaired to the court of Spain, whether to be married to the Infanta, or upon what other design, I cannot well determine: however, all comedies, playes, and festivals (this of the bulls at Madrid being included), were appointed to be as decently and magnificently gone about as possible, for the more sumptuous and stately entertainment of such a splendid prince. Therefore, after three bulls had been killed, and the fourth a coming forth, there appeared four gentlemen in good equipage; not long after, a brisk lady, in most gorgeous apparel, attended with persons of quality, and some three or four grooms, walked all along the square a-foot. Astonishment seized upon the beholders, that one of the female sex could assume the unheard boldness of exposing herself to the violence of the most furious beast yet seen, which had overcome, yea almost killed, two men of great strength, courage, and dexterity. Incontinently the bull rushed towards the corner where the lady and her attendants stood; she (after all had fled) drew forth her dagger very unconcernedly, and thrust it most dexterously into the bull's neck, having catched hold of his horn; by which stroak, without any more trouble, her design was brought to perfection; after which, turning about towards the king's balcony, she made her obeysance, and withdrew herself in suitable state and gravity."

At the *jura* of 1833 ninety-nine bulls were massacred; had one more been added the hecatomb would have been complete. These wholesale slaughterings have this year been repeated at the marriage of the same " *innocent* " Isabel, the critical events of whose life are death-warrants to quadrupeds. Bulls, however, represent in Spain the coronation banquets of England. In that hungry, ascetic land, bulls have always been killed, but no beef eaten; a remarkable fact, which did not escape the learned Justin in his remarks on the no-dinner-giving crowned heads of old Iberia.

These genuine ancient bull-fights were perilous and fatal in the extreme, yet knights were never wanting —valour being the point of honour—who readily exposed their lives in sight of their cruel mistresses. To kill the monster if not killed by him, was, before the time of Hudibras, the sure road to women's love, who very properly admire those qualities the best, in which they feel themselves to be the most deficient :—

> " The ladies' hearts began to melt,
> Subdued by blows their lovers felt;
> So Spanish heroes, with their lances,
> At once wound bulls and ladies' fancies."

The final conquest of the Moors, and the subsequent cessation of the border chivalrous habits of Spaniards, occasioned these love-pastimes to fall into comparative disuse. The gentle Isabella was so shocked at the bull-fights which she saw at Medina del Campo, that she did her utmost to put them down; but she strove in vain, for the game and monarchy were destined to fall together. The accession of Philip V. deluged the Peninsula with Frenchmen. The puppies of Paris pronounced the Spaniards and their bulls to be barbarous and brutal, as their *artistes* to this day prefer the *bœuf gras* of the Boulevards to whole flocks of Iberian lean kine. The spectacle which had withstood her influence, and had beat the bulls of Popes, bowed before the despotism of fashion. The periwigged courtiers deserted the arena, on which the royal Bourbon eye looked coldly, while the sturdy people, foes—then as now—to

Frenchmen and innovations, clung closer to the sports
of their forefathers. Yet a fatal blow was dealt to the
combat : the art, once practised by knights, degenerated into the vulgar butchery of mercenary bull-fighters,
who contended not for honour, but base lucre; thus,
by becoming the game of the mob, it was soon stripped
of every gentlemanlike prestige.   So the tournament
challenges of our chivalrous ancestors have sunk down
to the vulgar boxings of ruffian pugilists.

Baiting a bull in any shape is irresistible to the lower
orders of Spain, who disregard injuries to the bodies,
and, what is worse, to their cloaks.   The hostility to
the horned beast is instinctive, and grows with their
growth, until it becomes, as men are but children of a
larger growth, a second nature.   The young urchins in
the streets play at "toro," as ours do at leap-frog;
they go through the whole mimic spectacle amongst
each other, observing every law and rule, as our schoolboys do when they fight.   Few adult Spaniards, when
journeying through the country, ever pass a herd of
cows without this dormant propensity breaking out;
they provoke the animals to fight by waving their cloaks
or capas, a challenge hence called el capeo.   The
villagers, who cannot afford the expense of a regular
bull-fight, amuse themselves with baiting novillos, or
bull-youngsters—calves of one year old ; and embolados,
or bulls whose horns are guarded with tips and buttons.
These innocent pastimes are despised by the regular
aficion, the "fancy;" because, as neither man nor beast
are exposed to be killed, the whole affair is based in
fiction, and impotent in conclusion.   They cry out for
Toros de muerte—bulls of death.   Nothing short of the
reality of blood can allay their excitement.   They despise the makeshift spectacle, as much as a true gas-
tronome does mock-turtle, or an old campaigner a sham
fight.

In the wilder districts of Andalucia few cattle are ever
brought into towns for slaughter, unless led by long
ropes, and partially baited by those whose poverty prevents their indulgence in the luxury of real bull-fights
and beef.   The governor of Tarifa was wont on certain

days to let a bull loose into the streets, when the delight
of the inhabitants was to shut their doors, and behold
from their grated windows the perplexities of the un-
wary or strangers, pursued by him in the narrow lanes
without means of escape. Although many lives were
lost, a governor in our time, named Dalmau, otherwise
a public benefactor to the place, lost all his popularity
in the vain attempt to put the custom down. When the
Bourbon Philip V. first visited the *plaça* at Madrid, all
the populace roared, *Bulls ! give us bulls, my lord.* They
cared little for the ruin of the monarchy; so when the
intrusive Joseph Buonaparte arrived at the same place,
the only and absorbing topic of public talk was whether
he would grant or suppress the bull-fight. And now, as
always, the cry of the capital is—" *Pan y toros ;* bread
and bulls ;" these constitute the loaves and fishes of
the " only modern court," as *Panes et Circenses* did of
ancient Rome. The national scowl and frown which
welcomed Montpensier at his marriage, was relaxed
for one moment, when Spaniards beheld his well-put-
on admiration for the tauromachian spectacle. Nothing, since the recent vast improvements in Spain, has
more progressed than the bull-fight—convents have come
down, churches have been levelled, but new amphitheatres
have arisen. The diffusion of useful and entertaining
knowledge, as the means of promoting the greatest happiness of the greatest number, has thus obtained the
best consideration of those patriots and statesmen who
preside over the destinies of Spain; the bull is master
of his ground. This last remnant and representative
of Spanish nationality defies the foreigner and his civilisation; he is a *fait accompli*, and tramples *la charte*
under his feet, although the honest Roi citoyen swears
that it is désormais une *vérité*.

In Spain there is no mistaking the day and time that
the bull-fight takes place, which is generally on Saint
Monday, and in the afternoon, when the mid-day heats
are past.

The arena, or *Plaza,* is most unlike a London Place,
those enclosures of stunted smoke-blacked shrubs,
fenced in with iron palisadoes to protect aristocratic

nurserymaids from the mob. It is at once more classical
and amusing. The amphitheatre of Madrid is very
spacious, being about 1100 feet in circumference, and
will hold 12,000 spectators. In an architectural point
of view this ring of the model court, is shabbier than
many of those in provincial towns : there is no attempt
at orders, pilasters, and Vitruvian columns ; there is no
adaptation of the Coliseum of Rome : the exterior is
bald and plain, as if done so on purpose, while the
interior is fitted up with wooden benches, and is scarcely
better than a shambles ; but for that it was designed,
and there is a business-like, murderous intention about
it, which marks the inæsthetic Gotho-Spaniard, who
looked for a sport of blood and death, and not to a
display of artistical skill. He has no need of extraneous stimulants ; the *réalité atroce*, as a tender-hearted
foreigner observes, " is all-sufficing, because it is the
recreation of the savage, and the sublime of common
souls." The locality, however, is admirably calculated
for seeing ; and this combat is a spectacle entirely for
the eyes. The open space is full of the light of heaven,
and here the sun is brighter than gas or wax-candles.
The interior is as unadorned as the exterior, and looks
positively " mesquin " when empty ; around the sanded
centre rise rows of wooden seats for the humbler classes,
and above them a tier of boxes for the fine ladies and
gentlemen ; but no sooner is the theatre filled than all
this meanness is concealed, and the general appearance
becomes superb.

On entering the ring when thus full, the stranger
finds his watch put back at once eighteen hundred
years ; he is transported to Rome under the Cæsars ;
and in truth the sight is glorious, of the assembled
thousands in their Spanish costume, the novelty of the
spectacle, associated with our earliest classical studies,
and enhanced by the blue expanse of the heavens, spread
above as a canopy. There is something in these out-
of-door entertainments, *à l'antique,* which peculiarly
affects the shivering denizens of the catch-cold north,
where climate contributes so little to the happiness of
man. All first-rate connoisseurs go into the pit and

place themselves among the mob, in order to be closer
to the bulls and combatants. The *real thing* is to sit
near one of the openings, which enables the fancy-man
to exhibit his embroidered gaiters and neat leg. It is
here that the character of the bull, the nice traits and
the behaviour of the bull-fighter are scientifically criticised. The ring has a dialect peculiar to itself, which
is unintelligible to most Spaniards themselves, while to
the sporting-men of Andalucia it expresses their drol-
leries with idiomatic raciness, and is exactly analogous
to the slang and technicalities of our pugilistic craft.
The newspapers next day generally give a detailed
report of the fight, in which every round is scientifically
described in a style that defies translation, but which
being drawn up by some Spanish Boz, is most delectable
to all who can understand it; the nomenclature of praise
and blame is defined with the most accurate precision
of language, and the delicate shades of character are
distinguished with the nicety of phrenological subdivi-
sion. The foundation of this lingo is gipsy Romany,
metaphor, and double entendre; to master it is no easy
matter; indeed, a distinguished diplomat and tauromachian philologist, whom we are proud to call our
friend, was often unable to comprehend the full preg-
nancy of the meaning of certain terms, without a reference to the late Duke of San Lorenzo, who sustained
the character of Spanish ambassador in London and
of bull-fighter in Madrid with equal dignity; his grace
was a living lexicon of slang. Yet let no student be
deterred by any difficulty, since he will eventually be
repaid, when he can fully relish the Andalucian wit, or
sal Andaluça, the salt, with which the reports are
flavoured : that it is seldom Attic must, however, be
confessed. Nor let time or pains be grudged; there is
no royal road to Euclid, and life, say the Spanish fancy,
is too short to learn bull-fighting. This possibly may
seem strange, but English squires and country gentlemen assert as much in regard to fox-hunting.

The day appointed for a bull-feast is announced by
placards of all colours; the important particulars decorate every wall. The first thing is to secure a good place

beforehand, by sending for a *Boletin de Sombra,* a shade-ticket; and as the great object is to avoid glare and heat, the best places are on the northern side, which are in the shade. The transit of the sun over the Plaza, the zodiacal progress into Taurus, is decidedly the best calculated astronomical observation in Spain; the line of shadow defined on the arena is marked by a gradation of prices. The different seats and prices are everywhere detailed in the bills of the play, with the names of the combatants and the colours of the different breeds of bulls.

The day before the fight, the bulls destined for the spectacle are driven towards the town, and pastured in a meadow reserved for their reception; then the fine amateurs never fail to ride out to see what the cattle is like, just as the knowing in horseflesh go to Tattersall's of a Sunday afternoon, instead of attending evening service in their parish churches. According to Pepe Illo, who was a very practical man, and the first author on the modern system of the arena, of which he was the brightest ornament, and on which he died in the arms of victory, the " love of bulls is inherent in man, especially in the Spaniard, among which glorious people there have been bull-fights ever since there were bulls, because the Spanish men are as much more brave than all other men, as the Spanish bull is more fierce and valiant than all other bulls." Certainly, from having been bred at large in roomy unenclosed plains, they are more active than the animals raised by John Bull, but as regards form and power they would be scouted in an English cattle-show; a real British bull, with his broad neck and short horns, would make quick work with the men and horses of Spain; his " spears " would be no less effective than the bayonets of our soldiers, which no foreigner faces twice, or the picks of our *Navvies,* three and three-eighths of whom are calculated by railway economists to eat more beef and do more work than five and five-eighths of corresponding foreign material. By the way, the correct Castilian word for the bull's *horns* is *astas,* the Latin *hastas,* spears. *Cuernos* must never be used in good Spanish society, since, from its

secondary meaning, it might give offence to present
company : allusions to common calamities are never
made to ears polite, however frequent among the vulgar,
who call things by their improper names—nay, roar
them out, as in the time of Horace : " Magnâ compel-
lens voce cucullum."

Not every bull will do for the Plaza, and none but
the fiercest are selected, who undergo trials from the
earliest youth ; the most celebrated animals come from
Utrera near Seville, and from the same pastures where
that eminent breeder of old Geryon, raised those wonderful oxen, which all but burst with fat in fifty days, and
were " lifted " by the invincible Hercules.   Señor
Cabrera, the modern Geryon, was so pleased with
Joseph Buonaparte, or so afraid, that he offered to him
a hundred bulls, as a hecatomb for the rations of his
troops, who, braver and hungrier than Hercules, would
otherwise have infallibly followed the demigod's
example.   The Manchegan bull, small, very powerful,
and active, is considered to be the original stock of
Spain ; of this breed was " Manchangito," the pet of
the Visconde de Miranda, a tauromachian noble of Cordova, and who used to come into the dining-room, but,
having one day killed a guest, he was destroyed after
violent resistance on the part of the Viscount, and only
in obedience to the peremptory mandate of the Prince of
the Peace.

The capital is supplied with animals bred in the valleys
of the Jarama near Aranjuez, which have been imme-
morially celebrated.   From hence came that *Harpado,*
the magnificent beast of the magnificent Moorish ballad
of Gazul, which was evidently written by a practical
torero, and on the spot : the verses sparkle with day-
light and local colour like a Velazquez, and are as
minutely correct as a Paul Potter, while Byron's " Bull-
fight " is the invention of a foreign poet, and full of
slight inaccuracies.

The *encierro*, or the driving the bulls to the arena,
is a service of danger ; they are enticed by tame oxen,
into a road which is barricadoed on each side, and then
driven full speed by the mounted and spear-bearing

peasants into the *Plaza*. It is an exciting, peculiar, and picturesque spectacle; and the poor who cannot afford to go to the bull-fight, risk their lives and cloaks in order to get the front places, and best chance of a stray poke *en passant*.

The next afternoon all the world crowds to the *Plaza de toros*. You need not ask the way; just launch into the tide, which in these Spanish affairs will assuredly carry you away. Nothing can exceed the gaiety and sparkle of a Spanish public going, eager and full-dressed, to the *fight*. They could not move faster were they running away from a real one. All the streets or open spaces near the outside of the arena present of themselves a spectacle to the stranger, and genuine Spain is far better to be seen and studied in the streets, than in the saloon. Now indeed a traveller from Belgravia feels that he is out of town, in a new world and no mistake; all around him is a perfect saturnalia, all ranks are fused in one stream of living beings, one bloody thought beats in every heart, one heart beats in ten thousand bosoms; every other business is at an end, the lover leaves his mistress unless she will go with him,—the doctor and lawyer renounce patients, briefs, and fees; the city of sleepers is awakened, and all is life, noise, and movement, where to-morrow will be the stillness and silence of death; now the bending line of the *Calle de Alcalá*, which on other days is broad and dull as Portland Place, becomes the aorta of Madrid, and is scarcely wide enough for the increased circulation; now it is filled with a dense mass coloured as the rainbow, which winds along like a spotted snake to its prey. Oh the din and dust! The merry mob is every-thing, and, like the Greek chorus, is always on the scene. How national and Spanish are the dresses of the lower classes—for their betters alone appear like Boulevard quizzes, or tigers cut out from our East end tailors' pattern-book of the last new fashion; what *Manolas*, what reds and yellows, what fringes and flounces, what swarms of picturesque vagabonds, cluster, or alas, clustered, around *calesas*, whose wild drivers run on foot, whipping, screaming, swearing;

the type of these vehicles in form and colour was Neapolitan; they alas! are also soon destined to be sacrificed to civilization to the 'bus and common-place cab,
or vile fly.

The *plaza* is the focus of a fire, which blood alone can
extinguish; what public meetings and dinners are to
Britons, reviews and razzias to Gauls, mass or music
to Italians, is this one and absorbing bull-fight to
Spaniards of all ranks, sexes, ages, for their happiness is quite catching; and yet a thorn peeps amid these
rosebuds; when the dazzling glare and fierce African
sun calcining the heavens and earth, fires up man and
beast to madness, a raging thirst for blood is seen in
flashing eyes and the irritable ready knife, then the passion of the Arab triumphs over the coldness of the Goth:
the excitement would be terrific were it not on pleasure
bent; indeed there is no sacrifice, even of chastity, no
denial, even of dinner, which they will not undergo to
save money for the bull-fight. It is the birdlime with
which the devil catches many a female and male soul.
The men go in all their best costume and *majo*-finery;
the distinguished ladies wear on these occasions white
lace mantillas, and when heated, look, as the Andaluz
wag Adrian said, like sausages wrapped up in white
paper; a fan, *abanico,* is quite as necessary to all as it
was among the Romans. The article is sold outside for
a trifle, and is made of rude paper, stuck into a
handle of common cane or stick, and the gift of one
to his nutbrown *querida* is thought a delicate attention
to her complexion from her swarthy swain; at the same
time the lower Salamander classes stand fire much better
on these occasions than in action, and would rather be
roasted fanless alive *à la auto de fe* than miss these hot
engagements.

The place of slaughter, like the *Abattoirs* on the Continent, is erected outside the towns, in order to obtain
space, and because horned animals when over driven in
crowded streets are apt to be ill-mannered, as may be
seen every Smithfield market-day in the City, as the
Lord Mayor well knows.

The seats occupied by the mob are filled more rapidly

than our shilling galleries, and the "gods" are equally
noisy and impatient. The anxiety of the immortals,
wishes to annihilate time and space and make bull-
fanciers happy. Now his majesty the many reigns
triumphantly, and this—church excepted—is the only
public meeting allowed; but even here, as on the Continent, the odious bayonet sparkles, and the soldier pic-
ket announces that innocent amusements are not free;
treason and stratagem are suspected by coward despots,
when one sole thought of pleasure engrosses every one
else. All ranks are now fused into one mass of homo-
geneous humanity; their good humour is contagious;
all leave their cares and sorrows at home, and enter
with a gaiety of heart and a determination to be amused,
which defies wrinkled care; many and not over-delicate
are the quips and quirks bandied to and fro, with an
eloquence more energetic than unadorned; things and
persons are mentioned to the horror of periphrastic
euphuists; the liberty of speech is perfect, and as it is
all done quite in a parliamentary way, none take offence.
Those only who cannot get in are sad; these rejected
ones remain outside grinding their teeth, like the unhappy ghosts on the wrong side of the Styx, and listen
anxiously to the joyous shouts of the thrice blessed
within.

At Seville a choice box in the shade and to the right
of the president is allotted as the seat of honour to the
canons of the cathedral, who attend in their clerical
costume; and such days are fixed upon for the bull-
fight as will not by a long church service prevent their
coming. The clergy of Spain have always been the
most uncompromising enemies of the stage, where they
never go; yet neither the cruelty nor profligacy of the
amphitheatre has ever roused the zeal of their most
elect or most fanatic: our puritans at least assailed
the bear-bait, which induced the Cavalier Hudibras to
defend them; so our methodists denounced the bull-bait,
which was therefore patronised by the Right Hon. W.
Windham, in the memorable debate May 24, 1802, on
Mr. *Dog* Dent. The Spanish clergy pay due deference
to bulls, both papal and quadruped; they dislike being

touched on this subject, and generally reply " *Es costumbre*—it is the custom—*siempre se ha practicado así*—it has always been done so, or *son cosas de España,* they are things of Spain "—the usual answer given as to everything which appears incomprehensible to strangers, and which they either can't account for, or do not choose. In vain did St. Isidore write a chapter against the amphitheatre—his *chapter* minds him not; in vain did Alphonso the Wise forbid their attendance. The sacrifice of the bull has always been mixed up with the religion of old Rome and old and modern Spain, where they are classed among acts of charity, since they support the sick and wounded; therefore all the sable countrymen of Loyola hold to the Jesuitical doctrine that the end justifies the means.

CHAPTER XXII

WHEN the appointed much-wished-for-hour is come, the Queen or the *Corregidor* takes the seat of honour in a central and splendid box, the mob having been previously expelled from the open arena; this operation is called the *despejo,* and is an amusing one, from the reluctance with which the great unwashed submit to be cleaned out. The proceedings open at a given signal with a procession of the combatants, who advance preceded by *alguaciles,* or officers of police, who are dressed in the ancient Spanish costume, and are always at hand to arrest any one who infringes the severe laws against interruptions of the games. Then follow the *picadores*, or mounted horsemen, with their spears. Their original broad-brimmed Spanish hats are decorated with ribbons; their upper man is clad in a gay silken jacket, whose lightness contrasts with the heavy iron and leather protections of the legs, which give the clumsy look of a French jackbooted postilion. These defences are necessary when the horned animal charges home. Next follow the *chulos*, or combatants on foot, who are arrayed like Figaro at the opera, and have, moreover, silken cloaks of gay colours. The *matadores*, or killers, come behind them; and, last of all, a gaily-caparisoned team of mules, which is destined to drag the slaughtered bulls from the arena. As for the men, those who are killed on the spot are denied the burial-rites if they die without confession. Springing from the dregs of the people, they are eminently superstitious, and cover their breasts with relics, amulets, and papal charms. A clergyman, however, is in attendance with the sacramental wafer, in case *su majestad* may be wanted for a mortally-wounded combatant.

Having made their obeisances to the chief authority, all retire, and the fatal trumpet sounds; then the president throws the key of the gate by which the bull is to enter, to one of the *alguaciles*, who ought to catch it in his hat. When the door is opened, this worthy gallops away as fast as he can, amid the hoots and hisses of the mob, not because he rides like a constable, but from the instinctive enmity which his majesty the many bear to the finisher of the law, just as little birds love to mob a hawk; now more than a thousand kind wishes are offered up that the bull may catch and toss him. The brilliant army of combatants in the meanwhile separates like a bursting shell, and take up their respective places as regularly as our fielders do at a cricket-match.

The play, which consists of three acts, then begins in earnest; the drawing up of the curtain is a spirit-stirring moment; all eyes are riveted at the first appearance of the bull on this stage, as no one can tell how he may behave. Let loose from his dark cell, at first he seems amazed at the novelty of his position; torn from his pastures, imprisoned and exposed, stunned by the noise, he gazes an instant around at the crowd, the glare, and waving handkerchiefs, ignorant of the fate which inevitably awaits him. He bears on his neck a ribbon, "la devisa," which designates his breeder. The picador endeavours to snatch this off, to lay the trophy at

his true love's heart. The bull is condemned without
reprieve; however gallant his conduct, or desperate his
resistance, his death is the catastrophe; the whole
tragedy tends and hastens to this event, which, although it is darkly shadowed out beforehand, as in a
Greek play, does not diminish the interest, since all the
intermediate changes and chances are uncertain; hence
the sustained excitement, for the action may pass in an
instant from the sublime to the ridiculous, from tragedy
to farce.

The bull no sooner recovers his senses, than his
splendid Achillean rage fires every limb, and with closing
eyes and lowered horns he rushes at the first of the
three picadores, who are drawn up to the left, close to
the *tablas*, or wooden barrier which walls round the
ring. The horseman sits on his trembling Rosinante,
with his pointed lance under his right arm, as stiff and
valiant as Don Quixote. If the animal be only of
second-rate power and courage, the sharp point arrests
the charge, for he well remembers this *garrocha*, or
goad, by which herdsmen enforce discipline and incul-
cate instruction; during this momentary pause a quick
picador turns his horse to the left and gets free. The
bulls, although irrational brutes, are not slow on their
part in discovering when their antagonists are bold and
dexterous, and particularly dislike fighting against the
pricks. If they fly and will not face the picador, they
are hooted at as despicable malefactors, who wish to
defraud the public of their day's sport, they are exe-
crated as " goats," " cows," which is no compliment
to bulls; these culprits, moreover, are soundly beaten as
they pass near the barrier by forests of sticks, with
which the mob is provided for the nonce; that of the
elegant *majo,* when going to the bull-fight, is very
peculiar, and is called *la chivata;* it is between four and
five feet long, is taper, and terminates in a lump or
knob, while the top is forked, into which the thumb is
inserted; it is also peeled or painted in alternate rings,
black and white, or red and yellow. The lower classes
content themselves with a common shillelah; one with
a knob at the end is preferred, as administering a more

impressive whack; their instrument is called *porro*, because heavy and lumbering.

Nor is this bastinado uncalled for, since courage, address, and energy, are the qualities which ennoble tauromachia; and when they are wanting, the butchery, with its many disgusting incidents, becomes revolting to the stranger, but to him alone; for the gentler emotions of pity and mercy, which rarely soften any transactions of hard Iberia, are here banished altogether from the hearts of the natives; they now only have eyes for exhibitions of skill and valour, and scarcely observe those cruel incidents which engross and horrify the foreigner, who again on his part is equally blind to those redeeming excellencies, on which alone the attention of the rest of the spectators is fixed; the tables are now turned against the stranger, whose æsthetic mind's eye can see the poetry and beauty of the picturesque rags and tumbledown hamlets of Spaniards, and yet is blind to the poverty, misery, and want of civilisation, to which alone the vision of the higher classed native is directed, on whose exalted soul the coming comforts of cotton are gleaming.

When the bull is turned by the spear of the first picador, he passes on to the two other horsemen, who receive him with similar cordiality. If the animal be baffled by their skill and valour, stunning are the shouts of applause which celebrate the victory of the men : should he on the contrary charge home and overwhelm horses and riders, then—for the balances of praise and blame are held with perfect fairness—the fierce lord of the arena is encouraged with roars of compliments, *Bravo toro*, *Viva toro*, Well done, bull ! even a long life is wished to him by thousands who know that he must be dead in twenty minutes.

A bold beast is not to be deterred by a trifling inch-deep wound, but presses on, goring the horse in the flank, and then gaining confidence and courage by victory, and "baptized in blood," à la Française, advances in a career of honour, gore, and glory. The picador is seldom well mounted, for the horses are provided, at the lowest possible price, by a contractor, who runs the risk whether many or few are killed; they indeed are the only things economised in this costly spectacle, and are sorry, broken-down hacks, fit only for the dog-kennel of an English squire, or carriage of a foreign *Pair*. This increases the danger to his rider; in the ancient combats, the finest and most spirited horses were used; quick as lightning, and turning to the touch, they escaped the deadly rush. The eyes of those poor horses which see and will not face death, are often bound over with a handkerchief, like criminals about to be executed; thus they await blindfold the fatal horn thrust which is to end their life of misery.

The picadors are subject to most severe falls; the bull often tosses horse and rider in one ruin, and when his victims fall with a crash on the ground exhausts his fury upon his prostrate foes. The picador manages (if he can) to fall off on the opposite side, in order that his horse may form a barrier and rampart between him and the bull. When these deadly struggles take place, when life hangs on a thread, the amphitheatre is peopled with heads; every feeling of anxiety, eagerness, fear, horror, and delight is stamped on their expressive countenances; if happiness is to be estimated by quality, intensity, and concentration, rather than duration (and it is), these are moments of excitement more precious to them, than ages of placid, insipid, uniform stagnation. Their feelings are wrought to a pitch, when the horse, maddened with wounds and terror, plunging in the death-struggle, the crimson seams of blood streaking his foam and sweat-whitened body, flies from the infuriated bull still pursuing, still goring; then are displayed the nerve, presence of mind, and horsemanship of the dexterous and undismayed picador. It is in truth a piteous sight to see the poor mangled horses treading out their entrails, and yet gallantly carrying off their riders unhurt. But as in the pagan sacrifices, the quivering intestines, trembling with life, formed the most propitious omens—to what will not early habit familiarise?—so the Spaniards are no more affected with the reality, than the Italians are with the abstract " tanti palpiti " of Rossini.

The miserable horse, when dead, is dragged out, leaving a bloody furrow on the sand, as the river-beds of the arid plains of Barbary are marked by the crimson fringe of the flowering oleanders. A universal sympathy is shown for the horseman in these awful moments; the men rise, the women scream, but all this soon subsides; the *picador*, if wounded, is carried out and forgotten—" *los muertos y idos no tienen amigos* " —a new combatant fills up his gap, the battle rages— wounds and death are the order of the day—he is not missed; and as new incidents arise, no pause is left for regret or reflection. We remember seeing at Granada a matador cruelly gored by a bull: he was carried away as dead, and his place immediately taken by his son, as coolly as a viscount succeeds to an earl's estate and title. Carnerero, the musician, died while fiddling at a ball at Madrid, in 1838; neither the band nor the dancers stopped one moment. The boldness of the picadors is great. Francisco Sevilla, when thrown from his horse and lying under the dying animal, seized the bull, as he rushed at him, by his ears, turned round to the people, and laughed; but, in fact, the long horns of the bull make it difficult for him to gore a man on the ground; he generally bruises them with his nose: nor does he remain long busied with his victim, since he is lured to fresh attacks by the glittering cloaks of the *Chulos* who come instantly to the rescue. At the same time we are free to confess, that few picadors, although men of bronze, can be said to have a sound rib in their body. When one is carried off apparently dead, but returns immediately mounted on a fresh horse, the applauding voice of the people outbellows a thousand bulls. If the wounded man should chance not to come back, *n'importe*, however courted outside the *Plaza*, now he is ranked, like the gladiator was by the Romans, no higher than a beast,—or about the same as a slave under the perfect equality and man rights of the model republic.

The poor horse is valued at even less, and he, of all the actors, is the one in which Englishmen, true lovers and breeders of the noble animal, take the liveliest

interest; nor can any bull-fighting habit ever reconcile
them to his sufferings and ill-treatment. The hearts of
the picadors are as devoid of feeling as their iron-cased
legs; they only think of themselves, and have a nice tact
in knowing when a wound is fatal or not. Accordingly,
if the horn-thrust has touched a vital part, no sooner has
the enemy passed on to a new victim, than an experienced picador quietly dismounts, takes off the saddle
and bridle, and hobbles off like Richard, calling out
for another horse—a horse. The poor animal, when
stripped of these accoutrements, has a most rippish
look, as it staggers to and fro, like a drunken man,
until again attacked by the bull and prostrated; then it
lies dying unnoticed in the sand, or, if observed, merely
rouses the jeers of the mob; as its tail quivers in the last
agony of death, your attention is called to the *fun; Mira,
mira, que cola!* The words and sight yet haunt us, for
they were those that first caught our inexperienced ears
and eyes at the first rush of the first bull of our first
bull-fight. While gazing on the scene in a total abstrac-
tion from the world, we felt our coat-tails tugged at, as
by a greedily-biting pike; we had caught, or, rather,
were caught by a venerable harridan, whose quick perception had discovered a novice, whom her kindness
prompted to instruct, for e'en in the ashes live the wonted
fires; a bright, fierce eye gleamed alive in a dead and
shrivelled face, which evil passions had furrowed like
the lava-seared sides of an extinct volcano, and dried
up, like a cat starved behind a wainscot, into a thing of
fur and bones, in which gender was obliterated—let her
pass. If the wound received by the horse be not instantaneously mortal, the blood-vomiting hole is plugged up
with tow, and the fountain of life stopped for a few
minutes. If the flank is only partially ruptured, the pro-
truding bowels are pushed back—no operation in hernia
is half so well performed by Spanish surgeons—and the
rent is sown up with a needle and pack-thread. Thus
existence is prolonged for new tortures, and a few dollars
are saved to the contractor; but neither death nor lacera-
tions excite the least pity, nay, the bloodier and more
fatal the spectacle the more brilliant it is pronounced.

It is of no use to remonstrate, or ask why the wounded sufferers are not mercifully killed at once; the utilitarian Spaniard dislikes to see the order of the sport interrupted and spoilt by what he considers foreign squeamishness and nonsense, " *Ah que! no vale nā,*"—" Bah! the beast is worth nothing;" that is, provided he condescends to reply to your *disparates* with anything beyond a shrug of civil contempt. But national tastes will differ. " Sir," said an alderman to Dr. Johnson, " in attempting to listen to your long sentences, and give you a short answer, I have swallowed two pieces of green fat, without tasting the flavour. I beg you to let me enjoy my present happiness in peace and quiet."

The bull is the hero of the scene; yet, like Satan in the Paradise Lost, he is foredoomed. Nothing can save him from a certain fate, which awaits all, whether brave or cowardly. The poor creatures sometimes endeavour in vain to escape, and have favourite retreats, to which they fly; or they leap over the barrier, among the spectators, creating a vast hubbub and fun, upsetting watercarriers and fancy men, putting sentinels and old women to flight, and affording infinite delight to all who are safe in the boxes; for, as Bacon remarks, " It is pleasant to see a battle from a distant hill." Bulls which exhibit this cowardly activity are insulted: cries of " fuego " and " perros," fire and dogs, resound, and he is condemned to be baited. As the Spanish dogs have by no means the pluck of the English assailants of bulls, they are longer at the work, and many are made minced-meat of :—

> " Up to the stars the growling mastiffs fly
> And add new monsters to the frighted sky."

When at length the poor brute is pulled down he is stabbed in the spine, as if he were only fit for the shambles, being a civilian ox, not a soldierlike bull. All these processes are considered as deadly insults; and when more than one bull exhibits these craven propensities to baulk nobler expectancies, then is raised the cry of " *Cabestros al circo!*" tame oxen to the circus. This is a mortal affront to the *empresa*, or management, as it infers that it has furnished animals fitter for the plough than for the arena. The indignation of the mob is terrible; for, if disappointed in the blood of bulls, it will lap that of men.

The bull is sometimes teased with stuffed figures, men of straw with leaded feet, which rise up again as soon as he knocks them down. An old author relates that in the time of Philip IV. " a despicable peasant was occasionally set upon a lean horse, and exposed to death." At other times, to amuse the populace, a monkey is tied to a pole in the arena. This art of ingeniously tormenting is considered as unjustifiable homicide by certain lively philosimious foreigners; and, indeed, all these episodes are despised as irregular *hors d'œuvres*, by the real and businesslike amateur.

After a due time the first act terminates : its length is uncertain. Sometimes it is most brilliant, since one one bull has been known to kill a dozen horses, and clear the *plaza*. Then he is adored; and as he roams, snorting about, lord of all he surveys, he becomes the sole object of worship to ten thousand devotees; at the signal of the president, and sound of a trumpet, the second act commences with the performances of the *chulo*, a word which signifies, in the Arabic, a lad, a merryman, as at our fairs. The duty of this light division, these skirmishers, is to draw off the bull from the *picador* when endangered, which they do with their coloured cloaks; their address and agility are surprising, they skim over the sand like glittering humming-birds, scarcely touching the earth. They are dressed in short breeches, and without gaiters, just as Figaro is in the opera of the ' *Barbiere de Seviglia*.' Their hair is tied into a knot behind, and enclosed in the once universal silk net, the *retecilla*—the identical *reticulum*—of which so many instances are seen on ancient Etruscan vases. No bull-fighters ever arrive at the top of their profession without first excelling in this apprenticeship; then, they are taught how to entice the bull to them, and learn his mode of attack, and how to parry it. The most dangerous moment is when these *chulos* venture out into the middle of the *plaza*, and are followed by the bull to the barrier. There is a small

ledge, on which they place their foot, and vault over, and
a narrow slit in the boarding, through which they slip
Their escapes are marvellous, and they win by a neck;
they seem really sometimes, so close is the run, to be
helped over the fence by the bull's horns. The *chulos*,
in the second act, are the sole performers; their part is
to place small barbed darts, on each side of the neck of
the bull, which are called *banderillas*, and are ornamented
with cut paper of different colours—gay decorations
under which cruelty is concealed. The *banderilleros* go
right up to him, holding the arrows at the shaft, and
pointing the barbs at the bull; just when the animal
stoops to toss his foes, they jerk them into his neck and
slip aside. The service appears to be more dangerous
than it is, but it requires a quick eye, a light hand and
foot. The barbs should be placed to correspond with
each other exactly on both sides. Such pretty pairs are
termed *buenos pares* by the Spaniards, and the feat is
called *coiffer* le taureau by the French, who undoubtedly
are first-rate perruquiers. Very often these arrows are
provided with crackers, which, by means of a detonating
powder, explode the moment they are affixed in the neck;
thence they are called *banderillas de fuego*. The agony
of the scorched and tortured animal makes him plunge
and bound like a sportive lamb, to the intense joy of the
populace, while the fire, the smell of singed hair and
roasted flesh, which our gastronomic neighbours would
call a *bifstec à l'Espagnole*, faintly recall to many a dark
scowling priest the superior attractions of his former
amphitheatre, the *auto de fé*.

The last trumpet now sounds, the arena is cleared,
and the *matador*, the executioner, the man of death,
stands before his victim alone; on entering, he addresses
the president, and throws his cap to the ground. In his
right hand he holds a long straight Toledan blade; in his
left he waves the *muleta*, the red flag, or the *engaño*, the
lure, which ought not (so Romero laid down in our hearing) to be so large as the standard of a religious brotherhood, nor so small as a lady's pocket-handkerchief, but
about a yard square. The colour is always red, because
that best irritates the bull and conceals blood. There is

always a spare slayer at hand in case of accidents, which may happen in the best regulated bull-fights.

The *matador*, from being alone, concentrates in himself all the interest as regards the human species, which was before frittered away among the many other combatants, as was the case in the ancient gladiatorial shows of Rome. He advances to the bull, in order to entice him towards him, or, in nice technical idiom, *citarlo á la jurisdiccion del engaño*, to cite him into the jurisdiction of the trick; in plain English, to subpœna him, or, as our ring would say, get his head into chancery. And this trial is nearly as awful, as the matador stands confronted with his foe, in the presence of inexorable witnesses, the bar and judges, who would rather see the bull kill *him* twice over, than that he should kill the bull contrary to the rules and practice of the court and tauromachian precedent. In these brief but trying moments the matador generally looks pale and anxious, as well he may, for life hangs on the edge of a razor, but he presents a fine picture of fixed purpose and concentration of moral energy. And Seneca said truly that the world had seen as many examples of courage in gladiators, as in the Catos and Scipios.

The matador endeavours rapidly to discover the character of the animal, and examines with eye keener than Spurzheim, his bumps of combativeness, destructiveness, and other amiable organs; nor has he many moments to lose, where mistake is fatal, as one must die, and both may. Here, as Falstaff says, there is no scoring, except on the pate. Often even the brute bull seems to feel that the last moment is come, and pauses, when face to face in the deadly duel with his single opponent. Be that as it may, the contrast is very striking. The slayer is arrayed in a ball costume, with no buckler but skill, and as if it were a pastime : he is all coolness, the beast all rage ; and time it is to be collected, for now indeed knowledge is power, and could the beast reason, the man would have small chance. Meanwhile the spectators are wound up to a greater pitch of madness than the poor bull, who has undergone a long torture, besides continued excitement : he at this instant becomes a study for a Paul

Potter; his eyes flash fire—his inflated nostrils snort fury; his body is covered with sweat and foam, or crimsoned with a glaze of gore streaming from gaping wounds. " *Mira! que bel cuerpo de sangre!*—look ! what a beauteous body of blood !" exclaimed the worthy old lady, who, as we before mentioned, was kind enough to point out to our inexperience the tit bits of the treat, the pearls of greatest price.

There are several sorts of *toros,* whose characters vary no less than those of men : some are brave and dashing, others are slow and heavy, others sly and cowardly. The *matador* foils and plays with the bull until he has discovered his disposition. The fundamental principle consists in the animal's mode of attack, the stooping his head and shutting his eyes, before he butts; the secret of mastering him lies in distinguishing whether he acts on the offensive or defensive. Those which are fearless, and rush boldly on at once, closing their eyes, are the most easy to kill; those which are cunning—which seldom go straight when they charge, but stop, dodge, and run at the man, not the flag, are the most dangerous. The interest of the spectators increases in proportion as the peril is great.

Although fatal accidents do not often occur (and we ourselves have never seen a man killed, yet we have beheld some hundred bulls despatched), such events are always possible. At Tudela, a bull having killed seventeen horses, a picador named Blanco, and a banderillero, then leapt over the barriers, where he gored to death a peasant, and wounded many others. The newspapers simply headed the statement, " *Accidents* have happened." Pepe Illo, who had received thirty-eight wounds in the wars, died, like Nelson, the hero's death. He was killed on the 11th of May, 1801. He had a presentiment of his death, but said that he must do his duty.

Every *matador* must be quick and decided. He must not let the bull run at the flag above two or three times; the moral tension of the multitudes is too strained to endure a longer suspense; they vent their impatience in jeers, noises, and endeavour by every possible manner to irritate him, and make him lose his temper, and per-

haps life. Under such circumstances, Manuel Romero,
who had murdered a man, was always saluted with cries
of " *A la Plaza de Cebada*—to Tyburn." The populace
absolutely loathe those who show the smallest white
feather, or do not brave death cheerfully.

There are many ways of killing the bull : the principal
is when the matador receives him on his sword when
charging ; then the weapon, which is held still and never
thrust forward, enters just between the left shoulder and
the blade-bone ; a firm hand, eye, and nerve, are essential,
since in nothing is the real fancy so fastidious as in the
exact nicety of the placing of this death-wound. The
bull very often is not killed at the first effort ; if not true,
the sword strikes a bone, and then it is ejected high in
air by the rising neck. When the blow is true, death is
instantaneous, and the bull, vomiting forth blood, drops
at the feet of his conqueror. It is indeed the triumph of
knowledge over brute force ; all that was fire, fury, passion, and life, falls in an instant, still for ever. The gay
team of mules now enter, glittering with flags, and tinkling with bells ; the dead bull is carried off at a rapid
gallop, which always delights the populace. The
matador then wipes the hot blood from his sword, and
bows to the spectators with admirable sang froid, who
fling their hats into the arena, a compliment which he
returns by throwing them back again (they are generally
" shocking bad " ones) , when Spain was rich, a golden,
or at least a silver shower was rained down—*ces beaux
jours là sont passés ;* thanks to her kind neighbour. The
poverty-stricken Spaniard, however, gives all he can,
and lets the bull-fighter dream the rest. As hats in Spain
represent grandeeship, so these beavers, part and parcel
of themselves, are given as symbols of their generous
hearts and souls ; and none but a huckster would go into
minute details of value or condition.

When a bull will not run at the fatal flag, or prays for
pardon, he is doomed to a dishonourable death, as no
true Spaniard begs for his own life, or spares that of his
foe, when in his power ; now the *media Luna* is yelled
for, and the call implies insult ; the use is equivalent to
shooting traitors in the back : this *half moon* is the pre-

cise Oriental ancient and cruel instrument of houghing cattle; moreover it is the exact old Iberian bident, or a sharp steel crescent placed on a long pole. The cowardly blow is given from behind; and when the poor beast is crippled by dividing the sinew of his leg, and crawls along in agony, an assistant pierces with a pointed dagger the spinal marrow, which is the usual method of slaughtering cattle in Spain by the butcher. To perform all these vile operations is considered beneath the dignity of the *matador;* some, however, will kill the bull by plunging the point of their sword in the vertebræ, as the danger gives dignity to the difficult feat.

Such is a single bull-fight; each of which is repeated eight times with succeeding bulls, the excitement of the multitude rising with each indulgence; after a short collapse new desires are roused by fresh objects, the fierce sport is renewed, which night alone can extinguish; nay, often when royalty is present, a ninth bull is clamoured for, which is always graciously granted by the nominal monarch's welcome sign, the pulling his royal ear; in truth here the mob is autocrat, and his majesty the many will take no denial; the bull-fight terminates when the day dies like a dolphin, and the curtain of heaven hung over the bloody show, is incarnadined and crimsoned; this glorious finish is seen in full perfection at Seville, where the *plaza* from being unfinished is open toward the cathedral, which furnishes a Moorish distance to the picturesque foreground. On particular occasions this side is decorated with flags. When the blazing sun setting on the red Giralda tower, lights up its fair proportions like a pillar of fire, the refreshing evening breeze springs up, and the flagging banners wave in triumph over the concluding spectacle; then when all is come to an end, as all things human must, the congregation depart, with rather less decorum than if quitting a church; all hasten to sacrifice the rest of the night to Bacchus and Venus, with a passing homage to the knife, should critics differ too hotly on the merits of some particular thrust of the bull-fight.

To conclude; the minds of men, like the House of Commons in 1802, are divided on the merits of the bull-

fight; the Wilberforces assert (especially foreigners,
who, notwithstanding, seldom fail to sanction the arena
by their presence) that all the best feelings are blunted—
that idleness, extravagance, cruelty, and ferocity are
promoted at a vast expense of human and animal life
by these pastimes; the Windhams contend that loyalty,
courage, presence of mind, endurance of pain, and contempt of death, are inculcated—that, while the theatre
is all illusion, the opera all effeminacy, these manly,
national games are all truth, and in the words of a native
eulogist "elevate the soul to those grandiose actions of
valour and heroism which have long proved the
Spaniards to be the best and bravest of all nations."

The efficacy of such sports for sustaining a martial
spirit was disproved by the degeneracy of the Romans at
the time when bloody spectacles were most in vogue; nor
are bravery and humanity the characteristics of the bull-
fighting Spaniards in the collective. We ourselves do
not attribute their "merciless skivering and skewering,"
their flogging and murdering women, to the bull-fight,
the practical result of which has been overrated and
misunderstood. Cruel it undoubtedly is, and perfectly
congenial to the inherent, inveterate ferocity of Iberian
character, but it is an effect rather than a cause—with
doubtless some reciprocating action; and it may be questioned, whether the *original* bull-fight had not a greater
tendency to humanise, than the Olympic games; certainly
the *Fiesta real* of the feudal ages combined the associated
ideas of religion and loyalty, while the chivalrous combat
nurtured a nice sense of personal honour and a respectful
gallantry to women, which were unknown to the polished
Greeks or warlike Romans; and many of the finest
features of Spanish character have degenerated since the
discontinuance of the original fight, which was more
bloody and fatal than the present one.

The Spaniards invariably bring forward our boxing-
matches in self-justification, as if a *tu quoque* could be
so; but it must always be remembered in our excuse that
these are discountenanced by the good and respectable,
and legally stigmatised as breaches of the peace;
although disgraced by beastly drunkenness, brutal vul-

garity, ruinous gambling and betting, from which the Spanish arena is exempt, as no bull yet has been backed to kill so many horses or not; our matches, however, are based on a spirit of *fair play* which forms no principle of the Punic politics, warfare, or bull-fighting of Spain. The Plaza there is patronised by church and state, to whom, in justice, the responsibility of evil consequences must be referred. The show is conducted with great ceremonial, combining many elements of poetry, the beautiful and sublime; insomuch that a Spanish author proudly says: "When the countless assembly is honoured by the presence of our august monarchs, the world is *lost in admiration* at the majestic spectacle afforded by the happiest people in the world, enjoying with rapture an exhibition peculiarly their own, and offering to their idolised sovereigns the due homage of the truest and most refined loyalty;" and it is impossible to deny the magnificent *coup d'œil* of the assembled thousands. Under such conflicting circumstances, we turn away our eyes during moments of painful detail which are lost in the poetical ferocity of the whole, for the interest of the tragedy of real death is undeniable, irresistible, and all absorbing.

The Spaniards seem almost unconscious of the cruelty of those details which are most offensive to a stranger. They are reconciled by habit, as we are to the bleeding butchers' shops which disfigure our gay streets, and which if seen for the first time would be inexpressibly disgusting. The feeling of the chase, that remnant of the savage, rules in the arena, and mankind has never been nice or tender-hearted in regard to the sufferings of animals, when influenced by the destructive propensities. In England no sympathy is shown for game,—fish, flesh, or fowl; nor for vermin—stoats, kites, or poachers. The end of the sport is—death; the amusement is the *playing*, the *fine* run, as the prolongation of animal suffering is termed in the tender vocabulary of the Nimrods; the pang of mortal sufferance is not regulated by the size of the victim; the bull moreover is always put at once out of his misery, and never exposed to the thousand lingering deaths of the poor wounded hare; therefore we must not

see a toro in Spanish eyes and wink at the fox in our
own, nor

> " Compound for vices we're inclined to
> By damning those we have no mind to."

It is not clear that animal suffering on the whole predominates over animal happiness. The bull roams in
ample pastures, through a youth and manhood free from
toil, and when killed in the plaza only anticipates by a
few months the certain fate of the imprisoned, over-
laboured, mutilated ox.

In Spain, where capital is scanty, person and property
insecure (evils not quite corrected since the late demo-
cratic reforms), no one would adventure on the speculation of breeding cattle on a large scale, where the return
is so distant, without the certain demand and sale created
by the amphitheatre; and as a small proportion only of
the produce possess the requisite qualifications, the surplus and females go to the plough and market, and can
be sold cheaper from the profit made on the bulls.
Spanish political economists *proved* that many valuable
animals were wasted in the arena—but their theories
vanished before the fact, that the supply of cattle was
rapidly diminished when bull-fights were suppressed.
Similar results take place as regards the breed of horses,
though in a minor degree; those, moreover, which are
sold to the Plaza would never be bought by any one else.
With respect to the loss of human life, in no land is a
man worth so little as in Spain; and more English aldermen are killed indirectly by turtles, than Andalucian picadors directly by bulls; while as to *time*, these exhibitions
always take place on holidays, which even industrious
Britons bouse away occasionally in pothouses, and idle
Spaniards invariably smoke out in sunshiny *dolce far
niente*. The attendance, again, of idle spectators prevents idleness in the numerous classes employed directly
and indirectly in getting up and carrying out this expensive spectacle.

It is poor and illogical philosophy to judge of foreign
customs by our own habits, prejudices, and conventional
opinions; a cold, unprepared, calculating stranger comes

without the freemasonry of early associations, and criticises minutiæ which are lost on the natives in their enthusiasm and feeling for the whole. He is horrified by details to which the Spaniards have become as accustomed as hospital nurses, whose finer sympathetic emotions of pity are deadened by repetition.

A most difficult thing it is to change long-established usages and customs with which we are familiar from our early days, and which have come down to us connected with many fond remembrances. We are slow to suspect any evil or harm in such practices; we dislike to look the evidence of facts in the face, and shrink from a conclusion which would require the abandonment of a recreation, which we have long regarded as innocent, and in which we, as well as our parents before us, have not scrupled to indulge. Children, *l'age sans pitié*, do not speculate on cruelty, whether in bull-baiting or bird's-nesting, and Spaniards are brought up to the bull-fight from their infancy, when they are too simple to speculate on abstract questions, but associate with the Plaza all their ideas of reward for good conduct, of finery and holiday; in a land where amusements are few—they catch the contagion of pleasure, and in their young bias of imitation approve of what is approved of by their parents. They return to their homes unchanged—playful, timid, or serious, as before; their kindly, social feelings are uninjured: and where is the filial or parental bond more affectionately cherished than in Spain—where are the noble courtesies of life, the kind, considerate, self-respecting demeanour so exemplified as in Spanish society?

The successive feelings experienced by most foreigners are admiration, compassion, and weariness of the flesh. The first will be readily understood, as it will that the horses' sufferings cannot be beheld by novices without compassion: " In troth it was more a pittie than a delight," wrote the herald of Lord Nottingham. This feeling, however, regards the animals who are forced into wounds and death; the men scarcely excite much of it, since they willingly court the danger, and have therefore no right to complain. These heroes of low life are

applauded, well paid, and their risk is more apparent
than real; our British feelings of fair play make us side
rather with the poor bull who is overmatched; we respect
the gallantry of his unequal defence. Such must always
be the effect produced on those not bred and brought up
to such scenes. So Livy relates that, when the gladiatorial shows were first introduced by the Romans into
Asia, the natives were more frightened than pleased,
but by leading them on from sham-fights to real, they
became as fond of them as the Romans. The predomi-
nant sensation experienced by ourselves was *bore*, the
same thing over and over again, and too much of it.
But that is the case with everything in Spain, where
processions and professions are interminable. The
younger Pliny, who was no amateur, complained of the
eternal sameness of seeing what to have seen once, was
enough; just as Dr. Johnson, when he witnessed a horse-
race, observed that he had not met with such a proof of
the paucity of human pleasures as in the popularity of
such a spectacle. But the life of Spaniards is uniform,
and their sensations, not being blunted by satiety, are
intense. Their bull-fight to them is always new and
exciting, since the more the toresque intellect is culti-
vated the greater the capacity for enjoyment; they see
a thousand minute beauties in the character and conduct
of the combatants, which escape the superficial unlearned
glance of the uninitiated.

Spanish ladies, against whom every puny scribbler
shoots his petty barbed arrow, are relieved from the in-
fliction of ennui, by the never-flagging, ever-sustained
interest, in being admired. They have no abstract nor
Pasiphaic predilections; they were taken to the bull-fight
before they knew their alphabet, or what love was. Nor
have we heard that it has ever rendered them particularly
cruel, save and except some of the elderly and tougher
lower-classed females. The younger and more tender
scream and are dreadfully affected in all real moments
of danger, in spite of their long familiarity. Their grand
object, after all, is not to see the bull, but to let themselves and their dresses be seen. The better classes
generally interpose their fans at the most painful inci-

dents, and certainly show no want of sensibility. The lower orders of females, as a body, behave quite as respectably as those of other countries do at executions, or other dreadful scenes, where they crowd with their babies. The case with English ladies is far different. They have heard the bull-fight not praised from *their* childhood, but condemned; they see it for the first time when grown up; curiosity is perhaps their leading feature in sharing an amusement, of which they have an indistinct idea that pleasure will be mixed with pain. The first sight delights them; a flushed, excited cheek, betrays a feeling that they are almost ashamed to avow; but as the bloody tragedy proceeds, they get frightened, disgusted, and disappointed. Few are able to sit out more than one course, and fewer ever re-enter the amphitheatre—

> "The heart that is soonest awake to the flower
> Is always the first to be touched by the thorn."

Probably a Spanish woman, if she could be placed in precisely the same condition, would not act very differently, and something of a similar test would be to bring her, for the first time, to an English boxing-match. Be this as it may, far from us and from our friends be that frigid philosophy, which would infer that their bright eyes, darting the shafts of Cupid, will glance one smile the less from witnessing these more merciful *banderillas*.

CHAPTER XXIII

HAVING seen a bull-fight, *the sight* of Spain, those who only wish to pass time agreeably cannot be too quick in getting their passports viséd for Naples. A pleasant *country* life, according to our notions, in Spain, is a thing that is not; and the substitute is but a Bedouin Oriental makeshift existence, which, amusing enough for a spurt, will not do in the long run. Nor is life much

better in the *towns;* those in the inland provinces have
a convent-like, dead, old-fashioned look about them,
which petrifies a lively person; nay even an artist when
he has finished his sketches, is ready to commit suicide
from sheer Bore, the genius of the locality. Madrid itself
is but an unsocial, second-rate, inhospitable city; and
when the traveller has seen the Museum, been to the
play, and walked on the eternal roundabout Prado, the
sooner he shakes the dust off his feet the better. The
maritime sea-ports, as in the East, from being frequented
by the foreigner, are a trifle more cosmopolitan, cheerful,
and amusing; but generally speaking, public amusements are rare throughout this semi-Moro land. The
calm contemplation of a cigar, and the *dolce far niente*
of *siestose* quiet indolence with unexciting twaddle, suffice; while to some nations it is a pain to be out of
pleasure, to the Spaniard it is a pleasure to be out of
painful exertion : existence is happiness enough of itself;
and as for occupation, all desire only to do to-day what
they did yesterday and will do to-morrow, that is
nothing. Thus life slips away in a dreamy, listless
routine, the serious business of love-making excepted;
leave me, leave me, to repose and tobacco. When
however awake, the *Alameda*, or church-show, the bull-
fight, and the rendezvous, are the chief relaxations.
These will be best enjoyed in the Southern provinces,
the land also of the song and dance, of bright suns and
eyes, and not the largest female feet in the world.

The theatre, which forms elsewhere such an important
item in passing the stranger's evening, is at a low ebb
in Spain, although, as everybody is idle, and man is not
worn out by business and money-making all day, it
might be supposed to be just the thing; but it is somewhat too expensive for the general poverty. Those
again who for forty years have had real tragedies at
home, lack that superabundance of felicity, which will
pay for the luxury of fictitious grief abroad. In truth
the drama in Spain was, like most other matters, the
creature of an accident and of a period; patronised by
the pleasure-loving Philip IV., it blossomed in the sunshine of his smile, languished when that was withdrawn,

and was unable to resist the steady hostility of the clergy, who opposed this rival to their own religious spectacles and church melodramas, from which the opposition stage sprung. Nor are their primitive mediæval Mysteries yet obsolete, since we have beheld them acted in Spain at Easter time; then and there sacred subjects, grievously profaned to Protestant eyes, were gazed on by the pleased natives with too sincere and simple faith even to allow a suspicion of the gross absurdity; but everywhere in Spain, the spiritual has been materialised, and the divine degraded to the human in churches and out; the clergy attacked the stage, by denying burial to the actors when dead, who, when alive, were not allowed to call themselves "*Don*," the cherished title of every Spaniard. Naturally, as no one of this self-respecting nation ever will pursue a despised profession if he can help it, few have chosen to make themselves vagabonds by Act of Parliament, nor has any Garrick or Siddons ever arisen among them to beat down prejudices by public and private virtues.

Even in this 19th century, confessors of families forbade the women and children's even passing through the street where " a temple of Satan " was reared; mendicant monks placed themselves near the playhouse doors at night, to warn the headlong against the bottomless pit, just as our methodists on the day of the Derby distribute tracts at turnpikes against "sweeps" and racing. The monks at Cordova succeeded in 1823 in shutting up the theatre, because the nuns of an opposite convent observed the devil and his partners dancing fandangos on the roof. Although monks have in their turn been driven off the Spanish boards, the national drama has almost made its exit with them. The genuine old stage held up the mirror to Spanish nature, and exhibited real life and manners. Its object was rather to amuse than to instruct, and like literature, its sister exponent of existing nationality, it showed in action what the picaresque novels detailed in description. In both the haughty Hidalgo was the hero; cloaked and armed with long rapier and mustachios, he stalked on the scene, made love and fought as became an old

Castilian whom Charles V. had rendered the terror and the model of Europe. Spain then, like a successful beauty, took a proud pleasure in looking at herself in the glass, but now that things are altered, she blushes at beholding a portrait of her grey hairs and wrinkles; her flag is tattered, her robes are torn, and she shrinks from the humiliation of truth. If she appears on the theatre at all, it is to revive long by-gone days—to raise the Cid, the great Captain, or Pizarro, from their graves; thus blinking the present, she forms hopes for a bright future by the revival and recollections of a glorious past. Accordingly plays representing modern Spanish life and things, are scouted by pit and boxes as vulgar and misplaced; nay, even Lope de Vega is now known merely by name; his comedies are banished from the boards to the shelves of book-cases, and those for the most part out of Spain. He has paid the certain penalty of his national localism, of his portraying men, as a Spanish variety, rather than a universal species. He has strutted his hour on the stage, is heard no more; while his contemporary, the bard of Avon, who drew mankind and human nature, the same in all times and places, lives in the human heart as immortal as the principle on which his influence is founded.

In the old Spanish plays, the imaginary scenes were no less full of intrigue than were the real streets; then the point of honour was nice, women were immured in jealous hareems, and access to them, which is easier now, formed *the* difficulty of lovers. The curiosity of the spectators was kept on tenter-hooks, to see how the parties could get at each other, and out of the consequent scrapes. These imbroglios and labyrinths exactly suited a *pays de l'imprévu*, where things turn out, just as is the least likely to be calculated on. The progress of the drama of Spain was as full of action and energy, as that of France was of dull description and declamation. The Bourbon succession, which ruined the genuine bull-fight, destroyed the national drama also; a flood of unities, rules, stilted nonsense, and conventionalities poured over the astonished and affrighted Pyrenees: now the stage, like the arena, was condemned by critics,

whose one-idead civilisation could see but one class of
excellence, and that only through a lorgnette ground in
the Palais Royal. Calderon was pronounced to be as
great a barbarian as Shakespeare, and this by empty pre-
tenders who did not understand one word of either;—
and now again, at this second Bourbon irruption, France
has become the model to that very nation from whom
her Corneilles and Molières pilfered many a plume,
which aided them to soar to dramatic fame. Spain is
now reduced to the sad shift of borrowing from her
pupil, those very arts which she herself once taught,
and her best comedies and farces are but poor translations from Mons. Scribe and other scribes of the vaude-
ville. Her theatre, like everything else, has sunk into a
pale copy of her dominant neighbour, and is devoid alike
of originality, interest, and nationality.

It was from Spain also that Europe copied the arrangement of the modern theatre; the first playhouses there
were merely open covered court-yards, after the classical
fashion of Thespis. The *patio* became the *pit*, into which
women were never admitted. The rich sat at the windows of the houses round the court; and as almost all
these in Spain are defended by iron gratings, the French
took their term, *loge grillée*, for a private box. In the
centre of the house, above the pit, was a sort of large
lower gallery, which was called *la tertulia*, a name given
in those times to the quarter chosen by the erudite,
among whom at that period it was the fashion to quote
Tertulian. The women, excluded from the pit, had a
place reserved for themselves, into which no males were
allowed to enter—a peculiarity based in the Gotho-Moro
separation of the sexes. This feminine preserve was
termed *la cazuela*, the stewing pan, or *la olla*, the pipkin,
from the hodgepotch admixture, as it was open to all
ranks; it was also called " *la jaula de las mugeres*," the
women's cage—" *el gallinero*," the henroost. All went
there, as to church, dressed in black, and with mantillas.
This dark assemblage of sable tresses, raven hair, and
blacker eyes, looked at the first glance like the gallery
of a nunnery; that was, however, a simile of dissimili-
tude, for, let there be but a moment's pause in the busi-

ness of the play, then arose such a cooing and cawing in this rookery of turtle-doves,—such an ogling, such a flutter of mantillas, such a rustling of silks, such telegraphic workings of fans, such an electrical communication with the Señores below, who looked up with wistful glances on the dark clustering vineyard so tantalisingly placed above their reach, as effectually dispelled all ideas of seclusion, sorrow, or mortification. This unique and charming pipkin has been just now done away with at Madrid, because, as there is no such thing at Covent Garden, or Le Français, it might look antiquated and un-European.

The theatres of Spain are small, although called Coliseums, and ill-contrived; the wardrobe and properties are as scanty as those of the spectators, Madrid itself not excepted; when filled, the smells are ultra-continental, and resemble those which prevail at Paris, when the great people is indulged with a gratis representation; in the Spanish theatres no neutralising incense is used, as is done by the wise clergy in their churches. If the atmosphere were analysed by Faraday, it would be found to contain equal portions of stale cigar smoke and fresh garlic fume. The lighting, except on those rare occasions when the theatre is illuminated, as it is called, is just intended to make darkness visible, and there was no seeing into the henroosts towards which the eyes and glasses of the foxite pittites were vainly elevated.

Spanish tragedy, even when the Cid spouts, is wearisome; the language is stilty, the declamation ranting, French, and unnatural; passion is torn to rags. The *sainetes*, or farces, are broad, but amusing, and are perfectly well acted; the national ones are disappearing, but when brought out are the true vehicles of the love for sarcasm, satire, and intrigue, the mirth and mother-wit, for which Spaniards are so remarkable; and no people are more essentially serio-comic and dramatic than they are, whether in *Venta*, *Plaza*, or church; the actors in their amusing farces cease to be actors, and the whole appears to be a scene of real life; there generally is a *gracioso* or favourite wag of the Liston and Keeley species, who is on the best terms with the pit, who says and does what he likes, interlards the dialogue with his own witticisms, and creates a laugh before he even comes on.

The orchestra is very indifferent; the Spaniards are fond enough of what they call music, whether vocal or instrumental; but it is Oriental, and most unlike the exquisite melody and performances of Italy or Germany. In the same manner, although they have footed it to their rude songs from time immemorial, they have no idea of the grace and elegance of the French ballet; the moment they attempt it they become ridiculous, for they are bad imitators of their neighbours, whether in cuisine, language, or costume; indeed a Spaniard ceases to be a Spaniard in proportion as he becomes an *Afrancesado;* they take, in their jumpings and chirpings, after the grasshopper, having a natural genius for the *bota* and *bolero.* The great charm of the Spanish theatres is their own national dance—matchless, unequalled, and inimitable, and only to be performed by Andalucians. This is *la salsa de la comedia,* the essence, the cream, the *sauce piquante* of the night's entertainments; it is *attempted* to be described in every book of travels—for who can describe sound or motion?—it must be seen. However languid the house, laughable the tragedy, or serious the comedy, the sound of the castanet awakens the most listless; the sharp, spirit-stirring click is heard behind the scenes—the effect is instantaneous—it creates life under the ribs of death—it silences the tongues of countless women—on n'écoute que le ballet. The curtain draws up; the bounding pair dart forward from the opposite sides, like two separated lovers, who, after long search, have found each other again, nor do they seem to think of the public, but only of each other; the glitter of the gossamer costume of the *Majo* and *Maja* seems invented for this dance—the sparkle of the gold lace and silver filigree adds to the lightness of their motions; the transparent, form designing *saya* of the lady, heightens the charms of a faultless symmetry which it fain would conceal; no cruel stays fetter her serpentine flexibility. They pause—bend forward an instant—prove their supple limbs and arms; the band strikes up, they turn fondly towards each other, and start into life. What exercise displays the ever-varying charms of female grace, and the contours of manly form, like this fascinating dance? The accompaniment of the castanet gives employment to their upraised arms. *C'est*, say the French, *le pantomime d'amour*. The enamoured youth persecutes the coy, coquettish maiden; who shall describe the advance—her timid retreat, his eager pursuit, like Apollo chasing Daphne? Now they gaze on each other, now on the ground; now all is life, love, and action; now there is a pause—they stop motionless at a moment, and grow into the earth. It carries all before it. There is a truth which overpowers the fastidious judgment. Away, then, with the studied grace of the French danseuse, beautiful but artificial, cold and selfish as is the flicker of her love, compared to the real impassioned *abandon* of the daughters of the South! There is nothing indecent in this dance; no one is tired or the worse for it; indeed its only fault is its being too short, for as Molière says, " Un ballet ne saurait être trop long, pourvu que la morale soit bonne, et la métaphysique bien entendue." Notwithstanding this most profound remark, the Toledan clergy out of mere jealousy wished to put the bolero down, on the pretence of immorality. The dancers were allowed in evidence to "give a view " to the court: when they began, the bench and bar showed symptoms of restlessness, and at last, casting aside gowns and briefs, both joined, as if tarantula-bitten, in the irresistible capering—Verdict, for the defendants with costs.

This *Baile nacional*, however adored by foreigners, is, alas! beginning to be looked down upon by those ill-advised señoras who wear French bonnets in the boxes, instead of Spanish mantillas. The dance is suspected of not being European or civilised; its best chance of surviving is, the fact that it is positively fashionable on the boards of London and Paris. These national exercises are however firmly rooted among the peasants and lower classes. The different provinces, as they have a different language, costume, etc., have also their own peculiar local dances, which, like their wines, fine arts, relics, saints and sausages, can only be really relished on the spots themselves.

The dances of the better classes of Spaniards in private life are much the same as in other parts of Europe, nor is either sex particularly distinguished by grace in this amusement, to which, however, both are much addicted. It is not, however, yet thought to be a proof of *bon ton* to dance as badly as possible, and with the greatest appearance of *bore*, that appanage of the so-called *gay* world. These dances, as everything national is excluded, are without a particle of interest to any one except the performers. An extempore ball, which might be called a *carpet*-dance, if there were any, forms the common conclusion of a winter's *tertulia*, or social meetings, at which no great attention is paid either to music, costume, or Mr. Gunter. Here English country dances, French quadrilles, and German waltzes are the order of the night; everything Spanish being excluded, except the *plentiful want* of good fiddling, lighting, dressing, and eating, which never distresses the company, for the frugal, temperate, and easily-pleased Spaniard enters with schoolboy heart and soul into the reality of any holiday, which being joy sufficient of itself lacks no artificial enhancement.

Dancing at all is a novelty among Spanish ladies, which was introduced with the Bourbons. As among the Romans and Moors, it was before thought undignified. Performers were hired to amuse the inmates of the Christian hareem; to mix and change hands with men was not to be thought of for an instant; and to this day few Spanish women shake hands with men— the shock is too electrical; they only give them with their hearts, and for good.

The lower classes, who are a trifle less particular, and among whom, by the blessing of Santiago, the foreign dancing-master is not abroad, adhere to the primitive steps and tunes of their Oriental forefathers. Their accompaniments are the "tabret and the harp;" the guitar, the tambourine, and the castanet. The essence of these instruments is to give a noise on being beaten. Simple as it may seem to play on the latter, it is only attained by a quick ear and finger, and great practice; accordingly these delights of the people are always in their hands; practice makes perfect, and many a performer, dusky as a Moor, rivals Ethiopian " Bones " himself; they take to it before their alphabet, since the very urchins in the street begin to learn by snapping their fingers, or clicking together two shells or bits of slate, to which they dance; in truth, next to noise, some capering seems essential, as the safety-valve exponents of what Cervantes describes, the " bounding of the soul, the bursting of laughter, the restlessness of the body, and the quicksilver of the five senses." It is the rude sport of people who dance from the necessity of motion, the relief of the young, the healthy, and the joyous, to whom life is of itself a blessing, and who, like skipping kids, thus give vent to their superabundant lightness of heart and limb. Sancho, a true Manchegan, after beholding the strange saltatory exhibitions of his master, in somewhat an incorrect ball costume, professes his ignorance of such elaborate dancing, but maintained that for a *zapateo*, a knocking of shoes, none could beat him. Unchanged as are the instruments, so are the dancing propensities of Spaniards. All night long, three thousand years ago, say the historians, did they dance and sing, or rather jump and *yell*, to these "*howl*ings of Tarshish;" and so far from its being a fatigue, they kept up the ball all night, by way of *resting*.

The Gallicians and Asturians retain among many of their aboriginal dances and tunes, a wild Pyrrhic jumping, which, with their shillelah in hand, is like the Gaelic Ghilee Callum, and is the precise Iberian armed dance which Hannibal had performed at the impressive funeral of Gracchus. These quadrille figures are intricate and warlike, requiring, as was said of the Iberian performances, much leg-activity, for which the wiry sinewy active Spaniards are still remarkable. These are the *Morris* dances imported from Gallicia by our John of Gaunt, who supposed they were *Moorish*. The peasants still dance them in their best costumes, to the antique castanet, pipe, and tambourine. They are usually directed by a master of the ceremonies, or what is equivalent, a parti-coloured fool, Μωρος ; which may be the etymology of *Morris*.

These *comparsas*, or national quadrilles, were the hearty welcome which the peasants were paid to give to the sons of Louis Philippe at Vitoria; such, too, we have often beheld gratis, and performed by eight men, with castanets in their hands, and to the tune of a fife and drum, while a *Bastonero*, or leader of the band, clad in gaudy raiment like a pantaloon, directed the rustic ballet; around were grouped *payesas y aldeanas,* dressed in tight bodices, with *pañuelos* on their heads, their hair hanging down behind in *trensas*, and their necks covered with blue and coral beads ; the men bound up their long locks with red handkerchiefs, and danced in their shirts, the sleeves of which were puckered up with bows of different-coloured ribands, crossed also over the back and breast, and mixed with scapularies and small prints of saints; their drawers were white, and full as the *bragas* of the Valencians, like whom they wore *alpargatas*, or hemp sandals laced with blue strings ; the figure of the dance was very intricate, consisting of much circling, turning, and jumping, and accompanied with loud cries of *viva!* at each change of evolution. These *comparsas* are undoubtedly a remnant of the original Iberian exhibitions, in which, as among the Spartans and wild Indians, even in relaxations a warlike principle was maintained. The dancers beat time with their swords on their shields, and when one of their champions wished to show his contempt for the Romans, he executed before them a derisive pirouette. Was this remembered the other day at Vitoria?

But in Spain at every moment one retraces the steps of antiquity; thus still on the banks of the Bœtis may be seen those dancing-girls of profligate Gades, which were exported to ancient Rome, with pickled tunnies, to the delight of wicked epicures and the horror of the good fathers of the early church, who compared them, and perhaps justly, to the capering performed by the daughter of Herodias. They were prohibited by Theo-

dosius, because, according to St. Chrysostom, at such
balls the devil never wanted a partner. The well-known
statue at Naples called the Venere Callipige is the representation of Telethusa, or some other Cadiz dancing-girl. Seville is now in these matters, what Gades
was; never there is wanting some venerable gipsy hag,
who will get up a *funcion* as these pretty proceedings
are called, a word taken from the pontifical ceremonies;
for Italy set the fashion to Spain once, as France does
now. These festivals must be paid for, since the
gitanesque race, according to Cervantes, were only sent
into this world as " fishhooks for purses." The *callees*
when young are very pretty—then they have such
wheedling ways, and traffic on such sure wants and
wishes, since to Spanish men they prophesy gold, to
women, husbands.

The scene of the ball is generally placed in the suburb
Triana, which is the Transtevere of the town, and the
home of bull-fighters, smugglers, picturesque rogues,
and Egyptians, whose women are the premières dan-
seuses on these occasions, in which men never take a
part. The house selected is usually one of those semi-
Moorish abodes and perfect pictures, where rags,
poverty, and ruin, are mixed up with marble columns,
figs, fountains and grapes; the party assembles in some
stately saloon, whose gilded Arab roof—safe from the
spoiler—hangs over whitewashed walls, and the few
wooden benches on which the chaperons and invited
are seated, among whom quantity is rather preferred to
quality; nor would the company or costume perhaps be
admissible at the Mansion-house; but here the past
triumphs over the present; the dance which is closely
analogous to the *Ghowasee* of the Egyptians, and the
Nautch of the Hindoos, is called the *Ole* by Spaniards,
the *Romalis* by their gipsies; the soul and essence of it
consists in the expression of certain sentiment, one not
indeed of a very sentimental or correct character. The
ladies, who seem to have no bones, resolve the problem
of perpetual motion, their feet having comparatively a
sinecure, as the whole person performs a pantomime,
and trembles like an aspen leaf; the flexible form and

Terpsichore figure of a young Andalucian girl—be she
gipsy or not—is said by the learned, to have been designed by nature as the fit frame for her voluptuous
imagination.

Be that as it may, the scholar and classical commentator will every moment quote Martial, etc., when he
beholds the unchanged balancing of hands, raised as if
to catch showers of roses, the tapping of the feet, and
the serpentine, quivering movements. A contagious
excitement seizes the spectators, who, like Orientals,
beat time with their hands in measured cadence, and
at every pause applaud with cries and clappings. The
damsels, thus encouraged, continue in violent action
until nature is all but exhausted; then aniseed brandy,
wine, and *alpisteras* are handed about, and the fête,
carried on to early dawn, often concludes in broken
heads, which here are called "gypsy's fare." These
dances appear to a stranger from the chilly north, to
be more marked by energy than by grace, nor have the
legs less to do than the body, hips, and arms. The
sight of this unchanged pastime of antiquity, which
excites the Spaniards to frenzy, rather disgusts an
English spectator, possibly from some national mal-
organization, for, as Molière says, "l'Angleterre a pro-
duit des grands hommes dans les sciences et les beaux
arts, mais pas un grand danseur—allez lire l'histoire."
However indecent these dances may be, yet the performers are inviolably chaste, and as far at least as
ungipsy guests are concerned, may be compared to iced
punch at a rout; young girls go through them before
the applauding eyes of their parents and brothers, who
would resent to the death any attempt on their sisters'
virtue.

During the lucid intervals between the ballet and the
brandy, *La caña*, the true Arabic *gaunia*, song, is administered as a soother by some hirsute artiste, without frills, studs, diamonds, or kid gloves, whose staves,
sad and melancholy, always begin and end with an *ay!*
a high-pitched sigh, or cry. These Moorish melodies,
relics of auld lang syne, are best preserved in the hill-
built villages near Ronda, where there are no roads for

the members of Queen Christina's *Conservatorio Napoli-tano;* wherever l'académie tyrannises, and the Italian opera prevails, adieu, alas! to the tropes and tunes of the people: and now-a-days the opera exotic is culti-vated in Spain by the higher classes, because, being fashionable at London and Paris, it is an exponent of the civilisation of 1846. Although the audience in their honest hearts are as much bored there as elsewhere, yet the affair is pronounced by them to be charming, because it is so expensive, so select, and so far above the comprehension of the vulgar. Avoid it, however, in Spain, ye our fair readers, for the second-rate singers are not fit to hold the score to those of thy own dear Haymarket.

The real opera of Spain is in the shop of the *Barbero* or in the court-yard of the *Venta;* in truth, good music, whether harmonious or scientific, vocal or instrumental, is seldom heard in this land, notwithstanding the eternal strumming and singing that is going on there. The very masses, as performed in the cathedrals, from the introduction of the pianoforte and the violin, have very little impressive or devotional character. The fiddle disenchants. Even Murillo, when he clapped catgut under a cherub chin in the clouds, thereby damaged the angelic sentiment. Let none despise the genuine songs and instruments of the Peninsula, as excellence in music is multiform, and much of it, both in name and sub-stance, is conventional. Witness a whining ballad sung by a chorus out of work, to encoring crowds in the streets of merry old England, or a bagpipe-tune played in Ross-shire, which enchants the highlanders, who cry that strain again, but scares away the gleds. Let therefore the Spaniards enjoy also what they call music, although fastidious foreigners condemn it as Iberian and Oriental. They love to have it so, and will have their own way, in their own time and tune, Rossini and Paganini to the contrary notwithstanding. They—not the Italians—are listened to by a delighted semi-Moro audience, with a most profound Oriental and melan-choly attention. Like their love, their music, which is its food, is a serious affair; yet the sad song, the guitar, and dance, at this moment, form the joy of careless poverty, the repose of sunburnt labour. The poor forget their toils, *sans six sous et sans souci;* nay, even their meals, like Pliny's friend Claro, who lost his supper, *Bætican olives and gazpacho*, to run after a Gaditanian dancing-girl.

In venta and court-yard, in spite of a long day's work and scanty fare, at the sound of the guitar and click of the castanet, a new life is breathed into their veins. So far from feeling past fatigue, the very fatigue of the dance seems refreshing, and many a weary traveller will rue the midnight frolics of his noisy and saltatory fellow-lodgers. Supper is no sooner over than "après la panse la danse,"—some muscular masculine performer, the very antithesis of Farinelli, screams forth his couplets, "screechin' out his prosaic verse," either at the top of his voice, or drawls out his ballad, melancholy as the drone of a Lincolnshire bagpipe, and both alike to the imminent danger of his own trachea, and of all un-Spanish acoustic organs. For verily, to repeat Gray's unhandsome critique of the grand Opéra Français, it consists of " des miaulemens et des hurlemens effroyables, mêlés avec un tintamare du diable." As, however, in Paris, so in Spain, the audience are in raptures; all men's ears grow to the tunes as if they had eaten ballads; all join in chorus at the end of each verse; this " private band," as among the *sangre su,* supplies the want of conversation, and converts a stupid silence into scientific attention,—ainsi les extrêmes se touchant. There is always in every company of Spaniards, whether soldiers, civilians, muleteers, or ministers, some one who can play the guitar more or less, like Louis XIV., who, according to Voltaire, was taught nothing but that and dancing. Godoy, the Prince of the Peace, one of the most worthless of the multitude of worthless ministers by whom Spain has been misgoverned, first captivated the royal Messalina by his talent of strumming on the guitar; so Gonzales Bravo, editor of the Madrid *Satirist*, rose to be premier, and conciliated the virtuous Christina, who, soothed by the sweet sounds of this pepper-and-salted Amphion,

forgot his libels on herself and Señor Muñoz. It may
be predicted of the Spains, that when this strumming
is mute, the game will be up, as the Hebrew expression for the ne plus ultra desolation of an Oriental city
is "the ceasing of the mirth of the guitar and tambourine."

In Spain whenever and wherever the siren sounds are
heard, a party is forthwith got up of all ages and sexes,
who are attracted by the tinkling like swarming bees.
The guitar is part and parcel of the Spaniard and his
ballads; he slings it across his shoulder with a ribbon,
as was depicted on the tombs of Egypt four thousand
years ago. The performers seldom are very scientific
musicians; they content themselves with striking the
chords, sweeping the whole hand over the strings,
or flourishing, and tapping the board with the thumb,
at which they are very expert. Occasionally in the
towns there is some one who has attained more power
over this ungrateful instrument; but the attempt is a
failure. The guitar responds coldly to Italian words
and elaborate melody, which never come home to
Spanish ears or hearts; for, like the lyre of Anacreon,
however often he might change the strings, love, sweet
love, is its only theme. The multitude suit the tune
to the song, both of which are frequently extemporaneous. They lisp in numbers, not to say verse; but their
splendid idiom lends itself to a prodigality of words,
whether prose or poetry; nor are either very difficult,
where common sense is no necessary ingredient in the
composition; accordingly the language comes in aid
to the fertile mother-wit of the natives; rhymes are
dispensed with at pleasure, or mixed according to
caprice with assonants which consist of the mere recurrence of the same vowels, without reference to that of
consonants, and even these, which poorly fill a foreign
ear, are not always observed; a change in intonation,
or a few thumps more or less on the board, do the work,
supersede all difficulties, and constitute a rude prosody,
and lead to music just as gestures do to dancing and
to ballads,—" que se canta ballando;" and which, when
heard, reciprocally inspire a Saint Vitus's desire to

snap fingers and kick heels, as all will admit in whose
ears the *habas verdes* of Leon, or the *cachuca* of Cadiz,
yet ring.

The words destined to set all this capering in motion
are not written for cold British critics. Like sermons,
they are delivered orally, and are never subjected to the
disenchanting ordeal of type: and even such as may
be professedly serious and not saltatory are listened
to by those who come attuned to the hearing vein—who
anticipate and re-echo the subject—who are operated
on by the contagious bias. Thus a fascinated audience of otherwise sensible Britons tolerates the positive
presence of nonsense at an opera—

> " Where rhyme with reason does dispense,
> And sound has right to govern sense."

In order to feel the full power of the guitar and
Spanish song, the performer should be a sprightly Anda-
luza, taught or untaught; she wields the instrument
as her fan or *mantilla;* it seems to become portion of
herself, and alive; indeed the whole thing requires an
abandon, a fire, a *gracia,* which could not be risked by
ladies of more northern climates and more tightly-laced
zones. No wonder one of the old fathers of the church
said that he would sooner face a singing basilisk than
one of these performers: she is good for nothing when
pinned down to a piano, on which few Spanish women
play even tolerably, and so with her singing, when she
attempts " Adelaide," or anything in the sublime, beautiful, and serious, her failure is dead certain, while,
taken in her own line, she is triumphant; the words of
her song are often struck off, like Theodore Hook's, at
the moment, and allude to incidents and persons present;
sometimes they are full of epigram and *double entendre;* they often sing what may not be spoken, and steal
hearts through ears, like the Sirens, or as Cervantes
has it, *cuando cantan encantan.* At other times their
song is little better than meaningless jingle, with which
the listeners are just as well satisfied. For, as Figaro
says—" ce qui ne vaut pas la peine d'être dit, on le
chante." A good voice, which Italians call *novanta-*

nove, ninety-nine parts out of the hundred, is very rare; nothing strikes a traveller more unfavourably than the harsh voice of the women in general; never mind, these ballad songs from the most remote antiquity have formed the delight of the people, have tempered the despotism of their church and state, have sustained a nation's resistance against foreign aggression.

There is very little music ever printed in Spain; the songs and airs are generally sold in MS. Sometimes, for the very illiterate, the notes are expressed in numeral figures, which correspond with the number of the strings.

The best guitars in the world were made appropriately in Cadiz by the Pajez family, father and son; of course an instrument in so much vogue was always an object of most careful thought in fair Bætica; thus in the seventh century the Sevillian guitar was shaped like the human breast, because, as archbishops said, the *chords* signified the pulsations of the heart, *à corde.* The instruments of the Andalucian Moors were strung after these significant heartstrings; Zaryàb remodelled the guitar by adding a fifth string of bright red, to represent blood, the treble or first being yellow to indicate bile; and to this hour, on the banks of the Guadalquivir, when dusky eve calls forth the cloaked serenader, the ruby drops of the heart female, are more surely liquefied by a judicious manipulation of cat-gut, than ever were those of San Januario by book or candle; nor, so it is said, when the tinkling is continuous are all marital livers unwrung.

However that may be, the sad tunes of these Oriental ditties are still effective in spite of their antiquity; indeed certain sounds have a mysterious aptitude to express certain moods of the mind, in connexion with some unexplained sympathy between the sentient and intellectual organs, and the simplest are by far the most ancient. Ornate melody is a modern invention from Italy; and although, in lands of greater intercourse and fastidiousness, the conventional has ejected the national, fashion has not shamed or silenced the old airs of Spain —those " howlings of Tarshish." Indeed, national tunes, like the songs of birds, are not taught in orchestras, but by mothers to their infant progeny in the cradling nest. As the Spaniard is warlike without being military, saltatory without being graceful, so he is musical without being harmonious ; he is just the raw man material made by nature, and treats himself as he does the raw products of his soil, by leaving art and final development to the foreigner.

The day that he becomes a scientific fiddler, or a capital cotton spinner, his charm will be at an end ; long therefore may he turn a deaf ear to moralists and political economists, who cannot abide the guitar, who say that it has done more harm to Spain than hailstorms or drought, by fostering a prodigious idleness and love-making, whereby the land is cursed with a greater surplus of foundlings, than men of fortune ; how indeed can these calamities be avoided, when the tempter hangs up this fatal instrument on a peg in every house? Our immelodious labourers and unsaltatory operatives are put forth by Manchester missionaries as an example of industry to the *Majos* and *Manolas* of Spain : " behold how they toil, twelve and fourteen hours every day;" yet these philanthropists should remember that from their having no other recreation beyond the public or dissenting-house, they pine when unemployed, because not knowing what to do with themselves when *idle;* this to most Spaniards is a foretaste of the bliss of heaven, while occupation, thought in England to be happiness, is the treadmill doom of the lost for ever. Nor can it be denied that the facility of junketing in the Peninsula, the grapes, guitars, songs, skippings and other incidents to fine climate, militate against that dogged, desperate, determined hard-working, by which our labourers beat the world hollow, fiddling and pirouetting being excepted.

CHAPTER XXIV

But whether at bull-fight or theatre, be he lay or clerical, every Spaniard who can afford it, consoles himself continually with a cigar, sleep—not bed—time only excepted. This is his *nepenthe*, his pleasure opiate, which, like Souchong, soothes but does not inebriate; it is to him his "Te veniente die et te decedente."

The manufacture of the cigar is the most active one carried on in the Peninsula. The buildings are palaces; witness those at Seville, Malaga, and Valencia. Since a cigar is a *sine quâ non* in every Spaniard's mouth, for otherwise he would resemble a house without a chimney, a steamer without a funnel, it must have its page in every Spanish book; indeed, as one of the most learned native authors remarked, "You will think me tiresome with my tobacconistical details, but the vast bulk of readers will be more pleased with it, than with an account of all the pictures in the world." They all opine, that a good cigar—an article scarce in this land of smoking and contradiction—keeps a Christian hidalgo cooler in summer and warmer in winter than his wife and cloak; while at all times and seasons it diminishes sorrow and doubles joy, as a man's better half does in Great Britain. "The fact is, Squire," says Sam Slick, "the moment a man takes to a pipe he becomes a philosopher; it is the poor man's friend; it calms the mind, soothes the temper, and makes a man patient under trouble." Can it be wondered at, that the Oriental and Spanish population should cling to this relief from whips and scorns, and the oppressor's wrong, or steep in sweet oblivious stupefaction the misery of being fretted and excited by empty larders, vicious political institutions, and a very hot climate? They believe that it deadens their over-excitable imagination, and appeases their too exquisite nervous sensibility; they agree with Molière, although they never read him, "Quoique l'on puisse dire, Aristote et toute la philosophie, il n'y a rien d'égal au tabac." The divine Isaac Barrow resorted to this *panpharmacon* whenever he wished to collect his thoughts; Sir Walter Raleigh, the patron of Virginia, smoked a pipe just before he lost his head, " at which some formal people were scandalised; but," adds Aubrey, " I think it was properly done to settle his spirits." The pedant James, who condemned both Raleigh and tobacco, said the bill of fare of the dinner which he should give his Satanic majesty, would be " a pig, a poll of ling, and mustard, with a pipe of tobacco for digestion." So true it is that " what's one man's meat is another man's poison;" but at all events, in hungry Spain it is both meat and drink, and the chief smoke connected with proceedings of the mouth issues from labial, not house chimneys.

Tobacco, this anodyne for the irritability of human reason, is, like spirituous liquors which make it drunk, a highly-taxed article in all civilised societies. In Spain, the Bourbon dynasty (as elsewhere) is the hereditary tobacconist-general, and the privilege of sale is generally farmed out to some contractor : accordingly, such a trump as a really good home-made cigar is hardly to be had for love or money in the Peninsula. Diogenes would sooner expect to find an honest man in any of the government offices. As there is no royal road to the science of cigar-making, the article is badly concocted, of bad materials, and, to add insult to injury, is charged at a most exorbitant price. In order to benefit the Havañah, tobacco is not allowed to be grown in Spain, which it would do in perfection in the neighbourhood of Malaga ; for the experiment was made, and having turned out quite successfully, the cultivation was immediately prohibited. The iniquity and dearness of the royal tobacco makes the fortune of the well-meaning smuggler, who being here, as everywhere, the great corrector of blundering chancellors of exchequers, provides a better and cheaper thing from Gibraltar.

The proof of the extent to which his dealings are carried was exemplified in 1828, when many thousand additional hands were obliged to be put on to the manufactories at Seville and Granada, to meet the increased demand occasioned by the impossibility of obtaining supplies from Gibraltar, in consequence of the yellow fever which was then raging there. No offence is more dreadfully punished in Spain than that of tobacco-smuggling, which robs the queen's pocket—all other robbery is treated as nothing, for her lieges only suffer.

The encouragement afforded to the manufacture and smuggling of cigars at Gibraltar is a never-failing source of ill blood and ill will between the Spanish and English governments. This most serious evil is contrary to all treaties, injurious to Spain and England alike, and is beneficial only to aliens of the worst character, who form the real plague and sore of Gibraltar. The American and every other nation import their own tobacco, good, bad, and indifferent, into the fortress free of duty, and without repurchasing British produce. It is made into cigars by Genoese, is smuggled into Spain by aliens, in boats under the British flag, which is disgraced by the traffic and exposed to insult from the revenue cutters of Spain, which it cannot in justice expect to have redressed. The Spaniards would have winked at the introduction of English hardware and cottons—objects of necessity, which do not interfere with this, their chief manufacture, and one of the most productive of royal monopolies. There is a wide difference between encouraging real British commerce and this smuggling of foreign cigars, nor can Spain be expected to observe treaties towards us while we infringe them so scandalously and unprofitably on our parts.

Many tobacchose epicures, who smoke their regular dozen or two, place the evil sufficient for the day between fresh lettuce-leaves; this damps the outer leaf of the article, and improves the narcotic effect; *mem.*, the inside, the trail, *las tripas*, as the Spaniards call it, should be kept quite dry. The disordered interior of the royal cigars is masked by a good outside wrapper leaf, just as Spanish rags are cloaked by a decent *capa*, but l'habit ne fait pas le cigarre. Few except the rich can afford to smoke good cigars. Ferdinand VII., unlike his ancestors Louis XIV., "qui," says La Beaumelle, "haïssoit le tabac singulièrement, quoiqu'un de ses meilleurs revenus," was not only a grand compounder but consumer thereof. He indulged in the

royal extravagance of a very large thick cigar made in
the Havañah expressly for his gracious use, as he was
too good a judge to smoke his own manufacture. Even
of these he seldom smoked more than the half; the remainder was a grand perquisite, like our palace lights.
The cigar was one of his pledges of love and hatred:
he would give one to his favourites when in sweet temper; and often, when meditating a treacherous *coup*,
would dismiss the unconscious victim with a royal *puro*:
and when the happy individual got home to smoke it,
he was saluted by an Alguacil with an order to quit
Madrid in twenty-four hours. The " innocent " Isabel,
who does not smoke, substitutes sugar-plums; she regaled Olozaga with a sweet present, when she was
" doing him " at the bidding of the Christinist cama-
rilla. It would seem that the Spanish Bourbons, when
not " cretinised " into idiots, are creatures composed of
cunning and cowardice. But " those who cannot dis-
simulate are unfit to reign " was the axiom of their
illustrious ancestor Louis XI.

In Spain the bulk of their happy subjects cannot
afford, either the expense of tobacco, which is dear to
them, or the *gain* of time, which is very cheap, by smoking a whole cigar right away. They make one afford
occupation and recreation for half an hour. Though
few Spaniards ruin themselves in libraries, none are
without a little blank book of a particular paper, which
is made at Alcoy, in Valencia. At any pause all say at
once—" *pues, señores! echaremos un cigarrito*—well
then, my Lords, let us make a little cigar," and all set
seriously to work; every man, besides this book, is
armed with a small case of flint, steel, and a combustible
tinder. To make a paper cigar, like putting on a cloak,
is an operation of much more difficulty than it seems,
although all Spaniards, who have done nothing so much,
from their childhood upwards, perform both with extreme facility and neatness. This is the mode:—the
petaca, Arabicè Buták, or little case worked by a fair
hand, in the coloured thread of the aloe, in which the
store of cigars is kept, is taken out—a leaf is torn from
the book, which is held between the lips, or downwards

from the back of the hand, between the fore and middle finger of the left hand —a portion of the cigar, about a third, is cut off and rubbed slowly in the palms till reduced to a powder—it is then jerked into the paper-leaf, which is rolled up into a little squib, and the ends doubled down, one of which is bitten off and the other end is lighted. The cigarillo is smoked slowly, the last whiff being the bonne bouche, the *breast*, *la pechuga*. The little ends are thrown away : they are indeed little, for a Spanish fore-finger and thumb are quite fire-browned and fire-proof, although some polished ex-quisites use silver holders; these remnants are picked up by the beggar-boys, who make up into fresh cigars the leavings of a thousand mouths. There is no want of fire in Spain; everywhere, what we should call link-boys run about with a slowly-burning rope for the benefit of the public. At many of the sheds where water and lemonade are sold, one of the ropes, twirled like a snake round a post, and ignited, is kept ready as the match of a besieged artilleryman; while in the houses of the affluent, a small silver chafing-dish, with lighted char-coal, is usually on a table. Mr. Henningsen relates that Zumalacarreguy, when about to execute some Chris-tinos at Villa Franca, observed one (a schoolmaster) looking about, like Raleigh, for a light for his last dying puff in this life, upon which the General took his own cigar from his mouth, and handed it to him. The schoolmaster lighted his own, returned the other with a respectful bow, and went away smoking and reconciled to be shot. This urgent necessity levels all ranks, and it is allowable to stop any person for fire; this proves the practical equality of all classes, and that democracy under a despotism, which exists in smoking Spain, as in the torrid East. The cigar forms a bond of union, an isthmus of communication between most hetero-geneous oppositions. It is the *habeas corpus* of Spanish liberties. The soldier takes fire from the canon's lip, and the dark face of the humble labourer is whitened by the reflection of the cigar of the grandee and lounger. The lowest orders have a coarse roll or rope of tobacco, wherewith to solace their sorrows, and it is their calumet of peace. Some of the Spanish fair sex are said to indulge in a quiet hidden *cigarilla, una pajita, una reyna*, but it is not thought either a sign of a lady, or of one of rigid virtue, to have recourse to these forbidden pleasures; for, says their proverb, whoever makes one basket will make a hundred.

Nothing exposes a traveller to more difficulty than carrying much tobacco in his luggage; yet all will remember never to be without some cigars, and the better the better. It is a trifling outlay, for although any cigar is acceptable, yet a real good one is a gift from a king. The greater the enjoyment of the smoker, the greater his respect for the donor; a cigar may be given to everybody, whether high or low : thus the *petaca* is offered, as a polite Frenchman of La Vieille Cour (a race, alas ! all but extinct) offered his snuff-box, by way of a prelude to conversation and intimacy. It is an act of civility, and implies no superiority, nor is there any humiliation in the acceptance; it is twice blessed, "It blesseth him that gives and him that takes." It is the spell wherewith to charm the natives, who are its ready and obedient slaves, and, like a small kind word spoken in time, it works miracles. There is no country in the world where the stranger and traveller can purchase for half-a-crown, half the love and good-will which its investment in tobacco will ensure, therefore the man who grudges or neglects it is neither a philanthropist nor a philosopher.

A calculation might be made by those fond of arithmetic—which we abhor—of the waste of time and money which is caused to the poor Spaniards by all this prodigious cigarising. This said tobacco importation of Raleigh is even a more doubtful good to the Peninsula than that of potatoes to cognate Ireland, where it fosters poverty and population. Let it be assumed that a respectable Spaniard only smokes for fifty years, allow him the moderate allowance of six cigars a day—the Regent, it is said, consumed forty every twenty-four hours—calculate the cost of each cigar at two-pence, which is cheap enough anywhere for a decent one; suppose that half of these are made into paper cigars, which require double time—how much Spanish time and private income is wasted in smoke? That is the question which we are unable to answer.

Here, alas! the pen must be laid down; an express from Albermarle-street informs us, that this page must go to press next week, seeing that the printer's devils celebrate Christmas time with a most religious abstinence from work. Many things of Spain must therefore be left in our inkstand, filled to the brim with good intentions. We had hoped, at our onset, to have sketched portraits of the Provincial and General Character of Spanish Men—to have touched upon Spanish Soldiers and Statesmen—Journalism and Place Hunting—Mendicants, Ministers and Mosquitoes—Charters, Cheatings, and Constitutions—Fine Arts—French and English Politics—Legends, Relics, and Religion—Monks and Manners; and last, not least—reserved indeed as a bonne bouche—the Eyes, Loves, Dress, and Details of the Spanish Ladies. It cannot be—nay, even as it is, "for stories somehow lengthen when begun," and especially if woven with Spanish yarn, even now the indulgence of our fair readers may be already exhausted by this sample of the *Cosas de España.* Be that as it may, assuredly the smallest hint of a desire to the flattering contrary, which they may condescend to express, will be obeyed as a command by their grateful and humble servant the author, who, as every true Spanish Hidalgo very properly concludes on similar, and on every occasion, "kisses their feet."

Postscript.—In the first number of these Gatherings (see page 49) some particulars were given of Spanish Stock, derived, as was believed, from the most official and authentic sources. On the very evening that the volume was published, and too late therefore for any corrections, the following obliging letter was received from an anonymous correspondent, which is now printed verbatim:—

London, 30th November, 1846.

Sir,
       I have just perused your valuable and amusing work, "Gatherings from Spain;" but must own I felt somewhat annoyed at seeing so gross a misrepresentation in the account

you give of the national debt of that country; the amount you
give is perfectly absurd. You say it has been increased to
279,083,089*l.*—this is too bad. Now I can give you the exact
amount. The 5 per cents. consists of 40,000,000*l.* only; the
coupons upon that sum to 12,000,000*l.*; and the present 3 per
cents. to 6,000,000*l.*; in all, 58,000,000*l.*, and their own domestic
debt, which is very trifling. Now this is rather different to your
statement; besides, you are doing your book great injury by
writing the Spanish Stock down so; more particularly so, as
there is no doubt some final settlement will be come to before
your second Number appears [?]. The country is far from being
as you misrepresent it to be—bankrupt. She is very rich, and
quite capable of meeting her engagements which are so trifling
—if you were to write down our Railroads I should think you a
sensible man, for they are the greatest bubbles, since the great
South Sea bubble. But Spanish is a fortune to whoever is so fortunate as to possess it now. I am, and have been for some years,
a large holder, and am now looking forward to the realisation
of all my plans, in the present Minister of Finance, Señor Mon,
and the rising of that stock to its proper price—about 60 or 70.
I should, as a friend, advise you to correct your book before
you strike any more copies, if you wish to sell it, as a true
representation of the present existing state of the country. Your
book might have done ten years ago, but people will not be
gulled now; we are too well aware that almost all our own papers
are bribed (and, perhaps, books), to write down Spanish, and
Spanish finance, by raising all manner of reports—of Carlist
bands appearing in all directions, &c. &c. &c. &c., which is most
absurd—the Carlists' cause is dead.
I hope, Sir, you will not be offended with these lines, but
rather take them as a friendly hint, as I admire your book much;
and I hope you will yourself see the falsity of what has been
inserted in a work of amusement, and correct it at once.
              I remain, Sir,
                   Your obedient and humble Servant,
                            A FRIEND OF TRUTH.

To —— Ford, Esq.

It is a trifle "too bad" to be thus set down by our
complimentary correspondent as the inventor of these
startling facts, figures, and "fallacies," since the full,
true, and exact particulars are to be found at pages 85
and 89 of Mr. Macgregor's Commercial Tariffs of
Spain, presented to both Houses of Parliament in 1844
by the command of Her Majesty. And as there was
some variance in amount, the author all through quoted
from other men's sums, and spoke doubtingly and ap-
proximatively, being little desirous of having anything

connected with Spanish debts laid at his door, or charged to his account. He has no interest whatever in these matters, having never been the fortunate holder of one farthing either in Spanish funds or even English railroads. Equally a friend of truth as his kind monitor, he simply wished to caution fair readers, who might otherwise mis-invest, as he erroneously it appears conceived, the savings in their pin-money. If he has unwittingly stated that which is not, he can but give up his authority, be very much ashamed, and insert the antidote to his errors. He sincerely hopes that all and every one of the bright visions of his anonymous friend may be realized. Had he himself, which Heaven forfend! been sent on the errand of discovery whether the Madrid ministers be made, or not, of squeezable materials, considering that Astræa has not yet returned to Spain, with good governments, the golden age, or even a tariff, his first step would have been to grease the wheels with *sovereign* ointment; and with a view of not being told by ministers and cashiers to call again to-morrow, he would have opened the *negocio* by offering somebody 20 per cent. on all the hard dollars paid down; thus possibly some breath and time might be economised, and trifling disappointments prevented.

THE END